S

D1250508

DATE DUE

LITERATURE AND RELIGIOUS CULTURE IN SEVENTEENTH-CENTURY ENGLAND

Reid Barbour's study takes a fresh look at English Protestant culture in the reign of Charles I (1625–49). In the decades leading into the Civil War and the execution of their monarch, English writers explored the experience of a Protestant life of holiness, looking at it in terms of heroic endeavors, worship, the social order, and the cosmos. Barbour examines sermons and theological treatises to argue that Caroline religious culture comprised a rich and extensive stocktaking of the conditions in which Protestantism was celebrated, undercut, and experienced. Barbour argues that this stocktaking was also carried out in unusual and sometimes quite secular contexts; in the masques, plays and poetry of the era as well as in scientific works and diaries. This broad-ranging study offers an extensive reappraisal of crucial seventeenth-century themes, and will be of interest to historians as well as literary scholars of the period.

REID BARBOUR is Professor of English at the University of North Carolina at Chapel Hill. He is the author of two previous books on early modern England: *Deciphering Elizabethan Fiction* (1993) and *English Epicures and Stoics: Ancient Legacies in Early Stuart Culture* (1998). He has contributed articles to journals such as *English Literary Renaissance*, *Studies in Philology*, *Studies in English Literature*, the *John Donne Journal*, and *Renaissance Quarterly*.

LITERATURE AND RELIGIOUS CULTURE IN SEVENTEENTH-CENTURY ENGLAND

REID BARBOUR

*University of North Carolina
at Chapel Hill*

CAMBRIDGE
UNIVERSITY PRESS

PUBLISHED BY THE PRESS SYNDICATE OF THE UNIVERSITY OF CAMBRIDGE
The Pitt Building, Trumpington Street, Cambridge, United Kingdom

CAMBRIDGE UNIVERSITY PRESS
The Edinburgh Building, Cambridge CB2 2RU, UK
40 West 20th Street, New York, NY 10011-4211, USA
477 Williamstown Road, Port Melbourne, VIC 3207, Australia
Ruiz de Alarcón 13, 28014 Madrid, Spain
Dock House, The Waterfront, Cape Town 8001, South Africa

http://www.cambridge.org

© Reid Barbour 2002

This book is in copyright. Subject to statutory exception
and to the provisions of relevant collective licensing agreements,
no reproduction of any part may take place without
the written permission of Cambridge University Press.

First published 2002

Printed in the United Kingdom at the University Press, Cambridge

Typeface Baskerville monotype 11/12.5 pt.   *System* LATEX 2ε   [TB]

A catalogue record for this book is available from the British Library

Library of Congress Cataloguing in Publication data
Barbour, Reid.
Literature and religious culture in seventeenth-century England / Reid Barbour.
p.   cm.
Includes bibliographical references and index.
ISBN 0 521 00664 3 (hardback)
1. English literature – Early modern, 1500–1700 – History and criticism.   2. Christianity
and literature – England – History – 17th century.   3. Religion and
literature – England – History – 17th century.   4. Protestantism and literature – History – 17th
century.   5. Great Britain – History – Charles I, 1625–1649.   6. England – Church
history – 17th century.   I. Title.
PR438.R45 B37 2001   820.9'3823 – dc21   2001035688

ISBN 0 521 00664 3 hardback

*To Marion Durwood and Mary Anne Baker Barbour,
and Steven and Carol Arndt Wolfe*

Contents

Acknowledgments

Early versions of chapters 1 and 2 appeared as "The Caroline Church Heroic: The Reconstruction of Epic Religion in Three Seventeenth-Century Communities," *Renaissance Quarterly* 50 (1997), 771–818. An early version of chapter 3 was published as "Liturgy and Dreams in Seventeenth-Century England," *Modern Philology* 88 (1991), 227–42. I am grateful to the editors of these journals for permission to reuse this material.

The date of the earlier article, 1991, reminds me that I have been working on this book for ten years. Given the challenges presented by the material and by my own (often dull-witted) struggles over method and argument, I have been fortunate in the gifts of advice and encouragement from a number of friends and colleagues: Amy Dudley, Ellie Ferguson, Ian Finseth, Darryl Gless, Vicky Gless, John Headley, Christopher Hodgkins, Richard Kroll, Belinda McFee, Michael McFee, David Norbrook, Lalla Pagano, Kendrick Prewitt, and Victoria Silver. At Cambridge University Press, Ray Ryan has proved a wonderful editor – direct, talented, and kind.

In June 2000, I married a great woman and brilliant scholar named Jessica Wolfe. Our home boasts no "polished pillars, or a roof of gold," but it is a happy dwelling for us and for our little ones, two dachshunds. The greatest fortune of our estate is the pattern we have studied in our parents.

Introduction: spirit and circumstance
in Caroline Protestantism

In the decades of the 1620s, 30s, and 40s, authors attempting to secure
English Protestant orthodoxy against its critics undertook something
more daring in the process: a rich and complex inquisition into the wide
cultural constituents of religious experience itself. By and large, these
writers were less interested in articulating a core of doctrine than they
were in exploring and testing the very conditions in which their faith was
imagined, situated, and lived. From the publication of Bacon's last works
in the 1620s to the culmination of the Civil War in 1648, a spectrum of
writers took stock of what they tend to call the "circumstances" of their
faith, a term that ranges in meaning from the "pomp and circumstance"
of religious heroism and ritual to the analysis of the modes of reverential
thought itself. In these years, the term "circumstance" was applied to
the spiritual, social, and legal constituents of a "person" as well as the
cosmic or natural order enveloping a person. Carried out in print, in
small communities, from the pulpit, on stage, and at court, the Caroline
reexamination of English Protestant orthodoxy certainly generated its
own versions of dogmatism, but its main tendencies leaned toward the
intensive, probing scrutiny of the matrix of religious experience, lending support to Thomas Browne's contention that dogmatic appearances
notwithstanding, "the wisest heads prove at last, almost all Scepticks."[1]
Whatever their dogmatic way-stations, that is, these "heads prove" inventive seekers after the historical, imaginative, ritualistic, social, epistemological, and natural conditions in which English Protestantism tends
to lapse, struggle, and thrive.

In part, this stocktaking of the "circumstances" of English Protestantism was prompted by the Caroline writers' sense that their "true
religion" was increasingly humiliated by fleeing nonconformists and be-
sieged by foreign papists. Both these rival groups accused the Church
of England of becoming mired in the casuistry of circumstance. But
the critique of circumstance carried out by a wide spectrum of English

I

Protestant writers took aim at something much more familiar within the boundaries of what William Laud called the "hedge" and George Herbert the "double moat" of the church – namely, the criteria for assessing the sometimes mundane and palpable, sometimes elevated and elusive, conditions and instruments mediating God's gracious dispensations. At times, one circumstance of faith might be explored in isolation from all the others. A writer might review the conditions of religious heroism through the lens of recent developments in warfare, in colonization, and in the decoration of the church, or survey the past and future of the English church, the "circumstance of time." The habitually doubting conscience of these revisions often doubles as experimentation: thus Caroline assessments of the failures of recent Protestant heroics fertilize the intellectual and spiritual ground of such rich and unusual communities as Great Tew and Little Gidding.

But in Caroline religious discourse, one circumstance often leads to another. For instance, the search for the criteria of a heroic Protestant faith dovetails with debates over the status of ceremony in worship, a matter that reticulates with the interior workings of fancy and the senses, and generally with the newly sophisticated analysis of the epistemology of religious experience. In turn, this exploration of the benefits and liabilities of "fancy" in the practices of the church converges with the studies of the social category of the "person" – studies with far-reaching implications for Christian notions of social decorum or hierarchy, of ministry, and of the evidence for salvation. All the circumstances of faith – heroic, epistemological, cultic, and social – tend to merge in the extraordinary rereading of the Book of Nature carried out in the years after the launch of Bacon's Great Instauration. Adapting Seneca's notion that the *pneuma* surrounds or "stands around" us all, Caroline Protestant writers assemble all the other conditions of their faith as they rethink the constituents of nature and the methodology of natural philosophy. That is, the most explosive catalyst for the Caroline stocktaking of the state of English Protestantism is the study of that circumstance that challenges the centrality of the human condition itself in the landscape of God's providence – the circumstance of nature.

Despite the casuistic and interrogative thrust of so many Caroline writers, the stocktaking quality of English Protestantism in these decades has often been overlooked on the part of those church historians who seek to celebrate Caroline religion as the very "spirit" of Anglicanism or to vilify it as the corruption of that faith. Until the recent work of Achsah Guibbory and Kevin Sharpe, a major reason for such equally extreme, if contradictory, distortions of Stuart religion in the second quarter of the seventeenth century was that scholars commonly limited "religion" far too narrowly and apportioned their methods along rigid disciplinary lines.[2] Literary critics stuck mainly to poems and fictions, historians restricted themselves to sermons, visitation reports, and other "documentary" evidence. Meanwhile they often reduced the category of religion to narrowly doctrinal concerns, usually with the teleological aim of explaining the Civil War (1642–48) and its explosion of radicalism.

But the Caroline emphasis on the circumstances of English Protestant faith demands that the range of texts under consideration be expanded, together with the category of religion itself. As Guibbory has written, religious disagreements in the Caroline period must be understood in a "larger human and cultural" context than a "more narrow theological or political" focus will allow; what is more, this larger cultural understanding requires that the scholar gain "a better grasp of the symbolic meanings of the conflict over worship," which demands "a reinterpretation of seventeenth-century literature, so much of which is concerned with religion" (1). "Religion" comprises not just matters of salvation and worship but also the conflicts found in ethics, social dynamics, epistemology, and natural studies. Or, as Guibbory puts the point, Caroline authors understood that their religious conflicts "involved not simply rival conceptions of God, but conflicting constructions of human (and Christian) identity and of personal, social, and political relations" (4).

The best way to unpack the Caroline investigations of a broadly defined set of religious circumstances involves bringing to bear on English Protestantism a reorientation that Kevin Sharpe has urged on historians of early modern politics: "to pay attention to the representations that contemporaries presented of (and to) themselves," making sure that historians and literary critics join forces in an examination of "discourse and symbols, anxieties and aspirations, myths and memories" (*Remapping*, 3). Between 1620 and 1648, the "wiser heads" assessing and representing the circumstances of orthodox religious experience would not have agreed with some twentieth-century historians that their vein of Protestantism was so pure as an alchemical "spirit" or so debased as the devil incarnate. As William Chillingworth would argue in 1637, somehow the greatness of English orthodoxy was wrapped up with its fallibility. At the same time, recusant and nonconformist writers situating themselves outside the orthodox fold of English Protestantism boldly objected to a circumstantial religion, and even took action to remove themselves from its slough. But in their efforts at separation, recusants and nonconformists found in powerful and painful ways that the highly imperfect conditions of their faith could not be elided. They too came to terms with the imperfections to which the Caroline stocktaking of the circumstances of Protestant faith testified, and at which a rhetorically attentive study of that religious culture must take its aim.

I

It is Archbishop Laud, impeached and on trial for his life, who perhaps most emphatically insists on a careful assessment of religious circumstance. On the nineteenth day of his trial, he answers the charge "'that at the High-Commission . . . I did say that the Church of Rome and the Protestants did not differ in fundamentals, but in circumstances.'"[3] Allowing then setting aside the possibility that he, like anyone involved in theological speculation, might simply and earnestly have erred in this assessment, Laud proceeds to explain that it is wrong to minimize the value, weight, and status of circumstances, to assume that they matter little:

Thirdly, these two learned witnesses [Burton and Lane] (as they would be reputed) are quite mistaken in their very terms. For they report me, as if I said, 'not in fundamentals, but in circumstantials;' whereas these are not *membra opposita*, but fundamentals and super-structures, which may sway quite beside the foundation. (4.336)

Laud is ready with examples of those circumstances, neglected by or unknown to his opponents, "that many times . . . in religion do quite destroy the foundation. For example: the circumstances are these: *Quis? Quid? Ubi? Quibus auxiliis? Quomodo? Quando?*" Skipping the personal "who," Laud commences with the more clearly fundamental "what." "Place" seems less promising at first, "a mere circumstance; yet to deny that Christ took our flesh of the B. Virgin, and that in Judea, denies the foundation, and is flat Judaism." The means of belief – "by what helps a man believes" – can lead to heresy if one overemphasizes human self-sufficiency, a matter of central importance in the Antinomian trials held in Massachusetts, while a question of time, again "a mere circumstance," might arise in one's refusal to believe "that Christ is already come in the flesh," a position that "denies the foundation utterly, and is flat Judaism, and an inseparable badge of the great Antichrist, I John iv." Revisiting his favorite circumstances of place, time, and means, those sacraments and ceremonies so basic to his vision of the church, Laud reminds his examiners that each one of them considers the rite of

transubstantiation a crucial instance of the intersection between foundation and circumstance. Indeed his language almost reverses the normal
order in positing that such a rite is fundamental "upon the bare circumstance of *quomodo*," a point in keeping with his casuistical rule "that some
circumstances *dant speciem*, give the very kind and form to a moral action"
(4.337).

If Laud wants to ensure that his "Puritan" critics appreciate the pivotal
role of circumstance in salvation, worship, and moral action, recusants
deride Laud's church for being mired in fanciful, ecclesiastical, and epistemological accidents – indeed, never so forcefully as in the 1620s and
30s when, as some Catholics scoff, the Church of England has putatively
discovered its own deficiencies and is desperate to repair them. In the
1620s, 30s, and 40s, advocates of the Church of England are deeply
committed to the investigation of religious circumstance as the most pervasive and pious level of religious experience. But critics of their church
have a strong conviction that the bog of circumstance is stagnant and
debased, filled with the debris of the world's vanity fair. For these critics,
a focus on circumstance amounts to cunning policy at best, and hapless
perplexity at worst.

For the advocates of orthodox English Protestantism writing in the
1620s, 30s, and 40s, the conditions of English Protestantism are not newly
distilled into some purer form; "circumstance" is not narrowly political,
and not reducible to policies foisted on the public by a king's ideological
obsessions and personal paranoia. Rather, this generation of English
Protestants produces a far-reaching and exploratory reckoning of the
lived conditions and imaginative categories of their rich but beleaguered
faith.

Throughout the twentieth century, some very brilliant scholars of the
English religious imagination between 1625 and 1648 have tended to
reduce or ignore the inquisitive complexity of Caroline religious discourse. Sometimes reduction is ideological: advocates of "Anglicanism"
have distilled the very spirit of their faith into a world view attributed to
the "Caroline divines." In one famous instance of this scholarly alchemy,
The Structure of Caroline Moral Theology, H. R. McAdoo never explains why
his distillation of the spirit of seventeenth-century "Anglicanism" – and
really that of the late sixteenth and early eighteenth centuries as well,
perhaps simply "Anglicanism" for all time – should be called "Caroline."
The royal name is dropped from the title and contents of McAdoo's 1965
book, *The Spirit of Anglicanism: A Survey of Anglican Theological Method in the
Seventeenth Century*. But the later book is written very much as an extension

of the former, and both together on the foundation of a 1935 anthology compiled by Paul Elmer More and Frank Leslie Cross, *Anglicanism: The Thought and Practice of the Church of England, Illustrated from the Religious Literature of the Seventeenth Century*. With no more explanation than McAdoo provides in 1949, More and Cross conclude their volume with a section devoted to "Caroline Piety."

Sometimes reduction reflects a polarized state of scholarship: since the 1980s, the advent of the so-called Tyacke thesis, which argues for the hegemony of "anti-Calvinism" in the Caroline church, has lassoed scholars into a debate over the putatively core doctrine of English Protestantism under the rule of Charles I and William Laud. Still other scholars of English Protestantism have recoiled from what they consider the tyranny of state religion in the 1620s and 30s. In 1992, a compelling vilification of Caroline Protestantism was published, Julian Davies's *The Caroline Captivity of the Church: Charles I and the Remoulding of Anglicanism, 1625–1641*. Davies's title conceals no mystery: his book is dedicated to the argument that far from distilling the spirit of English Protestantism, "Carolinism" held that spirit hostage and amounted to "a very weird aberration from the first hundred years of the early reformed Church of England."[4] In contrast to McAdoo, for whom the "Carolines" represent English theology "at the apogee of its splendour and virility" (*Structure*, 13), Davies believes that the evangelical mainstream of earlier English Protestantism – "the more enthusiastic, evangelical type of Protestants" – was marginalized and suppressed by a king whose policies distilled an elixir of political ideology tragically poisonous to reformed spirituality.

Suspecting that the "spirit" of his "Carolines" has something to do with circumstance, McAdoo allows that "Sanderson . . . repeatedly stresses the importance of circumstances in cases . . . The phrases 'circumstances duly considered' and 'the infinite variety of human occurrences' are a thought never far from Sanderson's mind" (*Spirit*, 42–43). But in both of his books, McAdoo emphasizes how the "Caroline" divine examines then escapes the clutches of mere circumstance. Such a divine offers a practical and rational method governed by a humbly skeptical search for truth rather than doctrinaire systems; preserves scripture in its undeniable prominence and avoids arid rationalism and legalism; and marries critical freedom of judgment and wise obedience to authority in an eclecticism that nonetheless produces something of great permanance and observes the difference between fundamentals and *adiaphora*. Moreover, this divine knows when to be tolerant, when rigorous, and he is balanced in his optimism about human educability; is committed to the ancient and visible church but also to the modernized study of nature as part of a nexus of resources for religious devotion and method; is defined in habits of thought less by changing historical circumstances and personal idiosyncrasies than by those moderate qualities shared by the gathering at Great Tew, the Cambridge Platonists, Hooker, Andrewes, Laud, Sanderson, and Taylor, the latitudinarians and the new philosophers, and of the latter especially those of the Interregnum and Restoration; believes in a God more wise than willful and in accordance pursues holy living in action and discourse rather than subtle theological controversy; and builds guidelines for the average Christian by way of response to social, theological, and moral circumstances in what McAdoo calls their "relevance to the conditions of reality."[5] Historical circumstances only vaguely matter for McAdoo's alchemy. They are either the private, unknowable vicissitudes of daily living or the briefly listed parade of major events (314) that forced the otherwise peaceful "Anglicans" into controversy. In *Spirit* as in *Structure*, Charles I makes only a brief appearance.

For Julian Davies, however, Charles is the starring antagonist whose villainy consists of imprisoning the true spirit of English Protestantism. If for McAdoo Charles is a fleeting embodiment of the Anglican *pneuma*, for Davies, rich instances of Caroline spirituality such as Little Gidding matter only to the extent to which they supposedly enter Charles's imagination. And the king's is not an imagination for which Davies cares much. It is the narrow, self-serving, yet aggressive imagination of a paranoid tyrant, whose "obsessive drive [was] to eradicate 'profanity,' 'popularity,' and disorder" (3). Superimposing an ideology of sacrosanct kingship on the evangelical mainstream of English Protestantism, Davies's Charles is a lawless interloper whose chief ministers – while in considerable agreement with the king's desire for uniformity, reverence, and decency in worship – prefer more lawful and flexible modes of operation.

Recent "revisionist" historians are wrong, Davies argues, in maintaining that the conflicts developing into civil war were bureaucratic rather than ideological or that the Arminians upset a Puritan status quo. Before Charles, Davies believes, Puritanism was indeed the *locus amoenus* of clergy high and low, of monarchs and people alike; it was an English Protestantism dedicated to supplementing the ordinary means of spirituality with such other godly means as lectures and prophesyings. The revisionists are right, then, in their argument that the 1620s and 30s were critical years of conflict for the English church. Not Laud and the Arminians, however, but an atheological Charles and his personal magnification of a Davidic ideology were responsible for forcing good peaceful Christians into resistance. His target was, if not spirit, at least vital claims on the Holy Spirit, for Charles aimed "to marginalize and anathematize the most vital force within the Church as sectarian and subversive" (10). In a sense, Davies implies that McAdoo was right to emphasize the moral theology of Caroline spirituality; only, the king's is a moral standard of deference and sacralization that took its excuses from the jurisdiction of the temple but sought the utter destruction of any suspected enemy of a numinous court and a priestly monarch. What is more, virtually everyone was suspected – of disloyalty, irreverence, and anarchy.

For Davies, it is Charles (not Laud) urging the reissue of the Book of Sports; it is Charles (again, not Laud) who is obsessed with the rail and with altar policy. Both Charles and Laud want visible forms and accoutrements that will secure and manifest deference, order, and unity; but when attempts are made to bring iconoclasts, nonconformists, and the Scots into line with these ideals, it is Charles and not Laud who has no sense of tact, accommodation, or law. Concerned mainly with the status of the church and clergy and with lay interlopers in their domain, Laud is left to distort the truth in order to keep favor, minimizing the extent of nonconformity and maximizing the success of the royally mandated crackdown.

This last point – that Charles was basically out of touch with the religious realities that he sought so fervently to contain and to shape – raises a big question for the understanding of English Protestantism in the 1620s and 30s: what does it mean to say that the king, his ideology, and the policies that diffused it "captivated" the vitality of the church? Even if there is truth in Davies's compelling yet polemical argument about Charles, how much does it matter – for religion as practiced at Little Gidding, for example – what Charles had in mind or in store for "the Church"? It seems obvious that Charles's "personal stamp" was only one of the constituents of the religious imagination in the decades of his rule and that, as one sees with Little Gidding, this royal constituent had a way of contributing to the richness of contemporary spirituality, partly in the various and quite extraordinary reactions against the king's official ideology and partly in service to or imitation of his ideals. Davies values – but regarding the 1630s hedges on – the survival of the English Protestant mainstream. On the one hand, then, Charles's oppressive policies are said to be "illusory," unable to effect the reduction of the church that the king so fervently desired; on the other, these desires and policies are compared to a cancer so that whatever the vitality of religious culture under his rule, Charles infected the church and made it very difficult for godly ministers and lay people to remain healthy (171).

Davies is as little interested as McAdoo, then, in discussing the rich and various stocktaking of Protestantism in the 1620s and 30s. In *The Caroline Captivity of the Church*, a powerful chorus follows Laertes in rejoining that "the King, the King's to blame." When he sets aside Charles, Davies demonstrates as clearly as anyone the many practical variations that operated within the loopholes of policy. But variation in Caroline spirituality underwhelms Davies. Laud, who stayed away from court, nonetheless (Davies argues) was too indebted to Charles, too legalistic, and too paranoid himself to enjoy loopholes very much. No doubt he was having the nightmares recorded in his diary in large part because of the perils of high political and religious office under Charles. What about everyone else? Davies devotes an entire chapter to Arminianism and at times concedes a point that McAdoo resists, namely, that the intricacies of *ordo salutis* mattered to some Caroline religious writers. But his stress is unproductively on the overemphasis that soteriology has received from Nicholas Tyacke and the critics of his position that the Caroline church was overrun by "anti-Calvinists." It is Davies's tendency to insist that where Arminian questions of divine decree arose in the 1620s and 30s, the middle part of the spectrum was more commonplace than the polarities, the debates were nothing new, they were always subsumed by other ideological divides (to which in any case they have a relationship so uneven as to render it meaningless), and Charles only wanted to get rid of doctrinal controversies anyway.

Whether or not Charles "destroyed" or "captured" Caroline spirituality, Davies ironically follows in the footsteps of his least favorite king. For his is a book obsessed with policy rather than the exploration, opposition, or for that matter the middle ground that survived together with, despite, and against Charles's illusions of power and Laud's dreams of control.

In making a more positive case for Charles I, Kevin Sharpe's *The Personal Rule of Charles I* is much more attentive to the richness of the Protestant imagination in the years leading up to the Civil War. Sharpe concurs with Davies that order, decency, and conformity mattered more to the king than "fine theological distinctions," but unlike Davies, he assigns to the monarch religious motives that were at once a sign of "personal faith" and not altogether repellent to the English people. The faith of his Charles is not unlike the Caroline spirit of McAdoo's Anglicanism, pietistic and moral rather than theoretical and subtle. This

Charles is capable of theological debate but not interested in it, for he fills his life – both private and public – with ceremonies of sincere devotion.[6]

If there is a spirit to Sharpe's Caroline Protestantism, it is concocted with far greater parish-by-parish archival effort than McAdoo's, and with greater sensitivity to the nuances of rhetoric in which ideas are represented. Sharpe's key metaphor for his method of gaining access to this spirit is a tour rather than a concoction. For Sharpe, the variety of local circumstances *is* spirit, and the Caroline religious imagination is shaped by historical circumstances without really investigating the categories of circumstance. Unlike McAdoo, who showcases Sanderson's casuistry of circumstances but wavers on the relevance of factual change for the Anglican spirit, Sharpe honors historical circumstance with pride of place in the titles of one part ("'A Turn of All Affairs': Changed Circumstances and New Counsels") and one chapter ("'The Greatest Measure of Felicity'? Conditions and Circumstances") of his book. But in large part, his use of "circumstance" is not ideational but topical and narrative. It features "events ... unfolding – or not unfolding"; the fluctuating factors and priorities of policy; diplomatic maneuvering or "developments"; and material conditions. Sometimes it comprises the category of, "we might say, psychological circumstances." The latter range from the template of the "royal mind," with its "grammar of order, reform and efficiency," to the more widely spread perception of policies, whatever the political circumstances of their administration. But unlike some of his other works, which focus on the representation of ideas and ideals, Sharpe's *Personal Rule* is so intent on redeeming Charles and Laud that what Caroline writers imagined is usually a way of revaluing what they in fact lived. As in Davies's book, ideas are studied most often in the grammar of policy and in the uses of and responses to that grammar. So it is that Sharpe can ask the incisive question about Charles, Laud, and their relationship to Puritanism: did they "create the threat they had imagined?" (603–05, 732).

II

The Caroline religious imagination flourishes neither as the reified spirit of Anglicanism nor as the local permutations of policy but in its explorations of the conditions and circumstances of a Protestant life of faith. Given their tendency to believe that certainty derives mainly from outward conformity rather than from theological dispute, Charles and Laud might warrant the label of skeptics. But skeptical religious thought as we find it variously dramatized in the texts of the 1620s, 30s, and 40s is more exploratory and inventive than the king and his chief prelate would prefer. The writers of this period often focus their attention on some semantic field of the word "circumstance," a rich and complex nodal term that ranges across a wide spectrum of Christian concerns, agitates those concerns, but also laces them intricately together.

Thomas Browne opens his *Religio Medici* with this dilemma – "For my Religion, though there be severall circumstances that might perswade the world I have none at all . . ." – then orients circumstance toward natural philosophy and its relationship to faith.[7] Two paragraphs later he comes back to the word, only now in an ecclesiastical context: "I cannot laugh at but rather pity the fruitlesse journeys of Pilgrims, or contemne the miserable condition of Friers; for though misplaced in circumstance, there is something in it of devotion: I could never heare the *Ave Marie* Bell without an elevation, or thinke it a sufficient warrant, because they erred in one circumstance, for me to erre in all, that is in silence and dumbe contempt" (63). Contemporary explorations of the term agree with Browne that it is useful in working out the problems plaguing faith's interaction with natural philosophy and papist ceremony, but its usage extends to Caroline doubts about whether the Protestant faith has retained, refined, or squandered its heroic mission; and to their uncertainties about how social values articulate with spiritual ideals. Writing in the 1620s and 30s, Joseph Mede is typical of his contemporaries when in close proximity he enlists the term "circumstance" to depict the place and time of ceremony; the "pomp" associated with militarism; the holiness that sets religious persons apart; the events and details of historical discourse; and the ancillary issues of theology.[8]

In the Caroline stocktaking of the human experience and construction of Protestant faith, religious circumstance pertains to the discursive conditions of persons, places, and times (both past and future); to the circumscribing realities of matter and providence; to worship as decoration and as imagination; to the ways in which Protestants interact, institute their churches, think, solve moral and social dilemmas; and to the means through which they dramatize, spread, and heroize the faith, and find salvation. At a time when English Protestant writers are responding to a heightened Roman Catholic and nonconformist critique, to intellectual skepticism and philosophical revisionism throughout Europe, to the quagmire of religious warfare, to disillusionment over yet renewed hope in the colonial project, to reappraisals of decorum and dynamics in Christian society, to disenchantment with

doctrinal polarization and polemics, and to the accentuation of fault
lines within the *ecclesia anglicana* itself: in the years of the 1620s, 30s,
and 40s, that is, "circumstance" assumes a prominence in the English
religious lexicon, and gives coherence to the complex reinvestigation
of the aspirations and rites, the interior experiences and social signifiers, the natural framework and ministerial instruments of Protestant life in England. Caroline writers use the term "circumstance"
when reasserting or refashioning order or boundaries in their religious
culture, but also with a skepticism that suspects circumstantiality of
unsettling order and of crossing borders.

The Oxford English Dictionary (OED) is of considerable help in
sketching the range of concerns that agitate the Caroline examination of
the circumstances of faith.[9] One gloss (II.7.a) – "The 'ado' made about
anything; formality, ceremony, about any important event or action" –
encompasses two interlocking preoccupations: Protestant heroism and
ecclesiology. The more learned Caroline writers recognize that the Latin
terms *circumstantia* and *circumsto* often concretize the notion of "standing
around" or "surrounding" in terms of a military encirclement by hostile
troops around a town or army about to be invaded and occupied. But as
I argue in chapters 1 and 2, English Protestantism in the years 1620 to
1650 is deeply invested in a reconstitution of heroism, not least because,
like Othello's agonized farewell to the "Pride, Pompe and Circumstance
of glorious warre," there is a deep-seated fear that Protestant valor is
lapsing.[10]

In chapters 1 and 2, I argue that the 1620s and 30s bear witness to
a rich, wide-ranging, and skeptical review of the history and nature of
heroism in the church. At the Caroline court, at the home of the Ferrars
at Little Gidding, and at Great Tew, the estate of Lucius Cary, second
Viscount Falkland, communities of Caroline Christians reassert but also
question the status and conditions of the church heroic from a wide
variety of vantage points: the masques of "heroic virtue"; the history
of martyrdom; the paradigm of Charles V and his abdication from religious warfare; the colonization of Virginia; the Elizabethan past with
such heroic figures as Drake; church beautification; the English legends of
St. George; and skepticism itself. The chapters argue that Caroline religious culture is dissatisfied with its own heroism, with its relationship
to past forms of heroism, and with those old forms themselves. At the
same time, this culture struggles to make a virtue out of doubt by inventing composites of heroism but also by converting doubt into the
conscientious greatness of the Church of England.

For Caroline writers, however, questions of decorum in Christian worship and society are just as prominent as those of heroism. The usage of "circumstance" to mean "decorum" is well documented throughout the early seventeenth century: as a famous instance, Shakespeare uses "circumstance" to suggest formal, decorous, or ceremonial behavior of any kind in *The Winter's Tale* (v.i.90), when Leontes notes that Prince Florizel comes to his court "So out of circumstance and sudden . . . 'Tis not a visitation framed, but forced / By need and accident."[11] But when Laudian support for church decoration infuses the debates about heroism and ecclesiology alike, the two circumstances are united, if also competitive, in the Caroline exploration of what might elevate the English church to greatness. Moreover, both the beautification and the heroism of the church lead Caroline writers to decipher the circumstance of time, with critics of the English noninvolvement in the Thirty Years War looking to Drake for their model while the Laudians appeal to the medieval heritage of the church.

But, as I argue in chapter 3, church ceremony is itself a special "circumstance" often treated apart from questions of heroism and in the context of yet another gloss on circumstance having to do with perception and knowledge. When Hamlet speaks of "our circumstance and course of thought,"[12] his usage is philosophically rich: "circumstance" is the term to which skeptical critiques of human certainty classically revert; it is central to the work of Sextus Empiricus. But it has other influential classical legacies as well. Connecting the little world of man to the greater world of nature, the word often figures in the Stoic description of the pervasive *pneuma* that inhabits human beings as the faculty of imagination. In so many ways, the conditions of human knowledge, sense perception, imagination, and discourse are under review in religious writing of the 1620s, 30s, and 40s: in the Baconian revision of philosophical method and pneumatology; in the heroic skepticism to which Chillingworth and Falkland turn; and in the curious relationship between ceremony and "fancy" that chapter 3 unfolds. For those writers trying to consolidate and unify the identity and practices of the Church of England in the face of challenges by Puritan and papist alike, ceremony is conceived as very much surrounding the church in a defensive manner: in his conference with Fisher, Laud speaks of ceremony as the hedge around the church, while George Herbert writes of the Church of England as "double-moat[ed]" by the grace of God – this in a poem that celebrates the moderation of the Stuart church.[13] Meanwhile, "fancy" is customarily stereotyped as the amorphous, factious enemy to uniformity, order, and decency in church. But fancy is also the most intimate and active supplier of that holy passion and sensation necessary for ceremony to do its special work; and (as I discuss in the two chapters on natural philosophy) this faculty is often linked to the notion of a *pneuma* permeating and homogenizing the whole of the world. In short, the relationship between a putatively unpredictable, chaotic fancy and a uniform, decent ceremony is not so simple – in the diary of Laud, in masques at court, in the prose of Jeremy Taylor – as the polarities of Caroline polemicists often protest.

The Caroline meditation on ceremony and liturgy adds the circumstance of sacred place to the heroic circumstance of time. In chapters 4 and 5, the Caroline fascination with the status of personhood and with the nature of impersonation is added to considerations of time and place, in keeping with the rhetorical tradition that triangulates all three respects in a calculus of decorum. But "person" itself is religiously wide ranging in the discourse of the period, from moral casuistry to theoretical soteriology, and from the comedies about life in the town to handbooks about performance in the pulpit. Even more than with heroism or fancy, the category of the "person" illustrates how religious conflicts find their way into some of the most putatively profane texts of the 1620s, 30s, and 40s. It also corroborates Guibbory's argument that in the Caroline period, conflicts over religious ceremony had enormous implications for the broadly social organization of "human beings in relationship with each other".[14]

I have already noted McAdoo's emphasis on Sanderson's casuistry of circumstances, and in general early Stuart casuists are busy transforming the scholastic legacy of prescriptions for how the office of judging "That which surrounds [us] . . . morally" (OED, "circumstance," I) should be carried out by the individual conscience. Like Sanderson, Donne knows full well how crucial the exploration of circumstance is to the resolution of moral dilemmas. In an earlier but proleptic instance found in *Biathanatos*, he concludes of self-homicide that "to mee there appears no other interpretation safe but this, that there is no externall act naturally evill; and that circumstances condition them, and give them their nature; as scandall makes an indifferent thing hainous at that time, which, if some person go out of the roome, or winke, is not so."[15] Some circumstances of actions are external and performative, then, but some are internal, namely, those involving the motivations of self-homicides that help us decide whether or not an act is godly or sinful.

In his Caroline sermons, Donne joins Sanderson in being keenly provoked by "personal" respects. Prompted by the Bible's injunction against respect to persons, their contemporaries approach this circumstance of Protestantism from a variety of directions. For example, sermons *ad magistram* warn judges of their duty to deal decorously yet evenhandedly with the "persons" of various social rank brought to them. In the wake of the death of Andrewes and the ascendancy of Laud, sermons *ad clerum* are involved in contemporary debates over the distinctive marks and honors of the ministerial "person" or "parson" – a controversy that links questions of persons to those of heroism and ceremony in the matter of what lends grandeur to the church. In the aftermath of the Synod at Dort other works respond to the question of how exactly God places value on persons, and their attempt to construct a genealogy of God's decrees and of the processes of salvation intersects with the efforts of those Caroline playwrights and social theorists concerned in the aftermath of the inflation of honors with the decorum of everyday life.

In the matter of personal respects, then, circumstance can involve, apart or together, religious questions as diverse as "what does God see when He looks at our souls" to what kind of language a godly subject must use when he or she addresses an equal, a superior, or an inferior. In this respect, circumstance helps Caroline writers gauge how believers can mitigate offenses to God but also how citizens of the world can mitigate offenses to other human beings – as when Ben Jonson notes in line with OED II.6 ("circuitous narration; circumlocution, beating about the bush, indirectness") that sometimes one must "speak that in obscure words, or by circumstance, which uttered plainly would offend the hearers."[16] The casuistry of personal respects becomes all the more complex when the avoidance of spiritual offense produces social offense and vice versa.

In Caroline discourse, the circumstance that reticulates all the others is nature itself, what the OED calls "That which surrounds materially" ("circumstance," 1). In *Naturales Quaestiones* (II.6.7.1), Seneca gives this usage its most simply physical, pneumatic gloss: "Our Stoics call this [i.e. *pneuma*] *circumstantia* ['encirclement'], the Greeks *antiperistasis* ['replacement']. It occurs in air as well as in water, for air encircles every body by which it is displaced." The term is well known in the 1620s, 30s, and 40s; Bacon, for example, uses it in his studies of "the measure of surrounding circumstances [*de mensura peristaseos*]."[17]

With Bacon's public launching of his Great Instauration in the 1620s, Stuart readers are made privy to an extraordinary call for natural circumstance to be studied anew. This means, of course, that human beings must reexamine their cosmic habitation whether pneumatic or particulate, but also that they must rethink their spiritual lives from the outside (concerning the character, reach, and visibility of providence) and from the inside (regarding the ways in which human beings think, believe, and imagine). In addition to pneumatic links between imagination and nature, Bacon's exploration of internal circumstance revisits the dialogue between fancy and ceremony – in the idols of the mind, for instance. But the most significant heritage behind the Caroline exploration of internal circumstance connects Bacon more fully to Edward Herbert and William Chillingworth than to Laud, namely, the critical legacy of skepticism.

In *Outlines of Pyrrhonism*, Sextus Empiricus reviews those modes of critique by which the skeptic questions human certainty about whether knowledge captures or at least is commensurate with the underlying reality of the objects of human perception. Of these modes, all of which issue in the suspension of judgment, the fourth – "based, as we say, on the 'circumstances' [*peristaseis*]" – encapsulates many of the others:

And this Mode, we say, deals with states that are natural or unnatural, with waking or sleeping, with conditions due to age, motion or rest, hatred or love, emptiness or fulness, drunkenness or soberness, predispositions, confidence or fear, grief or joy.[18]

The skeptical critique maintains that human knowledge is always disposed or conditioned by a matrix of circumstances; or, put differently, that knowledge is circumstance – irreducibly differentiated according to age, physical welfare, wakedness, consumption, time, movement, and bias. Health does not amount to a condition for certain and confident judgment; it is rather a circumstance as productive of epistemological variation as sickness. In fact, our knowledge is so completely constituted by circumstances that we are in no position to assess the truth value of any one circumstance.

Under the influence of such Continental skeptics as Montaigne, Charron, and Descartes, English writers in the 1620s, 30s, and 40s are newly alert and responsive to the power of epistemological critique, including the terms of the fourth mode. Increasingly in the seventeenth century, skepticism affects the way in which evidence is measured, probability calculated, institutions and conventions assessed, and the mind itself situated. "Circumstance" is a word to which Stuart skeptics often return when characterizing human rationality, developing the implications of Donne's earlier summation in *Biathanatos* that "scarce any reason is so constant, but that circumstances alter it" (*Prose*, 66). Knowledge is mediated not just by internal circumstances but by the context and impressions tendered by the object of perception. In this skeptical context, circumstance is often a reminder of human imperfection. But in the wake of Bacon's full-scale promulgation of the Great Instauration in the early 1620s, the doubting conscience is increasingly a tool for attending more rigorously to natural circumstances; for improving the way in which human beings know things; and for repairing the way in which human beings live, interact, and aspire to the heroic stature originally bestowed on them by God. In the 1620s, 30s, and 40s, that is, doubt is more than ever a scourge and a minister for English Protestants.

In his last works, Bacon deploys but also surmounts the skeptical critique of the circumstances of thought and imagination on his way toward a full-scale reinvestigation of the natural circumstances surrounding human perception. In Bacon's work and in that of his contemporaries, however, natural circumstances are also intricately linked to the mythical, temporal, social, ecclesiological, and soteriological circumstances of English Protestant faith. That is, nature is the hub of a wheel around which the most problematic conditions of Protestant faith in the Thirty Years War generation tend to revolve: how do the heroic past and the millennial future of Christendom help shape and guide the present Church of England? Is true religion inclusive or selective, is it ceremonial or plain, and what are the principles according to which these matters can be settled? What is the relationship between fortuitous second causes and supernatural, providential forces? What is the equitable place (if any) for respect to persons in the life and thoughts of the English Protestant? What are the criteria that set apart the clergy, or that validate the performance of righteousness? How does human "fancy" interact with the phenomena – natural, ceremonial, artistic, and spiritual – that envelop and stimulate it? So it is that the Caroline imagination flourishes in its stocktaking of individual circumstances – history, heroism, thought, fancy, place, person, decorum, natural phenomena, ceremony, salvation, and providence – but also in networks traceable in such writers as Thomas Browne and George Hakewill. And in this stocktaking, the intense and unsettled interrogation of the conditions of religious faith contends with the highly inventive attempts to compose and stabilize the circumstances of English Protestantism into an impressive defense against the highly aggressive assaults of violence, doubt, external rivalry, and the factious enemy within.

III

In Caroline literature, the category of "circumstance" evokes complex imaginative work not least because it gravitates toward that fertile area where the indifferent and the fundamental converge. The OED corroborates this point by noting that "circumstance" can indicate a matter of great importance but also any "non-essential, accessary, or subordinate" detail. Just so with the Caroline Protestants: the vitality of their literature derives from what Donne calls an "agitation" provoking the faithful to move back and forth between the simple core of their catechisms and the trying conditions of their lives, at times uncertain of which is core and which condition, at times transforming one into the other.

In *Death's Duel* (1631), Donne provokes his auditors into examining their sins before they come to their Judge: "Hast thou been content to come to this *Inquisition*, this examination, this agitation, this cribration, this pursuit of thy *conscience*, to *sift* it, to follow it from the *sinnes* of thy *youth* to thy *present sinnes*, from the *sinnes* of thy *bed*, to the *sinnes* of thy *boorde*, and from the *substance* to the *circumstance* of thy *sinnes*?" (*Prose*, 326). As Laud reminds his prosecutors, circumstance sometimes bears directly on the fundamentals of doctrine and sometimes pertains not at all to the doctrinal core; one must work carefully to decipher the logic or the equity that conditions the relationship between the two.[19] Through the sifting of circumstances, Caroline Protestants are as eager to shore up the foundations of their church as they are worried that those foundations are either eroding or fraudulent. The result is a literature far-reaching in its inquiries yet focused on the problems of everyday Protestant faith.

There were many factors – and kinds of factors – contributing to Caroline religious agitation. Some were generational. By the 1620s, English Protestantism was mature enough to have become entrenched but also to have developed a sense of decadence, belatedness, and shortcomings – of promise unfulfilled and, as a corollary, of vulnerability. By contrast, Caroline religious and moral culture was bolstered by a growing awareness of the church's vast resources – from the medieval liturgies to sixteenth-century controversialists, and including such prominent modern and native authorities as Foxe, Hooker, Perkins, and Andrewes. There was also a confidence among theologians that they were capable of advanced critical modes of assessing those resources.

Another powerful constituent of the generation of the 1620s was, as Hugh Trevor-Roper has argued, the Thirty Years War, an experience that shaped Caroline treatments of heroism, the millennium, and even natural philosophy.[20] But other factors were more accidental and personal, and not just the character of the monarch and his chief ministers with their rage for conformity and decency. For example, the impeachment of Bacon lent him time to present his Great Instauration to the world and so radically altered the way in which the study of natural philosophy was understood. The Caroline fascination with the status of personhood emerged from a variety of contexts: from the elevated attention to Arminian soteriology at the Synod at Dort; the alternative styles of clerical vocation represented by the great and abundant Jacobean preachers but also by the rise of and conflict over Laudianism; by the development of the "town" as a laboratory for social interchange; by the great dramatic and ceremonial imagination of Ben Jonson; by the development of the technological means of colonization; by the sale of honors in Jacobean England; and by the development of the chancery courts, the aim of which was to oversee an equitable regard for personal circumstances.

As some of the accidental factors anticipate, there were pronounced ideational or ideological components to the religious imagination of Caroline writers: the ripening and diffusion of Continental skepticism; the consolidation of and polemical response against Arminianism; the elusive Rosicrucian call for the reformation of the world; the Caroline court's allegorical preferences in the masque; the Little Gidding fascination with the history of Christian heroism; the devotion to Erasmus by the uncommonly appealing patron, Lucius Cary; the struggle of a Puritan gentry between spiritual vocation and social respects; the church-less rational theology of Edward Herbert; and the acute critiques of church infallibility by Chillingworth. In 1625, Charles came to the throne, the Ferrar family moved to Little Gidding, the Montagu affair was in an uproar, a new breed of playwrights was emerging, Sanderson attempted to map God's decrees as he would a family tree, and Bacon's five most productive years were coming to an end, having changed the face and course of English philosophy for evermore.

No one kind of cause – rather every kind – contributed to the extraordinary review of the circumstances and conditions of holy living that took place in the years in which Charles and Laud attempted to capture and to sublimate the spirit of English Protestantism. From Rome and Massachusetts, critics of the Church of England tried to convert this agitation of circumstances into the clearest evidence of all that the death bell was ringing for the church of Donne and Sibbes. In writing the

Religion of Protestants, however, Chillingworth argued that any church modestly yet sincerely working through the challenges of circumstance was only just beginning to thrive.

Unlike James, Charles found theological and ecclesiastical controversies suggestive of a church spinning out of control. If he attempted to capture and hold the church in place, his program is not so much reflective of a theological dyslexia[21] – about which historians disagree – as it is indicative of the irreducible complexity of that Protestant stocktaking carried out under his watch – from Bacon's New Atlantis to Ferrar's Little Gidding; from Laud's diary to Sanderson's casuistry; from Donne's pulpit to Eleanor Davies's prophecy; from the collapse of the Virginia Company to Mede's calculations of the millennium; and from the rebuilding of the visible church to Lord Herbert's churchless common notions. The lapses of consensus in the Caroline church meant not only that the church would be haunted by its own skepticism but also that it would be well stocked with alternatives for rebuilding a consensus more lasting than before. Indeed skepticism itself was the basis for one such alternative. Our finest historians continue to contend over the person of Charles; but even more than the character of Charles, the imaginative habits of those Christians that he governed have eluded the distillations of spirit, the records of policy, and such catchall nets as the "persecutory imagination."[22] Between "substance" and "circumstance," writers in the decades leading up and into the Civil War reconceived the faith of their people in brilliantly clear but also obscure and crosshatched patterns. Thus, the dispensations of Charles and the visitations of Laud affected but hardly imprisoned what Thomas Carew called – in reference to Donne – the "giant fancy" of those Caroline writers whose hope and labor it was to secure the English church as the epitome of true religion.[23] As their church came of age, the Caroline writers felt very deeply both the authority and the responsibility that attend maturity, no longer green and "unsifted in such perilous circumstance."[24]

CHAPTER I

The church heroic: Charles, Laud, and Little Gidding

Of the circumstances of English Protestantism explored in the 1620s, 30s, and 40s, the reckoning of heroism requires from authors the greatest engagement with the past, with the circumstance of time. Overshadowed by their sense of an Elizabethan heyday for the honor of Protestant aggression, these writers struggle against the suspicion of their own belatedness, decadence, and paralysis. Far from collapsing under the pressure of the Elizabethan ethos, however, Caroline Protestants respond to the past of their own faith with an acute skepticism toward its myths and with richly inventive revisions of the heroic pomp and circumstance of faith. For heroic circumstance, they understand, comprises the various means – practical, ceremonial, or imaginative – through which the advocates of a church secure its singular elevation and, therefore, its warrant as the best of all possible churches.

Insofar as heroism comprises the means of ecclesiastical elevation, the warrant of tradition, and the claims of superiority, it dovetails with all the other circumstances of Protestant faith. Most clearly, the constructions of heroism contribute to, and depend on, the inner and outer conditions of worship – the circumstances of thought and place to be discussed in the third chapter. But as Guibbory has shown, presuppositions about ceremony are entangled with rival notions of how the social domain should be ordered and framed. So it is that the lofty authority of heroic religion makes an impact on the much more mundane ways in which human beings interact with one another in English Protestant society, in short, on the circumstance of persons.[1] As they are presented by enthusiasts for the Caroline court and the Laudian church, moreover, the assumptions behind religious heroism, worship, and social organization are corroborated by an image of the natural world according to which the ceremonies of the temple and the harmony of the social order find their counterpart in a magical, holistic cosmos whose forces are so often invoked in Stuart masques. With the Civil War and the collapse of orthodox religious heroism, the circumstance of nature substitutes for heroism as the enveloping non-divine condition of religious faith. But as later chapters will show, natural philosophy is even more unsettled by dispute than heroic religion.

In keeping with contemporary notions that heroic virtue is in some measure a ligament binding religious communities, the most extraordinary revisions of epic religion in these decades are produced among coteries of men and women – at the court of Charles I, at the Little Gidding estate of the Ferrar family, and at the Oxfordshire home of Lucius Cary. In their symbols, ceremonies, and masques, the cultural brokers for Charles I pursue the king's own obsession with redressing recent failures in Protestant aggression against the Catholic forces of the Antichrist. Somehow the vehicle of redress must indirectly criticize Elizabethan military Protestantism, yet also distill its moral and spiritual vigor. Hailed even by its critics as more morally and aesthetically elevated than its Jacobean predecessor, the Caroline court promulgates a comprehensive heroic synthesis centered on a godly prince but including the heightened ceremony and beautification of the church. In response, critics both within and outside the court detect and accentuate the fault lines and contradictions in this idealized synthesis. In no small measure, the Ferrar family members living at their Little Gidding estate operate in response to major alterations in the Caroline/Laudian church, both in imitation and in opposition. They deliver scathing criticisms of a Stuart, especially courtly, culture in love with the wrong (romantic) traditions of heroism, but in their staged dialogues the Ferrars epitomize the arduous and multifaceted Caroline search for the elusive marks of the genuine church heroic. In turn, the chief brokers of the Caroline/Laudian church are curious about the heroic codes and patterns being established at Little Gidding too. Both communities fear the loss of Protestant heroism; both are prepared to criticize the agents of this loss; and both strive to rebuild epic religion through discourse, ceremony, and action.

Yet a third Caroline community, that brilliant coterie gathered around Lucius Cary, second Viscount Falkland, in the 1630s, responds to the many versions of Christian heroism past and present. Principally housed at Falkland's Great Tew some twenty miles from Oxford, this coterie proves as vibrantly exploratory regarding the problem of a lapsing Protestant heroism as the manor at Little Gidding. Their chief contribution – that skepticism itself might serve as the most godly form of Protestant heroism – is worked out in the context of yet another heroic synthesis, the active constituents of which do combat with one another.

In the Caroline search for the genuine church heroic, then, there are many strong contenders – old and new, courtly and anti-courtly, Laudian and Foxeian – fracturing the perceived Elizabethan and Jacobean consensus that Protestant heroism demands violent and colonial opposition to the papal Antichrist. This consensus had been unsettled by Jacobean pacifism and James's opposition to the Virginia Company late in his reign. But it is under Charles I that the loss of a consensus on Protestant heroism is deeply felt and that strenuous, elaborate efforts are made to reassemble synthetic archetypes for this heroism or to justify a heroism committed to abdication from and critique of the old myths. Moreover, far from negating ecclesiastical heroism, the competition over and dispersion of its constituents contribute to the apologetic formation of a skeptical and fallible heroism, with an earnest but mistake-ridden endeavor after true religion becoming the diacritical honor of the Church of England. In this version of religious heroism, however, the circumstances of thought come very close to supplanting the specific dispensations of worship in a church – come very close, that is, to something like the tolerant and reasonable faith that some philosophers were seeking in the minimal common notions of all religions.

In their attempts to reclaim heroic Protestantism, the three extraordinary Caroline communities – the royal court, Little Gidding, and Great Tew – capture a much wider cultural search for the basis, scope, and strength of England's covenant with God. This search is worked out in action, in policy, and in literature. From the crisis over the Palatinate to the Order of the Garter; from the Laudian beautification of the church to the controversy over Neoplatonic demigods; from Virginia to Little Gidding to the battlefield at Newbury where Falkland was killed; from Agamemnon to Scylla and Charybdis to the Ovidian translation of epic combat into metamorphoses – the Caroline church is distinguished by its transmission, transformation, and urgent, creative analysis of interconnected but also hostile versions of religious heroism. The mediation between these heroisms results in impressive courtly spectacle but also in disenchanted bathos; in opulence but also austerity; in skepticism about the possibility of a justifiable Christian heroism but also skepticism as the very essence of that heroism; and in renunciation of the world but also renewed justifications of aggressive intervention throughout the world. In the three extraordinary communities in particular, the conviction that the contemporary English church is failing the conventions of Protestant heroism intertwines with the suspicion and the defense that those conventions have failed their church and must be recast.

I

As much as Charles cared about stabilizing the Christian creed of his people in their catechisms, he longed just as fervently for symbols and ceremonies that would bestow honor on that creed. For Charles, then, the heroism of the English church was a principal concern. Much more than his father, indeed in part because of his father, Charles came to power under the shadow of Elizabeth, who was hailed by such Stuart critics as Thomas Scot as more masculine in her aggression against the Antichrist than James with his accommodation of Catholic Europe. In 1624–25, after the return of Prince Charles and the Duke of Buckingham from Spain upon the collapse of the "match," Scot and others found reason enough to hope for the revival of the spirit of Francis Drake as a remedy for "this Dull or Effeminate Age."[2] Drake's was the spirit of the "righteous 'little David' setting off to beat down the abominable Iberian 'Goliah'" as Christopher Hodgkins puts it, and his legacy spoke to an Elizabethan conviction "that territorial expansion and fabulous wealth dovetailed neatly with chivalric virtue and apostolic zeal."[3] What made this legend all the more compelling, as Hodgkins reminds us, was "Spain's so-called Black Legend" as it was purveyed in "the graphic accounts by Bartolomé de Las Casas" of the Spanish atrocities in the New World (434). Set side by side with the martyrs memorialized by Foxe, the bloodletting dehumanization inflicted on the native peoples of "America" by the adventurers claiming authority from Charles V was starkly contrasted with "Drake's religious scruples." And even though Drake's reputation was controversial in the decades before the reign of Charles, "retellings of Drake's life and deeds constitute a minor publishing phenomenon" beginning with the death of James (Hodgkins, 436, 447).

Just before that death, an anticipated return to the militant Protestantism of an Elizabeth or a Sidney was briefly heralded in the post-Match figure of Prince Charles. As Mervyn James argues, this strategy would require a several-pronged attack: "a European Protestant league, a larger investment of resources in the war with Spain, wider military commitments abroad, westward oceanic expansion, and an extended naval assault on the Spanish empire."[4] According to John Reynolds – whose works zealously support the causes of the Elector Frederick and his wife Elizabeth, of New World colonization, and of the national honor to be derived from immediate and full-scale warfare against Spain – a heavenly congregation of monarchs from Henry VIII to Queen Anne would together indict James for seducing England away from religious warfare into the decadence of an impious peace, made palatable for the idle by the pastimes of "Stage-playes, Maskes, Reuels & Carowsing."[5] But not Charles whose mettle, according to one Spaniard in a Thomas Scot work, "is of another temper, and not so flexible as some take it."[6]

Just so, in the early years of his reign Charles's war with Spain and Buckingham's naval operations on behalf of the rebel Huguenots led to the report in foreign lands "that the days of Queen Elizabeth are revived."[7] At the start, as R. Malcolm Smuts puts it, Charles enlisted the Elizabethan cult of heroic monarchy, its capacity for ushering in a second golden age or the New Jerusalem, and its climactic role in the "great eschatological struggle between the forces of Christ and Antichrist."[8] Thereafter the king was shaken by his England's failure to revive the Protestant valor of his brother Henry, in whose honor a masque had celebrated the restoration of the "Fallen House of Chivalry" at a time when King James had reneged on heroic "austerity, military prepared-ness, and Protestant alliances" (29). Smuts has argued that the failure to secure a place "at the head of an international coalition" for the defense of Protestantism embarrassed Charles into "a decisive break with the religious and patriotic traditions that had grown up around Elizabeth" (7). A break was made, true, but it was not a decisive one: as Sharpe has shown, Charles continued to consider war a vital option, to blame parliament for the failures of the religious warfare under his watch, and to express the shame that he felt in their wake.[9] Other scholars, notably J. S. A. Adamson and Marlin E. Blaine, extend our understanding of this crisis in the royal leadership of religious heroism to a wide range of texts and practices in Caroline England, from "mock orders of chivalry" to poems such as Davenant's "Madagascar."[10] In many ways, Caroline cul-ture proceeds as if the epic-romantic dimensions of Elizabethan court culture and its satellites were simply dreams of the past: "there was no 'epic poetry' of the Caroline court," Adamson concludes, "and the already moribund Spenserian tradition of the chivalric epic was aban-doned." What is more, tournaments were jettisoned while "the image of the godly knight as the champion of the 'Protestant Cause'" was featured in mockeries of the stereotypical "Puritan" (161, 166).

But in the years of Charles I, Adamson explains, the ridicule of chival-ric conventions and pretensions is only half of a story whose other half is the "retrospective recasting" of Protestant valor; for "while Caroline courtly chivalry worked within the inherited language of the past, it simultaneously imposed new priorities on, and new standards for the reassessment of, that tradition's divergent elements and forms" (164). As a vital part of Charles's "major change in the cultural forms by which monarchy was presented," writers affiliated with the court found inventive ways in which to transform the representations of religious heroism in knighthood, "to reappraise and redefine the chivalric tradition," and to convert the military disasters of the 1620s into "a new, purified, chivalric ethos" so that the warfaring Christian is rendered preposterous and irreligious next to the holy chivalry of the Caroline court (161, 170–71). But Caroline court culture could not simply dispense with militarism, which had to be subsumed into a synthesis that abdicated from the atrocities of imperialism while attempting to disarm the charge that abdication permitted those atrocities. In the 1630s, Charles devoted himself to recasting a brave new ideal of religious heroism set forth in a ceremonial synthesis of power, virtue, and style – a holism from which no irksome component could wrest itself free and embarrass the lapsing prowess of the monarch. That is, he sought to create in symbol the honor that was languishing in military action and foreign policy.

The masques of the 1630s testify to Charles's commitment to a religious heroism, but also to his partial deflection of Protestant heroism away from the military cults of Queen Elizabeth and Prince Henry in two related directions. At the level of court ideology, the Carlo-Marian emanations of virtue, love, and piety are celebrated for revitalizing English morality and spirituality at large. This reformative influence, commonly hailed as "heroic," manifests itself in such exclusive circles as the newly spiritualized Order of the Garter, but it is also aimed at British subjects wherever they worship, at home or abroad. At a more material level, the Laudian restitution of the resources, ceremonies, and fabric of the church is linked by apologists and critics alike to the high cultural style of ancient epic so that the Caroline church heroic is as much a matter of beauty as it is of virtue. The beauty of holiness, the Laudians aver, will give the church a power to discipline and elevate souls that no hurly-burly violence or expensive, quixotic plantation could ever manage. The elevation of religion, that is, ought to have a wide and profound impact on the much more mundane regions of every Christian's thoughts and social interactions. But the Laudians themselves must have recourse to discursive, legal, even corporal force when beauty is underwhelming. Similarly, into the composite heroism of the court, poets and apologists inject transmuted forms of godly militarism, from the knightly and romantic to the nautical and colonial. The problem with the court's synthesis is that its elements are just as likely to conflict as they are to converge, and at any rate each element on its own is vulnerable to a criticism that the mysterious *pneuma* of holism is unable to silence.

In Davenant and Jones's *Britannia Triumphans* (1638), there is a prominent convergence between images of the king's "heroic virtue" and signs of the church's restored magnificence. The very first scene centers on the repaired and newly classical St. Paul's, "the symbol . . . of High Church Laudian reform."[11] Modeled on the temple of Antoninus and Faustina, its portico was held largely responsible for restoring St. Paul's to its proper status as the "principall ornament" of the English church.[12] However, in Stuart debates over the beautification of the church, while such a pagan genealogy and the epic analogues of English temples may be taken for granted, their spiritual benefits are not. Advocates argue that Christians have always borrowed architecture and prayers from the pagans who borrowed them from the Jews, that this is a perfectly acceptable practice and easily distinguishable from papist excesses and superstitions, and that the lineage of church ceremony will incite Christians to worship their true God more carefully and orderly than the heathens did their false deities.[13] Peter Heylyn traces the practice of setting aside sacred places – but also most sacred areas within those places – to classical culture, finding prime examples in the *Aeneid* and declaring that "there's no question to be made but many *Temples* of the *Gentiles* were, without any alteration of the Fabrick, converted into *Christian* Churches."[14]

Whereas Heylyn and John Cosin approve these grand resources for "replenishing" the church with "ornaments, utensills, and beautie" in "this last declyning age," the so-called "Puritans" whom they accuse of debasing the style of the church – and with it all uniformity, decency, and spirituality – argue against such conversions. In 1628, Peter Smart complains that Cosin would offer his flock the rites of Cybele or Bacchus, and transplant them into the high ritual "which the poett describeth in the 4th of his Æneidos."[15] The stances of other participants in the debate over the beautification of the church are sometimes hard to pin down. For instance, John Williams's love of rails does not prevent him from criticizing the paganism of Caroline altar policy.[16] Indeed, in the final chapter of *The Holy Table*, he concludes his attack on altars by deriving the church use of diptyches for the commemoration of noteworthy Christians from the *Iliad*.[17] Thus, for good or ill, Caroline efforts to dignify and decorate the church are measured according to epic proportions.

In *Britannia Triumphans*, then, the prominence of St. Paul's defines the church heroic in terms of the material enrichment, ceremonial elevation, and ancient catholicity of worship. This vein of heroism amounts to a

rearguard defense against papist attacks by shoring up the beauty of
the church from neglect and decay. As part of the synthesis between
the physical reconstitution of the church and the heroic virtue of the
king, the Banqueting House, as the political equivalent of St. Paul's,
is mentioned at the outset of the masque, which (the reader is told)
took place in a "new temporary room of timber" in order to prevent
damage to Rubens's recently imported ceiling and "other enrichments"
in Whitehall. The ceiling, moreover, features the apotheosis of Religion
among the other royal virtues named "heroic" in this and other Caroline
masques.[18]

In court entertainments, Graham Parry has noted, "Charles is generally presented as the embodiment of Heroic Virtue" – a virtue combining
contemplative depth and spiritual purity together with a military activism
in potentia.[19] In *Britannia Triumphans*, the figure of Action, whose motto is
medio tutissima ("safest in the middle"), is advanced in congruence with
a church balanced between the potential for military Protestantism and
the domestic rebuilding of the temple. What this balancing act means is
that Charles's synthetic ideal of heroic religion attempts to subsume its
more controversial elements in a larger, inestimable mythology. Nonetheless, the controversial element in Davenant's masque – the promotion
of Britain's naval strength – is notorious for its estimable cost, not just
because of the naval failures of the early reign but also because of the tax
on which that strength relied.[20]

In *Britannia Triumphans*, when Britanocles, the embodiment of royal
"wisdom, valour, and piety," gives way to Bellerophon or "Heroic
Virtue," the latter is associated with the reclamation of both reason
and chivalry from their debasement in the Socinian and magical impi-
eties into which the king's church, so critics argue, has a tendency to
slide.[21] The refined heroics of the court must be carefully separated from
certain problematic forms of heroism to which the king and his church
apologists nonetheless have debts. All in all, the court's religious heroism is said to combine the best of all other heroic codes, from chivalry
(including love and valor) to virtuous rationality, from wisdom and piety
to a St. Paul's evocative of ceremony and ornament in the grand style,
and from naval prowess in the vein of Elizabeth to the aura of Henrietta
Maria whose beauty, we are told, might serve as the inspiration for epic
poets such as Homer. "In this isle," Bellerophon concludes, the heroes
"old with modern virtues reconcile" in a catholicity of honorable traditions congruent with Laud's own commitment to the catholicity of
English ecclesiology.

The Caroline synthesis of traditions in reconstituting the church heroic is featured in other masques as well, and as often as not, its maker must find ways to subsume volatile ingredients in the amalgam. The very occasion of Davenant's *Triumphs of the Prince D'Amour* (1635) is challenging to a courtly formation of religious heroism. As they had done in 1613 at the wedding of Elizabeth and Prince Frederick, Palatine of the Rhine, the members of the Middle Temple staged a masque for the visit of the couple's son, Charles, who together with his brother Rupert, had made the journey in order to garner support for Charles's return to the Palatinate. Rather than monetary or military aid, the masque offers the beleaguered prince a chemical transformation of his otherwise limited valor into a holistic, numinous force that might somehow, magically, transmit English charity and valor over a distance.

In *The Temple of Love*, the Caroline court again is celebrated for its resourceful and sublime heroic synthesis; in this case, the Greek epic tradition, chaste love, and the conversion of Indians into "all soul within" are part and parcel of the king's depiction as "the last and living hero."[22] Similar is *Tempe Restored*, in which the king is featured as that heroic virtue combining "religion, justice, and all the other virtues joined together," with the masque assembling allegories from Homer – souls reclaimed from the wiles of Circe – and from the colonial enterprise of saving the impious Indians who appear in Circe's train. There is a contemporary logic to this conflation: authors such as Hugo Grotius envision the Indians and ancient Greeks in the same category of a paganism possessed with some basic religious values but in dire need of an enterprising Christianity. According to Thomas Morton, the Indians are offshoots from the demise and dispersion of the Trojans, at one time out there on those same seas over which Odysseus ranged and so not unreasonably imagined as encountering Circe.[23] As with naval prowess or the Palatinate, the epic venture of saving the heathens is a controversial vestige of the past – one thought by some to have been tragically jettisoned by the Stuarts when James disenfranchised the Virginia Company and Charles failed to revive its mission. The consequence of this betrayal was, it was complained, that the colonies were now fully given over to Spanish imperialism or to separatist errors. As usual, Charles made matters only worse, in the eyes of his critics, by his weak and misguided attempts to restore a colonial policy to the activism of the church, with Laud overseeing the (short-lived) committee responsible for ensuring conformity to the Church of England wherever British people worshiped.[24]

In *Coelum Britannicum*, magnificence figures centrally in the court's vision of heroic virtue. The reformation of heroism is at odds with poverty, the virtues of which are lazy, dull, and cheap. Approximating the ecclesiological position that God deserves in our services of worship the best and most that we can give, the idea of a plentiful and restorative heroic virtue suits the basic premise of the masque that Caroline England has inherited and must enrich a culture in ruins. Thus, a cautious "prudence" seems something of a misfit in the masque. But riches, we learn, are just as dangerous as poverty is undesirable: more often than not, the love of riches has induced the desecration of temples, vicious bloodshed, and erroneous colonialism. If this be so, the enrichment of the temple is in direct opposition to an interest in New England, which is disparaged in Carew's masque as a land to which some English Argo should transport the scum, humors, and vices rejected in the court-influenced reformation of Britain. But this divide between heroic goals is problematic for the court precisely because Charles putatively oversees the conformation of worship wherever there are British subjects. The immediate context of the masque drives home its colonial dilemma: three days after its performance the Privy Council discussed New England's descent into a separatist chaos.[25]

Whether or not domestic magnificence and a colonial mission can be reconciled – and writers such as Purchas argue that they can be – the court's heroic virtue is more securely triumphant in the mythology that unites conjugal love with wisdom and industry. But in Carew's masque the diachronic dimension of the synthesis – whereby modern heroes recreate the ancients in the same fashion that Laud would resituate the English church in a catholic tradition – remains in question. In the interest of reconciliation, Momus points out that some of the old constellations are worthy of retention, not least the dragon commemorating the legend of "a divine Saint George for this nation".[26] He comments further on the admirable recent habit of memorializing, in "embellished" form, the military heroism of the past. Whatever his penchant for criticism, Momus introduces the Order of the Garter as the most impressive Caroline synthesis of heroic traditions, uniting old and new but also Elizabethan – with its military, chivalric, and apocalyptic tendencies – and Caroline.

As Sharpe explains, Charles sought to endow the Order of the Garter with a religious significance at once deeply spiritual and grandly ceremonial.[27] But even the Armada is commemorated in the masque, suitably transformed into ornamentation in "the particular Christmas hangings of the guard chamber of this court, wherein the naval victory of eighty-eight is to the eternal glory of this nation exactly delineated" (Orgel and Strong, 574). Once again militarism and beautification converge, with the court's sponsorship of ecclesiastical reformation aimed as much at the body and ceremony of the church as it is at the refinement of its spirit.

Whatever Charles's love of St. George or the ongoing possibility of an English war in the 1630s, the military element fits uneasily in the context of virtually two decades of English abdication from any leadership in the Thirty Years War, seen by many Protestant commentators as the latest (if protracted and convoluted) installment in the apocalyptic battle against the Antichrist (Orgel and Strong, 574). In form and content, the ceremony of the Caroline masque epitomizes the court's reckoning with the problem that the spirit of its religious heroism is disturbed by the multitude of attractive but volatile competitors. But the masque also illustrates just how inventively the court's cultural brokers can work in redefining, expanding, and even humbling its own Christian heroism.

Mervyn James has argued that the Elizabethans and especially Sidney accomplished a "synthesis of honour, humanism and religion," whose legacy in the Caroline period was fractured between the court, which promulgated a version of that synthesis, and its critics, whose allegiance to a Foxeian vision of history was posed in opposition to those Laudians who had little patience for Foxe. To the Laudians, the "Puritan" devotion to Foxe was likely to result in ecclesiastical and social disjunction; it reinforced, that is, the Puritan mindset severing a community into the godly and the reprobate.[28]

From the beginning, it should be noted, the Foxe legacy itself was hardly univocal, as it supported the national church and even bishops on the one hand and stood critical of the persecutions sponsored by the state and its prelates on the other. But the rifts in the Foxeian heroic were not deeply felt until the reign of Charles, not least because this heroic stood in prominent opposition to the principles of the Laudian church. In the 1630s, Prynne was all the more irksome to Laud in claiming both sides of the Foxe legacy, supporting the monarch against an evil clergy and continuing a long line of heroic patience in the face of persecution. Critics indebted to Foxe also took aim at the assumption that the newly celebrated prelacy would be responsible for elevating the church to epic status; whereas Francis Markham could underscore the grand style of the Caroline temple by insisting on the "first Ranke in Honour" of its bishops, Lord Brooke subverted such a claim by enlisting his own aristocratic heritage against the modest origins and upstart mobility of prelates such as Laud.[29]

In turn, Laud's own preference for one aspect of the Caroline synthesis – ceremonial decency – over the others also demonstrates how multiple the church heroic had become. In a letter to William Kingsley, Archdeacon of Canterbury, he illustrates just how contentious the various constituents of the court's heroism might prove. Dated 29 April 1636, the letter instructs the archdeacon to hire a painter for the purposes of removing from a church monument "all that concerns the Fleet in '88, because that belongs to a foreign nation."[30] In his other letters, Laud vacillates between encouraging the Queen of Bohemia and expressing his opposition to any English involvement in wars that would work at cross purposes with his pursuit of the "honour of the Church" in terms of its beauty, catholicity, ritual, and wealth. Little interested in international Protestant coalitions, Laud shows an equally slight commitment to the business of regulating religion in the colonies: as early as 1626, he records a meeting with a Dutchman whose proposal to free the West Indies from the Spaniard involves religion "in a great measure" (3.184–85). But Laud is unconvinced that the man, John Overtrout, has a viable plan. In the notebooks kept by John Finet between 1628 and 1641, the master of ceremonies is compelled to divide his attention between the rituals of the court and the intricate diplomacy with European powers. But for Laud the latter concern, with its potential for warfare, is best avoided as a "laberinth" – no matter that Charles's sister and her children are the Protestants captured within. Laud is not interested in the court's synthetic (and costly) myths; for him the "labour" of churchmanship should be centered on "an orderly settlement of the external worship of God," or the protective "hedge" of the church, as he calls it elsewhere. With Humphrey Sydenham, Laud believes that ecclesiastical authority has awakened under Charles, since "canons, constitutions, decrees which were formerly without soul or motion . . . have recover'd a new life and vegetation" and "Ceremonies, harmless ceremonies . . . have gotten their former lustre and state again."[31] For these reasons and no other, Laud believes, the English church has attained heroic stature.

With the rise of the Laudians, then, no one constituent of religious heroism is a matter of widespread consensus, and none exists without its damaging or limiting components. In Peter Heylyn's defense of that "most excellent and heroicke institution" of the Garter, even St. George himself is scarcely beyond reproach. Among others, Calvin has denied his existence altogether. More intricately, some critics have challenged the historicity of the stories so that Heylyn is compelled to be scrupulous regarding the sources through which he must recover St. George. All the same, Heylyn insists on the uses of heroic fictions: in the *Iliad*, *Aeneid*, and Arthurian romances, poets embellish so that readers "might more constantly bee prompted to Heroicke undertakings."[32] He repeats the point later, when St. George is said to inspire Christians to emulation in much the same fashion that Homer's Achilles inspired Alexander. St. George has been identified, however, with a cruel and heretical bishop so that Heylyn must purge his saint of "unwarrantable" elements. Without St. George the New Jerusalem is "poorer" but a persecutory Arian hardly enriches it. In the 1630s, a consensus over religious heroism seems impossible when in 1636, the Foxeian Henry Burton can appropriate the church heroic from the Laudians in arguing that those godly saints with "a greater and more extraordinary measure of Christian zeale and courage for Christ" will always be persecuted by the merely ceremonial and largely papist prelates, and that such Christians of "heroick grace" – ironically like St. George – will find themselves condemned as dangerous heretics.[33]

For a number of reasons, then, Caroline court culture complicates heroic religion insofar as a brilliant and powerful synthesis of ideals encounters equally compelling critiques of and deep-seated fractures in that synthesis. Graham Parry has remarked of the differences between Jacobean and Caroline court cultures that the former iconography was more static, the latter more dynamic, and that Charles tended "to project himself in roles, either directly (as upon the Whitehall stage in masques where he appeared variously as a British Emperor, Heroic Virtue, or a heroic lover) or indirectly (by having artists – especially Van Dyck – depict him in dramatic circumstances, as St. George or as a triumphant Emperor)."[34] That is, Charles's heroism was set forth contextually, and it was dramatic in two senses: the king sought to play heroic parts to find those that best suited him; and this fashioning of a religious hero stressed the valor of the representational labors themselves. In liturgical contexts, the Caroline church heroic could approach a triumphant stasis, but given Laud's programmatic commitment to the notion that the ceremony and decency of the church must constantly be remade, even that aspect of the Caroline church heroic was always in the process of being established, lost, and reconstituted.

Between 1625 and 1640, this heroic process is widely acknowledged to be perilous and fallible as well as mediatory and reformative. Among those epic images to which Richard Montagu, William Laud, and other embattled apologists return, the English church is often imagined as a ship sailing in the treacherous waters between Scylla and Charybdis, assaulted contradictorily as true religion struggles to navigate between extremes. With Hercules the writers claim to be facing the unpleasant task of cleaning the Augean stables. Montagu in particular thinks of himself as a beleaguered epic hero, alone "in the gapp" between Puritan and papist. Comparing himself to those "old heroes" of the church, he often cites the words of Agamemnon from book one of the *Iliad*, according to which God and a good cause are said to justify the hero in the face of wretched betrayal and wild insubordination.[35]

Indeed the heroism of the Church of England is often characterized in this period by its fallible execution of a nonetheless sufficiently secure authority in assessing matters of faith and worship. Whatever the impressive mythologies of the court, then, other Caroline communities devoted to rethinking and remaking the church heroic must reckon not just with the bathetic failures of Stuart heroism but with heroism as failure in the processes of reformation. Even the stalwart Montagu draws his other "favorite tag" (as Trevor-Roper calls it) from Ovid's transformation of epic heroism into a series of metamorphoses.[36] And this is the very epic translated by the man (George Sandys) whose American adventures and friendship with Viscount Falkland connect those two Caroline communities producing the most complex and searching meditations on the church heroic, Little Gidding and Great Tew. These communities are dissatisfied with the official heroic postures of a masquerading court culture, but find it difficult to reinvent – and not just criticize – epic Protestantism.

II

In 1625, the family of Nicholas Ferrar pulled itself out of the political and financial wreckage of the Virginia Company and embarked on what its modern biographer has aptly called a "great adventure." Around thirty in number, their resolve was no less than to create their own religious community apart from, yet in keeping with, the Church of England as they construed it, so that they might concentrate on "complete self-dedication to God."[37] Finding neither their London nor Hertford domiciles appropriate for this design, the family found and secured in "Little Gidding, a tiny hamlet on the borders of Huntingdonshire . . . a large manor house in a shocking state of disrepair and, thirty or forty paces from it, a little church which had been converted into a hay barn."[38] In repairing the ruins of this one estate, the Ferrar family strove to rebuild English parish religion as they saw fit, without all the external depravity and political factionalism that had dismantled their involvement in that more obvious epic adventure, the plantation of true religion among the Indians in the New World. Theirs was not just a retirement from business; it was a kind of abdication from Stuart society itself, a society that nonetheless they hoped Little Gidding might come in some small measure to reconstitute.

Having spent their first few years at Gidding refurbishing the buildings and grounds themselves, the inhabitants of the community turned their attention to the establishment and development of a round of daily religious offices. Whereas these offices were the central feature of their lives, the family members kept themselves active, some with the ongoing affairs of Virginia, others with the crafting of the famous and beautiful Biblical concordances. They intervened with many charitable acts in the parish around their manor; at dinner, some worthy book was read aloud for the benefit of the diners; and for select audiences, they staged symposia on topics of Christian history that they left behind as dialogues in manuscripts, the so-called "story books." Each participant was assigned an allegorical name for her or his part in the dialogues of the "Little Academy," for example, the Guardian (John Ferrar), the Visitor (his brother Nicholas), the Chief (their niece Mary Collett), the Patient (her sister Anna), and the Moderator (their mother, Nicholas's sister, Susanna).[39]

At Little Gidding, then, "even the walls [were] not idle," as their dear associate George Herbert wrote of the parson's house in *A Priest to the Temple*.[40] But in everything they discussed or practiced, the Little Gidding community was concerned with the implications of their two main adventures: the spread of religion to the world, and the intensification of spirituality at home. And as Maycock understood, they cherished both endeavors as versions of Protestant heroism. Indeed, the preoccupation of their symposia was the problem of defining the very nature of epic religion in a Stuart society that seemed at once drastically unheroic in comparison to the Elizabethans and uncommonly inventive, even multiplicative in its revisions of Protestant greatness.

Like other Caroline communities invested in the reconstitution of Protestant heroism, the Gidding interlocutors cherish certain conventions of the past. For example, Nicholas Ferrar prizes Foxe's *Acts and Monuments* and the Little Academy's dialogues are filled with Foxeian narratives of "heroic suffering."[41] Beyond Foxe, the symposia concern themselves chiefly with the wonderful accounts of that heroic virtue, mortification, and faith manifested by exemplary Christians from the beginning of the church right up to the seventeenth century.

But in the Gidding story books Protestant heroism is as complex as it is pervasive. For one thing, the Little Gidding interlocutors are convinced that most of their contemporaries have no appreciation for the true heroism of the church, "hissing out as Folly & Fables all those Heroical Actions & Events of former Times, wch exceed that measure of goodnes, wch wee haue stinted out our selues by" (Blackstone, 191). For another, the story books mediate competing notions of Christian heroism and criticize even those heroic ideals dear to the interlocutors themselves – not least the epic odyssey of the Virginia Company.

In his *Acts and Monuments*, John Foxe divides the martyrdom of Dr. Robert Ferrar, Bishop of St. David's, into two phases. In the first and longer part, Ferrar is depicted in King Edward's time as the victim of slander – which includes allegations that the bishop has usurped the king's authority, fostered superstition against the king's injunctions, and proved himself a covetous, negligent, and popish prelate. Then, with the ascension of Queen Mary, Ferrar is burned for refusing to advocate the Mass and transubstantiation and to renounce justification by faith alone; for supporting clerical marriage; and for resisting papal authority.

In their story books, it is obvious that the participants at Little Gidding in the so-called "Little Academy" are deeply influenced by Foxe. Like Foxe, they celebrate "memorable example[s] of constancy" in the name of the faith in opposition to the flimsy world, and they read ecclesiastical history for signs of providence and for moral instruction. Replacing military heroism with martyrdom, Foxe bequeaths to Nicholas Ferrar and his family the simple idea that church histories make us "better in our livings," "better prepared unto like conflicts," and secure in the knowledge of "what true christian fortitude is, and what is the right way to conquer; which standeth not in the power of man, but in hope of the resurrection to come, and is now, I trust, at hand."[42] The legacy of Foxe is integral, then, to the heroic mortification so zealously acclaimed by the interlocutors at Little Gidding.

But as the case of Bishop Ferrar suggests, the legacy of Foxe is not altogether simple for the admiring inhabitants of Little Gidding. For one thing, Foxe supports both establishmentarians and nonconformists in the English church – and Little Gidding is at once conformable and irreducible to the Caroline version of the same. For another, the tale of Bishop Ferrar anticipates the martyrdom of slander despised and endured by the Little Gidding community itself, caricatured by some of their more biased contemporaries as papists and separatists alike. According to Barnabas Oley, Nicholas Ferrar once remarked "that to fry on a faggot was not more martyrdom than continual obloquy. He was torn asunder as with mad horses or crushed betwixt the upper and under millstone of contrary reports; that he was a Papist and that he was a Puritan."[43] As Elizabeth Clarke concludes, Little Gidding was committed not just to mediating between polarities but to achieving "a third position independent of them both." For the Ferrars, heroism at its simplest level amounted to the labors required to excavate, imagine, or attain this other ground.[44]

Even among the more careful and sympathetic spectators, Little Gidding provokes considerable bemusement on the part of English Christians, from the king and queen (who until the 1640s send messengers) to those many visitors – some official, some informal – who struggle to read the composite iconography and practices of the community against the backdrop of the Stuart religious landscape.[45] Some even defend the community against slander by insisting that Little Gidding itself is normative and not singular, "Orthodox, Regular, Puritan Protestants" as one gentleman categorizes it.[46] But the story books confirm what this interpretive quandary can only suggest, namely, that heroism at Little Gidding involves the adventure of reinventing the dignity of the Church of England itself, and that this adventure is characterized not by some confident, even magical technology of synthesis promulgated by the Caroline court, but by trial and error, dismay and hope, in the enrichment of worship and the reformation of spirituality.

In the story books at Little Gidding, then, Christian heroism is only in part straightforward, a matter of saintly patience and mortified opposition to the world. But it is also elusive because there are competing, sometimes failing, notions of heroism and each – including romance, colonization, and crusade but also peace and *contemptus mundi* – is subjected to criticism. As it is explored in the Gidding dialogues, heroism is offered as an epitome of what the Church of England ought to be or has failed to be – witness the collapse of the Virginia Company – and as a synopsis of what the church is: a critical and fallible negotiation between rival notions of the church and, as such, equivocal and mediating. As the interlocutors trade stories, religious heroism is not just undercut by a disenchantment over its illusory norms; it is also reconstituted in terms of the fallen world's inevitable recourse to incessant critique and to sometimes extraordinary, if also makeshift, reconstructions of its spiritual endeavors.

In their staged dialogues, the interlocutors concern themselves with correcting "misapprehension[s]" that inhibit the pursuit and perfection of virtue and devotion.[47] In contrast to the world's "opinions and practizes," they long to approximate the saints and their own allegorical titles in Christian faith, knowledge, and action. Keenly alert to their own shortcomings, and with an emphasis on the heroic execution of virtue and piety, the speakers tell noteworthy and illustrative stories from ancient to modern times. Some stories involve lapses from virtue: for example, as an emblem of the loss of charity to anger and revenge, the exceptional piety of a priest from Antioch is undermined by his envy for a protégé. Just as often in the stories, modern heroes endure the tumult of post-Reformation Christendom: Henry IV of France teaches a would-be assassin the difference between a church that harms the innocent and a church that forgives the guilty, while Katherine of Aragon suffers nobly in the rift between the pope and the king, her husband.[48]

For the most part, the applications are kept simple: enmity is bad, charity good, and Christian bliss is at odds with the world's false rewards. But problems small and large arise along the way. In the case of Henry IV, for instance, it is pointed out by one of the interlocutors that mercy is inferior to the "Conjunction of two so different Vertues," a compound of mercy and justice (Sharland, 34). Then there is the question of warfare and military heroism: at Little Gidding, romance in particular is condemned for its unholy marriage between Christian piety and violence, but the interlocutors also credit the idea that a king's charity now ensures his military victories later.

Throughout the story books, this problem of whether Christians can justify violence is linked to the larger question of just how Protestant heroism pertains to, or exists in, the political and even the natural world. At Little Gidding, the question of heroism centers on the problem of deciding just what holy enterprises can and should be accomplished in this world – on the battlefield, in the colonial search for a new Eden or New Jerusalem, in political and judicial actions, in acts of charity and worship, and in the perfectibility of virtue among the saints. It might even be said that heroism at Little Gidding comprises the laborious condition of striving to answer in life as in discourse the very questions that plague the straightforward validation of the resources of militant Christianity.

The interlocutors' most searching meditations on heroism involve enigmas as to whether utopias exist in the world, whether the miracles and wonders of saints' lives are either true or useful, and whether abdication from the world and its offices is desirable or even possible. Each of these problems impinges on the evolving enterprise of Little Gidding itself – on its involvement in colonialism, on its quasi-asceticism, on its relationship to the English world beyond its boundaries, from the parish to the court, and on its views of a Europe torn by over fifteen years of putatively religious warfare.

Many of these questions infiltrate what appears to be a straightforward (if long) celebration of Charles V's retirement from empire and the world. The abdication itself was a widely celebrated emblem in the seventeenth century of contempt for the world; in "Content," for example, George Herbert lauds "the pliant mind, whose gentle measure / Complies and suits with all estates; / Which can let loose to a crown, and yet with pleasure / Take up within a cloister's gate."[49] But as an important icon for Elizabeth I and Charles I, "this heroycall Emperour" (as he is applauded at Gidding) epitomized all the complexities of religious heroism that Caroline students of the emperor were coming to appreciate. As Karl Brandi explains, Charles V's Burgundian affiliations lent his imperial persona an air of chivalry, yet as emperor Charles wove his knightly values into a new heroic tapestry "with the conscientious piety of the Netherlands, with Spanish self-restraint and the universal traditions of the Romano-German Empire."[50] But the universalist scope of his conception of the Christian emperor made Charles vulnerable to the staggering vicissitudes of Euro-Christian politics; to complicity with those New World atrocities that were carried out in his name and denounced by Bartolomé de las Casas; and to contradictions between his Catholic convictions and his political alliance with Protestant rulers.

The abdication itself – to a villa near the monastery at Yuste – was a resolution that caused as much controversy for contemporaries in deciphering it as it did for Charles himself. Was it a repudiation of the profanities of the world in which he had been so intricately involved? Or was it a cowardly permission for those wars and atrocities to persist that he himself did much to unleash and could do much to restrain? Did the abdication make Charles a pious hero at last, or did it diminish whatever heroic stature he had ever claimed? As a ruler who had done so much to bridge past codes to the new heroism of the Renaissance, was Charles trying to cloister a valor that he had done so much to secularize as the prince under whom all God's children might be united? More than even the pope, was not he God's agent for unifying the church against heresy and political dissimulation, for planting religion among the heathens, and for combating the spread of Islam? Was not he the prince to whom Erasmus had looked for a way out of the impasse of religious conflict? Once the goals to "eradicate the Lutheran heresy and reform the Church" (Brandi, 258) were thwarted time and time again, was it righteous for Charles to commit himself to the solitary worship of God?

Biographers have disagreed about whether Charles's retirement was motivated by a series of disappointments late in his reign or by a medieval asceticism that he never abandoned. What the Little Gidding community emphasizes in its day-long dialogue on Charles's retreat from empire is how vexed and fitful the retirement was for Charles himself – indeed, this struggle over whether and why to retire, and over how to live once one has retired, is the most imitable and legible aspect of Charles's heroism for the Gidding interlocutors. On the day set aside for the story of Charles's retirement, the narrator (the Chief or Mary Collett) lays a trap for her audience. Charles V, she begins, ranks among the happiest of men because he combined noble blood, empire, and great actions with "the right Composure of an Inward Disposition to inioy them."[51] From his royal visage and equestrian skills to the excellence of his extended dynasty, Charles V is a perfect example, she concludes, of how external happiness complements internal virtues as the very essence of the "Heroical Prince."

But then the Chief springs the trap. Describing her discourse as a journey over seas, into creeks and channels in search of a haven, she undermines her own assertion that Charles V represents a perfect composite of internal and external blessings and, with it, her claim that such a composite defines happiness after all. Simply put, Charles becomes the true Christian hero when he renounces the world and all its politics and pomp, for only then does he acknowledge that "There's no happines at all in this World" (51). Even prior to his retirement, the Chief suggests, Charles himself has doubts about his place in the world, since in his "continual Exercize of Heroical Industry in most Noble & weighty Affaires," the emperor understands the political value of pomp and pleasures but he himself has little desire for these things. Yet Charles himself is fallible: for instance, his illegitimate children make him "a greater Example by his fall then perhaps he could haue been by his Integritie" (35, 56). This last statement is significant not just because it concurs with the point made so often in the dialogues – that stories about perfectly saintly virtue are less helpful than stories of the moderately virtuous and struggling wayfarer – but also because it broaches what proves to be an ongoing meditation on fallenness as a condition of religious heroism, with epic spirituality following the loss of – and preceding the recovery of – a pastoral Eden.

As he is presented in the story books, Charles is most heroic in distress –
witness "this Heroical Prince's Demeanour" in his noble retreat from a
disastrous military attempt on the Turkish stronghold at Algiers – and
in revision of himself (38). When the emperor lapses in choosing policy
over honesty, God refines him through punishment, a crucial point in
the auditors' understanding of "Heroical Vertues." So too the Chief's
strategy is to initiate the uprooting from the auditors' minds and hearts of
those "long rooted & fortified" misconceptions about happiness (41, 56).
More than anything else, then, Charles represents "the Reformation of
corrupted manners" and his renunciation of empire is the culmination
of a heroic life defined in terms of continual sanctification.

If Charles V comes to renounce "the imaginarie idol of Humane
Felicitie," it is strangely the case that he continues to strive for the
"revnitement of diuided opinions in the Church of Christ" (44, 67).
Pursuing the unity of religion in this world, his imperial life involves him
in diplomacy, warfare, and colonization, all at cross-purposes with retirement. And the relevance to Little Gidding of this aspect of Charles's
heroism unsettles the dialogue even more. After all, Nicholas Ferrar has
opted for semi-retirement over the offers of a diplomatic position in a
time of religious warfare; and despite his ongoing advisory role in colonial matters for Charles I, he and his brother John have been humiliated
and penalized under James for their leadership in the colonization of
Virginia. They have largely abdicated, that is, from a project of planting
true religion in opposition to the Spanish, an enterprise that ranks in the
Ferrar papers as the same kind of "Heroyicall Act" as support for the
Palatinate cause or opposition to the Spanish Match.[52] It was in fact this
tendency in their heroic code that led to their reputation as separatists – in
contrast to their more Laudian liturgical penchant that led to the family's notoriety as "Arminians." In a letter to Theophilus Woodnoth dated
30 January 1625, John Ferrar characterizes the move to Little Gidding
as a pastoral retreat from trouble through which means God "hath in
most vnexpected manner turned and refreshed vs."[53] Inventing there an
intensely spiritual and richly liturgical form of godly living – one that is
said to refine and elevate the religion of the parish radiating out from a
domestic retreat – the interlocutors nonetheless admire the providence
of God as it operates through Charles across the world and in pursuit
of Eden. Given this quandary over whether religious heroism thrives in
or against the grain of the world, the dialogue revisits the ruins of the
Virginia Company in what serves as a painful opportunity to rethink the
means and scope of heroic circumstance.

III

For John and Nicholas Ferrar in the early 1620s, the Virginia Company kept alive the Elizabethan heroic tradition of their father, along with Hawkins, Drake, and the other seamen who checkmated Spain by exporting Protestantism to the heathens of America. In addition, the company offered a new economic means of enriching and revitalizing the English church at home. As Samuel Purchas maintained in his defense of English rights to colonize Virginia, the enterprise resembled Solomon's journey "to fetch Ophir Materialls for the Temples structure, and to edifie Christs Church, with more full and evident knowledge of Gods Workes in the World, both of Creation and Providence."[54] As heir to his "Heroicke Brother" Henry, Prince Charles was hailed as the leader who might replenish the mother church while spreading true religion to America – hence the voluminous Ferrar papers "touchinge the Heroyicall Act and resolution" of the Virginia plantation.[55]

In epic terms, the Virginia enterprise was also construed as a cataclysmic movement of the European church westward – the *translatio ecclesiae*. For some, this *translatio* entailed a progression toward spiritual and ecclesiastical perfection in the New Jerusalem: consolidated by Spenser, the sixteenth- and seventeenth-century analogies between the English church regaining paradise with the grace of God and Aeneas's journey to *Roma Aeterna* were commonplace expansions of the medieval allegorization of the epic hero as "a Christian Everyman."[56] For others, America represented a nodal point in the ongoing struggles of the church militant. Indeed between 1619 and 1624, years of such pronounced factionalism in its ranks, the Virginia Company had offered little but turmoil for the Ferrars: more often than not, they found themselves defending those officials in the enterprise, especially Sir Edwin Sandys, that James himself distrusted or opposed, and this ideological and political tension, together with the Ferrar brothers' administrative burdens as successive deputies of the company, added insult to the injuries of the dearth, sickness, and bloodshed of the years 1622–23.[57]

All the same, Nicholas Ferrar understood the Virginia enterprise as largely responsible for the epic transmission of religion westward. It should be remembered that he fought to have Herbert's poetry published with the two infamous lines of the "Church Militant" intact: "Religion stands on tip-toe in our land, / Ready to pass to the American strand." In this poem, interpreted early on "as a 'heroic poem . . . which is partly *historical*, & partly *prophetical*,'" Herbert describes the progress of the church, together with the arts and power, in cyclical terms, with each cycle having its high points and low.[58] But in Herbert's poem each low point is more degraded than the previous one – a pattern crucial to the revision of colonial heroism at Little Gidding. Whatever their initial beliefs about the epic mission of the Virginia Company, the Ferrars came away from the massacres, diseases, famines, cost, and politics of the enterprise with a disenchantment about epic religion.

In Herbert's model of the translation of the church, heroism does not entail full restitution or perfection in a new Eden. Instead, the church's militancy always consists of metamorphosis, conflict, and decay as history spirals downwards toward the coming of Christ. In a similar vein, it is not surprising that George Sandys conceived of his translation of Ovid's *Metamorphoses* as an apt product of his travels to and troubles in Virginia. With Christian warfare taking place in a declining world, the painful irony of Herbert's poem is summarized in the words of Raymond Anselment: "Time . . . is the enemy of perfection, and any attempts to repair its ravages are doomed."[59] In this vein, heroism comes closest to the melancholy found in Chapman's *Odyssey*, as Colin Burrow describes it: Chapman's emphasis there is on "the painful and inescapable self-absorption of exile," on how "the whole lie of the world is against the success of virtue," and on "how grim it is to be good."[60] The best the church can hope for is temporary respite, brief periods of vitality, and the benefit of expiation in what A. B. Chambers calls "that longer and harder westward path."[61] But its battle against decay is endless and, until Christ returns, futile.

As is often the case in the Gidding dialogue on Charles V, the disenchantment over colonization checkmates an initial bout of optimism. Thus, following her source, the Chief at first declares that God saved "the full discouerie & subiection of the New-found world" for Charles V, who "was appointed to conioyne them not only by an intercourse of Ciuil Commerce, but by the farre more perfect Bond of Christian Religion, so he was to cleare those scruples, which had or might on either part disquiet." The so-called "scruples" pertain especially to the boastful and cruel Spaniards who deify their own "imaginarie All-sufficiencie," an idolatry which would appear to necessitate Protestant intervention in the New World.[62] But suddenly Charles assumes an extraordinary colonial position. His renunciation of the world disabuses the Indians of the idea that he is a god; they learn from him that all human beings are sinfully mortal, that the riches of the world are nothing, and that only God is sufficient in grace, wisdom, and power. In other words, Charles's retirement forms the basis of the heathens' admiration of him, and this the basis of their disillusionment about the idol of human sufficiency constructed by the Spaniards.

But the most ironic disillusionment produced by the great adventure of colonization belongs to the English and especially to the Ferrars who have learned that there is no perfect happiness in this world, and that any such pastoral fancy must be heroically uprooted:

The Remembrance of Eden, wherein our First Parents were sett, being propagated not only by sacred Historie, but by continued Tradition hath in all Ages brought forth a strong & rauishing conceit; That there was yet remaining in the world a place of Perfect Happines. Which because it appeared euidently false by the discouerie of that Portion, which wee inhabite, The Mainteners of this Fancie haue alwaies cunningly described it to ly hid in farre remoued Coasts & accessible only to the Possessours thereof. You shall not find any of the wise Naturalists, that haue recorded to Posteritie their knowledge of the seuerall parts & conditions of this world, but haue withall expressed the common report & beleif (wherein you shall easily perceiue their own credence implied) of certain people liuing alwaies in an vninterrupted Course of Felicitie, & vnder the influence of a benigne Heauen, which some of them haue pointed out to be vnder the Poles, other farre in the West in certaine Ilands of the Atlantique Sea, on which they haue imposed the Names of Happy & Fortunate. And herein for the better resemblance of truth, they haue boldly proceeded particularly to designe the very Climate, wherein they should ly. (70)

The heroism of Charles V does not consist of his pursuing this Edenic pipe dream, but rather in his exposing its sham through his renunciation of the world. Having surveyed the world with the help of his ministers in search of Eden, Charles returns not with "a greene oliue branch of Comfort & hope," but with "the Confutation of all those idle dreames, Assuring by the Experiment of Ten Thousand Eie Witnesses, That those Fortunate Ilands, which haue been so long boasted of by Antiquitie are but a few petty barren rocks yeelding a scanty maintenance to their short-liued inhabitants" (71).

For the historians at Little Gidding, the danger of such a critique is that it might lapse into the demolition of providence for the sake of tranquillity associated in the early Stuart decades with Epicureanism. For the ancient Epicureans, it is better to survey the vicissitudes of the world at a distance or with friends from a garden, to understand that no providence is guiding human affairs, and that the world is shot through with barrenness and monstrosity. Clearly, the interlocutors despise any such conclusion from their assessment of Virginia and would attribute the contemporary revival of Epicureanism to the degeneration of Stuart society. All the same, in this disenchanted vein of argument, the Elizabethan church heroic and its Jacobean descendants are deluded dreamers at best, greedy propagandists at worst; at best the New World offered them colorful trinkets, at worst a Circean seduction behind the gloss of "Cunning deuised Fables."

Far from dismantling the church heroic altogether, the Gidding dialogue poses the romantic ideal of the American mission against a lapsed form of heroism of which trouble, deception, and fallibility are the diacritical marks. This heroism amounts to an Odyssean battle against enchantment and degeneration without hope for peace or perfection in this world's "furious Gulf euer combated with Stormes & Tempests." Whatever its refreshments, Little Gidding is established in the dialogue as a microcosm of the world at large, "a vale of miserie & our whole liues a Continual exercize of Afflictions & Anguish" (71). That is, life in this religious house consists of a heroism meant to valorize disenchanted critiques of such fraudulent romances as the Virginia enterprise or, at least, as the credulous mindsets that the Ferrars took into that enterprise. Now religious valor consists of "a continual Exercize of Heroical Industry in most Noble & weighty Affaires," with the understanding that industry must be continued precisely because its heroes are defined by their fallen condition (35).

This is not to say that the utopian or romantic impulse is completely eradicated from the dialogues at Little Gidding. Like those Laudians who posit especially holy spaces in an admittedly fallible church, the interlocutors follow the historian Speed in celebrating the Isle of Man as a remarkably pious and just place that is, all the same, imperfect. The Manx have minimized lawsuits and crime, and they worship "with more sinceritie, then in most other places, though not wth that perfection, wch it ought. But men are frail. & They are to be deemed not only good but the best, who doe least amisse."[63] In this cautious paean on Man, we have the upshot of heroism at Little Gidding, as time and again the narrators mediate between models of perfection and the ongoing spiritual contests of the fallen world.

The Gidding mediation between perfect and lapsed forms of heroism appears in the narrators' caution regarding saints' lives. For the most part, their shorter dialogues center on the most "admirable passages that stand recorded in the ecclesiastical histories," that is, on examples of individual piety and virtue.[64] Some of the most "admirable" stories have two distinct sections insofar as they feature the conversion of some egregiously vicious sinner into an amazingly virtuous saint. But it is this very division into deeply fallible and superhumanly righteous halves that incites the interlocutors to reconsider the value and believability of such stories of "Admirablenes," with the Chief separating the account "of sinners Conversion wrought by meanes of Saints" from the narrative "of saints perfection encreased by meanes of sinners." Both halves relate the workings of the Holy Spirit, not least in the unpremeditated eloquence of the saints; and in the case of stories about prostitutes converted to honesty and godliness, the auditors insist on hearing both halves. Thus the interlocutors are unwilling to jettison the value of extraordinary virtue, with Foxeian heroes such as Bishop Ferrar himself serving as reminders to a decadent age of just how powerful Christian heroism can be. Although providence is consistent unto itself in ancient and modern times, God uses "strangenes" to provoke us out of the ordinary bondage of everyday life. It is wrong to expect extraordinary heroes from God, but it is equally wrong to rule them out according to the lapsed standards of one's times.

But while the Guardian chastises modern readers for discrediting heroic stories taken from antiquity, the narrators at Little Gidding concede their uncertainty about "the Authoritie" of such histories, even those with obvious value. As with the Virginia Company, so with romantic hagiography, the interlocutors convert doubt into the instrument of heroism itself, but at the risk of participating in their larger culture's erasure of awesome models for Christian aspiration (Sharland, 202).

On several occasions, the interlocutors bring home to Little Gidding the suspension of heroism between perfection and lapse. The Affectionate reminds the others that they must be "better off" than ordinary Christians, but on St. Luke's Day, 1632, the dialogue commences with a lament for their failure to execute their pious resolutions. As a physician, Luke represents the community's hope in "a lifting up, a rising againe, and a rising together" so that the Gidding church heroic is driven by a collaborative as well as an individual combat with lapse (243, 156). Notwithstanding the guarantee of election, each individual is exhorted to live up to his or her allegorical name, but it is together that they must battle human fallibility when the "beautie, the noveltie, and the honour of excellent things" give way to labor. When godly living "comes to the maine battail," then a congregational version of the Homeric shame culture must motivate the soldiers in their thirty-years war with "the paines, the patience, the difficulties, the hazards, that like so many dreadfull files of pikes and shott stand in guard of vertue, and deny the prize of worthy Actions except they be forced by Combate and Conquest." With

"Industrie, Humilitie, and Wisedome" and with their "shoulders to the wheel," the heroism of Protestants is simply "to gett out of the slough wherein [they] are fallen," an appropriate valor for the end of illusions (157–59).

Despite their deflation of the colonial enterprise, however, the interlocutors are only partly committed to retirement as an ascetic heroism. After all, it is still important that Charles V is responsible for converting the heathen, all the more remarkably so once his renunciation of worldly power disarms him of the cruelties of the Black Legend. The emperor's renunciation itself is fitful and vulnerable to critique. As the dialogue reveals, some have objected that Charles renounced the world only when he grew too old, tired, and melancholy to rule it. Moreover, as he is portrayed in the sources, it is difficult for him to leave behind his "vndefatigable course of serious Imployments for the Common good of Christendome" for the sake of "quiet, Rest & Peace." What is striking about the Chief's account of the emperor's journey to his retreat in Spain is how often the journey gets interrupted for the sake of religion in the world. When, in striking a truce with France, Charles is detained from sailing to his home in Spain, the Chief applauds the delay: "Hee shall better please & serue god, that condescends to serue & please his Neighbour in things, that truly edifie, then he, that in an intire retirement, liues to himself alone, though his Life be altogether in & vnto God."[65] Such a middle ground between cloister and activism is deemed suitable for Little Gidding, which was by the early 1630s established as a private estate with active and reformative involvement in the life of the parish. In the process of retreating, Charles pauses to educate his descendants, especially his son Philip, and so writes large those efforts made by the Gidding community to educate and catechize the children of their parish. Such reformative and charitable activities achieve a kind of epic stature for the interlocutors insofar as Charles himself "makes the Catechizing of his Grandchild . . . the Epilogue of all his Heroical Actions" (103).

The last section of the dialogue on Charles V – in which it is debated whether the Submisse should become a gentle servant in a noble household – summarizes the community's multisided relationship to the heroic codes of the world at large. When it is argued that her service in such a position would be both arrogant and humiliating, the Resolved complains that "The Contradiction of your discourses . . . intangle[s] my thoughts, as in a Laberinth; & though, mee thinkes, now & then I see light, yet it proues but like those foolish fires, that lead wandering passengers into further errours." The Guardian responds that they have been struggling with "seeming Contradiction" all along, especially in "that great Maze" which led to "Charles his true want of Happines in the appearent posses-sion of it" (141, 148). Ambushed by "Errour & Daunger," heroic exercise at Little Gidding proves to be discursive as well as practical. Given the material pitfalls, complex lineage, and ethical mazes of the various hero-isms, from Foxeian martyrdom and international warfare to colonization and Laudian beautification, the interlocutors acknowledge that skeptical questioning is as integral to the strength of the church as catechistical answers or romantic fancies. For the Ferrars, then, religious heroism is labyrinthine because its interrogative forms coexist with the family's commitments to honorable enterprises in the Church of England: the restoration of the church's catholicity; the beautification of worship as stimulus of the interior trials of mortification and sanctification; the care of sick bodies and of impoverished souls in the parish; and the conversion of the heathen in Virginia as part of the combat against the Antichrist.

In other dialogues, the interlocutors convey a similar combination of conviction and doubt regarding the violence undertaken on behalf of the faith, from the acts of iconoclasm that Nicholas Ferrar himself approved to the spectacle of bloodshed in contemporary Germany.[66] Does service to God include bloodshed? Violence, the Guardian protests, has wrongly found its way into representations of Christian heroism, especially in the chivalric romances of "fayned worthies so defective in Patience." The Chief extends this point: some romantic heroes such as Orlando and his Paladins are depicted as fighting against the Moors for the sake of reli-gion. Yet "Orlando and the rest of those renowned Palladines through the recompting of their worthy Action have beene made the destroy-ers of more Christian soules than ever they killed pagane Bodies." In turn, the Chief is eager to destroy these books in a planned "Bone-fire" (Sharland, 119). Thus, like Nicholas's declaration that he would disman-tle any room in which the Mass had been held, the punishment directed against romance is itself an act of godly violence meant to exorcise the false spirits of heroism from the estate.

IV

Such a bonfire was built near the end of Nicholas's life with the special purpose of burning, among other secular writings, romances and heroic poetry.[67] In the story books, the Chief is urged to elaborate on the evils of romantic fictions, especially since some members of the family have loved such books "from their Cradle almost." According to the Chief, "the world and the Devill owe to these Histories of Chivalry the making of that Match betweene Christianity and revenge, which could never, though diligently laboured from the very first, bee brought to passe till these last and perilous times of ours."[68] In attacking "the lying Patternes of Orlando and Rogero" in contradistinction to such early Christians as the patient Christopher, the Chief maintains that modern "Champions in the Fayth are produced compleat in all manner of Vertues, Patience excepted," and then that no such hero can ever teach "Temperance, Justice, Charity, or any other Vertue." Also, in modern times, the deformity of such heroism is hidden by the grand style – the pomp, flourish, and glitter – of its romantic accoutrements. As with the papist Mass, so too with devilish romance: at Little Gidding, the presence of false religious heroism is enough "to cause the burning of the House, or the unnaturall Death of the heire" (120–21).

But it is unclear what period is included in the interlocutors' own measurement of the apocalyptic "last and perilous times." As critics of Stuart court culture, which itself cultivates romantic images of the church heroic, the Little Gidding interlocutors might be focusing their attacks on the synthetic "heroic virtue" integral to the mythology of the Caroline monarchy. But the Ferrars themselves have encouraged a violence against the American Indians motivated explicitly by the appeal to holy and honorable revenge. The dilemma of justifying atrocity, or even of abdicating during the atrocities one has inaugurated, afflicts Charles V and the Ferrars alike. Does the Chief mean that the "last and perilous times" are indicated by the international quagmire entrenched on the Continent since 1618 – a war given some recent Protestant legitimacy by the appearance of Gustavus Adolphus? Or is the phrase broad enough to take in the Elizabethan ancestry of Stuart colonists and militant Protestants?

As critics and targets of what they take to be impiety, decadence, and malice in Stuart England, the family has sought in semi-isolation to reconstruct the Church of England at home, with a heightened commitment to its prayer book, creed, offices, and catholicity. On the other hand, their involvement with the Virginia Company and support of the Palatinate tend to implicate them in the violent opposition to papist idolatry. In search of a new ground on which to define what one visitor calls their orthodoxy, the family has a leader, Nicholas, whose early travels are spent in part surveying a wide range of religious practices; these range from Anabaptist to papist to Jewish.[69] Then, through the Virginia

Company, he has come to know Edwin and George Sandys, both of whom share his fascination with comparative religion. The Ferrars' understanding of iconoclasm, then, is as complex as their reconstruction of other forms of religious violence. Indeed, in the various stories that they narrate, the interlocutors have a keen sense of how motivation and context can differentiate one act of violence from another that might otherwise resemble it.

In the Gidding dialogue on the winding sheet, the complications of religious heroism are carefully studied through accounts of German history, an imperial legacy that is bound to come around to the European warfare of the 1620s and 1630s. The dialogue focuses on those rulers possessing an acute awareness of their mortality, especially Frederick III and his son Maximilian I, respectively the Habsburg great-grandfather and grandfather of Charles V. But far from reducing them to quietism, the dialogue clarifies that their constant attention to death strengthens these men in their active lives. Purged of their vices, they are all the more eager to act in the name of God, "Neuer at Rest, but when they are in Labor, not truly quiet, but when they are strongly exercized in weldoing." Some of their labors are more easily reconciled to Christian charity than others. In troubled Germany, for example, peacekeeping is as difficult a task as warfaring, since a peacekeeper like Frederick must "put the strength of his hand to the Rudder, as well as the Forecast of his head els he could neuer haue steered right in such an ouergrown Tempest as then raged vpon ye whole face of ye Earth almost."[70]

But of course aggressive peacekeeping (Frederick) or charity (Ferdinand) – in short, "Christian Affabilitie" – is easier to legitimize than Christian warfare, the justice of which is reasonably clear only if the enemy is not Christian. If the enemy is not Christian, there are the new casuistries of war like that written by Hugo Grotius against which to measure the putative validity and naturalness of one's religious cause. For instance, Frederick III must confront the usurpation of his lesser imperial principalities by the King of Hungary and Bohemia and by his brother and cousin. Having started to fight, the emperor realizes that too much Christian blood will be shed and so decides to join forces with the King of Hungary against their common enemy, the Turk. The lesson of this change in strategies is simple: God rewards those rulers who leave all to providence, forget petty revenge, and concentrate on the welfare of Christendom. Frederick's visit to an ambitious and covetous pope is somewhat more subtle with regard to the relative value of peace and war, as he wins the pontiff over with his mild disposition but keeps an army

behind him all the same. In a similar vein, the story of Rudolph's foundation of the Habsburg empire serves as a summary of how Christians
should eliminate most of their conflicts in order to focus on one. As the
Repeater puts it, ideally a Christian would live in peace: "But since few
aime & scarce any there be yt attaine this hight, it is necessarie yt there
should be Patterns of that Lower degree of vertue, wch the world is capable & willing to imitate" (144). Although they admire patient saints
and martyrs, the Gidding narrators read the persistence of Christian
warfare as a sign of the fallible and exploratory nature of the church
heroic.

Violence in general continues to occupy their attention as other stories are told "appliable to all manner of Contention as well as that, wch
is in warre"(148). But the shadow of the Thirty Years War itself looms
when we hear of "that strange Act & Resolution from Iohn Frederick of
Saxonie, one of the last, & vndoubtedly one of the Noblest and greatest,
yt euer came from him." The story goes that John Frederick, a deposed
elector, was Luther's greatest protector after God; aptly, he serves to illustrate Luther's belief that princes rely on reformed doctrine more than
reformers rely on princes – and he does so in battle by relying on God
and faith as "a stronger sheild . . . then power" (149). In the end he re-
tires to his remaining estate and refuses the military help of a powerful
Marquis; in his wake, this victim of Charles V's aggression leaves no
clear lesson about the justice of warfare, if little of the complexity left by
Charles himself or evoked by the recent war over deposition, empire, and
religion. There is no mention by the Gidding narrator of John George,
or the current Elector of Saxony's suspension between Protestantism
and nationalism, and none of the war's byzantine negotiations crossing religious boundaries while still maintaining, with the emergence of
Sweden, a powerful religious dimension. There is one mention of the
arrogance opening "one of the cheif sluces, through wch the bloud of so
many Emperors hath of late drayned," the point of which is that mortals
should always remember death and their God (150). But the hint of modern relevance makes Christian warfare only more difficult to evaluate
than the more safely remote crusades of the past.

Eventually in "The Winding Sheet," the interlocutors speak directly
to the enigma of deciding between renunciation and warfare. When
the pomp and treachery of the pope are condemned in contrast with
Frederick III's penchant for "warres and iourneys, & Treaties of weightie
& difficult businesses," the Apprentice spots a problem: "Why this
Passage very strangely setts of ye vertue, yt is in peaceablenes for the

prolongation of Life. when wee see yt this great Follower of Peace for
going but once aside out of the way had been well nigh supprized by
death for his Labor. I will not say, Error. For I know not whether any peace
ought to be preferred before this kind of warre" (156). It simplifies the
case that papal decadence is so unattractive even if the value of Christian
warfare is hard to measure. On request and with a glance at the blood
shed in Virginia, the Apprentice goes so far as to explicate the conditions
of a holy war: "This sacred warre, yt setts vp the crosse, not for a standard
to order ye March by, but for the maine end of all the designes & actions
of the whole attempt, wch intends not the enlargement of Territories &
Honors but ye propagation of Religion. Not the spoil of the conquered
but their enrichment, enfranchizing them vnto true Libertie by reducing
them to the subiection of the right Faith & putting them in possession of
Heauenly Treasures in exchange of a little worldly pelf, wch it may be
they come by this meanes to be depriued of" (157). Unlike the courtly
synthesis of St. George and St. Paul's, this paradoxical heroism admits the
brutal cost of an exchange whereby the heathens' material and physical
loss is supposed to translate into their spiritual treasure.

The Repeater also praises those wars undertaken for the sake of
"Pietie & Charitie, Gods Honor & Mankinds common Good." But actual wars fall short of their ideals, "the successe prouing alwaies wth
out exception almost cleane contrarie." It is added that some authorities take this critique further in charging the Crusades themselves with
"the ruine of our Church as well in Temporal as in Spiritual regards"
(157–58). Among other critics who, like Erasmus, sought to demilitarize
the weaponry of the Christian soldier, Etienne Pasquier is noted for his
conviction that saintly virtue will convert an infidel whereas war cannot.
For this reason, St. Lewis was successful in his mission until he embarked on two military "voyages" which proved ruinous for all his "pure
Deuotion." But more often than not, the circumstances of crusading and
the motives of crusaders are complicated in "The Winding Sheet," as
Lewis the Young's crusade is presented in the context of papal politics,
a controversial divorce, and the grievous memory of a horrible war at
home: "yt it was not pure Deuotion, not innocent but expiatorie Religion, yt induced Lewis the yong to this Attempt." Such shameful wars
re-create the fall of human kind all over again, substituting "Bitter &
deadly fruit . . . for such a plant of Paradise as Deuotion is." And these
combats remind the narrator of God's incomprehensibility, for instance,
when the relatively "innocent & pious" Conrad nonetheless encounters
"many hazards, miserie, & dangers" in crusade (161–66).

In "The Winding Sheet," then, the repudiation of a marriage between militarism and piety is compelling and leads to the rejection of romance in the name of a more skeptical heroism's mortification, charity, and peace. But the interlocutors also confess their fascination with romance and cannot altogether jettison holy violence. Instead they prefer to characterize religious heroism not as a clean divorce from the vicissitudes of life on earth, but as a laborious, resourceful, and vulnerable struggle in the fallen world over the terms and costs of an exchange between violence and spirituality. This struggle parallels the hardships of reinventing a church that must resourcefully navigate between rival creeds and disciplines or somehow locate another estate for the greatness of the church beyond the impasse of those rivalries. In turn, the attractions of retreat require modification; thus the "conceald Life" should be carried out "not in sluggish Idlenes but in happy quiet" and "Imployment." Meanwhile, in contrast to "the world now adaies," the interlocutors express nostalgia for those "Elder and better times" when godly warriors such as the Maccabees were divinely guided in conquering the impious tyrants of the world. The Learner takes this support for holy war quite far; at the outset of battle, a litany confessing one's weakness and reliance on God "is vndoubtedly a certaine way to obtaining of the victorie" or again "an vnfallible way to victorie in such warres as are iustly & Lawfully vndertaken" (171, 177–78, 181).

But the infallibility of heroic means cuts against the grain of heroism at Little Gidding, with its emphasis on the vulnerable and therefore boldly resourceful refashioning of the Protestant hero's credentials. Toward the end of "The Winding Sheet," the counterexamples to invincible Christian warfare are English and often contemporary, for it is Buckingham's disastrous expedition to Re that causes the Gidding community its greatest alarm. Buckingham's colossal failure to rescue Huguenots from oppression has become the stuff of popular derision: "The Inforcement of this Example were most necessarie perhaps for the present Age, on wch the Inheritance of this debauched Humor of our Ancestors is euidently fallen, & like a snow-ball much increased perhaps in ye descent. Whereof that prodigious Ballad made vpon the Expedition to the Isle of Ree" (183). In addition to their analysis of church heroism through the centuries, the interlocutors expose the Caroline synthetic mythology to ridicule by pointing to its popular reception as the kind of mock-romance permitted at court only in the antimasques of the 1630s. When the Apprentice curtails the discussion by remarking that their own weakness prevents them from doing the subject justice, we are left to decide whether they still support the pursuit of the Elizabethan church heroic against the idle, decadent hedonism of the mainstream of Stuart culture, or whether the failures of the Stuart regime are taken for synecdoches of an English church heroic that, including the community at Little Gidding and its parish, is defined by the fallible and ceaseless labors of godly living after Eden. If the latter view prevails, it is the vulgar ballad itself, and not the expedition to Re, that works against the valor of the English church. Thus the Repeater offers a prayer in support of those English soldiers who must work to "vnderstand & amend this dangerous Enormitie." Dismissing the ballad as a sign of "Common Impietie," the family devotes another prayer in honor of "our Deare Soueraigne, who hath so embellished his Crown wth Deuotion" (184). Whatever their criticism of the Stuart court, the modern aristocracy, and contemporary English manners, the family at Little Gidding expresses sympathy for the Caroline and Laudian efforts to re-create religious heroism at home so that its wars will be just, its ceremonies rich, and its failures noble and useful in "euery adventure" undertaken within the reach of the English church (187).

V

At Little Gidding, however, useful failure is most important of all. In the story books, the pomp and circumstance of war are converted not into a masque's beautiful myth but rather into casuistry and critique. As a form, dialogue is well suited for scrutinizing and refashioning the grounds and means for religious heroism, and for moving that heroism toward an irenic and a skeptical alternative to Protestant aggression and courtly pomp. The form also shifts the preoccupation of epic religion away from grand designs against the Antichrist or even relatively peaceful claims for the superiority of the national church. Instead, heroism is quieter, more local, and less sure of itself: it involves a small community staging, strengthening, and enriching its covenant with a God who expects an all-consuming – yet by no means perfect – devotion.

Remembering the reality of its "own Frailtie" as well as "others peeuishnes",[71] the Ferrar family carefully chooses "pious Resolution" over ascetic vows for, as they know well, resolve admits ongoing and earnest reformation, entrenched as it is in the trials of error and revision. Heroic resolve accentuates the notions that revision is fundamental to a Christian heroism always conditioned by misprision and fallibility, and that the epic adventure of Little Gidding demands above all the struggle of self-definition in a vacuum where, as one interlocutor puts it, there is "A Dearth of Patterns in an exuberance of Rules."[72]

Affectionate insists that it is their godly duty to establish a precedent for the future but knows that such leadership has considerable "hazard at first" and that, in short, the invention of Little Gidding is the most heroic enterprise that the family will ever undertake. "If wee had Authoritie," Mother Ferrar laments, "if wee might hope of companie, we would run where wee now goe creeping, wee should it may be reach that height, which wee now stand pointing onely at with our fingers." It is not enough, then, that they cautiously "stand inquiring right," as Donne urges young gallants to do in "Satire 3." "Wee are afraid to goe alone," the Affectionate chides her family, "Let vs not think so. There are others of our minds, if they had an Example to alledge for their opinion. Wee shall haue them, that will follow in the way assoone as they know there's any gone before. But we are loth to be the foremost. Why that's advantage, if wee well mark it. Wee shall thereby haue a double Benefitt, Not onely our own but others welldoing in Imitation of vs shall run to our Accompt. Wee want an Example, let's make one."[73] Even more than in the case of Virginia, that is, the Ferrar family construes the enrichment of English spirituality as a bold journey for which they stand alone at the Pillars of Hercules, with no one else yet at sea.

The theological studies carried out at that Oxfordshire community, Falkland's Great Tew, extend the Gidding meditations on the conditions of heroic faith to a general theory of valiant skepticism in the religion of Protestants. But once members of the Falkland community must leave their retreat for the fields of civil war, their revision of the criteria for elevating the Church of England above all contenders reaches an impasse much more insoluble than that imagined by the Ferrar family to have afflicted the retreating Charles V.

CHAPTER 2

Great Tew and the skeptical hero

Like Nicholas Ferrar, Lucius Cary presided over an extraordinary community in which the circumstance of religious heroism was eulogized, scrutinized, and recast. More than Ferrar, however, Cary embodied for his contemporaries both the legacy and the enigmas of that heroism. One sees this tendency in literature produced about Cary even in the years before he established his academy at Great Tew. In a Pindaric ode celebrating the friendship shared by Cary and Sir Henry Morison, Ben Jonson commences with a bold image of just how elusive an other-worldly heroism can be for even the wisest interpreter. Then over the course of the ode, he refashions that image so that Morison and Cary come to mythologize a well-rounded heroic friendship – at once contemplative and dutiful, rational and fervent – as a pious and honest alternative to the courtly composite staged by those masques from which Jonson was finding himself excluded.

Jonson's image of elusive heroism is the Infant of Saguntum, whose response to his birth into the chaotic, ignoble, and savage inception of the second Punic War is return into his mother's womb. The Infant's return, or antistrophe, is imputed perfect by the poet whose emblem for the return is so "summed a circle."[1] But no one, he says, not even the poet, can penetrate the center of that circle, and no one can foresee the future of catastrophe so readily as the Infant, whose self-immolation resembles two classical models, one morally vexatious (the Stoic's supposedly natural suicide) and the other mysterious (the Neoplatonic return to the One). Both models have heroic etymologies and resonance, and each is fraught with interpretive trouble for Jonson and his contemporaries. Suicide is precisely what Jonson is seeking to prevent the distraught Cary from considering, and Cary himself has explored and found wanting the hegemonic reason of the Stoic sage. At most, Jonson can wonder aloud about whether this suicide answers the call of nature, leaving the bizarre circumstances of the act to a casuist: "Did wiser nature draw thee back, / From out the horror of that sack" (212).

If Jonson begins his praise for Cary and Morison with an impossible, even suspect vision of retreat from cataclysm, the athleticism of his performance attempts to imitate, then trump the fashionable Elizabethan warrior ideal. After all, Cary and Morison know each other from the plantations and battle zones of Ireland, where Lucius's father, Sir Henry Cary, has been struggling to aggress against the Antichrist. With this military service as its most obvious constituent, Morison's heroic life is represented as a sphere, not a circle, for his is a legible, robust composite of all duties – to friends and family, to country and the God to whom he has zealously leapt after having compressed all honesty, piety, and beauty into the small container of his truncated life. Together, Jonson and Cary communicate in the sacrament of this newly declared norm, in celebration of a friendship now mythologized as those most famous of demidivine heroes, Castor and Pollux. Like the Neoplatonic allegory of such a hero, Cary and Morison continue to form a cosmic nexus that translates ideal virtue into human minds yet directs human minds toward their heavenly home; reinventing the myth of the Dioscuri, Jonson concludes that "fate doth so alternate the design, / Whilst that in heaven, this light on earth must shine" (214).

In 1629, the year of Morison's death, Cary was attempting to pass as an Elizabethan hero in the wake of his father's failure to extend the colonial glories of his Elizabethan generation.[2] In 1622, Sir Henry had assumed his office as Deputy of Ireland and, moved by James Ussher's sermon on the Biblical reminder that "he beareth not the sword in vain," he had campaigned for the expulsion of priests against the inauspicious backdrop of the Spanish Match. What followed next was perceived by critics of pro-Spanish policy as the mirror image of that policy in Ireland, namely, the court's pressure on Cary to restrain his aggression and to facilitate religious and agrarian concessions to the Old English Catholics.[3] According to critics, here was yet once more a Protestant humiliation on the order of Virginia, the Spanish marriage debacle, Cadiz, and Re, only the "Graces" could not be chalked up to incompetence. Rather, they sprang from a deliberate policy that could only embarrass Sir Henry, an Elizabethan holdover whose valor, according to an epigram by Jonson, had served to chastise the decay of that virtue in the early Stuart years. According to Jonson, Henry Cary's was a valor so extreme that it bordered on crime and could be undone only by accident.[4]

In 1625, however, there was insult together with injury, for Sir Henry's wife, Elizabeth, Lady Falkland, had declared herself a convert to Rome with every intention of taking her children with her.

Eventually, Elizabeth Cary alienated her eldest son, Lucius, with the dramatic liberation of her other sons from the clutches of the arch-skeptic Chillingworth. Until then, she had encouraged Lucius to experience his maturing faith as an intellectual and convivial exchange, in counterbalance to Sir Henry's colonial bravado. At his mother's table he discussed theology with learned priests; in his father's footsteps, he challenged an ingenuous soldier to a duel in a pique of honor that would have embarrassed Achilles while, just a year later, he sought in vain for military employment in the Netherlands. As Clarendon informs us, Lucius Cary defined himself as having a natural penchant for the soldier's profession; military Protestantism possessed Cary with a Sidneyesque spirit that Great Tew was in part meant to exorcise, a spirit decidedly at odds with the intellectual irenicism of his alter ego.[5] Cary's abandonment of poetry for divinity was italicized by his friends and correspondents, but he was never able to jettison the poesy of military honor and, a decade later at the Battle of Newbury, he was thought by some to have immolated himself out of a resolution from doubt and despair that this poesy helped generate.

At Great Tew, the philosophical enterprise of recasting religious heroism attempts to redress the failure of and challenges to those still very powerful conventions of Protestant aggression. Indeed, Great Tew shares with Little Gidding the distinction of having associates in the Virginia Company, George Sandys and Thomas Hobbes in the case of the former. Even Cary's famous physical deficiencies – his small body, unattractive face, and unpleasant voice – compose an emblem – part David, part Socrates – that both emulates and overturns the Elizabethan legacy. Sir Francis Drake – whose memory was being revived in the 1620s – was hailed as a David whose slighter stature made him all the more remarkably victorious against the gigantic and cruel Spaniard.[6] But Cary's improper masculinity renders his Elizabethan heroism at once miraculous and impossible. At Great Tew's *convivium theologicum* in the 1630s, David becomes Socrates for a few short years before Cary, plagued by his conscience, ventures off to expire in the wars of religion.

Unlike the Gidding story books, the dialogues that resulted from Falkland's retreat were informal and unrecorded. Indeed some of the evidence suggests that dialogue was secondary to private study among the visitors at Tew. All in all, the theological and philosophical work carried out at Great Tew was oriented toward a reconstitution of religion's heroic circumstance as more open-ended than ritualistic or formulaic; more epistemological than epic; and more metaphysical than militaristic. In short, the Tew circle pushed heroic circumstance toward exploratory forays into other religious circumstances – of thought, social interaction, and cosmology. All the same, its centerpiece, Lucius Cary himself, never outgrew the suspicion that the wars of truth shed blood and not ideas.

I

The writings of the Cary family in the late 1620s and early 1630s corroborate the family's central yet troubled role in transforming religious heroism. As with Little Gidding, part of the trouble derives from a complex and critical relationship between the family and the Caroline court with its ennobled temple.

Aside from Lucius Cary's own poetry, the work most indicative of the Falkland association with the exploration of heroism is a text whose authorship has been attributed to both his mother and his father, *The History of the Life, Reign, and Death of Edward II . . . with the Rise and Fall of his Great Favourites, Gaveston and the Spencers*. Unpublished until the two versions of 1680, *The History* is dated 1627 and attributed to E. F. in the folio edition and, as Elizabeth Cary's recent editors have argued, this date and attribution are probably right.[7] Whether it gives vent to Henry's derision of his maltreatment in Ireland or to Elizabeth's rebuke against the vanity of Protestant aggression, however, what matters for a study of Lucius Cary is that one of his parents allegorized the demise of English heroism in the years of Buckingham and Ré.

Early in the history, a paean for English honor is undercut by King Edward's abdication of his duties so that he might seclude himself in the fanciful cloister of his sexual desires. No matter how "many glorious and brave victorious Conquests [have] given this Warlike Nation life and spirit fit for present action," and no matter what the young monarch's early promise of mastering and advancing the military arts: all the same, "his inglorious Aims were bent another way."[8] Under Gaveston's influence, "Heroic Vertue" is basically interchangeable with pleasure, for both titillate the king's fancy and, therefore, solicit the favorite's flattery on the way to his consolidation of power. That is, English heroism has not simply been abandoned; it has been evacuated of substance, puffed into a gigantic idol, and converted into secondhand merchandise used in a barter whose main exchange is erotic gratification.

Meanwhile the once subjected Scots wreak havoc on their onetime English masters. When Edward's more conscientious advisors are not struggling to parse the circumstances that might preserve some modicum of their king's honor, they are orating on behalf of the English heroic spirit. But they too get entangled in the problem of exactly what constitutes a specifically Christian heroism. Thus the old Archbishop of York finds that whatever his military schemes,

there was a dangerous difference betwixt fighting and praying. The intent of this grave Bishop was certainly noble and worthy; but the act was inconsiderate, weak, and ill-advised. It was not proper to his Profession, to undertake a Military Function, in which his hope in reason answer'd his experience; neither did it agree with the Innocency and Piety of his Blood, though the quarrel were defensive, but by compulsion. But questionless he meant well, which must excuse his action. Too great a care improperly exprest, doth often loose the cause it strives to advantage. (46)

How much intention might count in a fallible, quasi-religious enterprise is a question that would preoccupy the Great Tew circle in its transformation of epic Protestantism. The narrator of *The History*, however, is certain that the archbishop should have deliberated the circumstances of his campaign, without which the balance of "so many Lives . . . at stake" is handed over to fortune (46).

What emerges most clearly from the Falkland *History* is the conviction reinforced by Hugo Grotius's work that wars require careful justification, or what the narrator calls "a well-grounded and warrantable reason for [an] Engagement" (47). Such a warrant does not ensure victory, but it guarantees honor. The potential conflict in heroic codes unleashed by this deepening of military conscience haunts the future of the Tew academy: on the one hand, specifically religious wars are rendered virtually always unnatural; on the other, the heightened pressure to ground warfare more systematically in natural law raises the religious criterion of future wars. *The History* cautions kings not to betray their righteousness and honesty, but it does not go so far as to declare that only by abdication of a court-centered fancy can a purely religious, if cloistered, honor survive. As in the case of the Gidding Charles V, any abdication by the Falkland Edward II from the atrocities of his realm would amount to abdication during those evils that he has created or permitted and that he might have some power to mitigate.

That warriors who are adept at the casuistry of violence will succeed in their own wars is a strange conclusion for a text that so emphatically segregates prayer and combat. Indeed, the narrator opines that Henry VI "was fitter for a Cloister than a Crown, being transported with a Divine Rapture of Contemplation, that took him off from the care of all Worldly Affairs." The narrator believes that the French are best at pursuing a "good Cause, in the integrity of time," a potent idea in the England of 1627 (157, 159). But the repetition of the word "integrity" – Clarendon's favorite heroic epithet – betrays the contemporary desire for a holistic or spherical religious heroism different from the official, spectacular, and conformist composite striven for among the advocates of the Caroline court and of Laudian church polity. The Falkland historian inspects, criticizes, and recasts the religion of a soldier at a complicated cultural moment: never before throughout Europe has religious warfare required so elaborate and cogent a justification; and never before in England have the justifications of religious warfare seemed so contestable and elusive. If on the Continent Gustavus Adolphus would soon stimulate the undeniable discursive power of a short-lived heroic integrity, in England it was Lucius Cary who came to epitomize the centrifugal pressures of the reformed and synthetic Protestant hero.

II

Like Jonson, whose Pindaric ode lends an athleticism and ritualism to a patriot's duty and zeal, Lucius Cary formulates Morison's exemplary life as a rare "Epick Poeme."[9] In one of two extant elegies for his friend, Cary constructs a synthetic hero for this epic. Part of the awkwardness of this construction is that the figure of Reason offers little comfort for Cary's grief beyond the observation that his life simply cannot get worse. In this melancholy vein, Cary locates his own mythical place in some imaginary supplement to Sandys's Ovid, in which he is metamorphosed into a pillar of grief. After Morison's death, then, it is love, or *eros*, that most characterizes the hero (*heros*) by shaming the weak if rational consolations of philosophy.

Even so, Cary makes use of the Senecan strains so central to Jonson's ode, namely, the topos according to which a short life can constitute human valor, virtue, and beauty at their best: "Hee had an Infant's innocence, and truth, / the judgment of Gray-Hayres, the witt of Youth. / Nor a yonge rashnes, nor an ag'd Despaire; / the Courage of the first, the Second's care" (283). Such a life is perfected by the legendary friendship that, in the death of one friend, comes to bridge the gap between two Neoplatonic entities, the daimonic heroes who shepherd souls toward transcendence and those souls that instantiate the purity of heroes in the conflicts of human life. When at last Cary turns to praise the qualities of his friend's life, he emphasizes not so much the daimon love that in Plato's *Symposium* motivates the earthbound soul to seek the Forms, but rather the longing for a whole so influentially allegorized by Aristophanes in the same Platonic dialogue. That is, Morison is heralded for his hermaphroditism: he was manly but not fearsome, beautiful and kind but not effeminate. These paradoxes open the way for Cary's own version of the synthetic heroism of his fallen companion. On the one hand, Morison's valor is imputed a greatness that has drained the rest of England of its heroism – just witness Cadiz and Re, Falkland protests. On the other hand, Morison is credited with a strenuous and polished wit that would have robbed Donne of his inventive poetry and Jean-Luis Guez de Balzac of his epistolary vein.

In his verses, Cary devises a similar heroic synthesis in his celebration of Hugo Grotius, who is praised for his lofty poetry, deep divinity, scholarly brilliance, and diplomatic aid to Sweden against the Habsburgs.[10] But his own life and ethos tend toward heroic conflict rather than harmony.[11] Indeed the poetry of his associates Thomas Carew and Ben Jonson exposes rifts rather than holism when they imagine the competing obligations that conscientious men owe to Charles on the one hand and to international Protestantism on the other. Carew's "In Answer of an Elegiacall Letter, upon the death of the King of Sweden, from Aurelian Townshend . . ." is so torqued about Caroline England's refusal to support the Protestant cause as to verge on satire against the court whose prosperity it surely supports.[12] Indeed it serves two masters, the "Heroique" ghost of Gustavus Adolphus at the expense of effeminate court lyricism, and the philosophical, pastoral, and masquerading monarchy of that same court, this at the expense of those warriors who "Bellow for freedome and revenge" (77). In Jonson's "An Epistle Answering to One that Asked to be Sealed of the Tribe of Ben," the heroic rifts in Caroline culture are more painful for the poet who italicizes his obligations to the centered integrity of a Stoic martyr. For such integrity convicts the gossipy and decadent court of shaming epic valor and athletic virtue in the masques that Jonson himself has produced. While Europe's religious wars rage, the English court is obsessed with the masque-maker's "Christmas clay, / And animated porcelain of the court." Ironically, the speaker indicts himself in expressing his longing for the masques and his indifference to the wars: Jonson's centered hero is ready to fight for honor in the Continental war, but it is a corpse and not a conscience that he is prepared to sacrifice.[13]

In the late 1620s and early 1630s Jonson and Carew delineate the fault lines in heroic values that Lucius Cary comes to embody. Simultaneously, the same poets – Jonson in *The New Inn*, Carew in his theory and practice of the masque – adumbrate a rationalist and Neoplatonic heroism meant to rise above the vicissitudes of court and camp. Cary's enthusiasm for his "kinsman's" *Coelum Britannicum* is recorded in his letters: the young lord requests a copy of the masque so that he might study it diligently, and having done so, he tells Carew that it has supplanted all other such court poesies in his mind. This rave review coincides with Cary's gift of the 1631 edition of Bishop Synesius's works to a friend.[14] Together, these exchanges suggest Cary's interest in a Neoplatonic heroism that serves as a transition from his early phase of military and poetic fancies (the late 1620s) to his famous conversion into what Suckling described as a philosopher "gone with Divinity."[15] That is, a poetics of Neoplatonic heroism is Cary's first step toward a Protestant heroism more salvific and irenic than his imitation of an Elizabethan planter-gallant toward the end of his years in Ireland.

Carew's *Coelum Britannicum* was based on one of Giordano Bruno's ethical treatises written in London for the Sidney circle. Carew found in this source a demanding, critical, yet suitably Platonic fable of the reformation of manners. He needed only to rewrite the fable so that Charles's court is held responsible for cleansing the nobility of its impurities. Like ancient and Renaissance Neoplatonists, however, Bruno's text centered his ethical – as against his cosmological – vision on a metaphysical category of dynamic spiritual and mental ascent that a Lucius Cary or Ben Jonson might displace from its courtly mythology. The name of this category in the differentiated ontology of the Neoplatonists was the "hero."

Clarendon's paean for the Great Tew community as a *convivium philosophicum* traces its legacy back to Plato's *Symposium*, in which Hesiod's golden race of heroes converted into a daimonic desire for ascent toward the Forms of Beauty and Goodness.[16] In their taxonomy of those numinous beings subsidiary to the One, Iamblichus and Proclus define the daimon as one scale above the hero in purity but also as responsible for subjecting souls to that labyrinthine physical world from which they long to depart. As Gregory Shaw has summarized this tradition, the heroes are situated one degree beneath the daimon, but their guardianship directs souls upwards and out of the corruption of matter. Theirs is a rational-cum-redemptive function for souls striving to transmigrate, and they gain a reputation for such an intellectual and spiritual striving.[17] For Lucius Cary and his associates, the ancient and Renaissance versions of this hero have a range of perils: idolatry, irrationality, eroticism, and heresy. Nonetheless, even Jonson's ode to Cary and Morison establishes a precedent for valorizing the Falkland coterie in Neoplatonic heroic terms. It is true that the choice of Castor and Pollux as mythical counterparts to the friends retains a commitment to military honor that the Infant has abandoned; but as the most prominent of the heroes in the Neoplatonic tradition, the Dioscuri also retreat from any politicized version of religious heroism.

For all the dangers of hero-worship debated by intellectuals in the 1630s, the demi-divinity of Iamblichus's "hero" – "life-sustaining, promotive of the reasoning faculty, and directive of souls" – befits the development of Falkland's touted conversion to Greek studies and to philosophy and divinity at his estates, Great Tew and Burford. Neoplatonic heroes can never retire into the tranquillity or stability of the putatively halcyon court; rather, they are "constantly in motion and . . . never exempt from change."[18] Such ongoing metamorphosis emphasizes the transitional, exploratory, and redemptive character of these heroes: their touch of fallibility belongs to the earthly vicissitudes and shadows from which they strive to free others.

In theurgical literature, the inauguration of heroic ascent is often characterized as a combat in which the initiate attains a watchword or *tessera* and must cope with "the violence inseparable from the magical operation," as Hans Lewy has it. Less combatively, the daimons and heroes guarantee what Shaw describes as "an unbroken continuity between the gods and man."[19] Whereas daimons, however, operate widely throughout the world of generation, heroes focus their animation, integration, and direction on the liberty of souls. This *epistrophe* (as it is called) reverses the movement of Jonson's Pindaric ode from the abortive Infant to the active Castor and Pollux, for the Neoplatonic Dioscuri abstract souls from the political, phenomenal, and violent world with little concern for the embodiment of moral norms. True, they are daimonic to the extent to which their impetus is to govern the world that they so halfheartedly, even mournfully have left. But as with Jonson's Infant, their efforts to redeem souls from the world transverse the maternal labor that might have generated a military hero, a Scipio Africanus.

Two related emphases of the sixteenth- and seventeenth-century transmissions of the Neoplatonic hero helped lay the groundwork for the charitable, skeptical heroism of the most theological phase at Great Tew. First, these transmissions accentuate the *eros* in the *heros*: heroism is the rational yet consuming desire to sublimate one's soul. But, second, love's pursuit of the divine truth that the loving soul does not yet possess converts into the nobility of failure. For Leone Ebreo, heroic love doubles as an extraordinary reason that sacrifices its own superficial welfare for an incalculable, inexpressible wisdom.[20] In *De Gli Eroici Furori*, Bruno celebrates what one scholar paraphrases as "the ascension toward God and the return to the supreme unity of the soul through love." But extraordinary or heroic rationality, if not reduced to the amorous disease of the medieval knight, pursues an enterprise so spiritually ambitious that its consummation is devout, even if imperfect.[21]

Dedicating his frenzies to the "heroic and generous" Sidney, Bruno consolidates and energizes an alternative Elizabethan legacy to the one that dreams of Sidney on the battlefield at Zutphen or of Drake sling-shooting the Spanish Goliath. In this less prominent, more heretical Elizabethan vein, Sidney is charged with the strenuous, limitless, and torqued speculation that strives on the threshold between souls and heroes. At this expanding horizon, moral thought must remain in "torment," wholly in love with "the future and the absent." The "heroic mind" is characterized more by endurance than by triumph, and is martyred by the pains of philosophy rather than the physical cruelties of papists.[22]

It was commonplace for Renaissance writers such as Tasso and Drayton to suppose the intimacy between epic, amours, demigods, wonder, and transformation.[23] But for two reasons, intellectual heroism grew controversial in the Falkland circle. On the one hand, it asserted a tolerant and skeptical freedom of discourse over and against the conformist mindset and censorial apparatus of the Laudian church. On the other, Falkland's Greek studies also led him to the church fathers that developed their own powerful critique of Neoplatonic heroics. In his *Preparation for the Gospel*, Eusebius offers guidance to those converts who must jettison their worship of such heroes as the Dioscuri, for such cults are bloody, idolatrous instruments of evil demons. This critique, popularized by Augustine in *The City of God*, is newly elaborated and invigorated in the heyday of the Tew community, beginning with Milton's 1629 nativity ode, then receiving more systematic and scholarly support in the work of Joseph Mede and Gerhardus Vossius.[24]

Both the revived critique of hero worship and its provocation of innovative defenses in the 1630s and 40s are readily glimpsed in the scholarship of Edward Herbert, who is elaborate in his reclamation of Neoplatonic heroism from its associations with idolatry, violence, and irrationality. Making use of Vossius's scholarship, Herbert seeks to cull a rational and impartial justification of heroic cults from their admittedly corrupt and priestly provenance. Thus in the eleventh chapter of *De Religione Gentilium* (1645), he argues that heroic symbolism would yield obvious spiritual fruit were it rid of the uncontrolled ritualism that sometimes comes with it. Giving a brief history of the controversy over these demigods, Herbert explains their "middle status between gods and men, who sometimes interacted with one another and from whom sprung a race of heroes."[25] Whereas such mingling can be read as evidence of the pagan gods' debauchery, Herbert prefers to allegorize this cosmic transaction in soteriological terms. Along with the "notion of divine grace going with heroism," he italicizes Cicero's classification of those heroes "whose assistance is necessary to obtaining divinity"; in Herbert's allegory, these heroes prove to be the abstractions leading the soul toward the common notions that ensure a peaceful, flexible, and anticlerical religion (192).

Herbert's heroes – in proper order, "Mind, Virtue, Piety, and Faith" – conduct the soul toward its own natural laws that God exists, must be worshiped, distributes reward and punishment in the afterlife, and expects us to live piously and virtuously. As John Anthony Butler explains, the Neoplatonic "Heroes and demigods" suit Herbert's conviction that the belief in one God need not produce bogus ritual, doctrinal controversy, and Christian bloodshed, but might instead make "a great contribution to the establishment of virtue" and to the evangelism of true religion after the demise of self-aggrandizing saints and priests. Indeed, in a later list, Herbert adds Concord, Peace, Chastity, Faith, Hope, Liberty, Safety, and Happiness to his nexus of heroic abstractions that offers to guide the soul in its return to those truths clouded by contemporary Christian discourse and practice.[26] But the heroic Mind is his favorite, at times approximating Chillingworth's nobly fallible and aggressively rational religion of Protestants.

III

Among Caroline intellectuals, then, the Great Tew circle was not alone in moving the pompous circumstance of heroic religion away from epic and toward epistemology; away from spectacular masques or conformist rituals and toward skeptical inquiry and dialogue; upward from the bloody battlefield into an exhilarating and challenging ascent through the cosmos, in search of a justification via strenuous thought surrounding an inclusive faith. Heroic Platonism was so compelling to intellectuals coming of age in the 1620s and 30s that it was made the subject of an epic and served as the cement for an informal philosophical group, the so-called Cambridge Platonists. According to one of them, John Smith, only true religion can produce the rational and spiritual hegemony that Stoicism so idly promises. Only true religion restores deposed reason back on its throne or "begets the most *Heroick, Free and Generous motions* in the Minds of Good men." Smith contrasts such true heroism with that all-too-familiar "*bravery* and gallantness which seems to be in the great *Nimrods* of this world," a shameless vanity parading in ornate disguise. Not far from the Ferrars' celebration of Charles V, Smith exposes beneath the triumphs of kings a desperate slavery to vice, their brave power "but a poor *confined* thing" reducible to the limits of "some *Particular* Cases and Circumstances." By contrast, "the *Valour* and *Puissance* of a Soul impregnated by Religion hath in a sort an *Universal* Extent, as S. *Paul* speaks of himself, *I can doe all things through Christ which strengtheneth me*; it is not determined to this or that Particular Object or Time or Place."[27]

That such a limitless heroic and rational soul must be stripped of external circumstance is in keeping with the denudement of ritual, politics, dogma, and militarism from Platonic religion in what Sarah Hutton has called "the golden age of English vernacular Platonic philosophy."[28] Henry More's epic account of the Neoplatonic soul expressly states this agenda. His stanzas will be Spenserian – for Spenser is his favorite model for a fanciful allegorical epic – but there will be no presiding monarch, no chivalric loves or wars, only the epistemological and spiritual quest for that "inward Fountain, and the unseen Seeds, / From whence are these and what so under eye / Doth fall, or is record in memorie."[29] By "memorie," More intends the Platonic remembrance of the Forms, not the patriotic record of "martiall deeds" in the Protestant advance against papist evil.

But as Hutton explains, such Platonic heroism did have its wars to fight and its circumstances to navigate. For one thing, it campaigned for "religious peace in an age of religious strife"; for another, it sought to resolve an "intellectual turmoil" that contemporaries believed unprecedented (73). Each in his way, Smith, More, and Nathaniel Culverwell joust with spectral presences of their philosophical culture, with Cartesian dualism, Epicurean materialism, Stoic monism, Socinian hyperrationality, and the factionalism of a civil war. On their one side is the Scylla of dogmatic wrangling, on the other the Charybdis of a newly resurrected and sophisticated skepticism.

The Neoplatonic hero embodied for the intellectuals of Falkland's generation both a vulnerability to and a mediation of the theological and philosophical enigmas of their day. In their minds, the Neoplatonic hero sacrificed its infallibility to a mutability that Plutarch compared to the moon. But this hero compensated for its defect with what the same writer celebrated as its uncommonly effective resolution of the theological extremism that continued to plague the contemporaries of Falkland, one extreme rendering the gods too irresponsible regarding human and mundane affairs, the other obliterating freedom by involving divinity too much in those affairs.[30]

As intellectuals and poets of the Falkland generation understood it, then, the Platonic hero represented the valor of intellectual strife in behalf of an embattled faith more than any one elaborate ontological scheme. Similarly, J. C. Hayward speculates that Falkland's own attention to the works of Synesius owes more to the ancient bishop's trials of conscience than to his subscription to theurgic dogma. Most importantly, Hayward argues, Synesius's Neoplatonism was less mystical and theurgic than that of Plotinus and Iamblichus; his was a Platonism that struggled to render accounts to Ciceronian duty, to understand the value of military courage, yet to express discontent with the conventions of the heroic mindset. So too, Hayward continues, "Falkland was not a pure Platonist" but contemplated Platonism against the claims of Roman moral philosophy and against the heroic provocation and problems of Greek and Roman history.[31]

For Synesius and Falkland alike, Platonism exacted great intellectual cost insofar as they were convinced "that a man could only by discipline be fit for revelation and that the path to that fitness was a slow one."[32] What Falkland found in the legacy of Platonism was a model for the spiritual and mental valor required for a theological critique, with the aid of which one might intervene in the gaps between worldly loyalties, ontological realms, and even competing notions of heroism. As a cultural hero who in the Caroline years was scrutinized for his negotiation of these divides, Falkland risked at every turn a loss of integrity in his vision of religious heroism, and once it was lost, his supporters were left to insist on the coherence in his persona.

Between the battlefield and the study, then, the ideal of the hero at Great Tew must glance Janus-like in two directions at once, as if he were a statue with "two pairs of eyes: the bottom pair must close whenever the top pair is open, and when the top pair closes, the bottom pair opens correspondingly." In the voice of Osiris's father, Synesius himself sums up the "riddle of contemplation and action": "The intermediate gods perform each alternately, while the more perfect gods are more often occupied with the better activity." In particular, heroes help those souls who would make a transition from the ceaseless combat of the world to the epic ascent of the mind.[33]

For Falkland, the community at Great Tew provided the opportunity to elevate the discourse of the Church of England and to lend assistance to its leading lights as they sought to liberate that church from its po-litical and ideational bonds. What is more, Neoplatonism served as a transition for Falkland from the Elizabethan conventions of heroism to the internalized, Erasmian, and skeptical valor that he developed with Chillingworth – this, despite the fact that Falkland never finally aban-doned the old warrior's mindset of his father. After 1629, the year in which Morison died and the estates of Tew and Burford were bequeathed to him, Cary embarked on an intellectual odyssey that led him from his stint as a feckless duelist in Ireland to the intellectual valor of the Platonic hero. Only – with Chillingworth's participation – this spiritual heroism came to rely on a powerful but fallible skepticism that could overwhelm the very peace, charity, and redemption that it was meant to sponsor. Distrusting the poesies, rituals, and eroticism that according to Robert Burton and George Sandys tended to vilify the putative "genealogies of the Heroes," Cary refashioned Bruno's model of the heroic and fail-ing philosopher, and his new confidante William Chillingworth came to embody it.[34] All the same, he never completely quashed the spirit of those other Elizabethan heroes within him, the ones who like Sir Henry Cary, Sir Henry Morison, and Sir Philip Sidney risked everything for a joust with the Antichrist.

IV

In a eulogy contributed to the 1633 edition of Donne's poetry, Cary ver-sifies why he, like Carew, credits Donne with a wit powerful enough to make the epic poets quake in their hexameter feet. In one passage, the eulogist imitates what he deems the crux of Donne's legacy, the strenuous message and style of the third satire, whose couplets – Falkland's own chosen verse form – can barely discipline the provocative and revision-ary energy of heroic skepticism. In particular, Cary praises the athletic and critical spirituality that Donne promotes against the mind-numbing customs of heroic and ecclesiastical prescription. If, as Donne claims, sin and custom make bogus heroes and churches alike, Cary embraces the skeptical recourse offered by "Satire 3,"[35] together with the corollary that true labor begins only once the false toils of the world have been shed.

Donne's "Satire 3" itself concludes with a carefully measured resistance to worldly authorities and pressures, but it begins with a fervent critique of Elizabethan assumptions about valor that speaks directly to the transformation of Falkland from gallant to scholar. In its opening lines, Donne's satirist finds himself torn between chiding and pitying a group of gallants of which he both is and is not a member. These spirited young gentlemen are oblivious to the courage required to find "our mistress fair religion"; theirs is the conventional and vacuous heroism of warfare and adventure. Religion concerns them only to the extent to which it lends a language of oaths or, more tragically, fuels insubordination, persecution, and war between iconoclastic Protestants and idolatrous Catholics. As a consequence, Donne proposes, those ancient philosophers gifted with right reason but not with Christian wisdom or grace will replace the gallant young men at the heavenly *convivium*, while the fathers of these young men will await the return of their prodigal sons in vain.

As John Klause has shown, Donne was generally skeptical of hero worship yet also derived his own sense of heroism in part from the critical thrust of skepticism.[36] Just so, Donne's clarion call to these mock-heroes of the putatively golden age of Elizabethan adventure requires not just the traditional combat against the world, the flesh, and the devil. More than this, it calls for a heroic brand of what Richard Popkin would name "mitigated skepticism."[37]

Cary's revision of heroism so that it is fallible yet faithful, cautious yet strenuously skeptical in its theological exploration, is imaged in Donne's poem, including the idea that the basic tenets of religion are as simple and plain as their circumstances are complicated or their mysteries are perplexing. What matters most is that each conscience undertake its own struggle for conviction in the truth, each to its own capacity.[38] Throughout the poem, Donne instructs the young men to question their fathers about church history and about truth's unfortunate proximity to falsehood; to avoid both running and sleeping in the business of the inquiry ("To stand inquiring right, is not to stray"); to explode the dichotomous fallacies so prominent in late sixteenth- century religious logic and rhetoric ("To adore, or scorn an image, or protest, / May all be bad");

to suspect the motivations of anyone who blindly or greedily embraces a moderate, officially sanctioned religion such as the Church of England; and to be wary of both skeptical and tolerationist positions that might also be fraudulently motivated or speciously deduced (Donne, 162–63).

Beyond the enigmas of this search for true religion, the gallants face the precarious brink dividing a retreat into God's bosom from the pressures of church and state authorities. Souls get quickly and irreversibly lost, Donne warns the newly fashioned heroes, in the relativism of politicized religion, the skepticism of which is finally spiritual lethargy or fear in disguise. Yet Donne leaves the individual conscience to manage this brink, like that flower which thrives best if it manages to root itself at the elusive interstices between divinity and policy. At this same border between the world and the divine, Donne's heroic rationality seeks to integrate, protect, and guide those souls that struggle so close to and yet so short of the ascent into ecstasy.

Although Cary had admired Donne's poetry in manuscript, his contribution to the 1633 edition emphasizes the coup de grace that the skeptical religion espoused in "Satire 3" delivered to his lapsing Elizabethan militarism. What at the outset of the 1630s seemed so natural to Lucius Cary – that he would respond (though in vain) to wounded honor with a duel, then (again in vain) with combat on the Continent: this humor (as Clarendon characterized it) was under attack by a valorized theological rationality that traced its roots to Erasmus and far beyond to Socrates.[39]

As European philosophers from Montaigne and Charron to Culverwell and Falkland himself knew, the complex relationship between skepticism and heroism has antecedents in Plato's dialogues. But the Christian skepticism produced in France offered special guidance to the English intellectuals of the Falkland generation who sought a clear understanding of how heroism and doubt inflect one another. Charron has no simple take on heroism and doubt, no great instauration on behalf of which he might project heroism beyond its own trade in doubt. In fact, Charron construes skepticism as the agent that demolishes the very rational heroism that it somehow comes to recast.[40]

There is much in Charron's heroic skepticism for the Falkland circle to admire: its liberation of thought, its charity and irenicism, its public decorum and yet its Socratic demolitions. But Charron's skeptic is too fideistic and conformist, too shy of imputed heresy, for the Tew circle's bold heroic reason. Falkland and Chillingworth want reconstituted, not blank, minds; they want wits that work dynamically if fallibly to "stand inquiring right." Charron wants an "extraordinarie and heauenlie reuelation" that translates Ebreo's erotic/heroic rationality into Catholic fideism (278). Away from the bloody battlefields of Europe, Falkland and Chillingworth want the agon if not the wars of truth.

Falkland's most attentive readers have underscored his love of Erasmus and of the tolerant spirits – Acontius, Castellio, Cassander, Melanchthon, eventually Grotius – that followed in Erasmus's footsteps. In his 1651 edition of Falkland's theological writings, Thomas Triplet sets the pattern for proclaiming Falkland's affection for Erasmus that resurfaces in Clarendon's comparison of Great Tew to the Erasmian "godly feast" as well as to the Socratic symposium.[41] In the twentieth century, such scholars as Kurt Weber, J. A. R. Marriott, B. H. G. Wormald, and Hugh Trevor-Roper have exfoliated the sympathies between Falkland and his convivial, skeptical, and pietistic model, cherished above all for his colloquies and letters. Both embrace a unity in Christian fundamentals; the excellence of charity and peace in all other, indifferent, disagreements; the preeminence of simple piety in everyday life; the fertility of Christian conversation and learning; and a modest, even sacred sense of one's own limitations. Neither the Eusebius of Erasmus's *Convivium Religiosum* nor the Falkland of Great Tew can even imagine boredom in a pious life of intellectual exchange and inquiry, and they both prize the ethical tenet that a man must learn "to live with himself."[42]

But the principal modes of inquiry promoted by Erasmus and Falkland differ in nuance, mood, or tone. Erasmus has the early humanists' tendency to lace serious inquiry with playful irony and sprezzatura, whereas the conviviality of Clarendon's Great Tew relieves what is clearly a more melancholy agenda, especially on the question of the justice of war. As Trevor-Roper has explained, the Falkland circle conceived of its informal mission as a response to the last fifteen years of "a watershed in the intellectual as in the political history of Europe," including the emergence of a powerful skepticism, an increasingly doctrinaire Calvinism, the resurgence of Catholicism, and the Protestant military losses of the 1620s.[43] Wormald notes that in addition to concerning itself with the complexity of religious warfare, the Tew circle recoiled from those fractures opening in the Church of England itself, for such inner turmoil exposed that church to the charge that doubt was its inescapable condition rather than its masterful instrument.[44]

One would not like to overstate the case that Great Tew was less tranquil, more burdened, as an academy than the garden setting of the Erasmian colloquy. Clarendon himself stresses just how amiable, witty, and refreshing Viscount Falkland was as a host, even with the most

boorish visitors. Indeed, Clarendon's portrait of the larger world of
Caroline England is conflictive on just this point: those years, he argues, were the most peaceful of times and the most internally divisive,
until finally circumstances and personalities, no doubt providence too,
tilted the balance toward tumult. But however much Clarendon models his portrait of Great Tew on the *convivia* of Erasmus and Socrates,
Suckling is not alone in sensing an extremism, however admirable, in
Falkland's obsession with theology in the 1630s. Not only are the intellectuals of Great Tew struggling to wrestle down the demons haunting
English Protestantism, but their critics soon have palpable recourse to
the demonization of Great Tew. Unlike Little Gidding, whose negative
stereotypes are so contradictory, the bogey projected on Great Tew is
more focused, like one of the characters in the microcosm of Falkland's
associate, John Earle. The loosely defined rationalism offering Falkland
a way out of polemics is readily converted by polemicists into an atheistic
sophistry from which no Christian could escape without some authority
larger than that of the self, without, that is, the miraculous grace of God
or the incontrovertible authority of a church.

With Erasmus, then, the key theologians of the Tew circle prized reason; combined obedience and reform; criticized the practices of violence;
encouraged doubt and even dissent; and embraced a universalist soteriology despite Cary's early education among the Calvinists in Dublin.
As Trevor-Roper has argued, Falkland opposed Laud to the extent to
which the archbishop sought to force conformity and to calcify super-
structure. True, Clarendon's portrait of Laud is more complex than that,
and Chillingworth's relationship to the archbishop was more intricate
and personal. All the same, the Tew circle found hope for the heroic
elevation of the Church of England in an exploratory skepticism and
rational "ecumenism" that subverted the agenda of Laud.[45] Falkland's
rationality is pitted against intellectual, doctrinal, military, and ecclesiological impasse – not least "how to find a basis from which to reason
which reason itself had not already undermined," as Trevor-Roper puts
it (200). And it must contend with the overwhelming suspicion that the
valor of religion in its various forms has proved fraudulent at best, and
savage at worst.

Characterized by Triplet as a courageous and learned David, Falkland
denounces religious persecution and force no matter who is to blame.
Like Grotius in *De Veritate Religionis Christianae*, Falkland is convinced that
any violent means of spreading faith transforms Christians into their very
rivals, the disseminators of Islam. But he has a more extended critique
in store for the tyrannical power of custom. Even if one's church were

infallible, Falkland argues, the person who simply accepts the religion of his parents or his country has less justification than the one who employs her reason in the search for truth. The fact that the search for true religion is enormously difficult might not please us, Falkland mocks; but "tumbling hard and unpleasant Books, and making my self giddy with disputing obscure Questions" have no infallible surrogate so that those labors might be eased.[46]

In his sequel to the *Discourse of Infallibility*, or his "reply" to Thomas White, Falkland advances reason as our best and inevitable, if also fallible, guide in dispelling our passions, divesting our interests, and emboldening ourselves to break the confines of habitual thought. It is, for Falkland, the freedom of opinion, speculation, and choice that justifies God's providence, which respects us with a liberty to cull the best from each position but also to envision possibilities not yet locatable on the intellectual globe. Falkland encourages a special vigilance against dichotomous thinking, urging his reader to follow Cassander and Melanchthon who set aside "particular interests" and sought truth "well in the mid-way betweene the Parties...nay in some points differ wholly from both."[47] By contrast, the Roman church has repudiated its own members – Erasmus especially – who suffer for the bigotry espoused by the putative heroes of infallibility, not least "your own Heroe" Cardinal Perron.

Throughout his reply, Falkland deflates false forms of grandeur in the church. For it is not Rome's "common Achilles" – the boast of infallibility – that lends a church greatness, nor is it magnificent ceremony or violence. Rather, "It is truely said, *Militia Christiana est Hæreses expellere*, but it needs this limitation, *sed armis Christianis*, that Christian warfare employ onely Christian armes, which are good arguments, and good life."[48] At Great Tew, the heroism of Henry Morison's patriotic stand "to the last right end" converts into Donne's injunction to "stand inquiring right," a heroism neither holistic in its claims nor worldly in its aims. Together Chillingworth and Falkland develop a heroic fallibility for their church, one unfinished rather than synthetic, conscientious rather than ceremonial, and critical rather than dogmatic. But in the writings of Chillingworth, the skeptical weaponry of the Christian soldier threatens at times to wound the hands that wield it.

V

In developing the skeptical-fallible heroism of their church, Chillingworth and Falkland collaborated in what their contemporary student of

Platonism called a "Heroick Friendship."[49] Reading through Falkland's library, debating points of emphasis or strategy, the friends forged a basic agreement over what should valorize the religion of English Protestants. According to Wormald, they recognized the need for champions in their church who would overwhelm the Catholic counterattack without either setting themselves up as idols or undermining their own foundation with doubt.[50] The campaign of such champions would oppose the contemporary habits and motives of controversy itself, and it would chip away at those traditions blindly and widely accepted in Christendom. The champions of the English church would help establish which truths are incontrovertible and which circumstances, among the rest, are worthy of debate. According to Chillingworth, this endeavor was the very essence of religious valor, for "he that could assert Christians to that liberty which Christ and his apostles left them, must needs do truth a most heroical service."[51]

In Chillingworth's *Religion of Protestants* (written 1635–37; first published, 1638), the English church is heroic precisely in refusing fraudulent claims of infallibility and in crediting skeptical criticism and earnest endeavor as integral to the Christian odyssey. Chillingworth confronts the Roman Catholic charge against the Church of England that it is stuck in an epistemological quandary, relying on the Bible for its prime authority but with no clear and stable authority for legitimizing interpretations or even the canon of the Bible. The English church is charged, moreover, that in its irresolution and uncertainty, "'Protestantisme waxeth weary of it self,'" with its moderates "'at this time more unresolved where to fasten, then at the infancy of their Church.'"[52] Having converted to and from Catholicism and remaining unevenly committed to the Thirty-nine Articles, Chillingworth himself is subject to being caricatured as an unstable skeptic; as his friend John Earle paints the picture, "Each Religion scares [the skeptic] from its contrary: none persuades him to itself . . . He finds reason in all opinions, truth in none: indeed the least reason perplexes him, and the best will not satisfy him."[53] Such instability is natural, critics charge, because Protestant churches such as the Church of England have had to invent themselves *ex nihilo*. This need explains, they conclude, why there is a "new face" of late on the Caroline church, a romish make-over in the beautification of worship and in the mitigation of rigid Calvinism.

In response, Chillingworth defends his church by transforming skeptical instability into godly heroism. So it is that he tends to compare his Catholic opponents to Achilles, a moniker suggestive of their delusions of infallibility. By contrast, the heroism of the Church of England is Odyssean, a perilous journey of which careful navigation, habitual error, and disenchanted revision are integral parts. Not only does Chillingworth situate the Roman church at the very epistemological impasse with which the papists charge the English church, but he also conceives of God as a merciful, reasonable being, one that credits the earnest, if mistaken, pursuit of truth. God measures the heart's sincerity, not the mind's infallibility, and does not expect an absolute certainty to which the human condition gives no access. Affording us all the saving certainty we need in the Scriptures and a confluence of helpmates in tradition, the church, and reason, God watches over us to see if we persist in the "constant and impartiall search of truth." In short, God demands "his servants true endeavours to know his will and doe it, without full and exact performance."[54]

When the papists accuse the Protestants of leading good Christians into profane heresies, Chillingworth retorts that the Church of England, like prudent Odysseus, navigates between the Scylla of foolish worship and the Charybdis of atheism. The apologist agrees that "the golden mean, the narrow way is hard to be found, and hard to be kept" (167–68). "Hard, but not impossible," and safer as well, with a God who saves us from our errors and credits earnest intention over lapsing success. Anyone hoping to prevent all error in the church militant "must be a meer stranger in the world" (217); indeed the papists "think simple errour a more capitall crime, then sins committed against knowledge and conscience" (214). Thus, Chillingworth converts the strategies of critical skepticism and the errors of fallen humanity into the epic stature of the English church, bound to make it home after its adventures between extremes, against enchantment and monstrosity, and despite error and delay.

In elevating "the narrow way of sincere and universall obedience, grounded upon a true and lively faith," Chillingworth recasts individual heroism in a reduced form: "it cannot but redound much to the honour of the truth maintain'd by me, which by so weak a Champion can overcome such an *Achilles* for error even in his strongest holds" (411). For Chillingworth, even the intentions behind Luther's solitary stand against Romish corruption must be weighed cautiously: "If he did so in the cause of God, it was heroically done of him." Individual conscience is of primary value to Chillingworth, for "in the Christian warfare, every man ought to strive to be foremost" (291). But Chillingworth opposes any deification of the individual and usually dogmatic authority as a misunderstanding of the skeptical church heroic.

Collaborating in the theological laboratory at Great Tew, Chilling-worth makes much of the notion that many people followed readily in Luther's footsteps, and that as "a man of a vehement Spirit" Luther himself tended at times to "over doe it" (Chillingworth, 381). "In the mean time," he allows, "I hope all reasonable and equitable judges will esteeme it not unpardonable in the great and Heroicall spirit of *Luther*, if being opposed, and perpetually baited with a world of Furies, hee were transported sometimes, and made somewhat furious" (312). With what Clarendon describes as a tendency to overdo the skeptical critique, Chillingworth insists that heroic faith is never a perfect thing, subject as it is to "augmentation and diminution" (326); human endeavor is integral to the church heroic, but individual or even ecclesiastical perfection is not its corollary. As Laud puts the case in his account of the conference with Fisher, "reformation, especially in cases of religion, is so difficult a work, and subject to so many pretensions, that it is almost impossible but the reformers should step too far, or fall too short, in some smaller things or other."[55] Reissued in 1639 under his own name, Laud's work responds to the charges also confronted by his godson Chillingworth in maintaining that the Church of England is at once safely redemptive and continually fallible. For Chillingworth, however, what is lacking from the courtly synthesis of heroic religion, or from the Laudian ceremonial and Puritan colonial extremes of epic Protestantism, is any sense of the skeptical, strenuous, and fallible practices of mediation at that horizon of experience where the Neoplatonic hero suffers mutation in striving to liberate human souls.

Like other apologists for English Protestantism, Chillingworth is motivated to distinguish the equivocal odyssey of his church from the also Odyssean shifts and dodges of the Jesuits, especially as the Greek hero appears in Ovid. Charged with wiliness, the Jesuit's "answer would be much like that which *Vlysses* makes in the Metamorphosis for his running away from his friend *Nestor*, that is, none at all" (410). But if the papist entrapment of Christians for the sake of religious imperialism is pernicious, then Chillingworth posits another, more tolerant approach to the heroic unification of the faithful. As the "most Heroicall service" to truth, the Protestant champion should reassemble Christendom around the countersign of apostolic liberty (197). With "Charity and mutuall toleration" for errors made by sincere pilgrims, controversy can be productive and redemptive, not disruptive and condemnatory.

Nevertheless, Chillingworth's appeal to Ovid, his residence at Great Tew, and his extended quotation from a book entitled *Europae Speculum. Or, a View or Survey of the State of Religion in the Westerne Parts of the World* all serve as reminders of his associations with the Sandys family whose deep involvement in the dismantled Virginia Company unsettles the spiritual and intellectual odyssey recommended in *The Religion of Protestants*. In the 1630s, after all, George Sandys is still involved with Nicholas Ferrar in the making of colonial policy, the delusions of which are underscored by the simultaneous rise of, on the one hand, the official desire to control the religious practices of New England, and on the other, the nonconformity of those practices.[56] The heroic thrust of the Stuart church is hard for its advocates to contain in the study or in the soul. With the Elizabethan colonial legacy still looming, the Odyssean legacy of the Caroline church owes as much to Dante as Homer, for like the Ulysses of the *Inferno*, the Elizabethan Protestant hero tirelessly urges his followers westward through the Pillars of Hercules and eventually to their demise. So too in Sandys's beloved *Metamorphoses*, the Trojan War figures in the cosmic history of ceaseless transformation.

It is a version of this metamorphic history on which Nicholas Ferrar insists when he overcomes those censors of Herbert's poetry who hope the poet to be no prophet. But it is Lucius Cary himself who most emblematizes the Caroline recognition that Protestant heroism has grown enigmatic and unstable – that a synthesis between conscience and militarism is as elusive as an infant's dream of return to his mother's womb.

VI

According to Clarendon, Falkland's conviction that "in religion he thought too careful and too curious an inquiry could not be made" included among its targets those conventional habits of thought regarding the political and military circumstances in which church history unfolded.[57] For the goal of the Great Tew academy as Clarendon understood it was to reexamine, sift, refine, and reject if necessary those received opinions that accrued around the theological core of the faith. Falkland's contemporaries and his finest modern scholars agree that the one set of values which he replayed time and again in the refashioning of his own public persona was that of the religious hero. Falkland took it as his life's office to inhabit the past but also to recast the future of the character of the valiant Protestant.

For this reason, no less important to the Falkland circle than Grotius's treatise on the truth of Christian religion was the Dutch lawyer's analysis of the natural warrant of a just war. In *De Iure Belli ac Pacis* (1625), Grotius performs a major service for his contemporaries that crave such a casuistry of war. But the lessons of this textbook for the lord of Great Tew are not easily digested, for Grotius offers a rational and natural rejection of the savage if superficially religious military politics that Falkland sought so urgently yet so futilely to exorcise from his championship of English Protestantism. Gustavus Adolphus himself is reputed to have trusted Grotius's handbook along with the Bible to guide him in battle, but in doing so the great Protestant Swede embodied the self-consciousness that his contemporaries shared over the circumstances of Christian bloodshed.[58]

As Richard Tuck has clarified, however, Grotius virtually eliminates the legitimacy of religious warfare by making all criteria of wartime justice a matter of natural rights – their defense, reclamation, and vindication.[59] When Grotius argues that not even the New Testament excludes the possibility of a naturally just war, he leaves no room for a specifically Christian or Protestant war, reminding his fellow Christians that their own obligations to peace are uncommonly strong.

Should offences to God be punished? Having listed arguments pro and contra, Grotius focuses on cases in which a false religiosity damages public morals. Thus, if a people transgress against the common notions of universal religion, theirs is a violation of natural law that might well threaten civil society. But Grotius protests against the violent plantation of Christianity, against persecution at home and against the pretext for war that singles out the self- contained immorality and impiety in a potential foe. And he emphasizes that the Apostles knew to concentrate on celestial concerns, those "not exercised by fire and sword, but by the word of God, proposed to all men and adapted to their peculiar circumstances." What this means is that war can never simply or justly redress evil with good; it must instead restore rights that have been unnaturally and irrationally deprived.[60] Conscience is especially required to assess those complex circumstances that usually render peace the safer course at long last.

With the outbreak of war with Scotland, however, Falkland's religion of a scrupulous conscience faced what many of his contemporaries deemed the very bankruptcy of religious warfare in Caroline England. This time, Charles I was not indecisive and weak in a good international Protestant cause but resolved (though still weak) in a dubious attack on fellow, even British Protestants and their church. With Falkland's enlistment in that war, he resumed the search for a synthetic heroic code with debts to Elizabethan chivalry and a planter's agenda. Only now his heroic code was largely counter-courtly and increasingly at odds with Laudian aggression against so-called Puritanism. In the 1630s, that is,

Falkland had rethought and recast the conditions of an acceptable heroic synthesis without effectively jettisoning the fictions of honor that the prick of skepticism was meant to deflate.

In the Scottish and Civil Wars, then, Falkland attempts to pass as a synthetic hero from the vantage point of an actor who has come to find the role decidedly suspect, perhaps even repulsive.[61] His reckless gallantry in those wars trumps the skepticism to which such careless instinct is also something of a standard response, that is, the notion that if one cannot arrive at truth via reason, then one had better follow creatural impulses or blindly adhere to custom. In the late 1630s and 40s, Falkland searches for a synthetic religious heroism; but if he represents the moral center of this synthesis, he also leads the skeptical charge whose mission is to destroy the heroic idol, together with all the other masques of infallibility plaguing the church in those decades. Thus Falkland's contemporaries read the amazing scene of his death in the gap of a hedge at Newbury as, in turn, the death of one last Philip Sidney, the world's fecal spoliage of a Platonic ideal, and a hopeless heroic impasse from which the tolerant skeptical impasse offers no tranquil escape. The synthetic religious hero makes one last wild appearance in Lucius Cary, then comes flying apart forever.

Falkland's own last hope for the recasting of a peaceful religious heroism was the Long Parliament in which he himself debated the immediate future of episcopacy and the recent past of domestic grievances. For a brief time, he participated in the composition of a reformative governing body that would activate the religious critiques theorized at Great Tew. As is typical of Tevian skepticism and of Chillingworth, Falkland began his parliamentary career with negation – especially his powerful and incisive attack on the bishops. He had resisted ship money, and poets Waller and Cowley urged him to resist the Scottish war as well.[62] Both poets agree that his learning ranks among the country's richest ornaments; and while insisting on his courage, they situate his value above the accidents of war: "He is too good for war," Cowley protests, "and ought to be /As far from Danger, as from Fear he's free. / Those Men alone (and those are useful too) / Whose Valour is the onely Art they know, / Were for sad War and bloody Battels born; / Let them the State Defend, and He Adorn."[63] There is no mention of the king's attempt to enforce church ornament and conformity through violence when the prayer book fails. There is little if any reflection of the widespread dismay that Charles could pursue such a dishonorable ecclesiastical war. But in his parliamentary speeches, Falkland himself assails in no uncertain terms those evils of a prelacy that nonetheless he hopes to retain and reform as an institution convenient to the English church. More than in Holland back in 1630 or in Ireland in 1629, Falkland's enlistment under the chivalrous Earl of Essex dramatizes the contradictions of a Protestant heroism that has a conscientious Socinian and Erasmian intellectual trying to pass as a warrior from 1588 when indeed England itself is the Armada or, to shift the allegory, the Goliath of the piece.

"Of all the important questions which came before the Long Parliament," Marriott stresses, "there was none to Falkland so important or so interesting as that of the Church."[64] Heroic service might be offered that church at last. In Falkland's view, Marriott continues, the Laudians had heightened division, hostility, ritual, and political clericalism in a church that could prosper only without a focus on these conditions. Denouncing the "many and great oppressions, both in Religion and Liberty" over the last few years, he urges the members of parliament to conduct a "little search" so that they might judge the Laudian prelates "to have been the destruction of Unity, under the Pretence of Uniformity; to have brought in Superstition and Scandal, under the Titles of Reverence and Decency; to have defiled our Church by adorning our Churches; to have slackened the strictness of that Union which was formerly between us, and those of our Religion, beyond the Sea; an Action as unpolitick as ungodly."[65] In these famous lines, Falkland contrasts the wrong way of making a church great – forced consciences and ornamented churches – with a refined composite that comprises freedom of conscience; a prudent and pious internationalism; and a flexible ecclesiology. For Clarendon, the English constitution requires that the state church remain very much as it has been. But even Clarendon knows that whatever the needs of political continuity, the spirituality of the English church has been too rigid, popish, and clerical.[66]

In the Long Parliament, then, Falkland seeks to transform Tevian heroic skepticism into palpable effects from the examination and reformation of religious institutions. Falkland is willing to attempt more radical reforms than is Clarendon, but all the same he fears the political version of his friend Chillingworth's tendency to throw good positions out with bad. At the outbreak of civil war, Chillingworth himself is recreating this tendency, with what we are told is his full-scale rejection of honest wars and with his uses of Roman military expertise to craft a machinery of combat that might end the war at hand with diminished savagery. But before the war breaks out, Falkland offers that heroic service of which Chillingworth has spoken in peacetime, namely, the extrapolation of apostolic liberty from the confines of Tew to the out-skirts of English church polity. In parliament he is able to decry those hegemonic Arminians of whom in private his friend George Morley so memorably quipped.[67]

Of course, the outbreak of civil war meant for Falkland that peacetime reform would be set aside for a casuistry of war. But the war also gave Falkland his most strained and dubious opportunity to fashion himself a synthetic religious hero – to embody and redeem the shadowy Caroline career of a romantic St. George. His biographers have captured this complex and poignant irony of a Falkland who would integrate a hero-ism according to the very conscience that insistently dismantled its in-tegrity. Marriott follows Clarendon's epic characterization of Falkland as a sincere man who like Cicero's Cato belonged in Plato's republic rather than among the Roman dregs. In this portrait, Falkland's con-science reproaches him into the duties of a secretary, the compromises of which that same conscience cannot endure.[68] As Falkland's hope for the Long Parliament fades, his own conflicts over religious heroism manifest themselves in an inappropriate honesty – the refusal to open enemy mail or always to use spies - - but above all in what Clarendon describes as "reckless courage and tender humanity" at Edgehill. Neither the crazily valiant royalism of Prince Rupert nor the conscience that makes cowards of us all can satisfy Falkland. He attempts to synthesize the two in a war that leads many participants to complain that they simply cannot act both honorably and honestly.

What Marriott, Wormald, Murdock, Hayward, and Coltman pur-sue in a variety of ways is a reversal of the eighteenth-century verdict that England would have been much better off had Falkland decided to remain in Plato's republic. According to this critique, he was a fine scholar and patron but no politician and, worse, his conscience made the secretary act a fool.[69] What Falkland's modern biographers accen-tuate instead is the agon in his self- destructive efforts to synthesize duty, courage, and conscience – to live out what Clarendon calls "integrity." What matters for the biographers, as it did for Clarendon himself, is the noble but failed assay. At the siege of Gloucester we see the viscount's most pronounced and deliberate fashioning of a doomed synthesis. Hav-ing argued down Chillingworth's Socinianism by night, he advises the king on tactics by day, and deals with the consequences of his possible failures by framing his own persona in response to his critics. Clarendon tells us "that it concerned [Falkland] to be more active in enterprises of hazard than other men, that all might see that his impatiency for peace proceeded not from pusillanimity or fear to adventure his own person."[70] Plunging through the gap in a hedge at Newbury, Falkland dies so recklessly that the event becomes a question for casuists of his day to debate. In this final act, Falkland's persona comes to encapsulate the dilemmas of religious heroism that the epic skepticism of Great Tew was meant to interrogate.

Clarendon himself tries to recuperate a synthesis between honor and conscience in characterizing the friend that (he knew) died between their millstones. In his paean, he chastises those supposed critics of the viscount who act "as if a man that was himself the most punctual and precise in every circumstance that might reflect upon conscience or honour could have wished the King to have committed a trespass against either."[71]

But modern scholars have captured the cultural rifts accentuated in the personae of Falkland and of that associate honored by Falkland, Clarendon, and Hobbes alike, Sidney Godolphin. From the two men who most epitomized their culture's penchant for locating heroes in unconventional packages, Irene Coltman generalizes a crisis of valor for an age coming to terms with the realization that "many troubles may befall a man who is not sure he is supporting a good cause."[72] Contemporaries complained that religion effeminized the warrior but also that the warrior sullied the conscience. Yet in the Civil War, they were thrown together with unprecedented urgency and enigma (12).

It is significant that Hobbes held his own associates at Great Tew in part responsible for the debacle of heroism. According to Coltman, the political philosophies of Hobbes and Anthony Ascham drew the conclusion that the Godolphins of the world – men uncommonly delicate in times of peace, uncommonly valiant in times of war – were destroyed by the social discord unleashed in those debates encouraged and refined by the likes of Falkland. That is, Falkland's death was not suicidal in being rash; it was self-immolation in being the product of the dissent engendered by the intellectual freedoms of Great Tew (23).

Whether from Hobbes's perspective or his own, the melancholy in Falkland's persona results, as Coltman argues, from a crisis over the conscience of heroism and the heroism of conscience: "[Falkland's] overpowering impulse was not to become an accomplice in crime; to have no part in the world's madness, yet he was not certain how he could stop himself... There were no perfect causes. It was not in the nature of things" (14, 17). It is Hyde who more than anyone else made epic material out of just this imperfection – about the men who could have avoided war, whose military debacle was the result of personalities and circumstances, who undertook the defense of king, constitution, and church as they felt "guided by [their] individual moral sensibility," and who expired under the weight of this "full burden of guilt" (17). By imitating Hooker in the opening lines of his history, moreover, Hyde recognized that the greatness of the church was especially distressed and in need of defense.

Clarendon knew, then, that (in the words of Coltman) the "Civil War was in part an extension of the dilemma of the popular hero from the favourite courtier, like the Elizabethan Earl of Essex, to the leaders of the gentry and to the gentry as a whole" (48–49). It has often been argued that Hyde's, Hobbes's, and Falkland's interest in Greek history amounts to their desire for a genealogy of an ambiguous and obscured modern heroism. As early as 1629, Hobbes prefaces his Thucydides with a lament for the obfuscation of "heroic virtue." No doubt for much the same reason, and to lend modern heroism some legibility, conviction, and integrity, Clarendon modeled his history on classical epic.[73]

But Coltman clarifies just how much the conservative Clarendon came over time to valorize in itself the active and tireless navigation of circumstantial ambiguity, and to prize not so much "the ultimate vindication of innocence" as the "faithful effort" carried out by public servants like Tacitus's Agricola between the extremes of servility and rebellion (129). Like Tacitus's father-in-law, whose portrait served as the chief analogue, Clarendon's Falkland protrudes from the backdrop of an unheroic age;[74] but more than this, he brilliantly constellates otherwise conflicting values for an age in which heroism has become obscure and dispersed like those atoms to which Hyde compares the men and events of the war.

Thus, in the late 1630s and 40s, the heroism of Protestant England became less and less a matter of pomp and circumstance, more and more the skeptical yet pious and loyal casuistry of the Christian soldier's circumstances. The leading lights of the Tew circle knew with Clarendon that "Courage is not the thing we take it to be" and that, in Coltman's paraphrase, "courage needed something beyond itself to be purely admirable" (144–45). But heroic casuistry was charged both with finding and with being that something, and with deciphering the status of military courage anew:

So those who wrote against the old heroes took up a new and heavy burden. The thoughtless courage of the hero gave way to a fastidious scrutiny of war's credentials. They thought that courage was still necessary – even more in fact – because the modern hero has to have both the courage to fight and the courage to commit himself to a cause, knowing he cannot escape the anguish of guilt if he chooses wrongly. (Coltman, 145–46)

Unlike Tacitus's *Agricola*, who at home frets the lethargy of that heroism that was so easy for him to unleash in Ireland,[75] Falkland embodies for his associates both the enigma of just what a godly, conscientious heroism might involve, and the hope that such a heroism might be legible in him – that the tolerant valor of spiritual and rational inquiry were not laid waste in the gap at Newbury.

VII

For a few years at Great Tew, Falkland attempted to live out a skeptical heroism of the mind and soul, free of arrogant claims, of war, politics, dogma, and prescription. His was a relatively open if intellectually elitist coterie, one suspicious of any precedent that, unlike convivial Socrates or Erasmus, was not itself a skeptical host. In a time of domestic peace yet of growing stress in religious and political culture, Falkland sought to convert honest misinterpretation into the very virtue of the Church of England – in contrast with the malicious misprision traded between "Puritans" and "Arminians" and productive, according to Clarendon, of the Civil War. By contrast to Tew, Little Gidding was more closed than open, more familial than friendly, more desirous of prescription and heroic precedents and almost plaintively critical of the same. People flocked to tour – and to be inspired by – the always remote and enigmatic "Arminian nunnery" run putatively by Virginia Company separatists; people came from Oxford to live, think, and breathe at Great Tew, but the heroic service of Tew could not be taken down in a prayer book formula. If Gidding was the distant yet luminous Castor of religious heroism of which people traveled for a glimpse, Tew was the imminent Pollux to which people looked for synthesis and leadership. Both groups responded in complex, critical ways to courtly and Laudian refashioning of religious heroism; both sought a middle ground but also a completely other ground on which to rebuild the fortress of their church. But their ideals eluded them, or so they worried. The little academy of Little Gidding – itself a version of the much-in-little topos – fretted its lethargy, inconsistency, family conflicts, lack of precedent, ill repute, and abdication. The core group at Great Tew promoted the liberation of conscience, only to find itself accused of atheism. Both groups realized that the circumstances of faith must be revisited rather than transcended; but both were hard pressed to find lasting satisfaction in the adventure of circumstantial imperfection.

Thus the Little Gidding inhabitants both imitated and recoiled from their saintly and ascetic paradigms; thus Falkland – whose sisters entered convents – felt drawn to Bishop Synesius, whatever his, Chillingworth's, and Hales's view of the impertinent authority of the past. In the Caroline years, when according to Clarendon, the heroic Falkland, Godolphin, and Chillingworth showed how "many great and wonderful men" came in improper containers, Gidding and Tew posed unconventional forms of heroism that pleased and served, but also subverted and criticized, the refashioning of religious heroism carried out by Charles and Laud.[76] Both communities straddled the gap separating a heroic religion that produced conformity to a corporate identity and a heroic religion that took a conscientious stand apart from that whole.

Outside the Ferrar and Falkland communities, writers boldly revised the circumstance of epic Protestantism. In 1642 Milton promised an epic of a knightly "Christian hero," an epic that, unlike Spenser who never finished his, Milton would never see his way to begin. But Milton was also exploring the possibilities of other, chiefly Biblical, models of epic, and sizing up their relationship to Greek and Roman poetics. Even more forthrightly than the Ferrar and Falkland circles, he was testing the limits of communal heroism – the shame culture that he derived from Homer but applied to Christian congregations – and of inward and rational valor, the esteem that the individual owes directly to God. In the years after Milton had abandoned his Arthurian hero to skepticism, Hobbes never gave up the obsession with the dream of heroic virtue that found such cramped quarters in his ship of a religious state.[77]

In their secular and Biblical directions respectively, Hobbes and Milton extended the Caroline reformation of heroic convention. It was Milton who in 1644 celebrated the spiritual and discursive valor of the "venturous edge"; it was of Hobbes that the onetime masque maker Davenant asked permission, "(remembering with what difficulty the world can shew any Heroick Poem that in a perfect glass of Nature gives us a familiar and easie view of our selves) to take notice of those quarrels which the Living have with the Dead."[78] Even in the courtly world of Charles, religious heroism provoked the tension and debate of which that heroism might be remade. And in that debate English writers were jarred awake from what Davenant criticized as Spenser's allegorical "continuance of extraordinary Dreams" (6). That they also longed for what they imagined to be the Elizabethan dream of heroic conviction and holism is manifested in Henry More's Spenserian stanzas, in the revival of Drake in the 1620s, in the mass movement westward in the 1630s, in Milton's 1644 praise for Spenser as more instructive than Scotus or Aquinas, in the obsession with Charles V, and in Davenant's own comparison of

Spenser's dream to what he now finds disappointingly weak instructors, those Caroline masques that were his own stock and trade (6–7).

In Davenant's belief that Christianity alone produces a heroism as guiltless as a "Village neighbourhood" yet still universalist in its pursuit of human welfare, one glimpses the little academies of Tew and Gidding in search of a local innocence coupled with an intellectual and soteriological catholicity whose unity, in their view, was not possible in the official grandeur of court and temple (10). What must be emphasized, however, is that Charles and Laud also strove against the demise and mistakes of religious heroism. So it is that in *Gondibert*, Davenant attempts yet once more to rewrite the heroism of "Courts and Camps"; but in such a way that, as Hobbes theorizes, fancy ornaments philosophy and judgment structures the fancy that "must take the Philosophers part upon her self."[79] It is just this combination of witty fancy and divine philosophy that Suckling and Clarendon attribute to Falkland even after his conversion to theology, just as the sympathetic Stuart commentators on Gidding apprehend the marriage of liturgy and iconoclasm officiated there.[80]

If Caroline communities such as the court, Little Gidding, and Great Tew strove to reassemble or to redefine the church heroic, these efforts were in part responses to the obvious failures of the Caroline church in military Protestantism. Charles never succeeded in restoring his sister's family to the Palatinate and he failed to oversee a colonial rebuff to Spanish imperialism. His efforts on behalf of the Huguenots reaped only ignominy and, unlike Gustavus Adolphus, he led no troops into battle against the Habsburg dynasts. Writers from William Alexander and Richard Eburne to Thomas Morton continued to promote the colonial enterprise as the chief means "to procure glorie vnto God, honour to [Charles], and benefit to the World." And they repeated the commonplace belief that "doubtlesse towards the end of the world, the true Religion shall be in America."[81] In the last years of James's reign, however, even the still hopeful Richard Eburne remarked that "We must not greatly maruell if our so long continued rest and peace from warres and warlike imployments, our vnspeakable idleness and dissolute life, haue so corrupted and in manner effeminated our people generally and for the most part, that they cannot endure the hearing, much lesse the doing of any laborious attempts, of any thing that shall be troublous or any whit dangerous vnto them."[82]

In 1629 there was an audience for the reissue of Edwin Sandys's *View or Survey of the State of Religion in the Westerne Parts of the World*, in which the controversial leader of the Virginia Company lamented the passing of heroic religion and its corollary, the disunity of Christendom. "They dreame of an old world, and of the heroicall times," he laments, "who imagine that Princes will break their sleeps for such purposes" as the war in Germany.[83] In *A Collection of Emblemes* (1635), George Wither also emphasizes the marriage between power and virtue in those "Heroicke-spirits" striving to produce "Great workes." In more witty fashion, burlesques of the Order of the Garter such as the "Order of the Fancy" and the "Order of the Bugle" mock an unheroic age – an age with no additional materials for a Hakluyt or a Foxe to celebrate.[84] Far from skepticism and failure, the "Epick Poeme" is often conceived as the remedy to ignorance and impasse; in defining his friend's life as such a poem, Lucius Cary writes of Henry Morison that he led "us on, to what we did not knowe: /And, being what wee were not, made vs see / What we should offer at; and sweat to bee."[85] Although "offer" and "sweat" suggest that the reader is credited for strenuous if failed endeavors, such an understanding of epic grandeur entails that the irresolution of English religion requires some heroic model but is none itself.

In his survey of contemporary religious practices, Edwin Sandys is not alone in his dismay over the decay of heroism. Prior to his adventures in Virginia, Edwin's brother, George, offers his own traveler's survey of decay in the Holy Land and surrounding areas, long ago "the seats of most glorious and triumphant Empires; the Theaters of Valour and heroicall actions," but now "the most deplored spectacles of extreme miserie."[86] As an officer and, after the massacre, a revenging soldier in Virginia, George is directly involved in the aspirations and frustrations of religion's transplantation by the English themselves. In other contexts, he is committed to bolstering Protestant heroism under the threat of its demise. For instance, in a poem honoring the Queen of Bohemia, he contrasts her fervent English supporters with the lotos eaters who forget their epic purpose, while his translation of Ovid's *Metamorphoses* is dedicated to those readers clothed "with all *Heroick Vertues*." For Sandys, the church heroic must ring its changes through earthly space and time: his commentary on Ovid is scornful of any allegorizing escape via "that multitude of Gods and Semi-Gods, which the Ethnicks adored." Citing Plato's and Seneca's denial that gods and mortals copulate with one another, Sandys participates in that iconoclasm that "cleane overthrowes the genealogies of the Heroes."[87]

But if the frontispiece of his Ovid resembles the set for one of Charles's masques, Sandys's dedication to Charles remembers the failures of the Virginia Company and the decay of heroism in Stuart England itself, when "we had hoped," he tells the king, "ere many yeares had turned about, to haue presented you with a rich and wel-peopled Kingdome." His Ovid, however, is all the American fruit he has to offer, "bred in the New-World, of the rudenesse whereof it cannot but participate; especially hauing Warres and Tumults to bring it to light, in stead of the Muses."[88]

In close proximity, then, Sandys positions the optimism of courtly syn-thesis – with Charles and Henrietta Maria representing the pantheon of heroic virtues – together with the history of heroism's decline, "tracing the almost worne-out steps of Antiquitie." But his master trope of meta-morphosis stakes a middle ground between optimism and pessimism, as the heroic is always defined by cycles of transformation so that de-cline leads to rise, westward movement back to east, especially in the Stuart imagination of what happens to the church as the "yeares had turned about." Not surprisingly, Sandys appeals to ancient and modern experience alike in glossing heroic virtue or ornament. Epic odysseys are therefore comparable to modern voyages and Ovid's description of the palace of the sun, modeled on Homer's account of Achilles's shield, "is imitated by the moderne in their Screenes and Arasses."[89] This cycli-cal view of history is the upshot of Hakewill's response to theories of decay – that decay together with reconstitution can be found in all ages. Similar is the Caroline church: from Laud's conference with Fisher to the emblems of Wither, it is recalled, with Augustine, that the church militant is like the moon, changeable, migratory, sometimes obscure, its light derivative yet sometimes splendidly full.[90] Typically, the Caroline church is defended as newly hopeful for, and therefore richly imaginative of, the heroic means of its own redemption and final triumph.

But the notion of a metamorphic church raises as many questions as it answers, leading once again to the possibility that the Caroline church is heroic mainly in the tricky, potentially sophistic sense of Plato's *Cratylus*, the hero as interrogator. Are failure and decay integral to religious hero-ism in this world, in line with Sandys's gloss on *Iliad* 14 that "no hu-mane felicity is either perfect or permanent" while the afflicted "wander through the aboades of burdned Earth, despis'd by men and Gods"? Even Herbert's "Church Militant" associates westward movement with a downward spiral.[91] Hoping that their lives might prove what Kenneth Murdock has called "an epic of ordinary men," the family at Little Gidding and the friends at Great Tew risked discovering the sad truth that solitary individuals or communities might fail in shaping or directing the church's mutations.[92] Might kings and ministers instead be trusted to reconstitute the body of the church and disseminate its spirit? In epic terms, George Sandys affirms that they can when he praises Laud, "Who through such Rocks and Gulphes, on either side, / So steadily the Sacred Vessel guide: / Repairs her bruised keile[sic], Close up her Rente; / New rigg and decke, wth her old Ornamente."[93] Might rulers and people alike contribute to the rebuilding of Solomon's temple or to the regaining of Eden? Or might the English people, their communities, and leaders be endlessly metamorphosed between the extremes of hope and despair, their church ever caught between the millstones of rival doctrines and disciplines?

It is just such a metamorphic epic that we find in such "godly" diaries as that of Richard Norwood, in the Chillingworth skeptic, and in the puritan-papist Ferrars.[94] Between its longing for order and its alertness to lapses and possibilities, the Caroline church remains committed to or nostalgic for those powerful heroic forms and legacies of which it is deeply, even heroically, suspicious. Caroline epic religion is at once catechistic and complex, synthetic and fractured, opulent and austere, hopeful and disenchanted, narrowly Protestant and broadly catholic. With the Civil War, Nigel Smith argues, there persists a broad range of political and religious uses of the epic tradition but the main direction of heroic appropriation is inward, "to refer to inward states of human constitution and consciousness."[95] In the heyday of the Caroline church, however, it is widely believed that religious heroism has been lost, but no one maintains that it has been simplified. In no small measure, its complications arise from the tendency of other circumstances – of worship, thought, social interaction, and the cosmic order - - to be bound up together with heroism and to exert the gravity of ordinariness on the elevation of Protestant experience.

CHAPTER 3

Between liturgy and dreams: the church fanciful

The Caroline fascination with the role of fancy in elevating the reverence of worship focuses on a circumstance of faith that shares many points of contact with the pomp and circumstance of epic religion. In both cases, a wide range of writers in the 1620s, 30s, and 40s answer the charge leveled at their church from Catholic quarters that theirs is an impoverished or a gaunt religion, a paltry showing for those talents divinely bestowed on the stewards of the church militant. In such cases, discussions of heroism and fancy mutually turn to the value and peril of ceremony. Accordingly, fancy is often held responsible for the heroic elevation of the faith, and even more often for the bankruptcy and bathos of epic inflation. Like heroism, too, the circumstance of imagination has both inward and outward manifestations.

Yet the skepticism of Tevian heroism notwithstanding, Caroline explorations of the assets and liabilities of imagination in worship are more intricately involved in the epistemology on which worship itself is premised, and thus in the uncontrollable ways in which the experience of faith unsettles the stability of English Protestant identity. Every seventeenth-century writer knew that fancy had a tendency to take flight, but with its strong links to ceremonial worship and to Stoic notions of the material *pneuma*, the faculty has a way of landing Caroline explorers of religious circumstance in the more mundane realms of the social order and of the body. For as Guibbory has written, the Laudian "ceremonialist ideology valued the ties to the past, the submission of the individual to humanly instituted power, and the analogous connection of body and soul within the human being".[1]

The role of fancy in religious experience was an official and unofficial concern for William Laud himself. Officially, he oversaw the enforcement of what Guibbory has called "the new ceremonialism" (13), which strenuously insisted on the grounding of religious worship in the ritualized body, the stimulated senses, and a disciplined imagination.

Unofficially, he was a painstaking student of his own dreams. From his earliest foes to the most recent and sympathetic scholars, observers of the archbishop have been fascinated by the careful notations in Laud's diary of his dreams – of personal but also political dreams, of anxious but also remedial dreams, of dreams with a hint of deep significance and dreams without any apparent significance at all. But for the most part these students have neglected the wider religious context of Laud's oneirocriticism even though his enemies used it as a smoking gun betraying the archbishop's popish, dictatorial crimes. As they are interpreted by both Laud and his foes, the dreams epitomize a problem at the very core of Caroline assessments of religious experience and worship, namely, the pivotal yet unstable role of human invention in the apprehension and worship of the Christian God.

It is commonplace for Caroline apologists urging conformity on the liturgy and ceremonies of the established church to vilify the loose extemporaneous prayers and variegated spiritual conceits of "Puritans" in terms of "fancy." By these terms of abuse, they understand unruly separatists and cancerous rebels worshiping the private idols of their own minds in opposition to the corporate body of the church, the holistic harmony of the cosmos, and the seamless past of the English church. And some of Laud's most unsettling nemeses – for instance, the prophetic Eleanor Davies – lay claim to the spiritual authority attained by dreaming. No wonder then that Laud is troubled by his own nocturnal fancies, the elusiveness of which sets them in direct contrast to the liturgies and ceremonies that he hopes can stabilize and unify religious experience in the kingdom.

But Laud's fascination with his dreams results not just from his fear of insinuation by what he sees as the wild, destructive opponents of decency and beauty in worship. Laud's bemusement at the uncontrollable dreams that might undermine the conformation and authority of his church is even more ironic in the face of orthodox attempts to approve liturgy and ceremony as products and stimulants of a holy fancy. So it is that the unlikely relations between liturgy and dreams emerge: in the work of Caroline theologians but also in the secular rites of the court masque, authors justify ceremony in a fashion that suggests its kinship to dreams – to official, uniform, and beautiful dreams. Meanwhile, the dreams of latter day prophets and the extemporaneous prayers of nonconformists are not fully extricated from the controlling structures of the established church. What this means is that Laud's ongoing and cautious search for the significance of his dreams amounts to the prelate's second-guessing about the proper boundaries and true constituents of meaningful religious experience itself. It is, moreover, a search that he shares with a wide range of Caroline Protestants in pursuit of certitude about the conditions of holiness in human thought, affection, and imagination.

I

In a translation from Plutarch, Robert Herrick offers a fitting preface to Laud's fear of the private chaos into which dreams might very well fling us like so many atoms: "Here we are all, by day; By night, w'are hurl'd / By dreames, each one, into a sev'rall world."[2] Elsewhere, of course, Herrick finds considerable use for privacy, but he concedes little to persistent dreamers: Corinna is urged to leave her "sev'rall world" to "obay / The Proclamation made for May" while Herrick's vision of heaven allows no time for sleep in contrast to mortal life on "the Isle of Dreames" haunted by "monstrous fancies."[3] Laud, too, allows for the uses of privacy, in prayer, for instance, but he vacillates on the uses of fanciful dreams. Fascinated by the vague possibility that dreams might mean more than immediately greets the inner eye, he also tends to trivialize them on the basis of an uncontrollability that recurs as a dominant theme within the dreams themselves.

The very first known reader of Laud's diary – William Prynne – enjoys a prosecutor's special delight in the dreams. As the driving force behind Laud's trial, he extracts evidence from them for the ambitious popery of the prelate: "What a superstitious observer," he declares, "and diligent Register he [Laud] was, of his owne idle dreames; and how ominous some of them have proved."[4] Prynne has it both ways: he discredits the dreams as idols, then milks them for omens and signs. Indeed, Prynne returns to the point, so remarkable is it: Laud has taken "speciall notice of sundry Dreames, Presages and Omens of his owne downfall" (34).

At times, Laud himself discredits the dreams as idle nonsense, especially at his trial when they are selectively used against him. In one chief instance, the prosecution reports a dream about Laud's rise to power. At first, Laud denies ever having the dream, remarking that he has recorded too many dreams in his diary to omit such an important one. The archbishop further defends himself with a still weaker argument that even were he to have this dream, he would never tell it to subversives such as Prynne. As for the actual dreams used against him, Laud discredits them as "wild fancy," and their interpretation as empty opinion: "my Lords, if I had had any such dream, 'tis no proof of anything against me. Dreams are not in the power of him that hath them, but in the unruliness of the fancy, which in broken sleeps wanders which way it pleases, and shapes what it pleaseth."[5] Laud's demotion of the dream targets the fancy in traditional terms, insofar as this faculty is always considered to elude the rational control of the dreamer: in another case he directs the reader of his diary to regard a dream as nothing other than "wild fancy".[6] According to Laud, dreams must be dismissed because they have no meaning; and they have no meaning because we have no control over them. Meaning, in this view, must be intentioned. The use of the dream by biased prosecutors in his trial only magnifies for Laud its divorce from the dreamer's own regulatory conscience.

But his diary is only fitfully dismissive of the dreams, reporting them, sour and sweet, in vivid detail, and offering tentative appraisals of their meaning.[7] No doubt to Prynne's excitement, some of the bad dreams are scenes of professional mistakes or disappointments. For instance, on 16 January 1626/27, Laud records that "Tuesday, I dreamed that the King went out to hunt; and that when he was hungry, I brought him on the sudden into the house of my friend, Francis Windebank. While he prepareth to eat, I, in the absence of others, presented the cup to him after the usual manner . . . but it pleased him not" (Laud, 3.199). To Laud, court politics always seemed as labyrinthine and unpredictable as nonconformist prayers, the worst case scenario of the kind of uncontrollability depicted as a more mundane affair in his dream "that on the sudden all my teeth became loose; that one of them especially, in the lower jaw, I could scarce hold in with my finger, till I called out for help" (3.200). This sudden collapse of the body parallels those dreams in which Laud fears the destruction of the temple and the palace by forces beyond his control.

In several dreams, Laud fails to control the legal and ceremonial affairs of church and state. On one evening, he dreams about the troublesome business of a legacy that he has been asked to manage. In another dream, he cannot explain to himself "how it should happen" that he was "reconciled to the Church of Rome." So while he can mock the dream of some separatist as "overgrown with fancy" (3.221–22), his own dreams about religion perplex him. One dream is especially revealing insofar as it concerns the Prayer Book: at a wedding that he has been asked to perform, Laud cannot find the service book, "and in my own book, which I had, I could not find the Order for Marriage" (3.231). In another, dreamed at court, Laud envisions "that I put off my rochet, all save one sleeve; and when I would have put it on again, I could not find it"

(3.209–10). For Laud, the liturgy and ceremonies epitomize order and stability in ecclesiastical matters, yet his dream converts their stability into the frustration that results when ceremonies must be used or interpreted in surreal contexts outside the boundaries of law and beyond the regulation of church authority.

A few of Laud's dreams afford the busy churchman some respite from the challenges of making, justifying, and enforcing conformity. This is the case whenever Laud dreams of his parents. In these dreams his mother stands by his bed, or his deceased father appears in order to cheer him. Just as fancy can make matters worse than they are in life, so too it can make them better. "I am not moved with dreams," Laud says of one comforting dream, "yet I thought fit to remember this" (3.234). On a Sunday in late January 1624/25, Laud dreams of Jesus in "one of the most comfortable passages that ever I had in my life" (3.157).

Most of his dreams, though, are filled with disaster, death, and disorder. Laud records these, then on occasion proceeds to consider whether a dream has an allegorical key and, if so, whether its interpretation is obvious or requires mental exertion. Sometimes a pregnant dream is allowed to stand on its own: "Wednesday night, I dreamed the Parliament was removed to Oxford; the Church undone: some old courtiers came in to see me, and jeered: I went to St. John's, and there I found the roof off from some parts of the College, and the walls cleft, and ready to fall down" (3.246). Or in another: "The night following I was very much troubled in my dreams. My imagination ran altogether upon the Duke of Buckingham, his servants, and family. All seemed to be out of order" (3.172). But just as often Laud is alert to a very real possibility that his dreams are prophetic. On Sunday, 14 December 1623, Laud dreams "that the Lord Keeper [John Williams] was dead" (3.144); the day after, Laud notes that Williams is now "dead in [Buckingham's] affections." Of a dream had on 4 June 1623, Laud remarks some twelve days later that it comprised all "that followed in the carriage of E. B. towards me" (3.153). So too in the daily events of his life – the fall of a picture or the wreck of a coach – Laud is vigilant for and often fearful of those portents. But dreams and indeed unintended thoughts are more troublesome to him insofar as they suggest an uncontrollability at the most intimate level of spiritual experience.

A good example of intention and its discontents in Laud's religious life involves the naming of his new chapel in 1625. Having determined to consecrate the chapel in the name of John the Baptist, Laud reports that "on Saturday, the evening preceding the Consecration, while I was intent at prayer, I knew not how, it came strongly into my mind, that the day of the beheading of St. John Baptist was very near" (3.171). Here the liturgical calendar, intention, and the inexplicable and powerful insinuation of a thought are congruent with one another, almost as if the liturgical calendar itself had the power independently to form or corroborate individual conceptions and resolves. In another dream, in which he encounters a beloved servant left sick at home the day before, Laud blesses the man upon receiving his surreal supplication. Once awake Laud tells his attendants "that I should find Pennell dead or dying" (3.224–25). When this tragedy proves the case indeed, Laud remarks that "so my prayers (as they had frequently before) commended him to God" (3.225). The dream, in other words, extends the reach of Common Prayer beyond the physical and waking capacities of the prelatical dreamer himself.

Like liturgy, orthodox intention can overpower and structure the otherwise chaotic dream. From the dream about his conversion to popery, Laud remembers an element that Prynne has strategically omitted during the trial, namely, the dreamer's conscientious attempts to resist temptation. Within the world of the dream, Laud recalls, the reconciliation to Rome "troubled me much; and I wondered exceedingly, how it should happen. Nor was I aggrieved with myself [only by reason of the errors of that Church, but also] upon account of the scandal which from that my fall would be cast upon many eminent and learned men in the Church of England" (3.201–02). Still within the dream, he resolves to "go immediately, and, confessing my fault, would beg pardon of the Church of England." Indeed, the moral combat between the seemingly resolute acts of the dream and the dreamer's continual slippage into perplexing mistakes imprints on the prelate "such strong impressions, that I could scarce believe it to be a dream" (3.202). Later, when the diary is published, Laud hopes that the "reader will note my trouble at ye dream, as well as ye dream" (3.264).

Liturgy and orthodox intention can, therefore, fight back within the context of the dream. But Laud also tries to counteract the uncontrolled and extemporaneous thoughts of dreaming by recourse in his waking life to formal prayer. So it is that having dreamed of trouble and disorder in the Buckingham family, Laud resists the interloping dream with prayers for Buckingham in his private devotions. When, on one Friday night in 1636 he dreams of the king's mysterious offense at him, Laud prays in response that God might obviate such an event: "*Avertat Deus*. For cause I have given none" (3.227).

Indeed for Laud formal liturgy and decent ceremony stand in dia-metrical opposition to the wild, extemporaneous dreams and prayers of sundry heretics, false prophets, and melancholics. On 11 August 1634, Laud makes note of a visit to Croydon by one Rob. Seal, who

> told me somewhat wildly about a vision he had at Shrovetide last, about not preaching the word sincerely to the people. And a hand appeared unto him, and death; and a voice bid him go tell it the Metropolitan of Lambeth, and made him swear he would do so; and I believe the poor man was overgrown with fancy. So I troubled not myself further, with him, or it. (3.221–22)

By contrast, Laud directs his energy toward the perfection, conforma-tion, and enforcement of worship in the services of the national church to which all English Protestants have access. In essence, his commitment to controlling the liturgical stability and to reforming the immaculate beauty of the face, body, and gesture of the Caroline church is unset-tled by the unwarranted imposition of his dreams. With fascination Laud suspects that the dreams might signify heavenly dispensations in signs and omens as "unmasterable in this life" as the controversy over predestination (4.292).

If, by day, Laud attributes wild fancy to the ravings of those non-conformists who refuse to go away in his own province and diocese, it is strangely the case that by night, fancy refuses to surrender the jurisdiction of his very soul.[8] To make matters worse, it is not just the fractious "Puritans" who cause the archbishop such trouble in his pursuit of decency and conformity in worship. Just as challenging is his task of ensuring that the advocates of ceremony and of the beauty of holiness avoid illegal extremes, superfluous opulence, and singularity.

Recent scholarship on Laud has demonstrated just how complicated his interpretive and administrative acts of standardization were.[9] The prelate's austerity sets him at odds with the masque-bound culture of courtly magnificence; his legalism compels him in some cases to let time, not persecution, decide whether a decent practice would live or die in popular favor; and his penchant for uniformity and order in worship induces the prelate fervently to argue that if private men are inevitably responsible for the invention of liturgy, this does not mean that liturgy is reducible to the individual conceits of "some private spirit." These problems – the encroachment of needless physical op-ulence in the ceremonies of the national church; the trials of interpre-tation in its ecclesiastical controversies; and the source of liturgy in the private wits of churchmen: all suggest an unintended discourse in which dreams and liturgy meet face to face, with fancy mediating between them.

Liturgy and dreams appear to be completely at odds in Laud's vision of the way the church should be. In their turn, Laud's foes confirm this polarity inasmuch as they claim the prophetic dream and extemporaneous prayer as their authoritative answer to the filth of set and regulated forms. But in his diary, in prominent and not so prominent defenses of ceremony, and in the masques of the 1630s, fancy ranks among those "many superfluities which," according to John Hales, "creep into the Church under the name of *order* and *decency*."[10]

Far from its reducibility to any "character" of the Puritan, then, "fancy" often elicits the charge – for example, from Sibbes – that its proper habitation is Babylonian Rome. From there it is but a step to the indictment that the Laudian church is addicted to images, carnality, and human invention at the expense of the preaching, the Holy Spirit, and the Bible. The tendency of fancy to waft across the wide cultural space separating Laudian ceremony and nonconformist dreams corroborates what William Lamont and Gerald R. Cragg have argued about Laud's trial. That is, Prynne simply miscalculated in enlisting Laud's diary in the case for the prosecution, for the image it leaves of the prelate's mentality is not so much one of perversion as it is of a vulnerable and "honest perplexity."[11]

II

In the 1620s and 30s, the negative associations of Puritanism with fancy are commonplace. In his apologia for the rituals, ornaments, music, and liturgy of the English church, Ambrose Fisher protests against the "windie fancies" of his opponents; so too Peter Heylyn protects the king's temple from any basis in "the particular fancie of one private man." Time and again, Heylyn decries what he takes as heretical thought in terms of "dreames," "wits and fancies," or "conceits and fancies." The placement of the table or altar, he insists, is not to be decided by "the particular fancy of any humorous person."[12] So too Cosin attacks supposed zealots for confusing inspiration with "their own fleshly will and fancy only."[13] In a preface to the Scottish prayer book Charles himself recollects an Elizabethan tradition for establishing the liturgy against "the fancy of extemporaneous prayer" and "the sudden and various fancies of men."[14] In defending the English church from its papist critics, Richard Montagu is virtually obsessive in distancing his church from "priuate Fancies, or peculiar opinions": "the Church is not tyed, nor any man that I know, to make good their priuate imaginations. Nor can or ought the seuerall fancies of men, to be imputed vnto the authorized and approued Doctrine of the Church."[15] On some indifferent matters of controversy, Montagu is prepared to leave "each one contenting himselfe with his own priuate: sobeit hee disturbe not the peace of the Church" (*New Gagg*, 157). But more often than not, "priuate fansy" should be dispelled by "receiued and decided doctrines": thus, rigid double predestination "is not the doctrine of the Protestants . . . It is the priuate fansie of some men, I grant: but what are Opinions, vnto Decisions? priuate Opinions, vnto receiued and decided doctrines?" (*New Gagg*, 179).

Montagu has even less patience for the appeal to dream visions in settling controversies. Defending the belief that the saints in heaven pray for human beings, he admits that the particulars of the controversy are difficult to determine. When his opponent tries to refute the prayers of saints with a reading of Revelation 5:8, Montagu complains that this text only makes matters more obscure:

So the Doctrine is a Dream; the proof, a Dream: a Dreamer related it: a Dreamer recorded it; and a Dreamer doth tell & beleeue it. So, *Qui amant, ipsi sibi somnia fingunt*: men are apt to beleeue Dreams, when the Dream is for their purpose. (*New Gagg*, 218)

In general, Puritans "vent, publish, and tender their many idle dreames, fancies and furies into the world, under pretext of the doctrine of our Church" (*Appello*, 114). Worst of all, the international community finds it convenient to believe that fancy tyrannizes over the Protestant Church of England so that, according to Montagu, the "plaine and easie *Articles* of [the English] CREED [are] disturbed and obscured by the wild dreames of little lesse than blasphemous men" (*Appello*, 226). In short, these men have replaced physical idols with mental ones, a disease much more difficult to eradicate.

For church apologists, the unorthodox love affair with fancy is utterly divisive and arrogant, especially given the faculty's tendency to grow (in Thomas Fuller's words) "too wild and high soaring."[16] But just as often (Fuller adds) fancy makes one's spiritual state "too low and groveling," producing a relentless fear in Christians that "every creature they meet [is] a sergeant sent from God to punish them" (2.177, 180). According to Michael MacDonald, the physician Richard Napier was in sympathy with Robert Burton in attributing such melancholy enthusiasm to zealots.[17] Napier's attribution of fanciful anxieties to extremist nonsense is, however, a wishful attempt to contain what moderate contemporaries believed to be a widespread horror about reprobation. Robert Bolton warns that the devil "hath great advantage to raise and represent to the fancy many fearful things, terrible objects, grisly thoughts, hideous injunctions, and temptations to despair, self-destruction, etc."[18] If some types of people – women, for example – were thought more susceptible to devilish fancies, it was nonetheless "widely recognized" that, in the words of John Stachniewski, the doctrine of reprobation was "conducive to despair" in imaginations as vastly different as Donne's and Bunyan's.[19] Dreams acquire a special status in the search for signs of election or damnation: Richard Norwood is haunted by the nocturnal recurrence of the "mare" while Ralph Josselin – critic of Laudians and Anabaptists alike – assiduously records and struggles to interpret in his diary the dreams of his entire family.[20]

Laud's fascination with his dreams, then, is part of what Stachniewski would consider his commonplace Puritanism. When Calvin wishes to epitomize his argument that the faster we run from God's judgment, the more surely God infiltrates our consciences, he compares the mental state of reprobates to the "dredfull dreames" of besotted men.[21] But for Laud, this shared mental torment is especially vexing because wild, peculiar fancy is supposed to be characteristic of his ecclesiastical nemesis, of faux prophets such as Eleanor Davies. For the nonsectarian, unaffiliated Davies, dreams acquire a special authority for those children of Daniel whose destiny it is to show as much disdain for imposed liturgies as Montagu does for extemporaneous prayers. Affording the visionary with what Nigel Smith calls "genuine intimations of the proximity of the divine," the appeal to dreams serves to challenge the set forms of the established church as the legitimate expressions of faith.[22] It is ironic that these set forms, dubbed the "imaginary" externals of the Church of England, are degraded by their critics to the status of perverse fantasies promoted by those "filthy dreamers," the hireling bishops.[23]

For Laud, the worst case of a "fantastical" dreamer's laying claim to divine insight was Lady Eleanor Davies. As she liked to point out, Davies's prophetic life began in the very year of Charles's ascendancy and lasted until just three years after his death. First there was the visit of the "Scotish Lad" George Carr who, it is said, could discern with his mental powers whatever Biblical verse a person across the room had open, the contents of "Letters enclosed in Cabinets," and the number of "pepper corns in a Bag or Box before it was opened." Then, according to her own account, "the Spirit of Prophesie" visited her as a voice from heaven, after which she commenced a conversation with the prophet Daniel.[24] Thus dreams and their interpretation operate at three levels in the prophecies of Davies: Daniel interprets the dreams of Babylon, Davies the dreams of Daniel, and George Carr together with various interested parties – prelates, commissioners, and courtiers – the dreams of Davies herself.

Not surprisingly, given her indebtedness to Daniel, Davies directs her "wimzees" and "fancies" – as they are often called – chiefly at the court and its temple. In 1627, already famous for having predicted her first husband's death, she interests the queen in her forecasts concerning the royal offspring, the fortunes of Henrietta Maria herself, and the military affairs of Buckingham. Not long thereafter, Charles has had enough, sending one Mr. Kirk to oust Davies from her residence nearby the court. In carrying out his office, Kirk nonetheless seeks answers from the latter day Daniel.[25]

It is, however, with the metropolitan ascendancy of Laud that the so-called "fancies" of Davies become a matter for the High Commission. The official view is summarized by Laud's biographer, Heylyn, who writes that Davies was "so mad that she fancied the spirit of the prophet Daniel to have been infused into her body."[26] As far as Heylyn is concerned, the highlight of the trial takes place when her anagrammatic fancies are answered by one witty commissioner who devises his own anagram out of her name, "Never So Mad a Lady." This commissioner (Lamb, Dean of the Arches) so pleases "that grave court" because in Heylyn's view, he substitutes a "happy fancy" for the mad ones of Davies. But ironically Lamb's witty reshuffling serves to underscore how integral a potentially nugatory fancy tends to be in Caroline court aesthetics, especially given its preference for masques, love lyrics, and other "fleeting things."[27]

In the 1630s, Davies's prophetic visions center directly on Laud (the "beast" emerging "out of the bottomless pit") and his church. Predicting Laud's imminent death according to the "handwriting on the wall" is criminal enough for the archbishop. Worse still, in 1636 she executes her campaign against the Laudian church by desecrating Lichfield Cathedral in a mock ceremony, which Laud describes to the king as "the gross abuse committed in the cathedral church by the lady Davis, who, I most humbly beseech your majesty, may be so restrained, as that she may have no more power to commit such horrible profanations."[28] According to Esther S. Cope, Davies had already joined forces with other women in causing trouble in the church, but alone she "sat upon [the bishop's] throne one morning, declared herself primate and metropolitan, and poured hot tar and wheat paste upon the new altar hangings that she later described as being coarse, woolen, and purple."[29] The size of Laud's displeasure at this appropriation of power is measured in the hefty fines and incarceration inflicted on Davies.

As the affair at Lichfield Cathedral makes plain, the relationship between Davies and the Caroline church is not simple – and not just because the court was fascinated by her prophecies. In her earliest prophecies, Davies heralds Charles as the Michael envisioned by Daniel as the liberator of God's people at the end of time. And while her visions are somewhat comparable to those had by sectarian seers, it is nonetheless the case that her language is at times liturgical and, as Cope puts it, like Lancelot Andrewes's, "focused upon the feasts of the liturgical calendar" (13). For Laud the dreamer, Davies is horrible not just because she disrupts the Caroline church, but because she represents the infiltration – perhaps just the habitation – of a potentially wild and seductive fancy within the walls of the temple itself. In a way not intended by the witty commissioner who answers Davies's anagram with his own, the Laudian church is constituted not so much as the fortress of reason against madness as it is the domicile of a holy fancy surrounded all around by its profane siblings. For the iconoclasts, of course, the reverse is true: their prophecies are divinely intended to replace the profane and trivial fantasies of the Laudian tribe. And there is a wide ground between the two polemical notions of profane fancy on which relatively moderate and orthodox "Puritans" seek not so much to destroy the forms and icons of an established church as to revise and redeem those forms and icons in a range acceptable to the spirit of the Reformation. Thus, attempting to situate himself somewhere between iconophobia and idolatry, Sibbes applauds a man who "studied by lively representations to help man's faith by the fancy."[30]

Whatever the middle ground between them, the supposed opposition between liturgical forms and inspired dreams intensifies just before, during, and after the Civil War. Especially at the end of Charles's reign and just after, such radical men as Gerrard Winstanley and Abiezer Coppe promulgate their dreams in order to challenge the forms of the national church, be it prelatical or Presbyterian. According to Winstanley, for instance, the Diggers are instructed "by Vision in Dreams, and out of Dreams" to challenge the private ownership of property.[31] In each case, a "pure experience" of dreams is juxtaposed with the travesty of external and internal idols. But while it is horrible enough for their Laudian and

Presbyterian enemies that these men boast divine favor on account of their dreams, it is immeasurably worse to the ilk of Thomas Edwards that the radical women have their dreams as well.[32]

To Laud and Edwards, whatever their differences, such women are not just ineffective when they preach, prophesy, or lead a congregation in prayer; more importantly, they are insubordinate and even insane for basing their religious authority in dreams. No wonder that in the late 1630s, the Winthrop faction did everything in its power to protect the settlement of Massachusetts Bay from those recriminations that were bound to follow once critics of the colonial enterprise heard about Anne Hutchinson's claims on the immediacy of the Holy Spirit. No wonder, too, that it was just such claims that elicited her banishment from the colony itself.

But Hutchinson's wide appeal among the colonists evinces that radical visions are hard to refute or assail as mere fancy. More than this, they permit the women to assume roles that are scripturally defined rather than culturally delimited, and they lay claim to a sentience at once mysterious and familiar enough to interest such prominent courtly persons as Queen Henrietta Maria. As Nigel Smith has shown in his study of Ranter language, the imaginary world represented in the reports of radical dreams is vivid and dynamic. For the Ranter women as for Eleanor Davies, the dreams promise a true freedom from the bondage of bishops, presbyters, and all their imaginary carnality.[33]

Not surprisingly, radicals of whatever sect or gender attempt to distinguish their authentic visions from false dreams and carnal fantasies. Such distinctions allow completely different critics of the established religion – Eleanor Davies of the Laudians, Abiezer Coppe of the Presbyterians – to claim the importance of dreams in their writings while other critics dismiss or vilify (as Prynne does) the dreams of Archbishop Laud as private symptoms of popish infections. But the need for a polemical division between the prelate and his nemeses is sealed by an irony of illegitimate family resemblance: nonconformist fancy is often charged with adopting duller "formalities" than the liturgies and ceremonies of the established church. Meanwhile, the theologians defending the liturgy and ceremony of the Caroline church habitually applaud their exterior forms as the products and stimulants of fancy. In the Stuart promotion of church beauty, Laud's fascination with his dreams gains a new and productive impetus, for like their critics, apologists for the established church are compelled to insist that one dream is certainly not another.

III

In seventeenth-century religious psychology, "fancy" or "imagination" is considered as serviceable as it is dangerous. In this, as in so much else, Sibbes says best what so many of his contemporaries attempt to articulate. In "The Soul's Conflict," he comforts his auditors and readers with an analysis of how fancy can magnify the divine sweetness and love so necessary for saving (and easing) each soul. First there is St. Augustine whose love of eloquence opens the way for holy matter to reach his heart. Then there is the Italian marquis, Galeaceus Caracciolus, who avers that just as the sight of dancers divorced from the sound of music makes those dancers seem crazy, so too with those Christian practices that at a cursory glance seem foolish; a closer look reveals "a gracious harmony betwixt their lives and the word of God" and stimulates a love of "the beauty of holiness."[34] The prominence of God's love in Sibbes's notion of salvation coincides as Janice Knight has argued with the preacher's lyrical style, one which gained him admirers at the Caroline court.[35] What is more, Sibbes believes that human fancy and divine love are meant to accommodate one another. As Luther understands that fears of predestination should send us back to the wounds of Christ, so "the putting of lively colours upon common truths hath oft a strong working both upon the fancy and our will and affections" (Sibbes, 1.184).

Sibbes elaborates the point. Reminding us that Christ himself refreshed his auditors' fancies with "a lively representation" and "an earthly, sensible manner," he features the sacraments among those Christian practices that appeal to human nature's physical side. But far from dwelling on the accoutrements of the church, Sibbes points to the down-to-earth language of the Bible and to all the little, everyday phenomena in God's creation as "matter to a holy heart to raise itself higher" and as encouragement that we can "make our fancy serviceable to us in spiritual things." "A sanctified fancy," he continues, "will make every creature a ladder to heaven." But there are warnings: the appeal to fancy is especially apt for children and its benefits are always contingent. "As the soul receives much hurt from imagination," Sibbes concedes, "so it may have much good thereby" – but only if it serves faith and avoids actively devising the substance of religion (1.184–85). In defense of fancy, however, the preacher notes that reason is charged with obedience to faith as well.

As William Rossky explains, Renaissance theorists of the faculties tend to feature the imagination as a mediating agent in the human system of mental apprehension, which means that fancy's duties to receive, re-shape, and transmit data from the senses to reason and from reason to the will are as crucial to thought as they are fallible and whimsical.[36] In this view, thought cannot take place or effect in bifold human nature without the magical mediation of fancy – and indeed its ties to sympathetic, pneumatic magic more fully implicate fancy for better or worse in the dispensations of ceremony.[37] But given fancy's tendency to misshape or distort information in its image-making capacity, thought can be crippled or compromised by the fancy that it needs. More often than not, it is argued, fancy sponsors and even composes images that are untrue, disorderly, or sinful.

A large part of fancy's instability and excess is derived from the body and its humors.[38] But given fancy's inhibition, misdirection, or contamination of religious meditation, Caroline religious writers often attribute the whims and obsessions of the faculty simply to sin. In *The Vanity of Thoughts Discovered: With their Danger and Cure* (1638), Thomas Goodwin discusses at length those "vaine, light, wanton, prophane, dissolute thoughts" otherwise known as "fancies."[39] Independent of our intentions and deliberations, these thoughts are "those *fancies, meditations*, which the understanding by the *helpe of fancie frames within it self of things*; those wheron your minds ponder and pore, and muse upon things . . . I meane those *talkings* of our minds with the things we know . . . those same parleys, enterviews, chattings the minde hath with the things let into it, with the things wee feare, with the things wee love" (6). We require no help from Satan in inventing these fancies – at times highly various or "vagrant" ("more evidently in dreames") and at other times obsessive (*"too fixed and intent"*), but always worldly and flimsy; but we do need a "heart sanctified" in order to distill from our thoughts whatever is good, holy, and useful (23). Goodwin reminds his reader that the vanity of thought can be extremely subtle, sometimes involving a right thought had at the wrong time, for example, if in prayer one is distracted by the desire for a sermon. More often, fancy stages what Goodwin calls *"speculative* wickednesse," the imagination of sins beyond our capacity to indulge and again most "evident to you by your dreames" (30).

If, as Lancelot Andrewes puts it, the essence of profanity is the replacement of God's law with one's "own fancy and affection," it is widely recognized in the period that fancy or imagination is powerfully instrumental in the maximization of devotion.[40] According to Bacon, who also explains how the faculty is poised between the senses, reason, and will, fancy has an especial value in the stimulation of worship, for

> it is either invested with or usurps no small authority in itself . . . For we see that in matters of faith and religion our imagination raises itself above our reason; not that divine illumination resides in the imagination; its seat being rather in the very citadel of the mind and understanding; but that the divine grace uses the motions of the imagination as an instrument of illumination, just as it uses the motions of the will as an instrument of virtue; which is the reason why religion ever sought access to the mind by similitudes, types, parables, visions, dreams.[41]

The spiritual authority allowed for fancy here resembles Thomas Fuller's claim that the faculty "is free from all engagements," "by a kind of omnipotencie creating and annihilating things in an instant."[42] But Bacon and Fuller fail to explain how it is that fancy operates so vitally in the sensory and emotional experience of liturgical ceremony, nor for that matter do they clarify how dreams come to be likened to the high services of the Laudian church. In fact, Fuller's emphasis on the "boundles and restlesse" energy of fancy suggests the impossibility of such a merger.

The improbability of the merger notwithstanding, advocates of church ceremony from John Cosin to Jeremy Taylor purvey many of the same arguments in favor of beautiful, formal worship, and against extemporaneous prayer and conceited preaching. We cannot afford, they argue, to offer God a dough-baked, ill-considered prayer, to worship God off the cuff. Instead, we should bestow more care on our worship than upon any other facet of our lives. Yet (continue the apologists for ceremony) the nonconformists fail to see that their roughshod worship restricts the souls of the congregation all the more severely, inasmuch as their prayers derive from nothing other than their preachers' singular or fantastical humors. Liturgy and ceremony ensure national and spiritual unity, and they preserve peace and order, qualities to be valued in any Christian community. They awe the common people into a proper trust for authority, and reap benefits from the learning and spirituality of the greatest men of the church over the centuries. Above all, liturgy and ceremony are productive means for worship. They memorialize the vital past of the church militant; they edify the understandings of the participants; they stir up the affections in a decent yet fervent devotion; and they accommodate the limitations of worshipers by appealing to the physical senses from which no mortal can escape.

This last advantage of ceremony, the appeal to the senses, is complicated for those seventeenth-century theologians who know their Erasmus. In his influential *Enchiridion*, Erasmus allows the senses their role in sacramental worship, yet he platonizes the division of the human self to such an extent that the spiritual goals of worship are emphasized at the expense of the flesh.[43] But in later English theology, the appeal to the senses persists in defenses of *adiaphora*. In an often quoted passage, Edwin Sandys "highly commend[s]" the papists for the stimulation afforded by "their musicke, perfumes and rich sights," remarking that in temples as in courts, "this outward state and glorie being well disposed, doth engender, quicken, encrease and nourish, the inward reverence and respectfull devotion which is due vnto so soveraigne Maiestie and power."[44] What is more, this appeal must justify the role of fancy in worship, the very faculty that ostensibly runs amuck in the madcap Puritans. Indeed the great irony of these defenses of elaborate ceremony is that their grounding in fancy can be turned against them as it is in the homiletic indictment, quoted by Henry Burton, against "such gay gazing sights, as their grosse fantasy was greatly delighted with."[45] Just so, when John Williams seeks to speak the worst that can be said about the Caroline replacement of tables with altars, he attributes the policy to "fancy and imagination," to a "curious composition . . . hatch't by the winde of [the Laudians'] imagination": "And when men in their *nominations* of things do vary from the *Law*, which is the Quintessence of *Reason*, they doe it in a humour, which is the Quintessence of *Fansy*."[46] To clinch his point, Williams cites Hooker's view that there is no way to achieve "peace and quietness, unless the probable voice of every entire Societie or Body politick, over-rule all private of like nature in that Body" (142). To Williams's argument that Christianity allows no material but only allegorical or metaphorical altars, Heylyn responds that all metaphors and allegories elaborate on material realities as "fancie serves" the allegorist, an answer that admits the vital role of fancy in the newly beautified worship of the Caroline temple.[47]

What emerges from the many defenses of ceremony is an intermittent and somewhat nervous apology for fancy and the dream. As we have seen, there is more to fear from the fancy in seventeenth-century England than just a general distrust of imagination. Apologists for the established church often couple nonconformist dreams with irregular fancy; thus Joseph Glanvill summarizes an entrenched tradition when he assails the religious radicals for the "imagery of dreams, and the pleasant delusions of their fancies."[48] And Jeremy Taylor, like Cosin and Montagu, multiplies instances in which he can scold disruptive extremists for their "wild and impious fancy" or "the fancies of any peevish or mistaken priests." These unregulated fancies, the ones presumably mistaken for the inner light in dreams, are allegedly factious and dangerous rather than creditable. But Taylor also finds uses for the fancy in church discipline. For instance, he faults the Directory of Worship for having "no external forms to entertain the fancy of the more common spirits."[49] In *Holy Living*, moreover, he exposes a strange kinship between fanciful dreams and church ceremony.

Describing the utmost love we should feel for God, Taylor pauses over the "little things ... and little accidents" that are the concerns of fervent love. Love tries to "muster" all its infirmities in the name of God, but it thereby slides all the more readily into impurities, including "an idle word" or "the impurity of a dream." According to Taylor, fervent love must struggle to maintain its decency as well as its passion. The cleansing of love is abetted when the soul minimizes its love of the world, for which it should "lay fetters and restraints upon the imaginative and fantastic part; because our fancy, being an imperfect and higher faculty, is usually pleased with the entertainment of shadows and gauds: and, because the things of the world fill it with such beauties and fantastic imagery, the fancy presents such objects, as are amiable to the affections and elective powers. Persons of fancy, such as are women and children, have always the most violent loves" (4.196–98). These women might be misguided worshipers of the Virgin Mary or sectarian prophets. Nevertheless, Taylor exhorts his reader to pity, to help, and even to admire their violent loves, though these amorous dreamers fasten on the "gauds" of the world. As with the awe that fancy can arouse in the common people, so here with the fancy of women: Taylor wants to find a safe place for the endangered imagination in legitimate worship.

Fancy is stamped with approval when Taylor turns the discussion of violent love into an apology for ceremony. If controlled, the power of imagination offers the advocate of church beauty an argument for the ceremonies that are simply the "transplant the instruments of fancy into religion" (4.198). Music, adornments, perfume, vestments: all entice the receptive fancy into proper worship and prevent the distorting fancy from erring into impurities. Among these impurities are the dreams that Taylor sometimes considers *adiaphora*. Thus he ascribes a washed fancy to the Church of England, and contends that formal ceremony prevents the "busy and less discerning fancy" from often daydreaming in the service of God.[50] Or as Donne puts it, the imagination is so voluble and giddy in its non sequiturs that "an anything, a nothing, a fancy, a Chimera in my braine, troubles me in my prayer." According to their apologists, however, the forms and accoutrements of public worship provide the fancy with structure and stimulation enough to concentrate its energies on the divine. As Horton Davies says of Jesuit meditation, seventeenth-century theologians inherit the belief "that the clue to the changing of the will is to be found in the imagination."[51]

Taylor's recommendation for the "removal" of fancy means, then, not so much its good riddance as its transplantation out of the world and into the sacred and beautiful space of the church. It is widely recognized in the period that fancy ranges between the extremes of mental elevation and humiliation, both of which are required by the stirring forms of liturgy. What is more, fancy is often characterized by its attraction to Edenic or utopian spaces, a penchant ideally suited to the Laudian postulation of singularly holy places within the already differentiated space of the consecrated temple. Fancy is especially equipped to appreciate the idea that as Horton Davies summarizes it, churches "are not merely convenient, or their fittings didactically valuable, or the encouragements from the example of others worshipping, or even the place where angels join with humans in worship, but they are the places of God's presence and most fully in the Body and Blood of Christ in the Eucharist centred on the elevated and enclosed altar."[52] But as George Herbert laments in "The Forerunners," fancy is prone to backslide after its baptism in the beauty of holiness; the faculty is full ready to return to her brothel or his sty, especially if its guardian – whether poet or priest – lapses into decrepitude.[53]

Taylor's baptism of fancy updates the heritage of Stuart apologies for the faculty's spiritual uses. Lancelot Andrewes has much the same "removal" in mind when, in a sermon, he modifies his attack on the "worshipping of imaginations." In regard to ceremonies, Andrewes announces that "First, I take it to be a fancy to imagine there needs none [imaginations]; for without them neither comeliness nor orderly uniformity will be in the Church."[54] These decent fancies are indispensable while the extemporaneous ones are insane. What this means, according to Davies, is that "Ceremonial, so Andrewes teaches, is based upon the threefold foundation of the nature of man and his activities, as soul and body and as having worldly goods. Man must worship with each of these instruments." After Andrewes, writers such as Herbert Thorndike and Foulke Robartes legitimize ceremony "as suited to the mixed spiritual-sensuous nature of man, as reminders of the homage due to the King of Kings, as pedagogical incentives to adoration, confession, or aspiration, and as means of encouraging the common people to respect their leaders in civil, and religious life." As John Barnard recognizes in 1641, fancy is situated at the very heart of all these experiences; indeed decency and reverence in the forms of worship are charged with taming the "rough and boystrous fancies of a Nation."[55]

In the years of Charles and Laud, somatic fancy comes out of the corner into the center of religious controversy. The problem for the Caroline defenders of a physical, imaginary worship is that they have staked so much polemical stock on vilifying the unruliness of fancy in their opponents. As part of their defense, divines frequently liken the awesome experience of elevated presence in the temple to the dream work of Jacob. Sometimes, as in Barten Holyday's 1625 sermon, the link between ceremony, imagination, and Jacob's ladder is simple enough: Jacob and Paul alike, we are instructed, learn "by the phantasie" about ascension into heaven.[56]

But the network of concepts can prove quite elaborate. In a sermon preached before Charles in 1636, for example, Thomas Lawrence builds a case for the proper reverence we owe holy places from Jacob's declaration about his vision in Genesis 28 that "surely the Lord is in this place, though I knew it not."[57] The preacher opens with a pun: "*God* came indeed to him in a *dreame*, but if we dreame while we are here, he will not come so to us." What this means is that the reception of God's "peculiar dispensations of his residence, and graces in the place" of the altar is best experienced in a state of mind less rational than surreal (2–3). We are not supposed to sit there in the pew, Lawrence insists, and analyze just how God has magnified his presence; rather, we should "clothe our phansies in *generall*, and *indefinite expressions*" (17). Fancy comes into play because the beauty and power of worship are mysterious as matters of faith, not scholastic debate. As Lawrence puts it in a 1634 sermon: "Againe, thou wast, o Lord, *in nubibus*, vnder the Law; and appearedst oftner in dreames then visions, and why should I then dreame of visions, vnder the Gospell? Where thou intendest night, why should I looke for noone? Why should I long to see, what the Cherubins saw not, which covered their faces, and opened their mouthes at once."[58] Given the mysteries of divinity, this passage suggests, the ceremonies in which God's holiness is most present should remind the laity of "the priviledge of the clergy" and of their own limitations in the practices of the national church (20). Once again, fancy has the capacity to shame us into conformity and to humble us into reverence, even as it offers to accommodate the most modest devotional needs.

In a related defense of the role of the body along with the soul in ceremonial worship, Foulke Robartes is generally dismissive of "fancy." But when he attempts to characterize the fervent devotion involved in bowing at the communion table even when the communion is no longer on it, he recalls how God showed Jacob "speciall signes of his speciall presence" in a dream, the passing of which made no difference to the patriarch who held the place consecrated forever more.[59] Such dreaming of God avoids the arrogance of those Puritans overwhelmed by their own "fancy and selfe-conceit," which will "take up that roome and power in their hearts, and that authority over their affections and practises which belong properly to almighty God." Robartes concludes by suggesting that such zealots intend the idolatry that seems to overpower them: "And so Conceit and Fancy is obeyed and followed, and become an Idoll, shutting out the Soveraignty of God, and placing it selfe, or rather placed by men, as a God in their hearts" (95). In other words, these men are held responsible for their nonconformity to the beautiful dreams that surround Laud's altar – to dreams as allegedly comforting as the parental images that revisit Laud's nocturnal fancy.

In sum, defense of a ceremonial imagination challenges apologists for the English church to discipline a transgressive fancy as well as to explain the origin of all ceremony's benefits in terms of fancy, that mediator between the body and soul. This question of origins leads us not just to what for Laud must be an ironic kinship between dreams and ceremony but also to the brink of an equation between them. The equation also encompasses the spectacle of state religion – of poetry, dance, music, and gesture – otherwise known as the masque.

There are many ways in which Caroline defenders of fancy are prepared to bridge the ceremonies of church and state. Take the problem of pagan origins: along with Thomas Fuller, John Aubrey, Peter Heylyn, and others, Andrewes was fascinated with the pagan history of Christian ceremonies. Like poetry, ceremony could be chastised or approved all the more for its pagan origins. Thus an analogy obtains between the masque and church ceremony, not just because of the cultic origins of drama, nor just because the historian of *homo ludens* links play and ritual, but also specifically because the Laudians loved to superimpose palace and temple and were attacked by William Prynne and his associates for the two excesses of stage plays and papist formalism.[60] To the judges in the Star Chamber, this puritanical conflation of ceremony and the theater was simply a sign of poor judgment: "Bayes in windowes, new yeres guiftes, May games, danceing, pictures in churches, &c. all [Prynne] comprehendes vnder the title of stage playes, which he dothe to withdrawe the people's affection from the Kinge and Governmente."[61] To Prynne, however, the shoes fit: plays and masques were defiled by the same pitch that tainted church discipline in the new popish branch of the Church of England.

Indeed the Caroline establishment did not often conceal the identification it made between the ceremonies held at St. Paul's and those performed at Whitehall Palace. Laud – no friend himself to the excesses of court life – preached that according to Old Testament precedent, palace and temple should be inextricably joined. And in their masques, the Stuarts offered a number of striking parallels between the spectacles of the masque and the ceremonies of the church. For instance, Inigo Jones's designs for *Salmacida Spolia* (1640) include the figures of Doctrine and Discipline, as well as the descent of the Queen in a cloud of "Celestial prospect," surrounded by lines and ranks of subdeities, and emitting a "transparent brightness of thin exhalations, such as the Gods are feigned to descend in."[62] Just such pictures or sculptures of the Virgin, angels, or Christ descending or ascending at the east end of the church drew the fury of Prynne, Peter Smart, and Henry Burton. In fact, the stage design of this masque could be superimposed on that for the chapel found in Prynne's *Canterburies Doome*, each receding back toward the altar or the cloud. As R. Malcolm Smuts remarks, there is a "parallel between these stage sets and Baroque altar paintings, whose illusory space removes the wall of a church to reveal an image symbolizing a religious mystery."[63]

Often the same terms were used to praise both masques and church ceremonies (e.g. "splendor"); and in its ornate beauty, the church was compared to a court, while the court was compared to a temple. As a nodal term in this shared lexicon, the court masque and the temple ceremony are joined at the hip by their appeal to the restive "fancy" that worries Laud. Stuart masques are cautious about fancy in the way that the theologians are. Sometimes the issue is skirted. Jonson's preference for "more removed mysteries" over the ephemeral constructs of lumber and paint in the masque is well known. Masques lay claim to the highest truths and virtues in their partisan defense of a peaceful and abundant Stuart England, but they also indulge the senses to the amazement of Bacon or the disgust of Prynne.[64] In James Shirley's *The Triumph of Peace*, however, the problem of fancy's place in the court mythology is treated forthrightly.

According to Clifford Leech, *The Triumph of Peace* (1634) was produced by the Inns of Court in response to the controversy over the lawyer Prynne's *Histriomastix*. The Inns of Court men wanted to show their devotion to the king with an "infinite splendor."[65] Fancy first enters the scene when, in his preface, Shirley humbly offers the masque as an "oblation," a word much hated by Prynne, and as the product of his own "weak fancy" (282). The author's fancy is effaced to prepare for the moment when the king will be credited with creating the splendor of the masque and the bounty it represents. But when we come to the antimasques, "Fancy" is the chief protagonist; as a nimble and inventive faculty, dressed in "several-coloured feathers, hooded; a pair of bats' wings on his shoulders," Fancy invents on the spot an astonishing number and variety of antimasques (283).

Much is made of his extemporal imagination by the several lightweight attendants, Laughter, Opinion, Novelty, and the rest. But when the heavenly strains and presences filter into the room along with the emerging masque, Fancy is sent packing as a "profane" annoyance who must be dismissed before we enter into the court of Irene and Eunomia, the latter of whom will "make a temple of a forest" (297). Eventually, the king and the queen are worshiped as Jove and Themis in the very temple for which they are praised.

There is, then, a double creation of his masque and its temple whose ceremony excels in "curiously wrought" ornament (301). The masque depends on fancy and the king, just as the sacrament looks through fancy back to God. Masques are formalized mysteries and extemporaneous shows; sacraments convey grace yet rely on an appeal to the senses. Indeed in their set designs masques often are said to feature "fancies": in *Tempe Restored* the description tells us that the "rest of the border was filled up with several fancies."[66] Even so, in *The Triumph of Peace*, there seems to be little confusion between the two creators.

But Shirley is not finished with what seem to be neatly divided origins. Toward the end of the masque, the carpenter, painter, tailor, and property man, among others, rush on stage in order to reclaim their creation. Their invasion is too violent for the guards to restrain, and "a crack is heard in the works" that totter on the brink of collapse. "Those stairs were of my painting," the painter cries, leading the charge.[67] His is the voice of the profane fancy, now emitting from the mouths of people who are represented in one antimasque at a tavern, happy with their lot in Caroline England. Here, however, they want credit for their common fancies, and so force the audience to remember not just the mechanisms and materials of the masque but the alternative theory of its origins, the giddy and extemporaneous fancy that favors the senses – or even discord – over mystery, grace, and order. The possibility of disorder in the fanciful basis of the masque is spelled out at the end of *The King and Queenes Entertainement at Richmond* (1636), when "every man fitted his part to his owne fancy, and the constitution of the whole tending to a greater bulke, it came to be what it is, without any designe, but rather a kind of necessity vrging it."[68] As with Laud's liturgies, so with the Carlo-Marian masques: their claims on conformity and unity are enabled yet also unsettled by their invention and execution according to the imaginations of private men.

Like the theologians, then, the masque writers are fascinated by the up-start claims of fancy to an integral position in the aesthetics of Caroline ceremony. According to Michael Neill, "fancy" is closely tied in the Caroline period to that "compendium of all literary virtues" wrapped up in the notion of "wit."[69] Clearly, the aesthetic values of structured formality, stylistic elegance, and involving passion might readily be trans-ferred to the liturgical ceremonies of the church. But as Neill points out, there is a negative potential in these Caroline aesthetic principles, not least a "sterile formalism" (360). Shirley's *Triumph of Peace* suggests the further irony that along with its appeal to the body and its passions, cer-emony must admit its reliance on the fancy's mercurial energies, that is, on the faculty's extemporaneous resistance to conformity and order. It is not surprising that in a play commissioned by Laud to be performed at Oxford, a chaotic "fancy" is defeated by a prudent king and his chief minister.[70] For Laud, fancy introduces the bogey of papal excess and Puritan chaos into those ceremonies that must steer between the orderly beauties of the one and the reformed spirituality of the other. The irony of the appeal to fancy at court and in church ritual is that it links cavalier wits to ceremonious divines, and both in turn to the zealots they love to hate.

Yet another convention of the Stuart masque identifies its fancies with the dream. In masque after masque, the participants are reminded that the performance, the masque itself, is coterminous with the night. At the end of *The Triumph of Peace*, Amphiluche, the goddess of twilight, enters to disperse the masquers with the darkness. Masquers are warned to seize the night while they can, then not to profane the sacred event by staying too long. At the end, too, they are commanded to "think a prayer," though the contents of the prayer are prescribed: "That all, that can make up the glory / Of good and great, may fill their royal story."[71] Here we have a version of the prayers so familiar in the Book of Common Prayer, for the welfare of the king and the queen. But this vespers is private, not just because it is located in the hearts of the masquers nor because it is staged indoors where the palace images the homes for which Cosin and Feltham composed private liturgies. Above all, the prayer is private because it is part of an official dream, the nocturnal masque, whose best spirits appear near dawn and then disappear with the morning light. On the force of these mysterious yet also nugatory connotations, Bulstrode Whitelock concludes his long account of Shirley's masque with this dubious benediction: "Thus these Dreams past, and these Pompes vanished."[72]

IV

Contemporary critics of the Laudian formalists are not alone in laboring to justify their dreams. No doubt in order to distance themselves from the "Puritans," apologists for ceremony in church and state are compelled to defend their own surreal yet disciplinary fancies. As Manfred Weidhorn has shown, the seventeenth-century fascination with dream theories yields an especially diverse set of explanations for the dream, some prophetic, others somatic.[73] But in religious contexts, ceremonialists and iconoclasts alike ponder with Milton the ideal circumstances required so that "if such holy Song / Enwrap our fancy long, / Time will run back, and fetch the age of gold."[74] It is helpful to remember that the young Milton praises Andrewes, devises masques, and celebrates in advance the apocalyptic demolition of fancy's magic and conformist structures.

In the Caroline years, religious fancy is habitually caught in that double bind of accommodation, having to purify the body in order to reap something of great constancy yet needing to concede the imperfections of the body so that worship is not barren. One Caroline oneirocritic, Thomas Browne, is especially committed to exploring fancy's overlap between church ceremony and private dreams, even as he mocks the insolence of zealots who miss entirely the proper devotional uses of imagination. Browne's treatise on dreams discusses all the theories and so illustrates that dreams are under review in the seventeenth century, not unlike those cousins of the dream including magic, imagination, and ceremony. But in *Religio Medici* he revels in the etiology that posits the magnification of reason in the fanciful work of the sleeper: "we are somewhat more than our selves in our sleepes, and the slumber of the body seemes to bee but the waking of the soule. It is the ligation of sense, but the liberty of reason, and our awaking conceptions doe not match the fancies of our sleepes . . . I am no way facetious, nor disposed for the mirth and galliardize of company, yet in one dreame I can compose a whole Comedy, behold the action, apprehend the jests, and laugh my selfe awake at the conceits thereof."[75] Browne does not always approve of dreams, and even here he concludes that the memory betrays his reason in its waking inability to report what "fancies" have achieved in the dream. Fancy's work is lost and gone, as Jonson says the images of the masque will be when the night has passed.[76] But Browne applauds the dream as an elevated performance, somewhere between those mysterious yet "outward and sensible motions" produced by church ornament and ceremony at which he kneels, and the ordered and witty surprise served up by a good Fletcherian comedy played extempore for a private audience of one in the theater of his bed.

To Browne, such dreams are the very apex of human existence – they enter our rooms like priests moving toward the altar or masquers across the platform and convey what is true, holy, and delightful. But like masques, they are also flimsy and ephemeral, sometimes constituted by the fabric of our bodies, the food that we eat or the business of the day now passed. And unlike the liturgical ceremonies "which misguided zeale termes superstition," they are not likely to pass our way again.[77] The dreams of Browne remove him from himself and therefore show the way down which a charitable, if mysterious, conformity might lie. But the dreams also italicize that amorphous singularity to which no one else asleep can gain entrance via fancy, and to which no one awake, not the dreamer himself, has access after the decay of that memory that is charged with guaranteeing traditions. As Herrick suggests in his little translation of Plutarch, dreams often rip us from the social hierarchy and even from the cosmic whole that lend our human experience its most reliable sanctity. The problem with reliability, though, is that it can restrict the heroic soul.

Given the perils and possibilities of fancy in Caroline religious discourse, it is no wonder that Prynne believes that Laud cannot control what he would, or that Laud indicts Eleanor Davies for ritualizing what she perhaps would not. Understood as a vital circumstance in the experience of worship, fancy can lend support to the heroic elevation of the church by means of ceremonies and sensations. But on its own, this particular heroic bent is controversial in the Caroline decades, and wherever stress is laid on its fanciful basis, Laudian heroism risks an ironic erosion into the inspired or haunted self that shows little regard for liturgical uniformity and cathedral contexts. Of course, a reconciliation between ceremony and spirit is best for Caroline writers: Milton's "Il Penseroso" manages to find personal raptures in a sensuous temple, and Browne likes to imagine himself a hybrid Christian, part melancholic Puritan and part Marian pilgrim. If, however, at its best fancy embodies the sort of pneumatic knot that conjoins external and internal reverence, it just as powerfully represents to Caroline polemicists the irreconcilable difference between the one true religion and its nightmares.

CHAPTER 4

Respecting persons

As circumstances of the faith, both heroism and fancy are nodal terms by means of which Caroline writers mediate the outward and inward conditions of worship and take stock of the rival ways in which their church might be projected above the gray shades of casuistry. When writers in the 1620s, 30s, and 40s attend to yet a third term, the category of the "person," their exploration of religious circumstance is no simpler even if at times it is more mundanely social. For that oft repeated Biblical stricture against respecting persons leads Caroline writers into a wide range of questions – about the criteria for ordination, for salvation, and for the appropriate interaction of saints and the worldly wise. The circumstance of the person has some points of convergence with other circumstances. With heroism, notions of the person bear the burden of accounting for what sets the church or its ministers apart from other churches or the laity. With fancy, competing definitions of the person provoke an inquiry into the inner human processes responding to or searching for saving grace. As Guibbory has argued,[1] attitudes toward religious ceremony have corollaries in attitudes toward social organization; and indeed the accommodation made by saints in navigating the social order is one of the primary motivations for investigating the circumstance of persons.

In Caroline England, the fascination with the status of the "person" centers finally on two often conflicting queries. Why and how does God set some human beings apart from the rest, either as persons saved or as persons consecrated? Why and how would God have holy men and women concern themselves with the niceties of social decorum and with the everyday drama of life's vanity fair? In the first instance, Christians are urged to understand the realm of experience with regard to salvation and to sacred offices. In the second, Christians are faced with the compromising prospect of living according to social codes and customs. More than any other circumstance, then, the personal respect makes its way into a widely ranging set of Caroline texts, from the most abstract taxonomy of God's saving decrees to the most geographically and socially specific comedies of the seventeenth-century stage. Time and again, Caroline theologians, preachers, playwrights, and social commentators attempt to come to grips with the warning that God will – and human beings should – respect no persons. The problem with that dictum is that it runs directly contrary to seventeenth-century norms, whether the Calvinist notion of predestination or the social signifiers of rank and hierarchy.

In his 1628 Christmas sermon at St. Paul's, John Donne pauses in the *exordium* to consider the Biblical repetition of certain phrases and maxims. Ordinary human beings have their own favorite habits of speech, Donne allows, but these interjections are commonly irrelevant at best, impious at worst. In contrast, he assures his audience that the Holy Ghost repeats phrases "out of an accommodation and communicablenesse of himselfe to man, out of desire, and a study, to shed himselfe the more familiarly, and to infuse himself the more powerfully into man."[2]

In order to show that what holds "for particular persons, and particular phrases," is extended in the Bible to include "certaine whole sentences, certaine entire propositions," Donne inserts a parenthetical mini-sermon on the Holy Ghost's reminder *"That God is no accepter of persons"*:

(for that is repeated in very many places, that every where, upon every occasion, every man might be remembred of that, that God is no accepter of persons; Take heed how you presume upon your knowledge, or your actions, for God is no accepter of persons; Take heed how you condemne another man for an Heretique, because he beleeves not just as you beleeve; or for a Reprobate, because he lives not just as you live, for God is no accepter of persons; Take heed how you relie wholly upon the outward means, that you are wrapped in the covenant, that you are bred in a reformed Church, for God is no accepter of persons) . . . (8.293)

As Donne would be the first to admit, this collection of glosses on those scriptural instances warning that God will accept no persons is hardly exhaustive of their possible meanings. In books of law, history, wisdom, prophecy, and gospel, and in epistles both universal and particular, the authors of the Bible maintain that in assessing the righteousness of others, mortals should disregard their poverty, wealth, might, flattery, bribes, friendship, and Judaism: to regard these accidents amounts to the ungodly acceptance of "persons."[3] But Donne's contemporaries recognize that the exhortations against accepting persons are as elusive, controversial, and intricate as they are crucial in the life of a Christian. After all, they knew, the Pharisees use the maxim in an unsuccessful attempt to trick Jesus, while it also figures prominently in the debate between Job and his visitors over the logic of divine punishment.

Here and often in his Caroline sermons, Donne corroborates the conviction of his fellow Protestants that the meaning of personal respects is implicated in a wide spectrum of doctrinal, ecclesiastical, moral, and social problems.[4] Thus scriptural iteration accommodates but also complicates the Caroline encounter with a set of recalcitrant questions about the constituents of personhood; the assets and abuses of impersonation in pulpit as well as on stage; the conditions of divine decrees, judgments, and mercies; the criteria of Christian duty and decorum; the status of the clergy and their various offices; and the respective genealogies of salvation and social privilege.

I

Between 1625 and 1642, a number of apparently unrelated events converged on the question of whether, how, and how much Christians are to regard "persons." The stormy English aftermath of the Synod at Dort regarding the means and scope of salvation; the late Jacobean and early Caroline restrictions on preaching; the self-examination and social experimentation of the drama; an accumulative cynicism from the sale of aristocratic titles; the decline of Ben Jonson and the death of Lancelot Andrewes; the ascendancy of Laudian churchmanship and its critics; the contradictoriness of a monarch at once the savior and nemesis of decorum; the competing devotional tendencies toward a heightened visible conformity on one side and an intensified spiritual experience of the Holy Ghost on the other: each and all produced a discourse of personhood that was equally apt to compound or isolate, to magnify or efface, incorporate or to abstract the identity of a "person." The discourse on persons concerns both divine and human judgments, and it is equally fascinated by "mysticall" and "historicall" genealogies.[5] With its various, even contradictory meanings, the word "person" recurs as often in Shirley's social comedies as in Donne's sermons. But it is Robert Sanderson whose frequent meditations on the question of personhood most fully integrate its spiritual, ecclesiastical, social, and moral aspects.

In 1625, the year of Montagu's *Appello Caesarem* and of Charles's succession to the throne, Sanderson undertook soteriological exercises in his capacity as Clerk of the Convocation. These exercises, one a manuscript entitled *Pax Ecclesiae*, the other a set of schemata mapping God's decrees, are potentially at cross purposes with one another in a fashion typical (as he himself remarked later) of Sanderson's religio-intellectual tendencies, one irenic in cautious defense of church unity, the other analytical in compulsive response to the intricacies of doctrine.[6] In his work on these exercises, Sanderson attempts to reconcile peace and analysis.

The *Pax* begins with a standard characterization of God's decrees. From God's perspective, the decrees have no distinction in time, but in human conception and in the order of nature, they unfold in a temporal sequence. For Sanderson, this means that Christian perplexity and schism derive from the increasingly dramatic contention over "the necessity, efficacy, and extent of Divine Grace, the concurrence of Grace with Free Will, the universality and application of Christ's Death," but also that peace might depend on a moderate and conciliatory diagram of decrees (5.257). There are, he adds, two illegitimate extremes: the "carnal Reason" of the Arminians aspires to the arrogance that their elevation of free will invites; but the so-called Calvinists have hurt their own cause against the carnal by responding feebly to charges that irrespective decree makes God contradict the many Biblical reminders that there is no divine acceptance of persons. Meanwhile, Sanderson laments, the Church of England finds itself in a tumult for lack of a legitimate genealogy of decrees.

That controversy over the *ordo salutis* requires mystical genealogies analogous to family trees is a case that Sanderson himself eventually makes. The five schemes of God's decrees were diagrammed, he wrote Henry Hammond, "much after the manner as I had used to draw Pedigrees, a thing which, I think you know, I have very much fancied, as to me of all others the most delightful recreation" (5.299). That is, Sanderson superimposed the legitimation of families – the putative guarantee of blood transmission in the face of marital and sexual contingencies – on the divine legitimation of souls with its questions of whether God accepts, disregards, or inspects the "person."

The logic of this conflation is at least partly clarified by other participants in the Arminian controversy just before and after 1625. Peter du Moulin's *Anatomy of Arminianism* (translated, 1620) assumes a sublapsarian stance on God's decrees similar to the temporary position adopted in Sanderson's *Pax Ecclesiae*. According to Du Moulin, God's decrees of election and reprobation are directed at the fallen lump of human nature embodied in Adam. Election is merciful, with reprobation amounting to a passover that cannot be said to have created sinners or sin. The problem with the Arminian position, this argument continues, is that it partitions God's will into antecedent and consequent wills, with the contingency of human will, belief, or endeavor thrust in between.

According to Du Moulin, the Arminian God is blameworthy not for accepting persons but for founding his decrees on the minute and on-going inspection of personal qualifications. If not hypocritical, this God looks foolish and weak, unable to effect his wishes without human per-mission, and with the genealogy of his decrees riddled at every level with the indignity of human imperfection and change. The Arminians think that belief elicits grace whereas, Du Moulin counters, grace yields be-lief. In its critic's final analysis, the Arminian recourse to genealogical explanations of damnation is as incoherent as it is debased; after all, family trees are hybrid things, a social or natural coincidence of spiritual opposites.

Whereas "the Arminians will haue euery particular person to be elected by God, for faith foreseene," Du Moulin believes that God singles out "particular persons" without conveying to us any method, manner, or rationale beyond the pleasure of God's will, which on faith we must take to be supremely wise, good, and just.[7] The Arminian God asks for qualifications; the sublapsarian God – or so his critics put the case – accepts persons, a state of affairs charged with painting an impious image of God's unjust favoritism but also with handing moral license to slothful ministers. According to critics of lump theology, its mysterious accep-tance of persons matters far more than it ought, the dignity and enter-prise of the clergy far less.

To the charge that his God accepts persons, Du Moulin retorts that the acceptance of persons presupposes some economic, social, political or tribal consideration that corrupts a judge, whereas human beings cannot bribe God – a point unsettled by the author's comparison of God to a king who pleases to condemn one man and redeem another for the same crime. But it is precisely God's singling out of persons from the lump – as Selden reminds us, the word *person* indicates something set apart – that leads Richard Montagu and Thomas Jackson to indict Du Moulin's God for an unjust acceptance of persons. Quoting Tertullian against the inevitable perseverance of the elect, Montagu poses, then answers a critical question: *"Doe wee estimate and approue Faith by Mens Persons, or not rather Persons by Faith? Onely the faithfull man is a wise man: Onely a Christian man is of accompt: No man is a Christian, but he that continueth vnto the end."*[8] In this instance "person" means not worldly status (as in the Bible) or a set of physical attributes (as is often the case in Caroline comedy) but something akin to individual substance.

This substance, Montagu maintains, amounts to the so-called Puritans' internalization of Peter's onetime sinful complacency about the salvation of Jews. In *Appello Caesarem*, he presses home the conviction that "person," that is, the unclean natural man, "with God must be made acceptable, then accepted, before any work of his become approveable or approved."[9] What this means according to Montagu is that as even Calvin knew, no person is accepted by God prior to the temporal and ongoing processes of justification and sanctification; by contrast, the "Puritan" has forgotten the fundamental, if troubling, contingency of the human beings on whom God's grace works.

Thomas Jackson offers a more sustained indictment of the construction of an unjust God who accepts persons – an image foisted, he says, on the divine by theologians who have miscalculated the significance of personal substance. In a sermon included in William Milbourne's compilation, *Sapientia Clamitans, Wisdome Crying Out to Sinners to Returne from Their Evill Wayes . . .* (London, 1638), Jackson argues that personhood is at once irrelevant to and at odds with the processes of salvation, precisely because God's decrees are directed at a more changeable "pedigree" in each person's life. Pharaoh is the famous example: "always one and the same man: yet . . . not alwayes one and the same object of the divine decree".[10] This claim suggests that theological pedigree resembles lunar eclipse; what matters is not an unchanging substance but a relationship over time – the soul playing moon to God's sun. Pharaoh was always the same person, but he had to become the reprobate "Pharaoh": "so doth the immutable rule of justice render unto every man, not according to the unitie of his person, but according to the diversity of his worke" until God reaches a "final induration . . . the just recompence of the full measure of iniquity" (183).

Yet even Jackson must dodge the objection that haunts sublapsarianism, the God of which appears to accept persons. The dodge is double: Jackson sends his readers to another text, presumably his *Treatise of the Times*, for assurance that God is no respecter of persons in meting out rewards and punishments to those persons "equally disposed"; but he also substitutes an easier question – about divine dispensations "in this life" – for the harder one about why God saves or damns this person or that.

Elsewhere, Jackson's answer to the harder question is that persons are not equally disposed and that no one person is evenly disposed over time. God is compared to an especially attentive astronomer watching the moon over a long period, not just its phases but all its motions, "So that

in one and the selfe same *Pharaoh* there might be more severall objects of
the eternall decree, than are minutes or scruples in forty yeares motion
of the *Moone*" (200). Jackson steers clear of God's treatment of "divers
persons" in order to map out the pedigree of divine judgment regarding
"the same persons, at divers times, according to a different measure"
(218). According to this argument, persons matter far less than their mutable habits in "the changes and chances of this mortall life" (228). God's
decrees are not "irrevocable sentences of salvation or damnation in respect of . . . individuall persons, but in respect of . . . present qualifications
in whomsoever constantly continued" (239).

Throughout his works, Jackson meditates on the acceptance of persons at two related levels, on the one hand regarding divine dispensations
and, on the other, measuring human, especially ministerial, duties.[11]
What is more, he investigates the linkage of these two matters as an
extension of the Book of James, which moves from the prohibition of
accepting persons in economic terms to God's inspection of our faithful works. Robert Sanderson is not alone, that is, in his fascination with
analogies between familial and mystical (moral, theological) genealogies.
As early as a treatise on faith first published in 1615, Jackson likens errors
in soteriology to mistakes in the "prosecution of genealogies in matters
moral." In particular, he criticizes those diagrams of the *ordo salutis* that
ignore contingent elements as dishonestly as those fictive genealogies
that elide the ways in which a noble family has squandered its status and
property by way of marital entanglements with lower families. Similarly,
Sanderson complains that whereas a cleanly bifurcated "table" of divine
decrees might be appropriate for accentuating God's supreme power,
this design can lead to the most absurdly reductive kind of mystical
pedigree.[12]

When in 1625 Sanderson sets down his five schemata, the transformation of theological maps into family trees can serve a wide range of
theological effects. A mystical pedigree of God's dispensations for human spirituality can admit but also manage contingency; can distribute
dignity and corruption flexibly or rigidly; and can intersect more or
less intricately with the social and moral duties of Christianity. Clearly,
Sanderson is compelled to design his maps of salvation by his sense that
in the 1620s, each genealogical jurisdiction – soteriological and social – is
undergoing a major and complex revision.

If the five diagrams of God's decrees are drawn up in an effort to
find a moderate and peaceful soteriological family to which England
can belong, their very form – the pedigree – betrays what Sanderson

admits to be an element of fanciful idolatry in his studies. As if to ensure that his humor cannot be satisfied, the pedigree is as flexible as it is monumental. If the best family of decrees can be found somewhere between rigid Calvinism and liberal Arminianism, it hardly helps that there are at least three intermediate distributions of the creation, the covenants, election and reprobation, of outward ordinances and inward progressions.

In a letter to Henry Hammond with a history of the changes in his own system of belief, Sanderson later confesses that he was never satisfied with his religious studies until he had migrated to what for him was the onetime "extreme" pedigree of the Arminians, leaving behind the sublapsarianism he had once found "more moderate, rational, and agreeable to the goodness and justice of God" (5.298). Indeed he suggests that the study of schemata was in part responsible for this fortunate drift, that his pedigrees allowed him to explore a version of the Arminian theology that privileges change over substance, and dynamism over essence. In the 1620s, however, English Arminianism has accrued illegitimacy by way of its exaggerated association with human will, fancy, pleasure, and idolatry. Ironically, Sanderson has the same suspicions about his own amateur love of "*Records, Genealogies*, and Heraldry" that we read about in Walton's life of Sanderson, itself a monument to the intersection between family history and church pedigree. If Catholicism has a greater investment in church pedigree – and it clearly does – Sanderson implies that Arminian doctrine has more to gain from the clarity of family trees, each in its turn running the risk of idolatry.

Sanderson relates to Hammond that over the years, family trees have entangled yet comforted, seduced yet redeemed, his thoughts on God's decrees. We learn of the redemption of these thoughts in a letter written by Dr. Pierce to Walton, which details Sanderson's eventual acceptance of the roles of free will and temporal change in the workings of God's grace. After the 1625 convocation and on into the 1630s, Sanderson remained restless over the doctrinal questions that he believed were dividing the church. According to his letter to Pierce, Sanderson underwent a final change in 1632 when, having read every word of William Twisse's *Vindiciae Gratiae* against the Arminians and "notwithstanding [his] former resolution" to leave such controversies behind, Sanderson "must needs be medling again" with the genealogy of salvation.

Surprised by the lapses in the admirable Twisse's argument, Sanderson writes that he was especially repelled by Twisse's diagram of the decrees, a schema intended by the theologian to avoid supra- and sublapsarian doctrine. This "new Device" situates God's glory not just chiefly but solely as the end of all decrees, rendering the subordinate decrees "one entire coordinate Medium," that is, each subordinate to God's glory but none – not the creation of man, permission of sin, the mission and death of Christ, the ordinances, election, or reprobation – to any other (5.300).

The upshot of Hammond's retrospective account is that in or soon after 1625, Sanderson came to see the decency of Arminianism and its good, just God. Moreover, this realization centers on Sanderson's revision of God's treatment of persons in the context of history, with sublapsarianism dictating "that the persons so left [in sin] are destined to eternal misery for no other cause, but this only, that Adam some thousand years since did eat the forbidden fruit, and they being yet unborn, could not help it" (5.301). But Sanderson's critiques of his own Arminianism make it clear that he was bothered by the inability of genealogies to settle soteriological questions; by his own compulsion to ask these questions in genealogical form; and by his deviation from the very irenic and cautious skepticism that seeks flexible boundaries "of sobriety and truth" rather than definitive schemes. The schemes convince Sanderson of the contingency that schemes are meant to manage, both horizontally in conjunctions and vertically in derivations.

Similarly, Hammond admits that Sanderson has continued to sense problems with Arminianism – problems both historical and spiritual. For example: if the object of God's election is not man fallen but "man preacht unto," what about those "nations or persons" to whom God's truth was not thus revealed? We cannot know, Sanderson concludes. What if the offer of grace proves "uneffectual to all persons"? One must have recourse – as does Sanderson – to a God who chooses "to confer [grace] upon such persons as it pleased Him to fix upon (without inquiring into under what qualifications, preparations, or dispositions considered)" – and this "without any thing on their part to deserve it." The ambiguity of this formulation is palpable: is it God or the theologian who does not inquire? Must we accept God without knowing at all in what sense he accepts us?

Sanderson is unhappy with this conclusion, but it is better than the Arminian possibility that all might be damned. In the face of mystery, it seems to him better also to err on the side of a suasive grace so attractive as to be effectively irresistible even if not theoretically compulsory. Still, he presses home the importance of the outward and inward means of grace in opposition to the "carnal security" that results the further toward rigid Calvinism one's soteriological pedigree advances.

Whatever the further troubles and insights elicited by the mapping of decrees, Sanderson's *Pax* operates on the assumption that the sub-lapsarian sequence legitimizes God's wisdom as it is demonstrated in electing "a certain number of particular persons out of the corrupted lump of mankind," in leaving the rest behind in the lump, and in con-ferring "in due season upon the persons so elected, all fit and effectual means and graces needful for them unto Salvation, proportionably to their personal capacities and conditions" (5.268). With its careful pro-visos regarding infants, irresistibility, and perseverance, this sequence skirts seeming contradictions and nagging questions about God's view of persons. Like Du Moulin, Sanderson refuses to linger on – though he mentions – the question of why God chooses one person and not another if that choice is not to be made on the basis of foreseen quali-fications. At the end of the *Pax*, as Sanderson builds a considerable list of deferred questions, one is not surprised to find an admission that the author's position is fallible if heuristic, at best decorous "within some competent bounds of sobriety and truth" (5.277). It is easy enough to see what Sanderson later admits, that his meddling with genealogies of sal-vation is at once a mode of establishing family boundaries within which impurities and tensions can be managed, and the clearest evidence that Sanderson himself cannot be satisfied with a relatively vague and fallible approximation of the family ties that bind and constitute divine decrees.

II

By contrast to the *Pax*, Sanderson's sermons tend to redirect the stipu-lation against accepting persons away from the *ordo salutis* and toward the dilemmas encountered by Christians in carrying out their social duties. This emphasis on assessing the social proprieties of holy living was no doubt more palatable to the decorous Caroline court for which Sanderson preached seventeen of his surviving sermons between 1631 and 1648. For Sanderson, however, the casuistry of persons is tortuous whether it concerns salvation, duty, ministry, or all at once.

Sanderson frequently invokes the Biblical injunctions against respect-ing or accepting persons in his sermons to court, clergy, and people. In a 1631 sermon to court on Ecclesiastes 7:1 ("a good name is better than precious Ointment"), he offers some standard remarks about the ideal match between goodness and reputation, together with a distinc-tion between good names and great ones, the latter available to persons regardless of their moral worth. But the preacher is as little satisfied with asserting the ideal marriage of morality and fame as he is with embracing any one genealogy of decrees, in large part because the ideal has so little bearing on one's lived experience of the world.

In the world one's success or failure can depend on reputation, even if it is unfairly gained and even though "we know well it should be otherwise":

As the magistrate that exerciseth public judgment should lay aside all respect of the person, and look at the cause only, so should we all, in our private judgings of other men's speeches and actions, look barely upon the truth of what they say, and the goodness of what they do, and accordingly esteem of both; neither better nor worse, more or less, for whatsoever foreconceits we may have of the person. Otherwise how can we avoid the charge of having *the faith of our Lord Jesus Christ, the Lord of glory, with respect of persons?* (1.16)

Sir Philip Sidney's famous notion of "foreconceit" justifies mendacious fictions by grounding them in Platonic ideas. In Sanderson's usage, however, human foreconceits are closer to Bacon's idols, those mental biases, predilections, and infatuations that keep us benighted in the tribe of our shared fallenness; in the cave of our peculiar humors and experiences; in the marketplace where a slippery but powerful merchant (language) trades us and not we it; and in the theater that seduces us with its neat logics and the authoritative persons whose names these influential lies bear. As for respecting persons, the Bible indicts a number of foreconceits at odds with righteousness and truth: one might favor those persons sharing one's own corporate identity; persons from whom one hopes to profit; and persons whose poverty clouds one's judgment.

Far from urging his audience to labor against such foreconceits, Sanderson finds it more practical to pursue their legitimate uses, especially "since men are corrupt, and will be partial this way, do we what we can" (1.16). *Pace* the Book of James, he believes that everyday charity is empowered by the redemptive use of personal respects, not justified in simple opposition to the carnality of these respects. But Sanderson understands that a proper respect for persons is exceedingly difficult to gauge and to instantiate. In his study of those gallants who care far too much about reputation, he explores the ironic convergence of extremes, namely, the gentleman whose rigid code of personal honor compels him senselessly into duels and the Puritan whose self-aggrandizing opposition to ceremony is unrelenting in the face of rational suasion. That is, rakes and zealots agree on this if on nothing else: that the acceptance of their persons should justify sin and error. By contrast, Sanderson believes,

God guides the human pursuit of a good name in the direction of charitable acts, a charity that discourages us from respecting persons for their
wealth, status, power, or purity.

As the sermon progresses, however, Sanderson's attack on those who
demand respect to their persons without due regard for duty, charity,
social harmony, or obedience narrows considerably to the self-righteous
Puritan. Such Christians are blinded by a foreconceit of their own perfection and fail to appreciate the decorous boundaries instituted to guide
us in the respect we can offer persons without losing our basic honesty or
piety. Promoting the singularity of their persons – in this instance, of their
purified substances – outside the heuristic boundaries of decorum, these
precisionists have "too much stiffness or peremptoriness either way concerning the use of indifferent things, without due consideration of times,
places, persons, and other circumstances" (1.28). Sanderson has no reason to elaborate on what is so clearly implied, that the failure to live
within the civil bounds of decorum regarding persons is linked to the
failure to believe within the sober boundaries of a decent soteriological
pedigree. Consequently, the Puritans reproduce their own foreconceits
in the minds of otherwise civil men, provoking "opposition against themselves, their persons, and good names" (1.28).

In subsequent court sermons, Sanderson returns time and again to
nagging questions raised by the scriptural treatment of persons. These
questions are variously social, soteriological, and ecclesiastical, but in
the 1620s and 30s, one genealogy implies the others, from charity and
ministry to social decorum and respective decree. What is more, the
category of persons produces moral dilemmas in Sanderson's sermons
no matter how hard he tries to set it aside or take it for granted.

In a sermon preached at Whitehall in November 1632 on Proverbs
16.7 ("When a man's ways please the Lord, He maketh even his enemies
to be at peace with him"), Sanderson glosses "ways" as "all his thoughts,
speeches and actions, whether good or bad," and sets this rubric in
contrast to *person* "because it is possible, the Lord may graciously accept
some man's person, and yet take just exception at some of his ways"
(1.33–34). Grace if not God, then, accepts persons, a premise that frees
Sanderson to distinguish three trajectories or "ways": the ungodly, the
godly, and the mixed if for the most part godly paths that people tread.

In the sermon *ad aulam* preached in Newark in 1633, Sanderson at-
tends to the social and ecclesiastical "person." His text from 1 Peter,
"Honour all men. Love the Brotherhood. Fear God, Honour the King,"
begs in the first two commands the questions of social decorum and

church identity, then juxtaposes in the second half the religious and political obligations of the subject.

In the Book of James, the first half of the chiasmus is vaguely treated in the contrast between *neighbor* and *person*, while in Christ's retort to the Pharisee's manipulation of his disregard for persons, the second contrast – between what we owe God as against rulers – is exemplified. The passage in Peter offers some foothold, if not pedigree, in its inversion, with love and fear representing relatively special and pre-emptive commitments. So it is sufficiently clear – if somewhat ruinous to aristocratic notions of honor – how one might act dutifully toward fellow human beings yet lovingly toward fellow Christians, setting aside for the moment the competing pedigrees of the true church in the early Stuart decades. Sanderson spells out how one is to fear as well as love the king but also how if king and God conflict, the fear of the latter should prevail. The major problem involves the gap between the honor we owe indiscriminately to people and the honor we owe specifically to the person of the king, especially if the king is as obsessed as Charles with the decorous protection of the king's personal sanctity.

Having offered a definition of honor proper – that owed to superior and excellent persons yet most of all to God – Sanderson admits that "so to take [honor] in this first precept would be subject to sundry difficulties and inconveniences; this, especially, above the rest, that the Scripture should here bind us to an impossible thing . . . not only *ex hypothesi* and by consequent in regard of the weakness and corruption of our nature, for so is every good duty impossible to be performed by us without the grace of God preventing and assisting us; but impossible *ex natura rei*, as implying a flat contradiction within itself" (1.56). Theological mysteries strike the preacher as straightforward when they are compared to the tensions between charity and decorum, the very partners married in the Laudian vision of a conformable and decent church. Sanderson underscores his logic of impossibility: "For honouring, in that notion, being the preferring of some before other some, we should be bound by this Text, were the word so to be understood, to prefer every man before every other man; which how it should be possible for us to do, is beyond the wit of man to imagine" (1.56). Leaving out further "absurdities," Sanderson betrays once again his desire for proper subordination in a pedigree; here we have the social version of Twisse's "one entire coordinate Medium," only made worse by the topsy-turviness of persons at once above and beneath one another.

Recourse must be had, then, to a sense of honor "somewhat looser and larger than the former, so as to import all that esteem or regard, be it more or less, which, either in justice or charity, is due to any man in respect of his place, person, or condition, according to the eminency, merit, or exigency of any of them respectively; together with the willing performance of such just and charitable offices upon all emergent occasions, as in proportion to any of the said respects can be reasonably expected" (1.56–57). But the elaborate gloss on the "looser and larger" sense of honor raises as many problems as it solves, not least because it works so well as a definition of the honor properly and unequally owed persons according to social decorum.

Nonetheless, this kinship between the loose and proper senses of honor brings to light how the heuristic flexibility of decorum can double as an unreachable ideal. Highly particularized in the service of social occasions and circumstances, decorum is no less rigidly prescriptive and ideologically primary in Caroline standards of behavior. So the term is helpfully loose and spiritually apt in its charitable embrace of high and low in the estimable image of God, but no less socially legitimate in its appeal to a just observance of degree. Honor slides through various criteria ("eminency, merit, exigency" but also "place, person, condition"), is performed in a multitude of contexts yet according to the measure of what is reasonable, and carries with it an uncertainty born of the scriptural concession to a charity that can modify that prohibition against accepting persons delivered by justice.

Admitting that "honour" is more commonly used in its narrower and "proper" sense, Sanderson clarifies the looser sense in the context of marital relations in which the ideal husband cherishes his wife and tolerates her "weaknesses whether of her sex or person," but does not relinquish his mastery over her. Such an honor – also that of parents for children, of masters for servants – amounts to "tender respect and loving condescension" (1.57). Again, Sanderson wants to reconcile charity and decorum with respect to persons, much as his theology must work out the proper measure of justice and love in those divine decrees that terminate in particular souls. All the same, he introduces – without reconciling – the rival criteria of place and merit, and concedes the impossibility of particularizing all the cases that arise in human relations. It is left to his readers to follow Sanderson's guidelines in their own affairs and to err on the side of generosity in bestowing honor when they are in doubt.

When, however, Sanderson further defines the honor owed to all persons by grounding it in justice, equity, and religion, it is religion that gives him pause. Most simply, the loosely defined honor owed to all persons is a function of their creation in the image of God, but it is God's good pleasure to provide whatever excellence a person has. That "excellency is twofold: natural, and personal," which means that nature sets human beings apart from animals whereas it is "the personal . . . whereby one man excelleth another" (1.62). So honor in the strict sense is precisely a respect owed to persons, that is, to the divinely dispensed constituents that set one human being above others.

But what are these constituents? Freely given by God, they comprise the "several gifts, and offices, and callings to several men, with admirable variety, and with no less admirable wisdom" (1.63–64). It is, moreover, through these distributions that God's government of the world operates. But Sanderson is uneasy with the tendency to elevate these attributes in metaphors that celebrate the human imaging of God. Instead, he prefers the metaphor of human shadows of the divine insofar as the argument that a king's power or priest's holiness bears the image of God verges on arrogance.

Does this mean that our closest approximation to God's image depends on our imitation of God's disregard for persons? But Sanderson has already evinced a tendency to reclaim personal difference and social decorum within the loose definition of general honor, and the two converge once again when he divides the value imprinted on us by God's stamp into "natural" and "personal" categories (1.64–65). For the most part, nature is subsumed by persons rather than persons by nature so that qualities that we all possess in some degree or other are simply converted into the category of merit or "particular graces, abilities, and qualifications." At times, to be sure, Sanderson's mixture of nature and persons serves to emphasize the tenet that all human honor is indebted directly to God. But personal merit gains legitimacy in functioning as an alternative to the respects of place, calling, and condition. In this vein, merit depends on spiritual qualifications, not on status, power, or office. Whenever natural merit complicates the assessments he must make of persons, Sanderson weakens the category of natural merit by concentrating on what for him are its meanest instances, the infants, fools, and insane whose only merits are defects, an argument for tender charity rather than judicious respect, for loose honor rather than proper.

But Sanderson cannot forget that the Bible forbids us to respect persons at all, and he stresses that charity is paramount for Christianity precisely because we are all defective, gratuitously rather than deservedly honored. We are all "infants, natural fools, and distracted persons" whose service to one another is to fill human meditations with fear and trembling. As Sanderson insists, the text "honour all men" allows for no distinctions, equivocations, or reservations but demands that we honor humanity for a merit that no one earns. Our sinfulness, moreover, entails that the truism – reward those who merit it – is essentially useless to us insofar as we are unable to judge the worth of others, in contrast to the earlier insistence that it is up to each of us to undertake the task of deciding what each person is owed in various contexts.

Over the course of Sanderson's sermon, decorum is constructed as obvious and elusive, integral and irrelevant to our lives, reasonable yet (given the difference between place and merit) conflictive. One way to simplify the question of respect to persons is to focus on the tribute and obedience owed by inferiors and subjects to masters, magistrates, and ministers, that is, to focus entirely on personhood defined as place, calling, or condition. Sanderson is explicit here (1.68) that our sin affects only our ability to judge merit. With the help of the often quoted 1 Timothy 17, however, he backs away from this reduction by arguing that single honor is owed to place, and double for meritorious performance by those who hold place. That is, personal merit is an adjunct of personal place, not a rival standard.

III

What we have seen so far is that Sanderson has a critical fascination with an oft-repeated Biblical injunction of which he seems equally intent on steering clear, those prohibitions against accepting or respecting persons. His treatment of the circumstance of persons covers a wide ground in religious culture, including the competing demands of scripture and decorum, the elusiveness of that evidence necessary for a sober genealogy of divine decrees, and conflicts over church pedigree. In turning to preach on the scriptural command "Love the Brotherhood," Sanderson confronts the difficult question of how a "person" should be gauged in efforts to define the boundaries of the church. One church is invisible, another visible, and each has its own set of impediments for the delineation of family: the visible church is always in danger of admitting rotten branches into its family tree while the invisible church is virtually impossible to delineate in confident genealogical terms. This dilemma is linked to soteriological questions about persons: as God alone is able to discern those persons whose grace is effectual, so God alone is able to apprehend the church invisible. One resort is to love those in the visible church and leave God to sort out the wheat from the chaff, but this strategy can make strange, even fatal bedfellows.

As Anthony Milton has demonstrated, the question of how to define the identity of the true church was complex and dynamic in the early Stuart period. Sanderson's emphasis on the visibility of the church is more anxious than the typical "Laudian" about what, as Milton shows, is finally a question about church ancestry and pedigree. Generally, the Laudians set out radically to redefine this pedigree. For all the conflicts and instabilities in Jacobean treatments of the ancestry of English Protestantism, their version of church pedigree tended to thrive on flexibility and vagueness – on a composite approach that preserved a basic consensus that the Church of England was defined as the polar opposition to Rome. In genealogical terms, this state of affairs suggested a pedigree at once promiscuous in its branches or fruit, and pure in its doctrinal roots and trunk. By contrast, Milton argues, the Laudians made irrelevant the pure doctrinal family core, refocused attention on visible, episcopal succession, discredited such heretical ancestors as the medieval proto-Protestants, and heralded medieval establishmentarians as a more dignified set of kin. The genealogical effects of Laudianism were conflicted. On the one hand, the Laudian notion of church pedigree was criticized for its own dalliance with papists while, on the other, the Laudians themselves saw their enterprise as ennobling the church in its ancestry, officers, and worship.[13]

One additional effect or goal of the Laudians was to isolate the Church of England from all other church families. As Milton shows, the Laudians also provoked their opponents into massive researches for the purpose of reasserting a strictly Protestant genealogy, so that Jacobean flexibility and negotiation were transformed under Charles into a cultural war over the pedigree of the church. The results of this war were hard to predict: indeed for Wat Montagu, a focus on church genealogy was significant in orienting discussion away from doctrinal squabbles, but while the historical dimension of religious conflict seemed to him much simpler as a starting point than soteriology, the simplicity of genealogy led in fact to his conversion to Rome.[14]

Like salvation and decorum, then, questions of church pedigree contributed to Sanderson's search for just the right value for persons. Directing us to love our brethren for their "goodness and nearness" (1.73), Sanderson runs into problems right away. At first "goodness" is defined broadly to include all created things, then we are said to owe "special Love" to those persons with "speciall goodness" (1.73), by which he means some moral, natural, or civil value. Yet we owe an even higher love to any person who "by the goodness of his conversation showeth forth, so far as we can judge, the graciousness of his heart," that is, *God's* grace. Sanderson never says, however, just how or how well we can judge such a manifestation.

As Sanderson remarks, the nearness of fellow Christians is a family matter: they share a father (God), a mother (the church), a sibling (Christ), an education (scripture), a covenant (baptism), and a household (again, the church). In addition to the double duty of the church in this family, there is the question of how the boundaries of the house are framed. Sanderson warns his audience against partiality, then declares it reasonable for his audience to love some Christians more than others. At first his reasons for this distinction are dissonant, one referring to a visible church at once national and local, the other directing us to assess goodness. But goodness is redefined as belonging to "a sober, discreet, judicious, peaceable, humble, and otherwise orderly and regular man," that is, to the conformable Christian who avoids arrogance, heresy and schism in the visible church.

It is typical of Sanderson, however, not to leave the question at that, but to prefer a casuistry of persons to a caricature. Acknowledging that there will be "emergent occasions" at which his audience will be obliged to treat "a mere stranger, a heathen, a notoriously vicious person" as a proximate brother (1.77), he exhorts his auditors to master rules of preference that are generally useful rather than absolutely true. Circumstances matter, even if they do not override habits. Still, he admits, there is a problem in deciding whether loving some brothers more than others is partial:

it may yet be demanded, where is this partiality to be found whereof we spake? what is it to *have the faith of our Lord Jesus Christ with respect of persons*, if this putting of a difference in our love between brother and brother, which we have now allowed of, be not it? I answer, it is no partiality to make such a difference as we have hitherto allowed, so long as the said difference is taken from other peculiar and just respects, and not from the very condition of brotherhood itself, or any distinction made therein. (1.78)

Sanderson's main point is that some distinctions are just, others are not, and he elaborates on the latter "evil partiality." It is one thing to love some brethren more than others, perhaps those in one's local church. But it is another thing to assume that the brethren you prefer are ultimately the only acceptable brethren, for this bias creates schisms. All in all, the Church of England's promotion of charity within the bounds of ecclesiastical decorum comes closest to Sanderson's rule for evaluating, and not respecting, persons.

In a sermon preached at court in July 1637, Sanderson focuses on the personal respects of the minister himself. In Caroline religious discourse generally, the question of the minister's person has social, moral, and spiritual branches, but at the root of all these branches lies the etymological kinship of *person* and *parson*.[15] So the search for the criteria of respecting persons has its microcosm in the debate over the respect owed to – and the constituents of – parsons, a question linked in turn to what James Bulman has called a stocktaking in Caroline theater and impersonation, the pulpit's longtime cousin and rival.[16]

Sanderson's text for the 1637 sermon is Philippians 4:2: "Not that I speak in respect of want: for I have learned, in whatsoever state I am, therewith to be content." Opposing those contemptuous and hypocritical "persons of quality" who would deprive the clergy of their maintenance (1.118), he frames this topical complaint with a digression on how unadvisable it is to turn the pulpit into a forum in which "to meddle at all with personal and particular things that concern either ourselves or others. Both because the more we descend to particulars, the more subject we are to mistakings . . . and the leaven of a little error or indiscretion in the pulpit will sour a great lump of truth and of wholesome doctrine." Personal particulars will, that is, work at cross purposes with the official late Jacobean and early Caroline program of restricting otherwise amorphous sermons to the foundations of creed and catechism, not least because audiences tend to filter a preacher's personal matter "through prejudices and the partiality of [their] affections" (1.118).

Nonetheless, he allows, it is not always possible to forbear personal respects in the pulpit, and "where a necessity lieth upon us" to handle them, the Apostle's utmost "caution and discretion therein" is exemplary in avoiding "misconstruction" and "offence" (1.118–19). The necessity of personal respects arises in those instances when "misconceits of the person may draw prejudice upon his doctrine, and consequently bring scandal unto the Gospel of Jesus Christ" (1.119).

As it turns out, however, personal concerns work at two levels in the sermon: Sanderson wants to justify a sermon about the exigencies of his office, which means that he must support the maintenance of the clergy yet steer clear of conveying discontent. But the call for financial maintenance is grounded in the central theme of charity, defined as our obligation to rejoice in a neighbor's prosperity and to counter self-love with brotherly love. Again Sanderson looks to the second chapter of James: *"If ye fulfil the royal Law according to the Scripture, Thou shalt love thy neighbour as thyself, ye do well,* saith St. James. Very well this. *But if ye have respect to persons*, especially if ye become partial once to your own persons, that is not well: then *you commit sin*, saith he, *and are convinced of the Law as transgressors"* (1.125). It is an appropriate context for urging charity: James goes on to exhort us to works in company with faith. But Sanderson glosses the strictures of James against the acceptance of persons so that they are directed as much at presumptuous views of oneself as they are at one's servile views of rich and stylish others. Perhaps this gloss is aimed as an attack on those godly gentry who withhold their support of the church on the basis of what for their critics is an insubordinate narcissism by faith. But in the sermon's earlier apologies and digressions, Sanderson directs his energy toward answering the "Puritan" objection that the Caroline clerical establishment is itself greedy and inflated.

For Sanderson's meditations on the ministry, then, James's attack remains as valuable as it is mysterious, a wisdom derived from the Holy Ghost yet via "the school of experience and of afflictions" (1.143). Personal respects for the minister – those regarding his evaluation by others and those concerning his evaluation of his auditors – are as perilous, Sanderson insists, as they are critical. In response to the problem of how congregations should assess ministers, there is a widespread enthusiasm in the Caroline decades for the notion that the performance in the pulpit demands the impersonation of a corporate priesthood that renders negligible and replaceable the person of any one minister. As Sanderson says in 1624 at Paul's Cross, this ideal runs at cross-purposes with those auditors of a sermon who pretend that they are witty critics at a play, judging each performance and each minister, even each passage of a sermon based on the protean criteria of a nonconforming fancy.[17]

Sanderson's 1624 sermon *ad clerum* explains the unprecedented contempt for clergymen with a taxonomy of the many reasons why the person of preachers is so intensely scrutinized of late. Far from simply blaming the critics of sermons, however, Sanderson urges "spiritual persons" to improve themselves by "prayers, care, and industry . . . as they that love not his coat may yet approve his labours, and not find any thing therein whereat justly to quarrel" (2.87). Those with slighter gifts should also remember Acts 10.34, which says that God is no accepter of persons, for God expects human endeavor from his ministers, not repayment which after all no minister, however talented, can bestow.

In Sanderson's account, the better sort among the laity can carp because thanks to the Reformation, they can take for granted a full supply of preachers. By contrast, John Selden's analysis of the causes of modern contempt for ecclesiastical persons centers on the origins of the Reformation and the struggle to cultivate that supply.[18] In the 1630s, the aristocratic contempt for parsons is made worse by the perception that there is an inverse proportion between the Laudian clergy's arrogance and its social lineage. That is, elite critics of the Laudians offer a social retort to the priestly refusal to situate ecclesiastical persons in "any lineall deduction from, and extraction out of, Wicklef, Huss, Abigenses" and other medieval heretics.[19]

From Laud's speech in the Star Chamber at the censure of Henry Sherfield (1632) to William Hardwick's 1638 visitation sermon, *Conformity with Piety*, divines take as one of their principal missions the denunciation of lay subjects who hold ordained ministers in as much contempt as the holy places in which, or holy services at which, they officiate. Never mind sufficient maintenance for the office or reverent accoutrements for the service, Hardwick mocks, the parson is held in greatest contempt.[20] Laud speaks even more sharply to the lawyer Sherfield who has appropriated the authority to take violent action against a pane of stained glass: "Thus much let me say to Mr. Sherfield, and such of his profession as slight the ecclesiastical laws and persons, that there was a time when Churchmen were as great in this kingdom as you are now; and let me bold to prophesy, there will be a time when you will be as low as the Church is now, if you go on thus to contemn the Church."[21]

Some less programmatic writers clarify just how taxing it is for ministers to maintain the proper respect for their persons, all the while having to assess the respect they owe to the variously stationed laity of their parish. By far the most vivid account of this double dilemma is George Herbert's *Country Parson* (1632). A handbook for the preservation of the minister's dignity in "his person and office," Herbert's manual devotes its twenty-eighth chapter to unfolding a parson's legitimate responses to contempt. The ideal parson knows that his profession will earn him scorn. All the same, he works hard to prevent or minimize this contempt in his parish by way of a "holy and unblameable life," "a courteous carriage, and winning behavior," and "a bold and impartial reproof, even of the best in the Parish, when occasion requires."[22] Thus the cultivation of respect for the parson turns into a study of how a parson should and should not respect lay persons.

For preachers as much as for justices, it is incumbent to understand in great detail just what personal authority and personal respects involve. Sermons *ad clerum* and *ad magistratum* stress the worth of those judges and ministers who respect no persons but these sermons seldom explain how such respect can be avoided. For instance, in *The Preachers President, or the Master and Scholler* (preached 21 April 1625), James Hyatt reduces the Pharisee's trap for Christ in Matthew 22.16 – "for thou regardest not persons" – to a third and last guideline for ministers who are to teach and practice God's truth *"without respect of men or persons."*[23] More than anything else, Hyatt's respecter of persons is idolatrous, but Hyatt is no Sanderson and conveys little sense of how divisive or complex this peculiar idolatry can be.

Increasingly in the 1630s and early 40s, Laudians and many moderates agree that addictions to ministerial persons cause division in the church no less than contempt for the same. That is, they criticize those nonconformist-leaning auditors who bestow the affection on the individual preacher that they have denied the priestly class. In the Christian tradition, there is a longstanding fascination with the theatrical charisma of certain preachers. In his study of the "antitheatrical prejudice," Jonas Barish discusses Augustine's famous celebration of those impressive preachers who, like a great actor, can unite as well as magnify an audience.[24] But Caroline writers such as William Hardwicke, Thomas Fuller, and again Sanderson decry the "love misplaced" that results when Christians excessively admire their individual preachers and hold all others in contempt.[25]

Sanderson's distaste for the admiration of ministers – which, he says, enslaves otherwise good and pious Christians – is that the admirers stop "questioning the truth of any thing they teach, or the lawfulness of any thing they enjoin" and – one suspects – truncate the valuable but difficult inquiry into the evaluation of personhood. Sanderson preaches to the court in 1640 that unlike God, who brilliantly and thoroughly scrutinizes human hearts, souls, and actions, human judgments are often mistaken "because themselves are partial and unjust, awed with fear, blinded with gifts, transported with passion, carried away with favour or disaffection, or wearied with importunity. But as for God, with Him is *no respect of persons*, nor possibility of being corrupted" (1.252). To accept persons is, in ungodly fashion, to assume in one's own self-interest that persons need no study or analysis within the difficult, particular, and shifting contexts of everyday life. Yet such a laborious genealogy of persons, he admits, is itself open to the charge of idolatry and timeserving, an elusive and worldly distraction at best. Sanderson recommends that Christians imitate those careful pilots who navigate in bad weather, in this case between the obsessive and negligent taxonomies of personal respects.

If an idolatry regarding persons is often treated as a form of "Puritan" histrionics, it is also commonly attributed to the rise of Laudian church-manship. Both sectors of religious culture confront problems in singling out ministers. Charity, catechisms, the visible church, the beauty of holiness, and the sanctity of clerical orders: for the Laudians, all are meant to magnify the value of ecclesiastical persons so as to factor out the vicissitudes and fancies of personal charisma and individual authority. As Robert Shelford puts it in *Five Pious and Learned Discourses* (Cambridge, 1635), the church should reclaim the status of the saints, the Virgin Mary, the name of Christ, and even the pope; but what matters even more is that Christianity be redirected away from the warrant of a solitary and an arrogant possession of faith and toward a religion more corporate and plural. Persons are not so much denied as multiplied, with the Trinity as the model for Christian community and spirituality – thus Donne's God has and prefers company.[26]

In sermons, in ministers, in God Almighty, Shelford prizes plurality because it jettisons the histrionics of insubordinate and chaotic humors. But he tends to legitimize those forms of plurality that involve an alterna-tive theatricality. If plurality allows for church hierarchy, it also stresses impersonation for the sake of conformity, with charity at the basis of the mysterious connection between rank and unity. In the 1620s, 30s, and 40s, we have seen, investigations of the personal circumstance can range from diagrams of God's decrees to expectations of the minister's performance, and from those decidedly religious concerns to the more clearly social affair of decorum. But just as staged dialogue is the medium through which the residents at Little Gidding unfold their questions about religious heroism, theatrical performance from the pulpit and the stage is the crucible in which the status of persons is most vibrantly tested. The more honestly Caroline writers confront the circumstantial status of their religion, the more prepared they are to concede its theatrical dimension, yet to differ over just what mode of acting God exacts.

IV

For all Donne's role in modeling the preacher's persona on the "three-person'd God," Caroline divines often derive the ideal of a composite ministerial person from Lancelot Andrewes, whose death in 1626 was a signal event for the development of preaching. Andrewes had a complex love affair with preaching. Biographers have noticed his early association at Cambridge with "markedly Puritan figures who met regularly for Scriptural study and discussion" and his lifetime commitment to the mission of preaching.[27] But these tendencies unfold side by side with Andrewes's ongoing critique of a sermon culture and of sermons heard either negligently or exclusively.

It is not hard to see why a man who cared greatly about preaching would criticize those audiences too disrespectful or blind to the full context and significance of Christian mysteries. Andrewes disliked those passionate preachers whose histrionics involved not so much unsettling the boundaries of self as overplaying an all-too-fixed humor, their sermons vapid, if showy, and productive of merely "sermon-warm" auditors.[28] In the performance of Protestant belief, Andrewes values a composite Christianity. For instance, disliking the prominence of the preacher's person, Andrewes has recourse to *prosopopeia*, giving voice to angels, God, Christ, and the congregation more often than directly to himself. Insofar as the sermon's mediation of the Holy Spirit belongs for him in the liturgical context of the Christian feast, Andrewes argues that preaching loses its power if Christians invert what he calls the synecdoche of the faith. What is needed instead is a plurality of persons, ordinances, and mysteries.

Both praised and indicted for his avoidance of self-dramatization, Andrewes locates the drama of Christianity in composite impersonation and in the interchangeability of agencies empowered by the context of mystery. To put this point in Barish's terms, Andrewes has less prejudice against expanding or shifting the self into other forms of personhood (impersonation) than he shows toward the overplayed self.[29]

As G. M. Story has written, one readily notices Andrewes's celebration of impersonation and of plural and converging persons in a sermon on the allegory of the meeting between truth, mercy, justice and wisdom. Reminding his auditors that "*Christianitie* is a meeting," Andrewes introduces his favorite rhetorical figure, synecdoche, which establishes the significance of each element by setting them all apart as "*Personages* . . . inasmuch as they have heer *personall acts* ascribed to them" (Story, 50). But each personage is meaningful only in a network with the others.

Not unlike James Shirley's plays, in which characters almost never speak in soliloquy,[30] Andrewes's Christianity is wary of isolates.

Synecdoche, he warns, or a one-entails-all spirituality, is easy to mistake for one-supplants-others. Heresies are born of this mistake, he adds, the Gnostics erasing all else except knowledge, the Encratite all save honest living: "*Christianitie* is a *meeting* . . . Err not this error then, to single any out, (as it were) in disgrace of the rest; Say not, one will serve the turne, what should we do with the rest of the foure; Take not a figure, and make of it a plaine speech; Seeke not to be saved by *Synecdoche*. Each of these [four virtues] is a *quarter of Christianity*, you shall never while you live make it serve for the whole" (72–73).

For Andrewes, then, each "person" is valuable yet none is singled out from the whole, "mixture," or "compound." So too with the various constituents of repentance (body and soul, anger and sorrow) or with our need for both sacraments and sermons; so too with Andrewes's sympathy for Arminian soteriology in which God respects no persons; so too in the liturgical emphasis of Andrewes's sermons: the personal becomes suspect when it individuates, and valuable when it congregates or hybridizes into a meaningful, if mysterious, whole. Thus, as Nicholas Lossky argues, Andrewes hesitates even to use the word "personal" in treating the "hypostatic union" typical of Christian mysteries because "of the ambiguity conveyed already in the seventeenth century by the use of the word 'person,' which tends to be identified with the word 'individual,'" whereas Andrewes thinks of "hypostasis or person . . . as a recapitulation of the whole." In theatrical terms, then, impersonation allows for historical continuity in the liturgical reiteration of a unique event much as synecdoche allows for cosmic holism at any one time, with singularity and separation as anathema.[31]

As contemporaries noticed, William Laud made it his habit as a preacher to impersonate the style of Andrewes, and Laud was joined in this practice by John Cosin and others.[32] In the 1629 Laud-Buckeridge edition of Andrewes's sermons, the editors participate in Charles's attempts to transform preaching and lecturing into the safe conformity of catechism, impersonation, and combination. Yet this editorial conversion of Andrewes into an imitable paradigm also betrays a sense that only Andrewes can impersonate himself. As early as 1609, John Chamberlain wrote to Dudley Carleton that a court sermon by Andrewes was greeted "with great applause, being not only *sui similis*, but more than himself by the report of the King and all his auditors."[33] At times, his unique style was criticized, most famously by a Scottish lord who told James that Andrewes simply played with scripture like so many pretty toys, and by George Herbert who in *The Country Parson*, without mentioning names, attacked those preachers who crumbled Biblical texts into pieces, such as the "Person speaking, or spoken to."[34]

Now the logical-rhetorical category of *persons* was commonplace in contemporary manuals for preaching and in sermons, too.[35] But the mixed reception of Andrewes in particular suggests that contemporaries had conflicting responses to the value and role of the *personal* in his sermons and preaching, if that term is taken simply to mean those tendencies to set something apart – a speaker, a word, an image, a doctrine. In Andrewes's sermons, the term *person* is neither ubiquitous (as in Donne or Sanderson) nor negligible (as in Sibbes). Andrewes is prepared to alert his auditor or reader that "the Person is here a weighty circumstance" (Story, I54–55), even as he resists the person-as-isolate.

Laud and Buckeridge celebrate Andrewes by noting that his sermons will readily identify their author and have required no editorial intervention. Andrewes is unusual, then, but only in a wisdom that amounts to the doctrinal conformity and sensible rhetoric of his sermons. Against a world overrun by a humorous and amorphous sermonizing made worse still by the partisan spirit in which sermons are received, the editors quote Acts I0.34, according to which Simon Peter learns that God is "no accepter of persons," in this case of Jews rather than Gentiles. For Laud and Buckeridge, Puritans are the modern Jews who destroy church order and unity in their addiction to self-righteousness, interior experience, and singular, charismatic preachers. A boon for "lawful authority," the "wise and discreet Sermons" of Andrewes are rendered all the less personal and all the more imitable by the removal of their author from life and the pulpit.[36] That is, the sermons have displaced the man so that "Andrewes" can take a place in the long line of Church Fathers.

Yet in his funeral sermon, Buckeridge captures the singularity as well as the doctrinal corpus and ecclesiastical family to which Andrewes lays claim. In praising Andrewes, Buckeridge dubs him "so singular a preacher" and "a great example example-less," even as the eulogist imitates his subject's attention to grammar and remarks how much Andrewes prized the "study of antiquity" in preparing his sermons. Liturgy is central to Buckeridge's association of Andrewes with historical and cosmic continuity, above all with what Anthony Milton identifies as the Laudian emphasis on an episcopal "personal succession" accompanied by minimal desire to know the actors in church history's play.[37] Still, as Buckeridge must allow in acknowledging his impersonation of the great Andrewes, some actors are simply distinctive: Andrewes "is the great actor and performer, I but the poor cryer, *vox clamantis*; he was the *vox clamans*, 'he was the loud and great crying voice,' I am but the poor echo" (*Works*, 5.287). Even here, however, the greater actor is just as disembodied as the lesser, consisting of voices more than persons.

As the Buckeridge-Laud edition purveys it, Andrewes's distinctive mark is to articulate the meaning of a Protestantism in a communal, historical, liturgical, and cosmic context, and in a synecdoche that loses its meaning when placed outside the integrating and impersonating tendencies of the figure. His celebration of Christian synecdoche was highly valued, if controversial, in the early years of personal rule when Charles and his chief ministers were attempting to regulate the "world of sermons." Charles loved the sermons of Andrewes but was also sympathetic, at least as prince and newly crowned monarch, to the Sibbes-Preston brotherhood of preachers. Some historians have stressed that sermons by the celebrated preachers of the Cambridge brotherhood continued to be published in multiple editions in the 1630s.[38] But in their detailed studies of the *Instructions* of 1629, Julian Davies and Patrick Collinson have shown just how fervently Charles and his clerical associates sought to render sermons and lectures less dominant and more conformable in English worship.[39]

It is well known that Charles was not the first English monarch to restrict preaching. Elizabethan policies reveal a queen nervous about sermons and especially about "prophesyings"; and while some recent scholarship has claimed a Jacobean consensus that ministers, even bishops, belonged in the pulpit, the political controversies of the early 1620s led James in 1622 to issue *Directions to Archbishop Abbot* prohibiting sermons on volatile religious and political subjects – especially involving questions of divine decree and of persons royal and otherwise prominent – and encouraging a catechism comprising the basic tenets of the faith.[40]

But Charles saw himself primarily as what Kenneth Fincham calls a "custodian of order," and some of his leading prelates and apologists followed suit, targeting sermons and lectures as prime suspects in bankrupting and fragmenting the church. Promoting catechisms, conformable prayer, reverence for the sacraments, and beautiful ceremony, Charles and his chief advocates made programmatic what Andrewes and Buckeridge had only urged of James, namely, a foreclosure on uncontrolled, amorphous, and provocative preaching by persons of suspicious doctrinal affiliation. Often, those preachers deemed suspect under Caroline regulations were rendered all the more dubious by their lay patronage; they lacked, moreover, an institutional mooring and a clear investment in the sacraments, prayers, canons, and performative regulations of the Church.[41]

Early in Charles's reign, critics of the so-called English Arminianism could have interpreted a number of events as omens that the heyday of preaching had passed. In 1628, Tobias Matthew died after twenty years as Archbishop of York and thousands of sermons. John Earle's eulogy characterizes Matthew as a miracle "in the pulpit."[42] By contrast, Cosin's 1626 sermon at the consecration of Francis White announced a major shift in the church's scheme of values according to which ecclesiastical "persons" would derive their dignity and sanctity: ordination, common prayer, charity, and the offices of ceremony and administration were promoted; preaching – especially if unlicensed – was resisted as too often chaotic, fraudulent, mercantile, and trivial.

This shift elicits something, but very little, of a protest from Cosin.[43] Citing Andrewes for support, Cosin associates wild claims on the Holy Spirit with a theatrical fraudulence no more defensible in his view than that bogey by his more zealous critics, the insincere and mechanical conformist who goes through the motions of, but cares little about, the service (1.124). According to Cosin, the spirit of God sets ministers apart by instituting them to preserve and execute the offices of sacred conformity, order, peace, and mortification, not to sermonize on behalf of factions and humors. Richard Tedder agrees that far from the bias against theater for which they are reputed, the Puritan sermon-mongers have introduced "such slovenly behaviour in the *Church* that there is no difference made between the *Temple* and the *Theatre*," with the novel result that "Never was there such a *Sermon age* as this is, and never was there such a *leannesse* in *Religion*."[44]

As other critics of the "Sermon age" construct the problem, Puritan theatricality is part and parcel of the rampant lay and heretical authorization of "particular, and private men" prone to error, disorder, arrogance, and partisanship.[45] In a 1636 sermon, Humphrey Sydenham laments the reciprocal rise of theatrical and personal authority in the church. Dedicating the sermon to Edward Seymour, the preacher complains that " 'Tis a criticall age we live in, where Divines and Poets have alike fate and misery, most men frequenting Churches as they doe Theaters, either to clap or hisse."[46] Sydenham believes that fickle and censorious popular pronouncements, not the motion of the Spirit, drive these hypocrites in the pulpit and the audience.

Sydenham connects such hypocrisy to a recent tendency to urge "Personall Authoritie" outside the composite boundaries of other forms of authority, including scripture, reason, councils, creeds, and ancient and modern theologians (240). In attacking bare personal authority, Sydenham appeals to the skeptical Charron to show how a man "in himselfe understands nothing perfectly, and purely, as hee should doe" (252). And it is the failure to situate the personal within the composite that ensures that our valuations will always be shams, and the world "a meere Play, where he that best dissembles, acts best: And such a one carries strongly the Applause of the multitude" (258). In such a world, error, fury, and faction prevail at the expense of the charity and "commendable *Rites* of an established Church" (258).

Sydenham thanks Laud for converting the critique of personal religion into a program for making the church lawful, reverent, and harmonious once again. In the wake of the 1629 *Instructions*, he believes, the dignity of ecclesiastical persons will be raised in like measure to the official ability to undo the mess left by a ridiculous theater of personal authorities. As Julian Davies summarizes them, the *Instructions* seek to counter-reform the church by outlining measures "to bind preaching to the liturgy and discipline of the Church" (Davies, 132). There is ambiguity enough in these *Instructions* to allow for variation in visitation articles and enforcement, but their upshot is to make catechisms, not sermons, the afternoon set piece; to require lecturers to read the service book prior to lecturing; to detach lecturers from their independent employment by lay patrons and to insist on their affiliation to the Church of England; and to plant monitors in the audience of lectures and to encourage lectures by combination.

As Collinson and Davies both note, lectures by combination previously supported the evangelical mission of ensuring effective preaching and abundant sermons in Jacobean England.[47] Yet Charles and his chief ministers seize on them as a way of ensuring orthodoxy and conformity and of discouraging singularity, heresy, or insubordination. The Caroline promotion of combination lectures epitomizes the cultural warfare over the nature, boundaries, and value of persons: in combination, that is, the ministerial person is framed as institutional, composite, and conformable.

As the parson is elevated by the sanctity of his office, Donne explains, the self is expanded into a person. Accordingly, each self is replaceable within the system, encased by the surplice and hood, and scripted by the canons and catechism. Each is subsumed by the combination, which ideally produces impersonations of conformity, not a dissonance of voices and interpretations. As Collinson says, combinations aim at the "successful containment of conflict" (469).

Accordingly, Laud urges the Bishop of Bath and Wells to permit lectures "not by any particular factious persons, but by a company of learned neighbouring ministers, which are every way conformable to the church."[48] But this so-called "Laudian" reconstitution of ecclesiastical persons insists on a hierarchy as much as it harps on the homogeneity ensured by impersonation. In the interests of clerical hierarchy, that is, the ideal Laudian minister is differentiated within the corporate "person," but given the tightening restrictions dividing priests from laity, that minister is fully and securely integrated with that composite person. In this latter instance, the person – the isolate – is priesthood itself.

The promotion of charity so common in these years italicizes the complex requirements made on ecclesiastical persons. In his sermon on Romans 14.1 ("Him that is weak in the faith receive, but not to doubtful disputations"), John Hales begins with an acknowledgement of his own imperfections; his voice (he says) is too weak for a large auditory, and he is neither ambitious nor skillful enough to garner popularity. Just so, the point of the sermon is to urge charity regarding another's flaws. Charity, we are told, is "a soft, and sweet, and flexible disposition," more valuable than great place or wealth or learning; for the respect earned by charity is loving and true, in answer to its sociable and communicable goodness. Unlike solitary melancholy, charity "rejoiceth in equalling others unto itself" so that Christians prosper best when "transfusing ourselves into others, and receiving from others into ourselves."[49]

Here then is the mystical yet social combination, the loving impersonation, that converts interior spirituality into meaning and purpose. Yet in Christian societies, Hales admits, charity is at cross purposes with the need for respect to persons defined in terms of rank and privilege: "One thing there is unavoidable, and natural to all societies, which is the greatest occasioner, yea, the very ground of disunion and dissent; I mean, inequality of persons and degrees." Hales adds: "All are not of the same worth, and therefore all cannot carry the same esteem and countenance: yet all, even the meanest, are alike impatient of discountenance and contempt, be the persons never so great from whence it proceeds" (398). Charity makes us conformable but somehow also equal, one communal person; yet inequality of persons is natural, even integral to charitable works, not to mention instrumental in mending the faults and redressing the trouble perpetrated by the weak who blindly throw themselves into disputes.

Despite his remarks on the weakness of all humanity, then, Hales seeks arguments for reconciling the two notions of persons that derive from love and status. As critics of the Laudian program emphasize throughout the 1630s and increasingly just before the war, Hales insists that for the best amalgamation of love and censure, "The teaching the people by voice is perpetually necessary" (405). Indeed this reminder is echoed in Fuller's recommendation that only assiduous preaching might "restore the honour and stature of the [prelatical] order"; in Falkland's 1641 joke, "at first [the Caroline prelacy's] preaching were the occasion of their preferment, they after made their preferment the occasion of their not preaching"; and in Ussher's view that for mutual tenderness between minister and people, "the work of government in the Church I confess to be great, but the work of the labouring minister a great deal more, and more to be respected."[50] But Hales disembodies the voice, then homogenizes it, converting the various weaknesses of individual preachers into an argument for the plurality of the clerical person. To the necessity of vocal teaching, Hales adds the desideratum that "all of us every where speak but the same things," for "our voices are confined to a certain compass, and tied to the individuating properties of *here* and *now*" (405).

If, as Hales notes, the very notion of a person requires some finesse in the 1630s, the picture is complicated further by the uncertainties and tensions at play in the so-called "godly" critiques of the Laudian church. If for Andrewes and Buckeridge the Trinity serves as a replicable (if mysterious) model for the corporate composition of the person, the Holy Spirit is featured in critiques of this model. As Geoffrey Nuttall writes, with its emergence in the seventeenth century as the most vital element in Christian thought and experience, "the doctrine of the Holy Spirit is a doctrine of a personal God, revealed in a Person and present in personal relationship with persons."[51] Many writers are convinced that the Holy Spirit must be lived as the principal agent in "the rediscovery of God as a Person."[52]

As Daniel Featley's preface to Phineas Fletcher's *Purple Island* puts it, the workings of the Holy Ghost in the individual soul situate Christianity exactly where it belongs, in "Autologie" or internal combat against sin. But as the foundation of theology, autology also affords a Christian with a way of severing as many ties as possible with an idolatrous and profane world. Sanderson himself remarks that our emplacement in historical, familial, and church genealogies is as likely to "bring judgments upon us, and enwrap us in their punishments" as it is to guarantee our redemption and happiness within the context of the "common and public good."[53]

But autology is only a starting point for the construction of a spiritual person. In itself, an inspired autology is fraught with problems, as Peter Lake explains. In sorting out the motions of the Holy Spirit from one's own thoughts and fancies; in coming to terms with the exact relationship

between Spirit and scripture but also between Spirit and reason or education; in measuring one's respect for clergy and community but also the
proper measures of fear and confidence: in all these challenges, Caroline
writers seek to validate autology by a "series of practical, institutional,
and emotional accommodations between the various parts of the Puritan
impulse and between that impulse and external reality."[54] In turn, the
need to legitimize autology is made all the more urgent in the face of the
Caroline–Laudian program for redrawing the genealogy of the church,
for restraining the lecture, and for incorporating spiritual personhood.[55]

The activities of the Feoffees of Impropriations from 1625 to 1633
were eventually prosecuted under Laud as a conspiracy to destroy the
church through the control of parliaments as well as church livings. The
Feoffees were thought especially dangerous insofar as they challenged
official sanctions about who was warranted to authorize ecclesiastical
persons; about the criteria according to which these persons should be
singled out and inspected; and about the kind of spirituality that ministers
should aim to instill in their auditors, "it being observed in England"
(according to Fuller) "that those who hold the helm of the pulpit always
steer the people's hearts as they please."[56] But as Paul Seaver notes, the
Feoffees conflicted not only with the Andrewesian subordination of each
Christian soul to an institutional composite, but also with Puritanism's
own supposed over-reliance on the personal authority of a minister. Thus,
the Feoffees can be seen as an attempt to guarantee the supply and
succession of ministers in that chain made famous by the celebrated
connections between Perkins, Baynes, Sibbes, Cotton, and Preston; but
it also attempts to "transcend the limits of the older personal following
because of its very impersonality; the Puritans gave their loyalty to certain
principles, not to a commanding ego, and therefore viewed themselves
as the impersonal agents of a divine will" (49).

Godly preaching, then, was also committed to impersonation – of
principles, paradigms, and (as Haller puts it) of the "spiritual biography"
projected onto "every man." In the early years of Charles, that is, the
Feoffees both extend and seek to modify one effect of the explosion of
sermons in Jacobean England, namely, the movement of "the center of
religious loyalty from the permanent structure of the Church – that is,
the parish – to the personality and capacity of the preacher."[57]

But godly ministers also resist this very shift in the direction of their
persons. In the prefaces and sermons of Sibbes, a great number of which
appeared with sermons by Dod, Downame, Preston, Thomas Goodwin,
and Thomas Taylor in the Caroline years, the category of a person is

largely overlooked. For a preacher who, as Nuttall has said, did more than anyone to personalize English Christianity within the triangle of heart, Holy Spirit, and Word, Sibbes tends to avoid the soteriological controversies, the testimonies of influence and allegiance, and meditations on the role of social decorum in Christian living that might unsettle his construction of "a platform of Christian doctrine, whereupon all persons and Christian churches might safely build themselves."[58] In his anxious sense of the demands of casuistry, Sibbes can resemble Sanderson. But unlike Sanderson, Sibbes can leave well enough alone: his ministry finds no use for or comfort in what Sibbes calls "respective religion, [which] is never a sound religion. A true Christian hath a single eye; he serves God for himself" (7.188, 411).

As Grosart said years ago, if it is true as Cotton Mather remarked that "persons truly converted unto God have a mighty and lasting affection for the instrument of their conversion," it is also true that Sibbes has little to say about his conversion by Baynes.[59] Perhaps the erasure of the problems of personhood in salvation, in the church, and in the social order allowed Sibbes to escape prosecution or disfavor when his participation in the Feoffees could have been construed as conspiratorial. But his own prominent place in the famous "Spiritual Brotherhood" contributes to the call for a "singular" godliness in ministers, the inspection of whom is as productive of controversy as the genealogy of divine decrees.[60] Between Sanderson and Sibbes, the network of questions about the "person" clarifies the central dilemma of a circumstantial faith: one can never be sure whether such a faith is inquiring rightly about salvation or missing the way altogether.

CHAPTER 5

Decorum and redemption in the theater of the person

At their best, the circumstances of *heroism* and *fancy* were believed to elevate English Protestantism. But no matter how much the circumstance of *persons* might factor into Caroline conditions for isolating and exalting the saint, church, or minister, the preoccupation with its complexities induced writers to consider the status of their Protestantism as implanted very much in the stage-play world. In the 1620s and 30s, the handbooks of manners, social comedies, and sermons address the problem of how the rejection of personal respects so critical to the God of the Bible can be reconciled with the social decorum so integral to early Stuart society. Whether it is Shirley staging comedies about the "town" or Donne preaching of conflict between a corporate and isolated soul, Caroline writers take stock of the proprieties governing their society.

So it is that the advocates of the Feoffees of Impropriations and, in general, of lay involvement in church affairs were compelled to grapple with the injunction against respecting persons as the Bible most often poses it: in social and economic terms. With St. Paul as their model, godly Christians attempted (in the words of Haller) "to adapt their teaching to the spiritual condition of all men" in a kind of "spiritual egalitarianism," the very essence of which was God's disregard for persons, Jew or Gentile.[1] Whereas Haller emphasizes the power of this Pauline model for giving voice and momentum to the oppressed, there is clearer evidence for the conflict over decorum that it provoked in the so-called "Puritan gentry" of the 1620s and 30s.

As godly members of the upper ranks strove to negotiate between, on the one hand, the strictures of their faith and, on the other, their aristocratic habits of thought or deeply entrenched expectations for their behavior, their chaplains and ministers often reminded them that God accepts no persons. In 1629, for instance, Roger Williams wrote a letter to Lady Joan Barrington in which he severely warns her against profane living and lukewarm spirituality, quoting the Book of Job to make his point that "'He with whome we deale excepteth not the persons of Princes nor regardeth the rich more than the poore; for they are all the worcke of his hands.'"[2] On either side of the dialogue between status and spirituality were simplistic extremes, on the one hand the view that God actually prefers the poor and, on the other, the notion that spiritual and social elections are fully reconcilable. But as Lucy Hutchinson wrote, it was up to God to save noble persons from the patently sinful tendencies of their group.[3]

In Caroline England, it was widely believed not only that aristocrats faced special temptations to sin but also that some members of the upper ranks had been distinguished throughout history for their piety.[4] At times, the two beliefs were connected insofar as the full-scale resistance of noble persons to worldly pressures produced great evidence of election, made all the more admirable in the face of public ridicule. For good or ill, however, ambivalence over the relationship between holiness and pedigree, or between mortification and decorum, affected every level of gentle living, from domestic habits to the specific offices of patronage and magistracy. In the first decade and a half of Caroline rule, these effects were complicated by a number of factors: the Laudian distrust of lay encroachment in the church; the mixed message about decorum sent by Charles to the great persons under his rule; the bitter aftertaste of the Jacobean inflation of honors; and, in the theaters, a social experimentation and religio-political criticism so attractive to the gentle Puritans. In this "difficult and anxious time for Puritan patrons,"[5] exegetes and casuists labored over the Biblical injunctions against respecting persons, especially in James.

In *Praxis Theologica: Or, the Epistle of the Apostle of St Iames Resolved, Expounded, and Preached upon by way of Doctrine and Use* (1629), John Mayer emphasizes the great relevance of this epistle but also the surprising dearth of commentary on it heretofore. As for the "respect of persons," Mayer is careful to read the words in context and to face head- on the questions, objections, and alternatives that they raise. The help of unimpeachable patristic and scholastic commentators notwithstanding, Mayer struggles with his own distinctions between inner and outer respects, and natural versus worldly honor, sometimes making much ado about the difference between prepositions in the Biblical formula.[6] For William Ames, etymology enables the casuist to understand that by "person," the Bible means something "externall or accidentall," including "such qualities [as] kindred, power, riches, and friendship; and hence in the Hebrew it is called . . . the respect of the *face*." But, typically, for every rejection of the honor paid this face, the casuist has a proviso: "It therefore hath no place, but in him who is oblig'd for some reasons to preferre one man before another, not according to his opinion, but according to some reasons and causes inherent to bee looked after in the very Persons."[7] A similar interpretive toil can be found in the gloss on *person* in Thomas Wilson's *A Christian Dictionary* or in the exhortations to holy living in Richard Braithwait's *The English Gentleman*.[8]

It is in the Caroline drama, however, that the spiritual, moral, and social struggle to define the meaning or to evaluate the status of persons is most experimental. Given the rivalry and kinship between pulpit and playhouse, this state of affairs is hardly surprising. But in Caroline England, the dramatization of this embattled respect is prominent and intricate.

I

By 1625, the "cultural interdependence" or "mutual influence" between pulpit and playhouse was well established, owing not just to the vitality of each but also to the theological problems that both mediated, most notably the psychology of election and reprobation.[9] But this kinship was always and increasingly nervous, competitive, and – according to some vocal critics both high church and low – sinful for the church to cultivate. By the outset of Charles's reign, William Prynne was preparing to wage his massive campaign not just against plays and actors, but also against the tenet "as *common as it is prophane*: That Stage-playes are as good as Sermons; and that many learne as much good at a Play as at a Sermon."[10] As historians of antitheatricality have remarked, there is virtually nothing new in Prynne's *Histriomastix*. But the endless and repetitious arguments against theater, acting, and players evince (as Barish puts it) "a staggering load of resentment and anxiety."[11]

The tremendous bulk of Prynne's assault on the stage is meant, then, to ensure that the exorcism or "divorce" of theater from the pulpit is complete.[12] To this end, he would have his reader believe in the unanimity of opposition to theater and, accordingly, in the minority of drama advocates. On page after page, Prynne denies or reverses the charge that critics of the stage are seditious "Puritans," for if this be the case, he quips, then "Puritan" is a highly amorphous label naming Christ and Ovid alike.

Indeed, whatever their own vague and atemporal use of the term "Puritan," historians of antitheatricality have been obliged to agree with

Prynne that some of the most virulent critics of the stage – Gosson comes
to mind – were establishmentarians, that these critics were only "Puritan"
to the extent that the establishment was, and that Prynne's judges (Laud
among others) were not at all interested in defending the stage and were
worried rather about Prynne's topical politics and social cynicism.[13] In
the age of Charles, moreover, the Puritan emphasis on preaching is just
as likely to be criticized for its theatricality as high church ceremony ever
was, in part because of the audiences of the sermons, in part because
(as Barish has shown) antitheatricality could be directed against exhibitionism as well as impersonation, and in part because Andrewes and his
followers caricatured Puritanism in terms of hypocrisy, a tendency that
according to Lucy Hutchinson and James Ussher ironically converted
the caricaturists' own pulpits into theaters.[14] In 1638, Bishop Henry
Leslie attacks the audiences who stay outside during the liturgy yet rush
in for the sermon by protesting that they have turned the church into
a playhouse. William Chillingworth and Henry Hammond had much
the same response to the shift of religious theater from altar to preacher
and from eye to ear, and Hobbes saw the shift as a major cause of the
war. But just as commonly, a so-called Puritan such as Richard Bernard
would object to the infiltration of the pulpit by onetime playwrights and
actors, a charge with a factual basis in the careers of several dramatists
who were concurrently or eventually preachers.[15]

Prynne was right, then, to argue that resistance to the blurring of
boundaries between preaching and acting was widespread. This non-
partisan critique of the theatricality of the church testifies in particular
to the intense examination of personal respects and even to the desire to
extricate the church from their purview. But Caroline writers respond to
Prynne with an equally strong advocacy of the theater, inventing defenses
for the theater's kinship to the pulpit and touting the drama's involvement
in the spiritual, moral, and social work of casuistry. In John Selden's
Table Talk, for instance, one finds an assertion that the pleasure taken in
sermons is easily converted into a pleasure taken in plays; mention of
how he convinced a Puritan to abandon antitheatricality; and analyses of
the rhetoric, tone, and performance of preaching, much like those found
elsewhere in the diaries and handbooks of the period. Selden draws
comparisons between the structure of romance and of sermons, and
assesses crowd responses to "the Preacher himself" – a concern with the
fixation on a minister's person to which whole pamphlets were devoted.[16]

In his *Resolves*, Owen Feltham prescribes strategies for lending theatrical vitality to the pulpit, and he elaborates on the benefits of doing

so; elsewhere, Donne and Cartwright are praised for the drama of their preaching, while Robert Gomersall defends plays against their sermon-centered critics by arguing that drama often preaches more effectively than sermons.[17] Celebrating a Caroline tradition of hybrid preacher-playwrights, Abraham Wright's *Five Sermons, in Five Several Styles; or Waies of Preaching* (1656) lumps together Jasper Mayne and William Cartwright as one of the styles, explicitly touting the power of the English clergy to "change the Theater into a Church; having a greater power over the passions of their Auditorie, then the Actor hath upon the stage."[18] Wright also promotes the preacher's impersonation of other ministers, especially as these ministers can be epitomized and stabilized as a method already shared among more than one "person." But in the Mayne-Cartwright contribution to Wright's anthology, the theater–pulpit kinship serves to consolidate the value of impersonation in both monitoring and interrogating the boundaries of a person.

Denouncing those hypocrites who are forever "making their Religion their part, and onely personating their godlinesse; their devotion being like the hangings of the scene, which they can take off and tack on as they list," the Mayne-Cartwright sermon is set forth in a book that invites the reader to impersonate its hybrid authorship, style, or method. Indeed, the sermon itself underscores a "sociable," protean, and diffusive personhood: "Insomuch that wee live not our own lives alone, but the life of the whole world; as if at our degeneration we took upon us no private persons, but the common nature, and were not baptized men, but mankinde: our actions being therefore not personal but oecumenical, & whether good or bad are held authentick" (52). Ironically, however, the anthology purveys Andrewes as *sui generis*, though readers might nonetheless attempt an impersonation.

Caroline writers in pursuit of conformity through impersonation support what Barish has noted is a positive iconographic tradition for Proteus and the chameleon. Yet they denounce the paradoxical tendencies of "Puritanism" toward hypocrisy and exhibitionism, the latter of which "merely carries truth to extremes" by way of the "emphatic maintaining of one's own person."[19] In the Caroline decades, the complexities of the person render any advocacy for theatrical religion a delicate affair. One of the trends of the period is to find some proper, limited, and monitored ground on which actor and preacher can meet: one sees this search, for example, in Braithwait's careful analysis of the uses and perils of drama, but also in Sir Richard Baker's response to Prynne's *Histriomastix*.[20]

The search for a middle ground between theater and pulpit is also illustrated by the records of the Master of the Revels, Sir Henry Herbert. According to his notes, Herbert conceived his mission as the institution of a moral rigor governing the standards in the theater. This mission was carried out in part in response to Prynne, but always in a complex negotiation with Charles, the churchmen, other officers, and patrons over judgments concerning indecency, irreverence, and slander – in short, questions more often than not about personal decorum and offence.[21]

It has long been established that so-called Puritans – Brinsely, Ames, even Prynne – found moral uses for theatrical impersonation.[22] But building on Haller's insight that the dramatic imagination is as integral to English Protestantism as impersonation and personal transformation are to Christianity itself, recent theater historians have made a case that Puritanism is a key (though also conflictive) component of Caroline theater and its treatment of the nature of persons.[23] Historians such as J. T. Cliffe have singled out the Puritan gentry as especially mixed in their views of theater. But Margot Heinemann and Martin Butler have argued that much of late Jacobean and Caroline drama was basically Puritan in its attitudes and concerns.[24] Far from simply serving an official court or "cavalier" ideology, Butler maintains, Caroline drama was often suspicious of official ideology and practice, and at its best was "critical and questioning, scrutinizing received platitudes, proposing alternatives, engaging most closely with the contradictions inherent in living in a time of change and uncertainty" (4). This critical edge is to be found, Butler argues, in courtly plays, Elizabethan revivals, and in new plays by such professionals as Massinger and Brome. The religious and political criticism offered in these plays is hardly unflinching or univocal; it is often torn between the claims of obedience and conscience. As Butler shows, the Puritan gentry's abiding investment in the English heritage of dramatic impersonation is aimed at preserving a lively if flawed vehicle for articulating dilemmas of the political and spiritual person within the social bounds of decorum (90–97).

In the reign of Charles I, the assessments of theatrical effects are exploratory and provocative. They bear witness to and consolidate the contemporary fascination with the question of how to accept, respect, and regard persons. At the same time, playwrights themselves show a heightened self-consciousness, boldness, yet uncertainty about their own enterprise of reforming their audience by way of fictive impersonation. For a variety of reasons, Caroline playwrights wrote plays reflective of their own self-evaluation or, in James Bulman's metaphor, their "stocktaking" of theater. These reasons include a palpable decline in court patronage from a king who nonetheless wants fully to control and censor the theater; the anxiety of influence by such masters as Shakespeare, Jonson, Beaumont and Fletcher; the tenuous relations between playwrights and audiences perceived to be more critical and partisan (if also more gentlemanly and decorous) in their aesthetic judgments; and the campaign against theater in the 1630s. But in the final analysis, Caroline playwrights simply feared "that the theatre was losing its credibility as a cultural force," and plays their status "as social and moral arbiters."[25]

At one level, Thomas Randolph's *The Muse's Looking-Glass* is a standard defense of the didactic power of theater, with the added bonus that it depicts two Puritans learning to appreciate this moral power. As Barish has argued, however, theater's *modus operandi* is undercut or at least obscured by the lingering figure of flattery, Colax.[26] Early on, the actor Roscius celebrates the remarkable ability of theater to teach virtue by way of laughter and impersonation – more effectively indeed than lectures. After the various dramatic genres have argued over their claims to perform this mission best, the allegory settles into an Aristotelian ethical framework that apparently crosses generic boundaries in constituting virtues between – or as a mixture of – extremes. The most important pair arrives first: Dyscolus (extreme disrespect or disregard for persons) and Colax, a slave to respect who stays around for the rest of the performance. Far from an impediment to the moral mission of the dramatic looking glass, however, Colax is the pivotal figure in Randolph's allegory of theatrical impersonation, for flattery pays his respects by way of impersonating all the humors and desires which he shamelessly applauds. In a poem addressed to the actor and "his dear friend, Thomas Riley," Randolph praises Riley as a Proteus who can assume any shape – "all professions and all passions"–and make the audience believe in the reality of each.[27] So too flattery: it is not surprising that Colax compares himself to Proteus or that he assumes the role of directing the various extremes to the looking glass offstage where they will see themselves for the vices that they truly are. But the mirror *is* Colax, whose praises are so extreme and protean as to teach the Puritan spectators what these vices really are, with the obvious danger kept in view that, as in Philip Massinger's portrait of a miser in *The Roman Actor*, extreme impersonation will be taken at face value.

Despite his moral relativism, then, and notwithstanding his own surprise in discovering that he has helped reform the vices that he would encourage and deceive, it is Colax who articulates the play's medicinal metaphor for comic reform.[28] His own extreme, tantamount to the courtly acceptance of persons, must be blended with the two Puritans' rancorous disregard of persons in order for virtue to be attained, and only a visit to the Muse's looking glass can effect the cure. In essence, the fictive actor and his fictive Puritan audience are converted to the value of moral impersonation by way of a medium with which they have previously allowed only the most superficial relations – the Puritans having supplied its feathers and pins.

Especially in the plays of Ford and Brome, Caroline theater unsettles the kind of casuistic and systematic attempt made by Sanderson soberly to resolve questions about the metaphysics and morality of personal respects. In *The Theater and the Dream: From Metaphor to Form in Renaissance Drama*, Jackson I. Cope situates such plays as Brome's *Antipodes* and Ford's *Perkin Warbeck* within a "broader tendency toward epistemological perspectivism – toward viewing the world as a theater in which man is a Protean perfomer who seeks his place endlessly among the credits, now as player, now as playwright, now as director of the whole and even – with Bernini in mind – as artificer of the scene itself."[29] As for the status of persons in this cosmic theater, Cope finds what the French historian Jean Rousset describes as a widespread fascination with "the inevitability of metamorphosis, the omnipresence of Circean and Protean figures and myths, and the reasoned dominance of ornamentation and surface. Moral and aesthetic appearance supererogates an often merely hypothetical inner being . . . This implies that man is a quick-change artist, a role-adapter, an actor" (3).

While much broader in scope, Cope's work is helpful for getting at the Caroline emphasis on the surreal mysteries of impersonation, for example, in pointing out that in contrast to Bacon's *History of Henry VII*, which keeps Perkin Warbeck's theatricality in the margins, "Ford grasped [Perkin's story] as a tragic paean to man's Protean ability to create himself in the image of his own imagination," with the haunting corollary "of autogenesis, the possibility that Perkin may have willed himself into reality" (127–30). According to Cope, Brome's *Antipodes* is as "complicated" in its theatrical "perspectivism" as *Perkin Warbeck* is occult, with its multiple layers of inset plays, "all simultaneously enacted," underscoring the ambiguous Caroline dramatization of the power that impersonation has to fashion, reform, or balance personhood (157).

As a bold and topical case of their concern with personal respects, Caroline plays explore both the constituents of royal persons and the extent to which those persons must be respected. In such plays the word *person* is tested both prominently and provocatively, for example, in Brome's *Queen and Concubine*, the heroic queen of which is banished by her tyrannical husband and learns that "'Tis then the Greatness of / The Person dignifies the Titles, not it the Person."[30] In many ways, Charles himself contributed to this complex imagining of royal and noble persons, especially given his contradictory relationship with principles of decorum. At court, and in reaction against his father, he was obsessed with the restoration of order, decorum, and protocol. "In March 1629," writes Kevin Sharpe, Charles "ordered greater care concerning the distinctions and degrees of rooms and persons."[31] The king's passion for decorum was protective not just – though principally – of his own sanctity and separateness; as Sharpe points out, he also oversaw "a return to the careful maintenance of aristocratic privilege"; attempted to end the sale of honors; and generally sought to resurrect "the old society of degree and deference," in the church as well as among the laity and at court (*Politics*, 108).

But notwithstanding his emphasis on what one ambassador called "a rule of great decorum," Charles's record of respect regarding the great persons of his kingdom was checkered, and not just in his eventual resumption of the sale of honors that his father had launched. The very insistence on and protection of his own sacred person meant that Charles distanced himself all the more from the very subjects for whom he would serve as a model and, according to Glenn Burgess, that he violated the decorum for articulating and observing the boundaries of a royal prerogative agreed on in Jacobean England.[32] Anthony Milton largely agrees in his treatment of Caroline official policies and discourse on the church: subjects were simply confused by what they perceived to be their monarch's indecorum regarding the usage of rules governing their liberties.[33] Thus, in such plays as *Perkin Warbeck*, the collapse of royal respect for and gratitude to great persons is as problematic as the question of defining and respecting royal persons.[34]

In *The Crisis of the Aristocracy*, Lawrence Stone has argued that the Caroline failure to reverse the collapse of aristocratic prestige begun under James was perceived by mid- and late-seventeenth-century commentators as a cause of the Civil War equal in weight to the decline in respect for the royal person and the breakdown of accommodation in the church.[35] Charles's response to the inheritance of this scandal was mixed. On the one hand, he prominently displayed his intentions to reverse the downward slide of honorific titles, placing a moratorium on their sale.

For Charles, this cessation of a trade on social rank was analogous to the restoration of respect owed royal and ecclesiastical persons as well. But on the other hand, Charles continued in his own way the cheapening of and offense to persons of substance, at first under Buckingham's sway then eventually under the pressures of fundraising without parliament. "In face of the mounting criticism of their privileges," Stone writes, "the growing contempt for their persons, and the erosion of the territorial foundations of their authority," aristocrats resisted their own demotion by way of everyday actions, social criticism, and genealogical self-consciousness (750–71).

Charles's obsession with personal decorum was similar to Sanderson's casuistry of personal respects: in both cases sacred and social concerns converged; in both cases, attempts were made to stabilize or reverse a trend toward confusion that was developing beyond control. The Caroline playwrights, however, were less fully committed to stabilizing and clarifying the respect owed to or even the very nature of persons. It is true that they held themselves responsible for addressing the challenges to and uncertainties about decorum within a relatively decorous medium; but they were also interested in exploiting those uncertainties about what a person is and what value should be placed on a person once it is isolated.

II

The playwright held most accountable for protecting yet also undercutting decorum was Ben Jonson. In a 1629 panegyric that Jonson prized, Nicholas Oldisworth expressed more than he knew in urging the famous playwright to die: "Die Johnson: crosse not our Religion so, /As to bee thought immortall. Lett us know / Thou art a Man. Thy workes make us mistake / Thy person; and thy great Creations make / Us idol thee, and 'cause wee see thee doe / Eternall thynges, thinke Thee eternall too."[36] In 1629, there was much ado about mistaking Jonson's person and Jonsonian persons, but not for the flattering – if oddly expressed – reason given by Oldisworth that unless Jonson dies, audiences will believe the poet as immortal as his works. By this inaugural year of Charles's personal rule, Jonson's health and career were sharply in decline; simultaneously, the career of Jonson's onetime servant, Richard Brome, was on the rise. In other words, Jonson's own personal authority was challenged in triplicate: the decline of Jonson's health removed him from his place as arbiter of manners in English society; the debacle of *The New Inn* signaled the playwright's own failing grasp on aesthetic and social norms; and Jonson's replacement by the upstart Brome served as a reminder that the master's own social status and cultural authority were themselves based on indecorum. That is, the Caroline Jonson elicited from his audience a heightened sense that normative authority over matters of decorum can depend on a strangely protean career of social impersonation.

At the end of his life, Jonson's eulogists made note of the strange truth that the great playwright's mastery of apt characterization ran counter to his life's unsettling of decorum. In *Jonsonus Virbius* (1638), Shackerly Marmion applauds Jonson for "Fitting each person to his *time* and *place*"; but Edmund Waller attempts to square Jonson's ability to dramatize all kinds of persons with the playwright's own elusive persona: "For as thou couldst all *characters* impart, / So none can render thine, who still escapes, / Like *Proteus* in variety of shapes, / Who was nor this nor that, but all we finde, /And all we can imagine in mankind."[37] Waller captures the irony that the playwright most authoritative in representing the distinctive humors is the very one that embodies the uncertainty, mutability, and capacity of a single actor in the stage-play world. Jonson the dramatist mastered the making of persons in their proper circumstances; Jonson the man was both all persons and no person at all.

Historians and critics of Caroline theater tend to agree that its social experimentation in large part centers on a new space, the town. For "Caroline high society," Butler explains, theaters helped the town to develop "standards against which forms and codes of behaviour could be established, scrutinized and adjusted."[38] In the context of a decorum under review, social status itself requires – but often lacks or even resists – an authority guaranteeing the normative value of persons; and Caroline theater clearly participates in this state of affairs.

As much as Sanderson, James Shirley is set on recovering or devising reliable formulae for navigating that circumstance in English values that is most vulnerable to the vicissitudes of everyday life. Among Caroline playwrights, Shirley deploys the word *person* most frequently and diversely, and has the most complex relationship to social regulation and experiment. It is noteworthy that the censors made Shirley into both positive and negative examples for other dramatists seeking a decent language and acceptable personations. Of *The Young Admiral*, Sir Henry Herbert raved that it was exemplary in its abstinence from "oaths, prophaness, or obsceanes" and, accordingly, a model for improving the

moral decorum of drama as well as "for the bettring of maners and language." But in 1639 Shirley touted his own refusal to flatter the court, no
doubt recalling his trouble with the censors over _The Ball_, a play deemed
offensive for its rude impersonations of prominent courtiers.[39]

It is understandable then that critics have differed over the social logic
of Shirley's plays. Ira Clark dismisses any evidence that Shirley was anti-
court, arguing that the playwright's "career exhibits consistent venera-
tion of degree and of court; it appears to have been a quest for courtly
approval and support unmatched by any other Caroline professional
playwright."[40] By contrast, Martin Butler's Shirley has his imagination
stimulated by the decidedly independent and experimental, if also highly
decorous, town (158). In a similar vein, Richard Morton finds the basic
ingredient of Shirley's London in the changes among those "conflicting
social elements" that interact but always misunderstand each other.[41]
Social degree, norms, hybridity, failure, conflict, and incoherence: taken
together, these critical emphases capture Shirley's dramatization of a
decorum in the remaking. As Gordon Braden has argued, Shirley's characters have little if any individuality and fumble any attempt to speak _sui
similis_.[42]

But if Shirley's is a drama resistant to isolates, its social logic of persons explores strange interstices – for example, in _The Lady of Pleasure_ –
as often as it inhabits familiar places. In _The Gamester_, Old Barnacle's
explanation of extraordinary social change from one generation to the
next serves as an amusing example of the Caroline search for some law –
any law – that can pose as the arbiter amid social flux or as a taxonomy
of social hybridity.[43] Especially in love plots, Shirley's habitual use of
the word _person_ is so malleable as to name, by turns, a character's physical attributes, family heritage, financial prosperity, behavioral carriage,
emotional sympathy, social office, individual being, ethical value, and
spiritual status. The implications of this flexibility are none too clear: either Shirley hopes for an ideal convergence of these personal accidents in
his logic of character, or he yields to the sheer multiplication of personal
respects that necessitates charity as a recourse from "the fierce vexation
of community."[44]

In Shirley's plays, then, a propriety of or respect for persons is taken
for granted as desirable. But as in Sanderson's work, this propriety is all
the more fervently reviewed inasmuch as its meaning is elusive and the
formation of its criteria is in progress. As portrayed by the playwright
whose plays both pleased and vexed the censors, the town becomes a

setting as much for social skepticism and exploration as it is for social abuses made right again.

III

In the formative years of the Caroline preachers, drama and pulpit were bound up in the search for the meaning of God's disregard for persons. On the one hand, divines concerned themselves with the theater of preaching: rumor has it that at Oxford, William Laud frequently reminded a young James Shirley that the future playwright's facial mole rendered him "an unfit person to take the sacred function upon him," for despite his other gifts, audiences would object to his deformity.[45] On the other hand, several contemporary playwrights went on to become parsons famous and infamous alike, and Caroline plays feature a number of decidedly unfit parsons – Parson Palate in *The Magnetic Lady*, of whom the garrulous Polish says "I respect no parsons, / Chaplains, or doctors, I will speak"; the lascivious titular character of Killigrew's *The Parson's Wedding*; and that paradoxical and musical reveler, Sir Christopher, of Cartwright's *The Ordinary*, a mock-Puritan as obsessed with the social status and financial maintenance of his order as he is with the source of his next drink, the strength of his next witticism, and the tune of his next song.[46]

If Caroline dramatists were involved in evaluating and fashioning acceptable norms for ecclesiastical persons, the most remarkable preacher of their time, John Donne, cut his social and intellectual teeth in the theater. And though he appears to have left the theater behind in the years of his search for employment, his critics ever since have singled out the theatrical qualities of his preaching.[47] Critics have disagreed about whether one should admire Donne the preacher's theatricality, and this debate usually centers on the difference between the sermons of Donne and Andrewes in their polarized treatments of persons and the personal. Such judgments pro and con are premised on relatively few and stable, if often illuminating, notions of rhetoric, theater, and personhood. But as William Mueller has noted, Donne is as likely to chastise his audience for regarding ministerial persons as he is to call attention to himself or to his flair for performance.[48] Thus Donne's 1628 sermon-in-parenthesis surveying the Bible's injunctions against accepting persons betrays a deep-seated ambivalence critical to his ministry and to the religious thought of his contemporaries: the Bible's repudiation of personal respects is as hard for Caroline writers to accept or to understand as it is for them to forget.

From his pulpit in the last years of his life, Donne embodies the full range of Caroline responses to the suspicion that the respect owed to persons must be reconceived, stabilized, and explored. Unlike the dramatists, he insists on reuniting the matters of redemption and of social interaction that came together in Sanderson's work; but unlike Sanderson, he projects rival and equally powerful notions of the person – one corporate, the other isolated – that elude all efforts at system-building and casuistry. Unlike Sanderson, Donne forces on his auditors the value of doubting any complacency they might feel about their personal status, all the while granting them a passionate hope that God's assessment of personal templates and isolates is mysterious rather than contradictory.

Like Andrewes, Donne advocates a plural and sociable template for the Christian person, its model a Trinity of divine persons at once variously employed and fundamentally conformable. This model, Donne reiterates, is as hard to fathom as it is necessary to believe: a belief in its plural-conformable person is not just the diacritical mark of the Christian but also the *sine qua non* of meaningful social relations and duties.[49]

For Donne the preacher, God's preference for communicable persons entails two corollaries of great comfort, one soteriological and the other vocational. Donne's soteriology is premised on the belief that "God never did it, God never meant it, that any should sin necessarily, without a willing concurrence in themselves, or be damned necessarily, without relation to sin willingly committed" (8.261). God is no hypocrite in his offer of salvation to all and each. More positively put, the grammar of salvation is Trinitarian: the soul of each person is made more surely and vitally precious to God by virtue of its almost inextricable station among all souls, for God so loves plurality that divinity itself is plural.

In speaking of one person of the Trinity, Donne observes, Church Fathers will often use the names of the others; in speaking generally of salvation, the Bible implicates each single in the plural. For Donne, the attraction of these grammatical shifts is that they articulate a paradox about God's mercy so as to minimize the contingencies of the single person who, in the Arminian scheme, has hope but no guarantee. So, he stresses, the mercy belonging to others belongs to each and vice versa: "God is a plurall God, and offers himselfe to all, collectively; God is a singular God, and offers himselfe to every man, distributively" (9.140). If God accepts no persons, then, it is simply because God wants and fashions each person in the plural. But for Donne, the theological shifts from this plural back to single persons is as haunting as it is hopeful.

The redemptive corollary of the Trinity is matched by a vocational corollary best seen in Donne's celebrations of the ordinance of preaching, about which he is much less critical and cautious – if much more excited and anxious – than Andrewes. For Donne, the person of the minister is subject to idealization if each man is divested of the singularly personal – "every man puts off his owne person" (7.204) – and is dilated into the dutiful shape, extended family, and spiritual sufficiency of the ordinance. What is more, the conformity, plurality, and dilation of the preacher's person demand impersonation now and across history. According to Donne, audiences should presuppose that each minister's dilation entails both his inspiration and replaceability.

In a sermon preached at Whitehall in February 1628, Donne claims that men achieve the status of a person only if they propose to themselves a pattern, example, or office. This pattern will often be embodied in some noteworthy figure or saint, but if we impersonate that figure, we are transformed into an office and not into an isolated self. That is, we come to inhabit a place, to acquire an inscription, and in this guise we are transmitted to posterity.

But Donne is careful to delineate the difference between natural or civil offices and religious vocation. "In nature," he explains, "the body frames and forms the place; for the place of the natural body is that *proxima aeris superficies*, that inward superficies of the air, that invests and clothes, and apparals that body, and obeys, and follows, and succeeds to the dimensions thereof." But if the physical person defines a place in nature, the reverse is true in religion: "In nature the body makes the place, but in grace the place makes the body: The person must actuate it self, dilate, extend and propagate it self according to the dimensions of the place, by filling it in the execution of the duties of it" (8.178). The person has much to do in expanding, multiplying, and adapting itself to office, but this much ado has a way of divesting personal agency of its contingencies. In sum, Donne concludes that dilation spreads us into our offices; our offices spread and grow when others dilate by or into our example; then over time conformable and dilatory impersonation becomes "a concatenation, a genealogie, a pedigree" of vocation.

Donne has as many emphases as he has metaphors for elaborating the person of the parson. For instance, in multiplying the tendencies of vocation in historical and generic terms, he prizes the pedigree of namesakes. That is, our own names accrue a history of offices; thus, the revelation of John and the sermons of John Chrysostom amount to Donne's own personal debts (8.181). As preachers multiply by names, so too the sermons that they preach: "And there is no exercise, that is denoted by so many names, as Preaching" (8.237–38). The nominal dilation of the sermon takes hold of various "Church-exercises" but also of moral treatises, academic orations, and even legal speeches, all expressive of the Holy Spirit's "recommendation of Bountie, of Munificence, of Liberalitie" (8.238). If the notion that "best things . . . are communicable, diffusive" has a way of integrating religious and civil forms, Donne especially thrives on imagining that each preacher's person is filled with the Holy Spirit, dilated into the holy office, and integrated into a holy pedigree. He tells an audience at St. Paul's in 1626 that neither his logic nor his rhetoric but "that Character, and Ordinance which God hath imprinted in me" enable the preacher to persuade others of supernatural matters (7.95).

Donne is prepared to mythologize the preaching ministry in such a way that no contingencies of history or of persons will disrupt God's dispensations. Lest the uncertain inspiration of the minister himself or the imperfect reception of an auditor introduce impediments for the diffusion of grace, Donne imagines the merciful Holy Ghost liquidly sliding "from those gray, and grave, and reverend hairs of his Ministers . . . downe to the *skirts of his garments,*" that is, "through us, upon you also, so, as that you may, so, as that you must finde it in your selves" (8.267). Infusive, diffusive, effusive: Donne's Holy Ghost and his ministers are divested of that person understood as a singular and contingent isolate. There is little chance of error in this pneumatic, almost oily conveyance. Indeed, the Holy Ghost and ministerial ordinance are linked by Donne in this sermon to the comforting Arminian emphasis on accepting at face value God's offer of salvation to all persons and on leaving questions of exactly how human will concurs with divine grace in some doctrinal waste pile.

The great conflict of Donne's Caroline sermons is suggested, however, by his movements from the minister's dilation, the sermon's multiplication, and charity's boundless diffusion back toward the minister's separation, the sermon's dramatic moment, and the judicial inspection of personal qualifications. Each of these latter isolates embodies a corollary drawn from Donne's Arminian God that rivals the former, plural, extrapolations of that God; but whereas the isolates stress God's justice, the pluralities italicize God's loving sincerity.

Donne's sermons dramatize a preacher's pursuit of comfort – made difficult by personal contingencies on both sides of the pulpit – as surely as they mythologize an almost compulsory rhetoric of comfort divested of personal variables. In a 1628 sermon preached to King Charles, Donne hypothesizes the consolation he receives back from his auditors who – not as sinful as he has been – have received consolation from him (8.249). But Donne's dilation of the person into an office, a history, the church, or a plural grammar is intricately tied to the contraction of office, history, church, and grammar into the frightening, frustrating, yet critical contingencies of the person. Once it is admitted that single persons are not foolproof, it is also allowed that such putatively isolated contingency involves larger – historical, social, doctrinal, and dramatic – respects.

One would expect from the third prebend sermon, preached on Guy Fawkes Day, 1626, an allegory of such larger respects, especially of national election. But the sermon opens with a critique of the rigidly predestinarian notion of a God who accepts persons:

First, that God in his punishments and rewardings proposes to himselfe Persons, Persons already made, and qualified. God does not begin at a retribution, nor begin at a condemnation, before he have Persons, Persons fit to be rewarded, Persons fit to be condemned. (7.238–39)

In repeating the point that first God "proposed Persons, Persons in being," Donne reminds his auditors of the plural grammar of a God who would have all souls in heaven. But the overriding thrust of the passage is toward contingency, even though God would rather omit all mention of damnation: "If his owne Glory, and the edification of his Children would beare it, he would not speake at all of judgements, or of those persons that draw necessary judgements upon themselves, but he would exercise our contemplation wholly upon his mercy, and upon Persons qualified and prepared for his gracious retributions . . . onely of Persons disposed, ordained, prepared for them" (7.238–39).

Donne's God looks for evidence in the qualifications and faithful works of persons, not in his own secret devices and desires. Predisposed to compassion, God is nonetheless a sharp-sighted reader of conditions in and actions by each and every one of us. But God's fixation on each person, together with the contingencies that any personal history proliferates, has momentous implications for the minister whose own performances are subjected to anatomy and critique by audiences.

At its most innocent, this anatomy requires each member of the congregation to divide the sermon in order to focus on the part that most applies to his or her own condition and history. Donne finds support for such piecemeal attention in the Gospels themselves (7.329–31, 393). At worst, however, the history of each listener and the mixed constituency of the whole congregation mean that the preacher faces a more vulnerable task. Indeed, in the very same sermon so elaborate about God's proposal of persons, Donne turns from the cosmic theater in which God watches us to the church theater in which Christians watch him. Suddenly questions involve not whether God approves a person but whether the audience approves "me." The grace dispensed by means of the preacher is not mythologized in some awesome colossus, not diffused through some flawless vessel, but hypothesized as the hopes and goals of a passionate "I."

The obsessive "I" – when it dominates stretches of Donne's sermons – is often framed as a hypothesis, an impersonation, or a "consideration" that multiplies not consolation but contingency from one person to all. "And then," Donne projects, "if I have done any good to any of Gods servants, (or to any that hath not been Gods servant, for Gods sake) . . .": thus begins a long sequence of conditional performances in life, print, and pulpit that is weighty enough to carry the preacher into an anticlimax at Judgment Day: "All those things that I have done for Gods glory, shall follow me . . . and meet me with their testimony, That as I did not serve God for nothing . . . I did not nothing for the service of God" (7.255). Thus God, minister, and congregation converge in the painful analysis of persons who cannot be accepted but must be scrutinized now and until the end of time.

However much the "I" in Donne's sermons parades in hypothesis or as a surrogate for every preacher and all Christians, the convergence of sinner and preacher – both with contingencies – tends to isolate the person and performance of Donne the preacher. Dilatory ordinance is never far from personal isolate in Donne's Caroline sermons; the corporate history of sermons is never far from the critical turning point for redemption, lived out by each auditor in every minute of each sermon. In a sermon preached at St. Paul's in 1628, Donne is especially alert to the gap between the dilatory and mythical person of the minister and the isolated auditor who would make use of specific sermons or passages in the temporal processes of spiritual education. Early on, Donne divests the minister of any inadequacies by situating him in the dilated space or genealogical succession of his office. But the minister has his own limits: he can work to make himself an "acceptable . . . messenger" yet this process is insignificant next to each auditor's application of the sermon.

As an example of such an application, Donne characterizes his own method of reading sermons, according to which the wit and power of the very best preachers matter far less than the attention to and use made of the scriptures that they unfold. Later, in celebrating how he himself expands the church through charity and preaching so as to "enlarge, dilate, amplifie God," Donne again modifies dilation by appealing to the work of application carried out by the audience (8.289, 283). Insisting that God's election terminates in persons – "for when he elected me, I was I" (8.282) – he includes the educative process and interpretive habits of his audience among the contingencies that an effusive image of the preacher cannot avoid. Both of these emphases, the struggle for salvation and the widening of its scope, are part and parcel of Donne's critique of rigid Calvinism.

At times, Donne tries to stabilize and guarantee the processes of spiritual education with analogies to the smooth, progressive matriculation of a person from parental nurture through grammar school on to university and a vocation. This seamless, cumulative genealogy of a soul might be consistent with Donne's claim that the Holy Spirit inhabits the iterations of memory more than the agonies of understanding (8.261), but it is at odds with the centrality of contingent persons and histories in Donne's conception of ministry and salvation. His image of mercy flowing without interruption from an effusive Holy Spirit through dilated ministers into all humanity, now and at all times, is countered by a more disruptive, uncertain, and individuated reception of grace at any one time and by the descent of spiritual pedigree through time.

Having fixed his critical eye on audience applications, Donne can blame or pity his auditors for their failure to make God's liberal mercies and ordinances their own. But his most searching and sometimes intemperate meditations on preaching explore the gap between two notions of the minister's own person, the office and the human isolate. Preaching before the king at Whitehall in 1626, Donne traverses the considerable ground from one to the other, beginning with a paean for the "inthronization" of ministers who – as royal priests in their pulpits, clothed in their ordinance "as with a Cloud" – are divested of inadequacies, no matter how "so poore a man . . . stands here." Through such a king, or rather through his non-material, official body, God will "drop raine, poure downe his dew, and sweeten that dew with his honey, and crust that honied dew into Manna, and multiply that Manna into Gomers, and fill those Gomers every day, and give every particular Man his Gomer, give every soule in the Congregation, consolation by me" (7.134).

But even in this sentence, a mythology divested of the contingencies of isolates begins to yield to the high but uncertain stakes of the isolated moment of preaching, with no persons and no ministers accepted by God. Whatever the set lineage and repetition of the liturgy, Donne's ministry – even his famous habit of preaching from notes – keeps reminding auditors of its extemporaneousness, not that of a presumptuous and "mechanical" Puritan but that of a frail, if legitimate, priest. Unlike God, kings, or magistrates, Donne says elsewhere, the speech of a minister is not automatically an effective deed.

As the Whitehall sermon has it, Donne the preacher represents a hem in the garment unfolding the pedigree of priests whose office it is to convey the uninterrupted flow of a liberal grace over time: the perfect family tree from which Donne derives his ordinance can be superimposed on the cosmic garment into which Donne is stitched. But this is Donne's prayer rather than his presupposition, and soon he has returned to the preacher's difficult charge of transforming human animals into godly saints. Especially in his office of shedding mercy on the king, Donne consolidates both the mythological power of ministerial persons and the tireless labor of a human minister whose God accepts no persons. Toward the end of the sermon, he describes himself not as one in a line of kings but as one – perhaps the worst – in a line of sinners.

In the sermons discussed so far, Donne often diverts attention away from the personal isolate of the minister by celebrating his dilatory and multiplicative ordinance. But in many Caroline sermons, Donne admits and studies – even where he rejects or criticizes – the isolation and reception of the minister's own person.

In the fourth prebend sermon (28 January 1627), he chastises his auditors for their simultaneous obsession with and disrespect for the person of their minister. Taking their miscue from the ironic Biblical notion of the foolishness of preaching, auditors usurp

so much liberty in censuring and comparing Preacher and Preacher, nay Sermon and Sermon from the same Preacher; as though we preached for wagers, and as though coine were to be valued from the inscription meerely, and the image, and the person, and not for the metall. You measure all by persons; and yet, *Non erubescitis faciem Sacerdotis, You respect not the person of the Priest*, you give not so much reverence to Gods Ordinance, as he does. (7.319–20)

Whereas (Donne continues) English ministers "preach uncovered" and so show more humility than those of any other church, English auditors are perversely disrespectful to preachers and sermons, the keys to their salvation. But ministers too must have their limits: instructed to preach to everyone, they are also commanded not to cast pearls before swine.

Defenses of ministerial persons are common in Donne's sermons: a sermon at Whitehall (30 April 1626) warns that those who "Lay imputations upon the person [of the minister] . . . will evacuate and frustrate all his preaching; for whether it be in the corruption of our nature, or whether it be in the nature of the thing it self, so it is, if I believe the Preacher to be an ill man, I shall not be much the better for his good Sermons" (7.151). In an Easter sermon at St. Paul's, in 1630, he assails the insincere Christians whose faith is "conditionall" on how much they "like the Preacher . . . the place . . . the company . . . the weather" (9.194). In another sermon, Donne blames the devil for corrupting sermons into ripe occasions for sin, either by leading auditors into misinterpretations or, conversely, by encouraging affectation in a speaker whose gifts supplant his mission in the minds and hearts of the congregation (10.58). In his 1628 sermon on St. Paul's valedictory address, Donne not only claims a rising authority for the ministry as a whole; he also engineers a growing credibility in the lives of each and every minister. For just as preaching has an unprecedented fertility and dignity in Stuart England, so too a preacher near death acquires so much authority that Donne beckons his audience always to pretend that pulpits are deathbeds (8.171).

In the same sermon, however, he admits that preachers, like dying men, can tell lies, all the more reason to separate the message from the messenger. If auditors face this challenge, preachers like Paul had their own burden of persuading wildly different "persons" – some "Persons of better quality" (8.165–66), others whose "Prejudices, and disaffections, and under-valuations of the abilities of the Preacher . . . disappoint the purpose of the Holy Ghost, frustrate the labours of the man, and injure and defraud the rest of the Congregation" (8.166). As ministers, like Paul, must strive to make love to each audience without contaminating the integrity of their mission, so (Donne argues) audiences must respect the minister with "a holy Nobleness . . . A religious good nature, a conscientious ingenuity" but without lapsing into dotage or complacency. Like the Bereans who "searched . . . for confirmation, and not upon suspition" (8.166), congregations must navigate the thin line between too much leniency and too much skepticism.

The Bible itself warns ministers against preaching about themselves, "yet" (Donne responds) "to preach out of our owne history, so farre, as to declare to the Congregation, to what manifold sins we had formerly abandoned our selves, how powerfully the Lord was pleased to reclaime us, how vigilantly he hath vouchsafed to preserve us from relapsing, to preach our selves thus, to call up the Congregation, to heare what God hath done for my soule, is a blessed preaching of my selfe" (9.279). For Donne and his contemporaries, the Solomon of Ecclesiastes makes the most complex example of preaching the person insofar as Stuart readers of the book disagree about whether the royal preacher impersonates an evil man or makes an example of his own evil.[50]

This controversy over Solomon – both interpretations of which Donne allows to stand – clarifies the divide between the competing notions of acting argued among Prynne, Baker, Massinger, and Randolph: is acting at its moral best or worst when it is *sui similis*? Do actors become their parts? Are actors arbitrary and protean impersonators of some other? On one side of the controversy, Solomon impersonates the Epicure and so displaces or subsumes himself; on the other, Solomon confesses his own sins, seeks grace for himself, and pours out himself for all to see. In the rival persons of Donne's Arminianism there is a similar, if not equivalent, distraction between the dilated, mythic preacher who impersonates the idea of his office, and the sinner who unfolds the contingencies of his own transgression and redemption. Thus, he says, searching for the person of the preacher resembles the search for Plato in Socratic dialogues: in some ways nothing could be simpler, in other ways nothing could be more frustrating. Similarly, George Herbert compares catechisms to Socratic dialogues, for the former are designed (he says) not just to instill conformable truths in a child but also to isolate each auditor on the spot.[51]

If a congregation's examination of the minister's person is so dangerous as to warrant its own resistance, the Christian guidelines for ministerial decorum towards persons are no less fraught with traps and enigmas. At the simplest level, Donne preaches, the Bible is at once the most deferential and the most familiar text in its grammar of persons (9.358); among religions, Christianity is the most and least respectful of persons defined as social status. Given these interpretive and behavioral burdens on decorum, Donne returns on a number of occasions to a meditation on the vexed kinship between theater and pulpit, and even more frequently to considerations of the minister's respect to persons defined in various worldly contexts.

On occasion, Donne is intent on divesting the sermon of any theatrical vestige, even when his gloss on a Biblical text sustains a parallel between the theater and pulpit. On Easter day 1628, his sermon on 1 Corinthians 13.12 appears to divide the two quite neatly: whereas nature is likened to a theater and to mirrors, the church is compared to an academy or university. Yet, Donne stresses, both nature and the church are worldly media whose illumination of God is imperfect and obscure. By contrast, in the 1629 sermon preached on the day of Paul's conversion, Donne compares the logic of divine retribution set forth in sermons to the representations of that logic in revenge tragedy, and imagines that an atheist would scoff equally at the political agenda of the one – "to souple and regulate Congregations, and keep people in order" – and at the anthropomorphism of the other.

Ironically, much of the sermon is committed to the natural but contradictory and sinful errors that people make in imposing logics of retribution and prosperity on persons and events. Errors of this kind, Donne says, amount to wrong interpretations of Deuteronomy 10.17 – that God "regardeth no mans person" – and motivate such wildly different figures as the mythographers who invent the Furies and those friends of Job who accuse him of transgression. Our applications of this logic – as hasty as they are neat – come close to the fictional status of Bacon's Idol of the Theater; and in repudiating our mortal and flawed attempts to systematize God's dispensations in this world, Donne anticipates the atheist's critique of those dramatic plots and pulpit logics that dare to judge a "mans person and actions" (8.317). But he also criticizes the atheist's extrapolation of godlessness from human uncertainty and, by implication, the atheist's blindness to the logic of providence unfolded from the pulpit and on the stage.

Donne tends to divest his religion of those theatrical residues that find their way back into his ministry. His stocktaking of the dramatic impersonation as it relates to preaching is most elaborate in those two sermons in which he offers historical discussions of audience reception in theaters and churches: his 1627 Christmas sermon and an undated sermon at St. Paul's. The Christmas sermon examines Moses' excuses for resisting his divine vocation, the fourth of which – the fear that he will not be believed – leads Donne to review the patristic critique of the popularity of plays as against sermons. We hear of the Fathers' earnest complaints about the "scarcity" of their audiences but also of their self-effacing strategies for keeping their audiences in place. In the vein of a passage written by Augustine and explored by Barish,[52] Donne confesses his envy regarding the transfer of theater dynamics to the audiences of the early church, for then more audiences "did countenance that which was said, with a holy murmur, with a religious whispering, and with an ocular applause, with fixing their eyes upon the Preacher, and with turning their eyes upon one another; for those outward declarations were much, very much in use in those times" (8.148–49).

If theatrical effects effaced the malleable and humble Pauline preacher as much as they earned him approval, the Fathers themselves (Donne continues) had conflicting attitudes toward theater's infiltration into the church, sometimes assailing the demonstrative excesses of their audience yet generally approving "a holy delight to be heard, and to be heard with delight. For . . . No man profits by a Sermon, that heares with paine, or wearinesse" (8.149). Disbelief, Donne concludes, is simply the worst in a long series of negative audience responses, including nonattendance, inattentiveness, and noncomprehension, most of which result from responses to the preacher's person as it is defined in performance.

In triangulating relations between the "persons" of God, a minister, and the laity, Donne's undated sermon on 2 Corinthians 5.20 begins with the discrepancy between the honor of the minister's embassy and the foolish humiliation that its zealous performance often yields the person of the minister. Once again, Donne offers a critique and a history of audience reception, beginning with his scorn for members of the congregation who believe they have the leisure and warrant to pick and choose among available sermons. But Paul once again provides the great example of the Christian preacher who would act virtually any part to gain the hearts and minds of his audience. In what amounts to a history of applause in theater and the church, Donne composes a hybrid person of the minister who is as glorious as he is foolish.

Reviewing the evidence of the primitive church for the value of audience response, Donne especially looks to Augustine for an understanding of how the psychology of the theater can strengthen the vital work of the preacher (10.132–33; cf. Barish, 58). But Donne's analyses suggest that applause for the person of the actor is as seductive as it is functional: it can inform the minister that his point is understood, or it can lead a member of the audience to believe a point just because it is applauded. Donne's model, John Chrysostom, is noteworthy for his impatience over an applause that he never succeeded in prohibiting. The closer that audience responses approximate the work of a catechism, Donne allows, the more acceptable they are. But like his model, he is impatient over "those impertinent Interjections" so common (he says) among audiences.

Donne is largely negative, then, if partly wistful, in his assessments of a crowd psychology once powerfully – if always fitfully – useful for spiritual work. For Donne, theatrical effects can impede that work, made more urgent and fragile by the assumption of ongoing contingencies in the processes of salvation. But these very contingencies also single out the performing parson as, in Milton's phrase for Samson, a "person separate to God."[53] The Caroline preacher's vexation over the demands of social decorum in the face of his privileged auditors' contempt adds yet another level to what is already Donne's complex regard of persons.

In puzzling over persons – in the Bible or in the Trinity, in polemical warfare over heresy and in prayer for the dead, in the contingencies of history but also in the dramatic moment of the sermon – Donne shares with Sanderson and Shirley the tireless search for a schema, theory, or standard that might stabilize the most socially implicated of religious circumstances. In the wake of the Civil War, Hobbes attempts to systematize the question of what "A Person . . . is"[54] by subjecting that question to the criteria of geometry and natural philosophy. But well before *Leviathan*, Caroline writers put great stock in the possibility that a right understanding of nature might resolve those dilemmas explored in the myths and ceremonies, imaginations and impersonations forming the circumstances of their Protestant experience.

CHAPTER 6

Nature (I): post-Baconian mysteries

In the 1620s and 30s, the various respects of English Protestantism tend to converge in the study of nature, so that a radical reconsideration of what Seneca calls the pneumatic "circumstance" of human existence serves to center the stocktaking of all the conditions of Protestant faith and practice. With nature as their chief concern, writers trace the network of connections between the advancement of natural studies and all the modes in which they live out their religion: in time (the heroic past, the pivotal present, and the apocalyptic future); in thought (the internal respects of logic, knowledge, error, language production, and imagination); in worship; in the search for salvation; and in a society respectful of persons.

Fully launched in the 1620s, Bacon's Great Instauration prompts the painstaking and complex investigation of religious circumstances – the respects of person, place, time, heroism, thought, and ceremony – through his clarion call for the transformation of natural philosophy.[1] From his announcement of a new method and a comprehensive plan in 1620, through the natural histories and the *De Augmentis* of the first half of that decade, leading up to that recasting of a religious society in the *New Atlantis* of the early Caroline years: Bacon's transformation of the study of nature magnifies the stakes, complicates the dynamics, and promises unprecedented resolution of the intellectual labors taken over the conditions of holy living. This transformation stimulates the naturalized stocktaking of religious circumstances carried out by such diverse writers as George Hakewill, Edward Herbert, William Harvey, and Thomas Browne.

I

As Graham Rees has recently reminded us, Bacon had sketched out the basic six-fold plan of his Great Instauration by the close of the century's first decade. In the second decade, he worked on a number of valuable manuscripts in which he drafted parts of the project.[2] But as William Rawley first averred in his life of Bacon, the crucial years for the composition and publication of the Great Instauration were 1620–26.[3] It has often been argued that King James was Bacon's principal reader; but when it came time for Bacon to justify the new ways of science before God, prince, and public, that honor might just as well be awarded the less intellectually traditional Charles.

After all, Prince Charles was the dedicatee of Bacon's inaugural installment in what was the third, yet in some ways the foundational, part of the Instauration, the natural history. As king, Charles was Rawley's dedicatee for the posthumous *Sylva Sylvarum* (1626), of which there were six Caroline editions and in which Bacon attempted to collect experimental histories of the widest possible range of phenomena, from percolation to imagination. The 1622 *Historia Naturalis et Experimentalis*, in which Bacon features a suitably meteoric *Historia Ventorum*, is prefaced by one of Bacon's most powerful attempts to explain the singularly Christian legitimacy of a natural history without metaphysics, final causes, or any fictional superimposition on phenomena.

Bacon tells Prince Charles that this first installment of the natural history is "like a grain of mustard-seed, very small in itself, yet a pledge of those things which by the grace of God will come hereafter," in this instance the monthly installments of the history to which Bacon has committed himself in the name and for the glory of God. And there might be, he hopes, further work by those others who come to grasp the signal value of "a sound and well-ordered Natural history" as "the key of all knowledge and operation" (Spedding, ed., *Works*, 9.367). The mustard-seed comparison is Bacon's way of formulating the resemblance of true natural philosophy to true faith, both of which involve a humility rewarded with an exponentially heightened power to control phenomena (to move mountains) and to purify the mind (to exorcise demons).

Bacon makes it clear that the circumstance of time demands a directive for philosophical heroism with a religious orientation. He sees himself as part of the production of the "true circumstances," of the mental and methodological re-edification that both requires and creates heroic philosophers in an epic venture not identical to, but still overlapping with, the colonial-cum-skeptical heroism of the church. A philosophical navigation through the pillars of Hercules onward to the New Atlantis – the philosopher's Virginia – is in no way guaranteed; the journey is as fallible as that spiritual search in Chillingworth's theology.

According to the outline of the Great Instauration, the future of heroism depends seriatim on an analysis of the historical conditions of learning; a tour of the circumstances of thought together with strategies for changing those circumstances; a collection and tabulation of all the phenomena of nature; an application of the new epistemological strategies to selected titles from the natural history; some provisional anticipations of abstract conclusions that are subject to further critique, are stepping stones for climbing the pyramid of knowledge toward the axioms of nature, yet are speculative enough to produce what Graham Rees has called a doubleness in Bacon's philosophy;[4] and finally the New Atlantis itself, a religious society living up to its potential.

Every one of these six stages works from the conviction that a re-edified mind and a reconstituted natural philosophy will be more deeply and truly holy than any thinking done before. Thus, there is providence to consider as well as phenomena, the circumstances of time, and the conditions of thought; as Rees puts it, natural philosophy is not to be invaded but is rather to be "bounded" by the provenance of theological legitimacy.[5] Yet in *De Dignitate*, the proper relationship between matters of faith and philosophical inquiry is as difficult for Bacon to articulate as the marriage between mind and nature is for him to effect. And the next generation of natural philosophers understands the accomplishment of this propriety as his most provocative challenge to them. Producing great conflict as well as urgency in this generation, Bacon catalyzes an exacting, complex, and momentous account of the theological circumstances of natural philosophy, and he demands that at long last human beings rightly calibrate what Rees calls its "theological respectability."[6]

Throughout *De Dignitate*, Bacon's reevaluation of how human beings do and should explore the creation in the context of divine providence highlights its double tendencies to segregate and reintegrate the religious and phenomenal circumstances of human learning. In redefining metaphysics so that it is neither prime philosophy nor natural theology but rather the home of formal and final causes apart from a physics of material and efficient causes; in constructing a pyramid of natural knowledge with its base in history or experience and its ascent through physical, then metaphysical causes, and onward to the pinnacle or "summary law of nature" which, according to Ecclesiastes 3.11, is "the work which God worketh from the beginning to the end"; in recommending a properly holy and humble attitude toward our ascent up this scale; in applauding Democritus (against Plato) for having "removed God and Mind from the structure of things"; and in justifying the wisdom of providence for disposing a universe whose material causes are perceived at considerable remove from God's largely hidden intentions for the same: in all these ways, Bacon opposes the Aristotelian suggestion that one can be rid of God by embedding final causes wholly in nature's "figures and motions." Accordingly, particle physicists ought to cherish the secrets of divine design and to posit that material causes lack providence in themselves but require from beyond themselves a "Providence at the last" (Robertson, ed., *Philosophical Works*, 471–72).

From *De Dignitate* to the final paragraphs of the *Sylva Sylvarum*, it is the imagination or the fancy that so often tests the boundaries and proprieties of Bacon's coordination between natural philosophy and theology. Bacon concedes that all good physicians take into account how the mind affects the body. Yet much less studied or understood is the problem of "how far (setting the affections aside) the very imagination of the mind, or a thought strongly fixed and exalted into a kind of faith, is able to alter the body of the imaginant" (Robertson, ed., *Philosophical Works*, 482). Can such a thought-becoming-faith benefit as well as impair our physical welfare? Bacon compares this question to the inquiry into "pestilent" and "sovereign" airs, adding that research into the status, power, and reach of imagination is as profound as it is useful.

Imagination accentuates how the soul-body connection makes an uneasy fit in Bacon's plans for natural history – as surely as the almost endless deferral of the final chapter on revealed religion uneasily fits the survey of historical circumstances and intellectual cartography. In another context, Rees has metaphorized this unease in terms of Bacon's amputation of a religious limb that nonetheless continues to hurt: "the phantom limb still aches."[7] In the *Sylva Sylvarum*, imagination is the Great Instauration's phantom released from the attic at last. Bacon is at pains to sort out how philosophy must thrive without the faculty that, like faith, can convert philosophy into a mustard seed capable of producing enormous, virtually miraculous results from a decidedly finite effort. That is, he studies imagination in order to denude it – this, out of fidelity to nature and as a benefit to deluded minds. But as with church ceremony, so with natural philosophy: fancy is the one delightful, expansive, and powerful faculty that might serve to make the Instauration great. Indeed, the *Sylva*'s final paragraphs – on imagination and its relationship to belief and action – take up the question of how fancy pertains to religious faith and heroic hope. The persistent question in *Sylva* is whether faith-qua-imagination can compel the circumstances that it desires, a question that links natural history not just to the Caroline fascination with the shape, power, and cosmic reach of fancy but also to the heroic utopia of the *New Atlantis* published posthumously with the *Sylva* in 1626. In its assessments of imagination, the *Sylva* places Caroline readers at a cultural crossroads where they might continue without agitation or risk a choice with profound ramifications for how they live and think, even worship, believe, love, and hope.

Bacon's analysis of imagination is only a small portion of his overhaul of the internal and external circumstances of human thought carried out in his assault on the idols in the *Novum Organum*. One of the externals – the Idol of the Theater – was interpreted in the Caroline decades as a version of partiality and, withal, as a respect for persons.[8] As the *New Atlantis* shows, Bacon is committed to refashioning the decorum of Christian society, and such change must commence with the fanciful mind itself. For internal idols – our habits of thought – also involve partisan respects, for instance, the Idol of the Cave, or the individual's addiction to what John Worthington calls "a Pile of private Fancies."[9] Rounding out the idols with the pervasively human or "tribal" diseases of thought and perception, and with the unmoored and unstable language that we exchange in the marketplace of human society, Bacon challenges the readers of his 1620 volume to find hope in the drastic message that "the whole course of the mind must be completely re-started."[10] What is needed is a Virginia Company of the daunting, wretched mental frontier.

As explained in the 1620 volume, then, the six parts of the Great Instauration schematize a comprehensive redefinition of the circumstances of human life in a religious society. The past is rethought in part one's survey and critique of the intellectual globe, and the future is projected in part six, when a fully revised natural philosophy will have transformed the goals and conditions of human society. Then there is the mind in part two, purged and disciplined as much as possible but never entirely, a mind that is still allowed to dream in part five, to theorize in anticipation of what true induction might one day legitimize. Part three focuses on the stuff of nature itself – on its collection and tabulation – though even here subordination of the mind to natural phenomena as they truly are involves sifting through natural histories of the past as well as applying in part four the mind's true method or "legitimate form" of judgment to selected cases.

In all six of its parts, Bacon's Instauration attempts a clarification and stabilization of the relations between faith and philosophy, but it also helps produce the extraordinary Caroline search for the rightful place of natural inquiry within the circumstantial network of English

Protestantism. The complexity of this search derives in part from the multiple appropriations of Baconian thought, in part from the Christian resistance with which the secular intimations of the Instauration met, and in part from Bacon's accentuation of the gulf between what Brian Vickers has dubbed the occult and scientific "mentalities."[11] Far from simplifying the religion of Caroline natural philosophy, Bacon's critique of Paracelsian analogical thinking was strident enough to embolden some of its most impressive representatives in the last phase of this thinking, and it was nuanced enough to encourage those latter day Paracelsians to work at accommodation with dull sublunary induction. The most remarkable instance of this rivalry-cum-accommodation is that figure whom one mid-century polemicist named Bacon's polar opposite, Robert Fludd and his "Mosaical philosophy."

Fludd's was a natural philosophy that in the 1620s and 30s demanded a reckoning, for it retained the greatest possible intimacy between the imaginary and natural circumstances of Protestant belief. As William H. Huffman has accentuated, Fludd was no outsider to the medical profession, no freak in early Stuart philosophy.[12] Quite the contrary, he was a well born, properly educated, royally patronized, orthodox, and licensed member of the College of Physicians. His synthesis of alchemical, Paracelsian, Neoplatonic, and Cabalistic thought coincided with then outlived the zeal both pro and contra the Rosicrucian call for universal reform. Following the work of Allen Debus, Huffman argues that Paracelsian speculation did not translate necessarily into outrageous practice; its chemistry had a practical bent, could be reconciled with Galenic medicine, and would scarcely prevent Fludd from working as a censor for the College.[13]

In short, the natural philosophy of the 1620s and 30s was made all the more complex by virtue of the fact that none of the contestants could be sent packing as an obvious quack. Fludd's "Mosaical philosophy" is unflinchingly theological and occult. With Bacon, then, Fludd embodies a turning point for the study of natural philosophy within English Protestantism, for his insistence on an alchemical philosophy serves two conflictive purposes: it stands in bold opposition to those more mechanically minded philosophies that uncomfortably situate providence and spirit rather far outside natural processes; yet it caricatures those various quasi-theological philosophies whose presuppositions are uneasily subject to a naturalizing critique by mechanical, Baconian, or traditional Aristotelian and Galenic thinkers. Thus, Kepler's accentuation of the difference between his and Fludd's cosmic harmonies is meant to erase traces of similarity; meanwhile, Fludd criticizes what in his view is erroneous alchemy – for example, Patrick Scot's contention in *The Tillage of Light* that the philosopher's stone is predominantly allegorical – as much as the empirical approaches to the weapon salve. Between Bacon and Fludd, natural philosophy in the 1620s and 30s has what for modern readers are both clear and curious logics: no one would mistake Bacon for Fludd, but the latter can speak of "atoms" in a pneumatic, magical context, and Bacon cannot get spirits off his naturalizing mind.[14]

Written throughout the 1630s and published in 1638, Fludd's final synthesis of his philosophy proposes scripture as the guide *nonpareil* for leading "judicious" students "through the confused Labyrinth of the creature, unto the bright Essence of the Creator." Moving up and down between the creatures and their Creator, and with careful study of the spiritual emanations, alchemical mysteries, and analogical patterns along the way, the Mosaical philosopher works with Genesis in one hand and a weather glass in the other "to search out the mysteries of the true Wisdom in this world, and the creatures thereof; but by penetrating with a mental speculation and operative perfection into the earthly Circumference or mansion thereof, and so to dive, or attain by little and little unto the heavenly Pallace."[15]

What makes the weather glass especially apt for Fludd is its encapsulation of cosmic design, spiritual contrariety, and divine alchemy. "In strict adherence to the microcosm–macrocosm correspondence," Huffman writes, "the rule is: as above, so below" (131). Thus, in those rarefactions and condensations of air prompted by the movements of the Sun, the weather glass measures the world's but also humanity's spiritual pulse. Tracked by theology from center to circumference, God breathes out, dispensing warmth, light, good spirits, medicinal winds, sympathy, concord, life, purity, humility, sweetness, justice, and action. Traced by philosophy from circumference to center, God breathes in, condensing the opposites of all these qualities in much the same alchemical separation that results from the Spirit's creative fiat. One glimpses this alchemy in the delicate, pneumatic balance in human functions but also in the operation of the winds, in the interlocking and pyramidic proportions of the created world, and in the human arts, those apes of nature such as the "artificiall Machin" of the weather glass in which the larger world is contracted. God's breath is all and does all in the sympathies and antipathies at work in the cosmos.

In defending such magical phenomena as the weapon salve, Fludd envisions a rapprochement with Bacon that might keep the heroic, social, and imaginative thrust of natural philosophy centered squarely where it belongs: on the religion of Protestants. After all, in the final paragraph of the *Sylva Sylvarum*, Bacon investigates the validity of sympathetic cures at a distance. But the heated and notorious controversy over the salve that erupted in the 1630s also drove a wedge between those naturalists who would focus on material causes and those who always look to the first (divine) and final (providential) causes. The salve, supposed to cure wounds at a distance from the wounded, pushes the metaphysical and operational limits of natural agency to the brink of mystery. Is nature enigmatic or rational? Is its rationality mechanical, pneumatic, or scriptural? Are its subtleties of sympathy and antipathy comparable to or far removed from the conceptions of the human mind? In the 1620s and 30s, many writers believe that human beings stand at a crossroads regarding the circumstances of their own position in God's creation.

On one road Fludd represents the conviction that the circumstances of Protestant living are welded together by God's own spirit. On the other road, Bacon maintains that the hope of Protestant society requires a new understanding of how God's providence frames the heroic labors undertaken among those circumstances. In between the two, natural philosophers struggle to map out a space in which atoms can be magically animated by God and spirit can be parsed to the brink of particulate physics. Certainly writers as diversely qualified as John Hales and William Harvey agree that the role of nature in the experience of faith is often mysterious and epitomizes an English church in search of its own spirit.

Indeed the salve controversy has a way of reminding the medical thinkers of the 1620s and 30s that natural philosophers should cultivate their own casuistry of circumstances – and not just because the weapon salve offers a case of conscience. This classical approach to the burden of curing human beings is elaborated in James Hart's KLINIKE, *or the Diet of the Diseased* (1633), the introduction to which criticizes interlopers in the field of medicine. A recurring claim in this critique is that the properly trained physician possesses a mastery of therapeutic variables or what Hart repeatedly calls the "severall circumstances."[16] Not unlike the Arminian "person," the transmutable church heroic, or the protean fancy, variation in medical procedure tests the limits of the rule of reason, a state of affairs made worse (Hart laments) by the commonplace tendency for parsons to double as physicians. Indeed it is imagination more than anything else that challenges the talent of the circumstantially savvy doctor. Rejecting Oswald Croll's idea "*that the whole heaven is nothing else but mere imagination, sending downe upon this inferiour world*, fevers, pestilences, *and the like, without any corporeall instruments*," Hart rebukes those supposedly powerful magi who claim control over this pervasive spirit: where were they (he mocks) in 1630 when there was a critical drought (360–61)?

Hart also suggests that the death of the salve and of magic somehow follows from the recent disappointments in Protestant heroism. This point emerges when, unhappy both with the interloping parsons and theological physicians of his time, Hart appends to his critique of imagination and spirit an extended repudiation of the weapon salve, including the Fluddean conviction that it is divinely inspired or scriptural. Again following Libavius, he adds that it is the Protestants who claim miraculous powers over and above those of Moses: in the vein of Paracelsian bombast, advocates of the salve maintain that they can make an instrument effect whatever they desire via spirits and imagination – that they can heal at a distance, restore severed heads, raise storms, awaken the dead, crown a man with horns, force people to love or hate, and scatter armies so that "It is a wonder the Emperour can find none of these so usefull artificers now in his so great need" (381). This last quip about the Thirty Years War is Hart's most devastating proof that fancy's power is sorely limited. For Hart, it is all the more offensive for Mosaic philosophers to exaggerate the powers of fancy when Protestant heroism has been languishing on the battlefields of Europe.

II

For Bacon, efficient and material causes are the domain of physics, in contrast to the metaphysics of formal and final causes. For Fludd, Jehovah is *the* "essential efficient cause."[17] For Bacon, *pneuma* is mysterious only so long as natural inquiries are insufficient. For Fludd, the winds and other meteorological phenomena amount to "an airy spirit, of a mean consistence, inspired and animated by the breath or inspiration of JEHOVA, the which he draweth forth of his treasury, to execute his will and pleasure, either by way of malediction and vengeance, or of benediction and misericord." Not exhalation from below but mysterious emanation from above, wind is inextricable from God's wisdom, or at least "there appeareth no difference between an angelicall creature, and the aire, so divinely inspired" and responsible for exacting justice and distributing mercy (*Mosaicall Philosophy*, 91).

For alchemists supporting Fludd's approach to nature, physical circumstance threatens to debase the method that would sublimate it; for advocates of Baconian induction, epistemological circumstance threatens to neglect or distort the elemental world that God has wrought. But if Fludd and Bacon represent the polarities of natural philosophy in the 1620s and 30s, they also indicate a large field in which Caroline writers explore the interstices between the human mind, the efficient and material causes of nature, and the hieroglyphs of divinity.

In resisting physical circumstance, alchemists looked inward, for example in Patrick Scot's *The Tillage of Light, Or, A True Discourse of the Philosophicall Elixir, commonly called the Philosophers Stone* (London, 1623), one of the "spiritual alchemies" of the early seventeenth century.[18] In the 1620s, furthermore, the perception that an inductive natural philosophy is awash in material causes and physical structures provokes some religious writers to caution against the encroachments of atheism. One prominent example is Thomas Jackson's commentary on the Apostle's Creed. Jackson is famous for the Arminian notions unfolded in his twelve-book exposition (1613–57), especially in parts five (*The Originall of Unbelief* [1625]) and six (*The Treatise of the Divine Essence and Attributes* [1628–29]). But, as Sarah Hutton has argued, no less critical in Jackson's scheme of values is his natural theologian's strident opposition to logical induction, which is driven in part by his sympathy for Neoplatonic illumination and the intuition of the so-called ancient theologians (Moses, Orpheus, Hermes, Pythagoras).[19] Under the category of induction, Jackson includes Aristotelian scholasticism but surely also the recently unleashed Great Instauration.[20]

But Jackson's opposition to induction diverts attention from his own promotion of human involvement in the *ordo salutis*. In chapter 12 of the treatise on divine attributes, he attempts to reconcile divine providence with an element of fortuity in the claim that God has decreed mutability in human affairs (5.292). Given the Epicurean legacy of the fortuitous universe – a legacy increasingly vigorous in the 1620s and 30s – Jackson worries over the respectability of his case. He insists that arguments allowing for some measure of both free will and chance are mistakenly deemed interchangeable with the irreligious assaults on providence made famous by Epicurus. Meanwhile, fraudulent arguments from necessity are mistaken for lineal descendants from the certainty of God's decrees.

If Jackson risks the charge of Epicureanism in his theology, his interpretation of nature in matters of worship again deflects profanity to his iconoclastic critics. In *The Originall of Unbelief*, he notes that rural scenery is conducive to true devotion as well as pagan idolatry, a point that reduces sermons to surrogates for flowers and trees (4.186). In a paean for simple wonders of the countryside, Jackson offers the obligatory warning against pagan idolatry, but his main targets are those jaded souls for whom God's creation and mundane operations have become too familiar or have simply been muted in the tumult of urban life. Hence, he surmises, we are compelled by a need for retreat from the noise of everyday life to escape into that urban *locus amoenus*, the temple (4.186–87). Jackson's conception of the temple as a surrogate Forest of Arden harmonizes ecclesiastical and seasonal cycles as do Herrick and other Caroline preservers of merry old England. But Jackson offers more: he conflates cathedral and pastoral so that as in Milton's "Il Penseroso," a contemplative soul fancies an inviolate forest at the very moment that he enters the temple. In resisting the irreverence of the 1620s, he suggests, an urban Hermes or Orpheus might find much for his delectation in stained glass or a pretty altar.

Jackson aims simply to applaud how the pastoral temple encourages us to fashion "our behaviour and affections, as if we had gone out of an old world into a new, or travelled from one kingdom to another people" (4.188). The temple, then, is the only true Virginia, and it requires not colonization or nonconformity but humility and reverence. Yet Puritanism, he laments, has ruined the church pastoral as surely as induction threatens the creed, so that even those clergy who should defend the church lack the spiritual means, sense of honor, and mental fortitude. In short, naturalists and iconoclasts have produced the very pluralists and impoverished church that they decry – or so Jackson believes, ignoring the hexameral model, Protestant warrant, and Edenic aims of the decade's great proponent of induction.

Jackson's opponents retort that his theology of will and his emphasis on the landscape of the temple are mired in the carnality of human and ecclesiastical circumstance. But even writers less committed to the beauty of holiness worry that in the 1620s, a newly revived attention to the circumstances of nature detracts from English spirituality. In writing about nature at its ugliest – during a time of plague – George Wither offers what might be called a foil to Bacon's new natural histories, emphasizing the supernatural dispensations of the plague over recent tendencies to naturalize its contagion into secondary causes. First in the manuscript *History of the Pestilence* (1625), then in the elaborated print version, *Britain's Remembrancer* (1628), he presents his work to the dedicatee of Bacon's histories, Charles, but shifts the meaning of "history" away from "inquiry" toward a diachronic and prophetic account of divine justice and mercy. Accordingly, his refrain condemns those naturalists whose explanations of disease are unable to account for the selectivity of contagion.

Like Jackson, however, Wither wishes not to appear naive, especially not before the sophisticated Charles; in both versions but more elaborately in print, he concedes the validity of studying natural causes and even maintains that such a pursuit needs to be carried out more diligently as well as more piously. Much more than Jackson, Wither seeks to analyze the entanglement of two contemporary problems: the question of which causes signify most in the case of nature, and the problem of which ecclesiastical means most facilitate salvation. Just as it is mandatory to use all ordinary and licit means of escape from the plague, he argues, so too one should resist rigid views of reprobation and deploy all ordinary means to work out salvation.[21]

In addition to caricatures of the impious "naturalist," Caroline writers offer reductive critiques of Bacon himself. One noteworthy example is Henry Reynolds's *Mythomystes* (1633?), a counter to Bacon's surveys of learning and evaluations of myth. In his "survay" of ancient and modern poetry, Reynolds supports the arguments for the decay of nature by focusing attention on the decline in the "frute of the Fancy," especially mythic theology.[22] Contending that modern learning is degenerate, he hearkens back to the ancients now libeled by those wits who vainly imagine they hold the keys to the advancement of the arts. Poets, he says, have largely reneged on their duty to decipher and preserve the natural and divine mysteries encoded in the mythic hieroglyphics of the ancients. In their place, "many Prose-men excellent naturall Philosophers in these late times" have taken up the hieratic mantle and are seeking the difficult truths hidden in ancient myth and primordial nature alike (162). Some of these latter day magi understand that "there is nothing of greater efficacy then the hymnes of *Orpheus* in naturall Magick, if the fitting musick, intention of the minde, and other circumstances which are knowne to the wise, bee considered and applyed" (166). Thus prose magicians have supplanted modern poetasters in the imaginative work of transmitting ancient philosophy, including those myths that preserve the exemplary virtue of ancient "Heroes" but featuring those that spell out chemical and natural mysteries.

A number of Bacon's earliest readers contest the Great Instauration – as an atheistic trap for the soul; as a cultural and philosophical quagmire; and as a strange new discourse surpassing understanding. But even Bacon's sympathetic readers were keen to fashion some ready and easy courses out of the natural and methodological labyrinth in which his Instauration had landed them. In the 1630s, the most noteworthy example of the latter are the associates of Samuel Hartlib. Reacting against the specters of skepticism, Protestant disunity, and the trauma of losses against the imperial forces, Samuel Hartlib, John Dury, and briefly John Amos Comenius looked to England for a haven in which the general reformation of religion, learning, and nature might be initiated.[23] Central to their post-Rosicrucian, wartime schemes of unification and reform was the formulation of a method by which the human mind might know all things – certainly, expeditiously, and synthetically. The Hartlib papers make it clear that Bacon's new organon, while by no means the only method and perhaps not even the best, was credited with momentously altering European consciousness about the key to apocalyptic reformation.[24]

Given their master plans, however – the unification of the churches; the communication of all real and fruitful knowledge, both spiritual and natural, to all Christian people; the apocalyptic reformation of society; the *coup de grace* delivered on skepticism – Hartlib and his affiliates respond in two ways to the complexities and labors of Bacon's Instauration. One, as Hugh Trevor-Roper has argued, is to reduce Baconianism to a heroic, apocalyptic, and technological caricature.[25] Another, contrary to those who like Pym urged a full and vigilant reading of the *Novum Organum*, expresses dissatisfaction with the difficulty and intricacy of Bacon's project.[26] What these thinkers wanted in the face of massive warfare, heightened skepticism, and Protestant fragmentation was a force at once more ambitious and more efficient, a method aimed at the acquisition and communication of all knowledge and efficacious in redressing the woes of Christian society now, not at some uncertain time in the future.

In turn, their notion of "pansophia" was accused of ignoring the burden of circumstance. In response to Comenius's work, Philip Müller contended that those "matters in hand are not all . . . constituted in that way, since they depend on an unstable principle, the will of man, varying motion, etc.; how then can we hope for an infallible science in everything, especially in Ethics? Laws too are valid according to circumstances of time, person and place; a fact which Comenius recognises when he excludes the study of jurisprudence from his *Pansophia*."[27] If Hartlib and Dury hoped to advance English Protestant society beyond the burden of circumstances, then this was a project that only a severely reduced Bacon could be thought to support. Having criticized Bacon for his method's labors, uncertainties, and narrow materialism, then, advocates of pansophia had to deflect the charge that their project was an impossible fancy. For, they urge, pansophia "is no dreame, but a reall worke."[28]

III

If some critics and advocates reduce Bacon's grand proposition to a manageable size, other cultural brokers demonstrate that after the 1620s, the religion of natural philosophy can never again be a simple or naive matter. The Caroline perception that the presuppositions behind natural theology are losing in unanimity and stability what they are gaining in sophistication is underscored by a correlative division in church polity. The two fissures – one in natural philosophy, the other in church polity – hardly map onto one another with neatness and precision. But as Guibbory has shown, Laudian support for conformity and ceremony stands in a mutually constitutive relationship with holistic, seasonal, and festive understandings of the natural world. For Thomas Browne, the reverse is also true: that those sectarian forces rending the Church of England into pieces are at least analogous to the atoms into which Epicureans would divide the world, and that their claims on superior holiness are in fact the ready and easy way to widespread profanity.

In *Religio Medici*, the hieroglyphic and flexible or metaphorical approach to natural wonders is interwoven with the desire to answer the main challenge delivered most famously by Bacon himself, namely, that the students of nature in the 1620s and 30s launch a new, and newly arduous, natural history, all the while refining a not so new, but newly rigorous, methodology. This challenge, however, is double, for the rigors of the new philosophy must fully support the providential assumptions of a largely deductive approach that speaks to, but not always from, the experience of mercury or silkworms. It is inevitable that at some level the rigorous and flexible desiderata would conflict. But Browne has tripled the challenge, for the *Religio Medici* interweaves the "severall circumstances" of his natural studies with the complicated circumstances of his faith – so that his spiritual recreations have as much to do with the church, the Bible, and salvation as they do with the expansive hieroglyphics of nature.[29]

That the practices of the church and the laws of nature might be co-defendants would surprise no one in post-Hookerian England; but Hooker is attempting to stand outside the circumstances of faith so that their universal (if diachronically flexible) warrant might be confidently asserted. Nature matters to Hooker only as a metaphysical law that lends support to English ecclesiastical polity. But in 1635–42, Browne urges on his reader two major modifications of the Hookerian argument: first, that authenticity depends on one's writing from within the circumstances

of nature and religion, a point shared by Lord Herbert, and second, that
the relationship between natural law and ecclesiastical polity can only
be complicated by Baconianism as well as by the complicated geography of wartime Protestantism. As Browne understands in composing the
Religio in the second half of the 1630s, then increasingly with his revisions
in the early 1640s, the wars of Protestantism are not at their grimmest
against a papal Antichrist. Rather, English Protestants are at war with
themselves to decide whether the spirit of ceremony or the violence of
iconoclasm best represents the Church of England. As Guibbory has
shown, Browne's positions on church polity and on natural theology often imply one another; but the problem with a correlation, say, between
church ceremony and natural holism is that Browne's position on each
is fractured, not to mention his view of how conflicts within church and
nature pertain to one another. To make matters even messier, Browne
is intent on engaging the circumstances defining human thought and
social organization at the same time. In short, "Browne's 'singularity'
and skepticism distance him from Laudian rigor and threaten to desta-
bilize the Laudian ceremonialist order that Browne would defend."[30]
Far more skeptical than the Arminian works of Richard Montagu and
the ceremonialist apologia of other Laudians with which, as Guibbory
has shown, his *Religio* dovetails, Browne conducts a dialogue between his
own thoughts over how a natural theology, ceremonial church, and cohe-
sive epistemology might guarantee each other in an age of materialists,
sectarians, and skeptics.

In the opening paragraph of the *Religio*, Browne's complex religion
and no less complex natural philosophy are joined in those "severall
circumstances" that threaten to drive them apart and, therefore, to leave
Browne with incoherence at best and atheism at worst. Thus, his implied
critic would take note not just of his natural and medical preoccupations
but also of his "indifferency" in religious manner, all in an effort to prove
Browne's lack of faith. For Browne, however, what critics might take as
a lack of spiritual conviction is in fact an irenic, composite, and true
religion, one that he justifies in terms of a cohort of religious authorities,
locates on a map of the faith, then hybridizes as the amphibious character
of a Christian.

In the instance of the cohort, Browne builds the case that religious
education, the self-evident truths of the Bible, and the instrument of
reason serve to differentiate the author from other Christians and religions, but that charity rejoins them again. The same double movement –
differentiate, then unite – is repeated when Browne maps contemporary

Christianity, with English reformed spirituality the marker that sets him apart but also situates him in a sameness that stretches from Christ through the Apostles, Fathers, and Martyrs. It is repeated again when Browne offers himself as the hybrid character, at first morose and severe like a "Puritan," then resourceful in converting noteworthy Catholic errors into *adiaphora* that might be put to good use.

Regarding papists, Browne emphasizes, one should pray either "with them, or for them" so that Catholic churches and habits of worship amount in turn to spaces that a good Christian might safely enter, to unfortunate customs that one might pity at a distance, and to the tendencies or humors of Browne's sociable disposition. Iconoclastic violence fails to set aside mere circumstance in ecclesiology, for whether it is holy water, the crucifix, or the Ave Mary bell, one should conclude with civility that "though misplaced in circumstance, there is something in it of devotion." Even though (he modifies the point) the papists have "erred in one circumstance," a true Protestant should not "erre in all, that is in silence and dumbe contempt" (63).

What is unclear in the opening paragraphs of the *Religio* is whether the "severall circumstances" of Browne's natural studies contribute mainly to the atomization of the church or to the reconstitution of its sameness and holism. This question is complicated once Browne's discussions of nature have mapped out the landscape of philosophy. Clearly Browne's charitable Protestant has a complex relationship to circumstance; as the context of belief, circumstance must be ignored if one's own faith and reason are to create spiritual fruits of potentially superstitious practices (thus, "misplaced"). But the Brownean Protestant must also rediscover the meaning and scope of context, with the charitable and civil Browne adaptable and sympathetic to any church, nation, or place. Speaking, kneeling, and loving, this Browne avoids error in all circumstance, that is, in the circumstance of all that surrounds us, from the churches of the world to the world-as-temple in which no creature is ugly or repugnant.

In natural philosophy, too, there is the Baconian call to decontextualize nature in order to rid it of the idols of human invention, error, and sin. But in the 1620s and 30s, there is a no less powerful and perhaps even more pervasive summons to recontextualize nature, to understand anew how nature articulates with human art, thought, aspiration, history, sociopolitical identity, cosmic destiny, and faith. For Browne, the atomic worldview unhinges meaningful natural context as surely as "atoms in Divinity" destroy the unified church. But he is no less interested in or committed to the questions raised, and meanings made possible, by the atomization of both nature and faith. With atomization, the circumstances of nature are expanded, rendered precarious, yet made more critically precise, while the circumstances of a singular faith are contracted, internalized, yet threaten to permit heresy in the church, with vacuous "gaps" the corollary of "atoms in Divinity."

In keeping with circumstance understood as unanchored particulars, Browne is always prepared to analyze his singular faith and to investigate the "strict particulars . . . dispersedly found" in nature.[31] Throughout *Religio Medici*, Browne contributes to the fissures in the church and in nature that he so strenuously resists. No less challenging for the pious doctor is the question of how Christianity and natural philosophy address the concerns of one another. In the wake of Fludd and Bacon, whose projects would serve to epitomize the rival "mentalities" of his time, yet whose pneumatic and even teleological commitments intersected, Browne maps the cultures of Protestantism and philosophy, apart and together. And he pursues his map in a searching, unsystematic fashion, with dogmatic attempts to hold intellectual and religious culture together but also with skeptical concessions to culture's nagging and undeniable incoherence – a skepticism that, converted into charity, can effect only a "soft and flexible" coherence.

First comes *religio* alone. Attempting to contract his own "into a lesser circle," Browne unfolds his "double obligation" to the Church of England, that is, his legal and rational-cum-devotional allegiance. So the "lesser circle" is a church, but it is also a complex Protestant who disclaims allegiance – to Luther, Calvin, Dort, Trent – and replaces blind affiliation with a hierarchy of authorities comprising the Bible, the church, and "the dictates of [his] owne reason" (64).

But this contraction of the religious circle is quickly reversed when Browne opposes scurrility and dispute among Christians. In the 1630s, the more zealous sort of English Protestant is apt to interpret Browne's emphasis on charity, harmony, and peace as code for crypto-popery and persecution. For Browne, however, charity and harmony are at once Laudian and non-partisan. He maintains that charity is made all the more appropriate insofar as most Christians have their full share of uncertainties. Skepticism can entail both a quiet allegiance to one's own church and an unwillingness to condemn any church.

But Browne's chief witness of the link between doubt and charity – himself – returns the focus of book 1 back to faith and reason – that is, to the inner search for certainty and truth – and with this return, neither questions of religious authority alone nor the vexed relationship between the faithful Christian and the rational philosopher can be dissolved into a soft allegory or flexible paradox. Some of Browne's doubts involve a question of method made all the more prominent after Bacon and integral to the controversies surrounding the revival of ancient atomism in the 1620s and 30s, namely, the question of what phenomena should be subjected to physico-rational analysis. Thus Browne has been tempted into the heresy that the soul enters the grave with the body, in part because philosophy cannot disprove it; and he is relieved by the lack of evidence for the very organic container of the soul for which his commitment to anatomy compels him to search.

Browne delights in the theologizing of natural philosophy – no one more so. Silkworms, the philosopher's stone, and mercury all serve as instances in which the alchemical experiences of the hieroglyphs of nature enrich and deepen his love of and faith in the mysteries of religion. But the subjection of theological matters to philosophical analysis is an impulse that disturbs Browne precisely because, as he portrays it, he has never quite been able to quash it. That Browne compares heresy to atoms is not just a popular metaphor of the 1640s; it also suggests an association in his mind between the gaps in religion (both personal and ecclesiastical) and the Epicurean subjection of even divinity to atomic and rational analysis. After all, "gaps" resemble that Epicurean vacuity or "empty cantons" of nature that many seventeenth-century writers, including Browne, resist *a priori*, even as they (Robert Burton and Henry More among them) are learning to baptize atoms and void in the name of Christ.

Browne's troubled relationship with the exposure of theological questions to the double-faced critique of philosophy is best glimpsed in his treatments of two problems, the nature of human rationality and the presence of monstrosity in God's creation. In paragraphs 8–10 of the first book, reason undergoes extraordinary and rapid-fire changes. First, reason is the candle of the Lord and approximates the kind of worshipful imagination that exfoliates in contemplating those "many things untouch'd, unimagin'd, wherein the libertie of an honest reason may play and expatiate with security and farre without the circle of an heresie" (69). With heresy suddenly in a circle, and orthodoxy permeating or bounding the virtually limitless space of the religious imagination, Browne echoes the language of Robert Burton at the outset of the "Digression of the Air," a text in which free expatiation journeys discursively through atomic theories, plural worlds, and conjectures of infinite space.

But Browne's muse takes flight at "wingy mysteries," with reason assuming the following values or identities: a faculty intimate with faith and impressive in its demonstrations of religion's "ayery subtilties"; an instrument of spiritual recreation that pursues mysteries but only to a limit, at which point only faith obtains; an extremely limited faculty that errs wretchedly in trying to force the certainty of "impossible" spiritual mysteries into arid definitions at the expense of evocative allegories and fanciful metaphors – and indeed its limits undercut reason's ability to understand even such "obvious effects" of nature as light; and at worst a rebellious secret agent of Satan that seduces the believer into naturalizing all phenomena (including miracles) and into raging for empirical proof when such ocular demonstrations in fact work at cross purposes with faith in the Trinity, Incarnation, and Resurrection. At best, reason has the pliability of a faithful imagination, at worst it is demonic, and in the middle its instrumentality, like that of a hawk, is variously effective and "haggard" or "unreclaimed" (71).

Unlike Fludd, however, who condescends to empiricism, Browne is compelled to take seriously a rationality that insists on experiential proof and an Epicurean critique of providence that stresses the imperfections and fortuities of the natural world. In claiming that it is "no vulgar part of faith to believe a thing not only above, but contrary to reason, and against the arguments of our proper senses," Browne has not entirely abandoned the right, pliable, and virtually fanciful rationality of "an easie and Platonick description" (72, 70).

Nonetheless, he splits reason into rationalities, one of which is decidedly inductive in orientation. It should be remembered too that nature and history, like nature and scripture, nature and art, and nature and the church, are mutually definitive in Browne's meditations. That is, nature is no separate issue for Browne but rather part and parcel of his exploration of the full circumstances constituting English Protestant faith – from the stuff of thought and imagination to the more "sociable" disposition of charity.

When he comes to God's attributes, especially eternity, Browne traverses the intellectual space from considerations of reason to a reassessment of natural theology. Given the additional mystery lent God's eternity by the doctrine of the Trinity, according to which no person has "priority," he somewhat ambiguously expresses wonder at Aristotle's notion of an eternal world. One might think that Browne would go on to repudiate these double eternities, but instead he considers various ways in which a philosopher might arrive at such a parallel, including the trinitarian structure of our souls and the Pythagorean "secret Magicke of numbers" but generally encouraging natural philosophers to read "this masse of nature" as a shorthand of, ladder to, and portrait of divinity (73). Browne's support of natural philosophy is not as enthusiastic here as it is elsewhere: the divine alphabet in nature is lower-case, the light that it provides is like a candle "in the abysse of knowledge," and the equivocation of its "shapes" is potentially as strained, even monstrous, as it is mediatory. Just so Browne's notion of "amphibious" man: the five natures and lives instantiated in human beings fill in the gaps of the scale of creation; in doing so, they prevent vacuity or cosmic gaps; and thus they guarantee the warrant of a providential view of the world: God's method is made good by this creature. But the existence of reason in "divided and distinguished worlds" suggests that the circumstances of human life are always divided, always incoherent or conflictive, caught between Fludd and Bacon, and like the emblems of monsters in this period, a ragtag assembly of various animal parts. As such, amphibious man is reminiscent of the cosmic imperfection that Epicureans invoke in undoing providential method (103).

In considering God's wisdom, Browne (like Bacon) conceives of natural studies as a properly humble jurisdiction for those Christians who would know themselves, discover something "asquint" about God, and rest contented with the method that explores "the obvious effects of nature," not "Contemplations Metaphysicall" (75). But any Baconian resonance evaporates when Browne revisits the Aristotelian four causes. Bacon segregates material and efficient causes from formal and final, emphasizes the need for attention to the former two, redefines "formal" so as to concretize it in the material constituents and structures of phenomena, and cautions against the hegemony of the final cause. But for Browne, it is the final cause that he will always "grope after in the workes of nature, on this hangs the providence of God"; structure matters less, that is, than "predestinated ends." If it is a fine thing to pursue the matter, form, and efficient cause of, say, an eclipse, it is better "to profound farther" into the reason why providence has set the planets in such a course (77). Natural philosophers from Aristotle to Suarez are to be judged according to their appreciation of the final cause.

In the *Religio*, then, the obvious and "onely indisputable axiome in Philosophy" is that nature does nothing in vain, nothing imperfectly or monstrously. In the *Religio*, this axiom leads to the unflagging attention to divinity – and the right understanding of it too – in nature's "common Hieroglyphicks," "mysticall letters," and "universall and publik

Manuscript" (78–79). Rightly understood, providence is more wonderful than matter in motion, and more artful and regular, if more circuitous, than miracles. Twice Browne insists that his focus on nature does not lead to the idolization of nature. But more worrisome to Browne than the replacement of first cause with second causes is the specter of the Epicurean critique according to which putatively honest assessments of nature reveal its imperfections. If Chillingworth focuses on an apology for an imperfect church, Browne must defend together an imperfect church and a flawed natural world, for as he never tires of repeating, their divine providence is one and the same.

Browne almost never simply asserts the beauty and purposeful perfection in things; no matter how elaborate his defenses of God's artistry in each of and among all the kinds, he usually lets on that God's providence is an embattled notion. Ruling out deformity even among toads, bears, and elephants, Browne defends the adherence of these species to God's will and the decorum with which their outsides manifest "their inward formes" (80). Even so, he considers two additional problematic cases of ugliness and deformity, namely, monstrosities (which are said to have their own remarkable ingenuity and singular contrivance) and the chaos (which possessed no deformity because God had not yet supplied anything with form).

In concluding his section on the providential art of nature, Browne proffers the Renaissance commonplace that both art and nature serve providence, with the corollary that nature is God's art and that human art is a constituent of nature. But lumped together with these received opinions is a theory nuanced rather differently, namely, the notion that art perfects nature, that art and nature create divided worlds, and that the world would remain disorderly without human artistry. This series of ideas opens up a range of possibilities for nature: that nature's perfection is a human invention, either in technology or in imagination; that nature is sufficient in itself but man can create other worlds either better or worse (more monstrous) than nature per se.

It might be argued, then, that art makes good the providence of God, either as a part of that providence or as the kind of fiction-making substitute for that providence that the Epicurean critique is meant to explode. In Browne's *Religio*, moreover, as in Caroline religious culture more widely, debates over the status of human invention have offshoots in the writings for and against ceremony in the church itself. Indeed, Browne's views of invention and ceremony are at times as polemical as the heated exchanges between, on the one side, William Prynne, Henry

Burton, and John Bastwick and, on the other, their Laudian critics, at times exploratory in the manner of Herbert's poetry. The nature-art debate and its theological pertinence are not new in the 1620s and 30s; but in Browne's text, as in Robert Burton's *Anatomy of Melancholy* and other contemporary dealings with the Epicurean revival, the debate is newly heightened and sophisticated. For these writers, the desiderata of church worship are inevitably caught up in the natural theologian's consideration of whether human art can improve on or even harmonize with divine creations.

Elsewhere Browne backtracks from a dalliance with putative monstrosity and disorder. On the matter of how our souls are transmitted to our bodies, he is inclined toward their direct and divine infusion, but this hypothesis is unsettled by the case of monsters, those products of human and bestial copulation that have some semblance of reason. This example hardly settles the question of how art relates to nature, for Browne hedges on whether he has observed or imagined these monsters. Natural philosophy fares no more clearly: anatomy positively presents us with "a masse of mysterious Philosophy" large enough to convert pagans; as Huntley has shown, Browne and William Harvey are indebted to the teleological impulses of Renaissance anatomy and in particular of Galen's *De Usu*.[32] But most significant of all is anatomy's failure to find evidence of an organ for the soul. It is both pleasing and unsettling to Browne that our souls appear to have no "history," that is, no clear past and, in Bacon's sense, no proper place in natural inquiry. Soul will not be joining wind, spirit, or density in the third part of the Great Instauration.

No less torqued is Browne's declaration that human sexuality is disgusting – part and parcel of the general "incurvate" sinfulness of human beings and especially of female crookedness. Immediately he retreats from this critique of artful nature and insists that he appreciates feminine beauty because he finds the idea of beauty everywhere – in a picture of a horse or in tavern music, for instance; these instances alike (Browne notes) stir up his devotion for the creator of cosmic harmony.

But the emphasis on the hieroglyphic idea of harmony is followed up by Browne's defense of the medical profession, namely, that it (like law and divinity) emerges from the condition of the fall and faces an enemy – disease, like dispute or vice – that cannot otherwise be beaten. Brownean art belongs in this category too as the capacity of the human imagination in spiritual recreation to transform tavern music into the music of the spheres. At one and the same time, fancy salves and exposes the flaws in the hieroglyphs of nature, just as it does with church ceremony. If, however, human imagination – like human copulation – can create monsters like so many endogenous "weeds and tares," then nature – its harmony, purpose, beauty – offers incurvate man a place in God's providence to which amphibious man was supposedly entitled.

Beyond monstrosity and deformity, there is the Epicurean theory that the world is governed by chance. Browne disposes of this charge by arguing that our "fortune" is really God's other, mysterious providence, one "full of Meanders and Labyrinths . . . and that is a more particular and obscure method of his providence, directing the operations of individualls and single Essences." This more "cryptick and involved method of [God's] providence" produces strange, incongruous events in the history of any individual – Browne included – or of any nation (England too) (*Religio*, 81–82). If Epicureans need to learn that such "fortune" is in fact a mysterious providence, Stoics need to realize that nature is not entirely and fatally predictable.

All the same, Browne meets these extreme natural philosophies halfway. Accommodating the Stoic tendencies of the age, he bestows on even the more opaque and irregular providence a certain legibility and predictability. Its surest sign is disproportion – when thanks to divine favor the slightest factor can make all the difference in the outcome of an event. But even the extraordinary rise and fall of nations is adaptable to a paradigm of cosmic "revolution and vicissitude" within a general economy of sameness (82). Even in "matters of greatest uncertainty," Browne asserts not a "loose and stragling" but "a setled and preordered course of effects," one that we often cannot detect but that, strangely, we might well influence through prayer (83).

So God's more labyrinthine ways nonetheless are somewhat accessible to us – legible, ordered, and flexible. The only silly human response is to make proverbs or poesies of fortune. *Pace* proverbs, Fortuna is neither unfair nor unavoidable nor immoral, and anyone who repines at the unjust division of earthly spoils commits "an errour worse than heresie, to adore these complementall & circumstantiall pieces of felicity and undervalue those perfections and essential points of happinesse, wherin we resemble our Maker." Browne offers two remedies for the sense of incongruity and injustice that "circumstantiall pieces" can provoke. One is to credit the cosmos, including the planets, with a compensatory system of distribution established by God's mercy, which regulates our nativities so that each receives some benefit from the planets, and birthrights are not simply "indifferent and uncertaine." It makes sense to pray before a card game, for at least one acknowledges that life's rounds "begin and end in the Almighty" (83–84).

But the second remedy offers concessions to the Epicureans. In this world, Browne reminds us, human beings confront the apparent injustices and incongruities of external fortune, "these complementall & circumstantiall pieces of felicity." What is more, it is internal incoherence that weakens human beings into error regarding nature and fortune; ignoring faith, philosophers are misled by those co-conspirators, reason and passion, that upset the balance of the inner commonwealth. Faith, reason, and passion all appear ridiculous to one another, unable to maintain the ideal rule with "every one exercising his Soveraignty and Prerogative in a due time and place, according to the restraint and limit of circumstance" (85). What the Epicureans understood – for all their anti-providential insistence on atomic chance and vacuity – was that there can be no happiness in the toils of external and internal circumstance.

As Christians can finally solve theological and philosophical doubts only on their knees, the Epicureans imagined their gods above and careless of the nitty-gritty circumstances of the world precisely because, Browne argues, they wanted to grant their gods the utmost happiness and majesty, "those perfections and essentiall points of happinesse, wherin we resemble our Maker" (86). As Stoic fatalism is an erroneous but understandable way to express God's lawfulness, so too the Epicurean denial of providence is an extreme but attractive way to protect God's grandeur. One might think that Browne has the "Epicure" in mind when he decries that "Rhetorick of Satan" enticing certain men into egregious atheism or abusing the natural studies of philosophers like Browne: "the villany of that spirit takes a hint of infidelity from our Studies, and by demonstrating a naturality in one way, makes us mistrust a miracle in another" (85–87).

But in fact it is a Paracelsian brand of medicine – via pneumatic sympathies – and not atomism that is said to vie so dangerously with miracles and first cause. The devil could never demonstrate that atoms assembled themselves into the orderly cosmos, but sympathetic spirits might work their own magic, whatever the piety of Fludd and the alchemists. As long as evil exists, Browne suggests, human beings must struggle with the circumstances of faith without access to the intermundane bliss of the Epicurean gods. As there are no empty cantons in nature (suggesting its providence), there is also no empty space into which one might remove oneself from the world. For as Hobbes and Marvell also know, plenism can entail tension and warfare as well as order and harmony.

Especially but not just in the case of natural philosophers, Browne dramatizes and explores the life of faith carried out within natural, social, ecclesiastical, and epistemological circumstances. No wonder, then, that skepticism – that philosophy most inclined to proclaim and investigate the circumstantiality of human experience and knowledge – is Browne's instrument and his bogey. In some instances, circumstantial doubt prompts Christian piety, unity, and charity, in some instances it haunts the same. There is scarcely any aspect of his religion that does not give Browne pause. Scripture itself can seem fabulously farfetched in its narratives, even as one can attribute its impossible logic to "a divine concourse or an influence but from the little finger of the Almighty." And its "irregularities, contradictions, and antimonies" produce more than one Baconian "catalogue of doubts," some but not all of which are pointless, nugatory "Atoms in Divinity" (87–88).

Browne avers that the more subtle a question, the more absurd its "history." More meaningful doubts, he says, have either rationally cogent explanations, the benefit of an allegorical ("soft and flexible") sense, or "the refuge of a Miracle." But the first of these recourses – cogent explanation in answer to glossatorial error – involves the Christian in the careful, skeptical interpretation of textual and historical circumstances: for instance, the notion that Babel was built to protect the people from another flood can be disproved as "improbable" according to the text itself and "from the circumstance of the place, that is, a plaine in the land of *Shinar*" (89–90).

But such questions are not "points of Faith, and therefore may admit a free dispute"; there is "no consequence" for souls, at least if one sets aside the overarching question of the status of the Bible itself (90). Considering even that status, Browne maintains, one can chalk up doubts to the "fallible discourses of man upon the word of God," which also happens to be the world's greatest book in contrast to the artless, sophistical, and ignorant Koran (91). One can readily argue too that frail human minds cannot grasp God's smallest miracles. But reaching for the significant mysteries of Christianity is integral to Browne's spiritual recreations from within the circumstances of faith, hope, and charity, even if it is incumbent on the player to cry "*oh altitudo*," to trust the scriptures and obey the church on fundamentals.

Close attention to the natural circumstances of life can enrich as well as distract from meditations on divinity, and Browne never lets us forget either state of affairs. The commitment in book 2 to a sociable-charitable disposition is founded at least in part on a pneumatic and holistic magic of sympathy – Donne makes a similar link between church unity and cosmic holism in the *Devotions* and the link is integral to the Laudian appropriation of Marcus Aurelius and Stoicism in defenses of conformity and ceremony.[33] But natural sympathy, however moral and rational, is not enough for Browne's personal divinity. It is not long after his praise for natural sympathy – with the whole more than the sum of the parts – that Browne offers his most compelling arguments for individuation, from the physiognomy that divides us all to the private wonder of his own dreams. Everything seems to support the value of charity – the dignity of friendship, the lack of knowledge about ourselves and others, the ridiculousness of polemical warfare. But the circumstances of charitable practices, Browne concedes, are often opaque, changeable, and compromised; one needs to develop private strategies for virtuous actions so "that where they are defective in one circumstance, they may repay their want, and multiply their goodnesse in another" (158).

As with cosmic holism, ecclesiastical unity, or epistemological coherence, charity requires that given the circumstances of faith, the skeptical but devoted Christian must labor to make good the method of God. Browne has recourse to simple notions – that charity amounts to love of God – and to simple obedience and contentment. But in disclaiming any pride for his considerable learning, he declares that all wise men are skeptics, for like a double-faced Janus they will always juxtapose one "common and authentick Philosophy . . . learned in the Schooles" and used to persuade others with "another more reserved and drawne from experience, whereby I content mine owne" (148). This skepticism divides Browne between a disdain for intellectual labor and sweat (with the corollary that true knowledge comes only with death and glorification) and the deep and sophisticated involvement that Browne shows from start to finish with the search for religious truth from within the hieroglyphs of nature, the microcosm of man, and the dispersion of the church.

The Brownean imagination, then, is both sympathetic and singular – reticulated with the network of correspondence and desirous to get beyond mental, natural, and ecclesiastical circumstance. This conflict emerges in his assessments of magic. Like Fludd, Browne harps on spirits and angels and is keen to build with them a holistic macrocosm or natural scale, yet unlike Fludd, he is decidedly pressured by the critical edge of skepticism.

Browne's desire to catch a glimpse of angels is more than just the commitment to a scale of creation. For the angels also "walke . . . freely exempt from the affection of time, place, and motion" (104). Angels affect but elude circumstance, in how they live and know alike. Theirs is a habitation that Moses failed to describe, indeed that he and John in

Revelation erred in wanting to concretize. At long last the only spirit of which Browne is sure is the Holy Spirit without which there is no life, heat, or light but which "makes no part of us" (100).

Browne's study of nature can double as a death wish, as a surrogate for those dreams that offer us the illusion of going beyond vexatious and restrictive circumstance. The heat of the sun is only a trope – a pleasant piece of rhetoric – for that Spirit of God that might thaw the winter of the soul and allow it to fly to heaven with fiery wings. So it is with silkworms and the philosopher's stone: Fludd traces the interlocking influences of spirits moving outward from God and then contracting back into God; but for all his disdain for ocular proof, Fludd is committed to the pleasant trope of correspondence to an extent that Browne is not. His second thoughts may tell him that the trope of the microcosm is real, but his first thought centers on the spiritual needs of a fancy with which no other spirit can ever quite sympathize.

So it is that the silkworm eludes reason and sight but manifests divinity "unto my owne fancie." Even when he is in the thick of his paean for a charitable-sociable disposition, Browne is always ready to turn attention to himself – to the personal struggle for charity; to the epistemological and spiritual battles that prevent peace and love from taking up residence within; to his singular devotions, storm of passions, and habitual vices; and to his own private and unlimited world. Awake, he is happy in God, but most happy in the dreams rejoining him with God, for dreams liberate his reason, transform a melancholic into a comedian, and expand his devotions. In dreams one breaks the ties that bind the soul, whether social or physical, epistemological or ecclesiastical.

But after Bacon's analysis of idols, and given the revival of skepticism, dreams either offer only a pretense of escape from circumstance – an internal stage play, as Browne describes it – or they take him so far to the edge of circumstance that they can never be remembered, never glimpsed among the hieroglyphs of a natural history or heard in the music of a church. For Browne, circumstance is deeply meaningful, with ceremony in the church, charity in social relations, and artful hieroglyphs in nature. In each case, contexts provide singular wits with a wonderful network of order and beauty.

But Browne is no Hooker, no builder of systems of law, purpose, and order so that the church in its own time and place might be defended in periodic sentences. From within the mutually constitutive landscapes of the church, epistemology, and natural philosophy, the most persistent notion in the *Religio Medici* is that the desire for an easy reconciliation between religion and natural philosophy – one that hinges on ecclesiastical unity, cosmic holism, and epistemological coherence – becomes all the more fervent when in a world far removed from Hooker's, systems organizing circumstance from without are self-evidently vulnerable like so many Idols of the Theater.

IV

Speculating on the reason why the William Harvey of *De Generatione* had developed into a dilatory essayist, Keynes hypothesized that the heart doctor was under the influence of the good doctor, Sir Thomas Browne, whose *Religio Medici* was lumped together with *De Generatione* and Bacon's *Sylva Sylvarum* for rebuke by Alexander Ross in 1652.[34] As Keynes notes, the Harvey of *De Generatione* is much more apt than the Harvey of *De Motu* to praise and to puzzle nature, to pursue natural mysteries to an *oh altitudo!* Together with Browne, William Harvey exemplifies just how intricately the natural philosophy of the period weaves together induction, imagination, and mystery.[35] His *De Generatione Animalium*, though published in 1648, was developed and drafted most likely from 1628 to 1642; there is some evidence that Browne saw a copy of it around 1638, and it refers specifically to events in 1633 and 1636, not to mention that a good deal of the experimentation takes Charles's deer as its subjects.[36]

The recent translator and editor of *De Generatione*, Gweneth Whitteridge, points out that for all its traditional pursuit of the efficient cause of generation, this text is more searching, imaginative, and digressive than the more systematic *Exercitatio Anatomica de Motu Cordis et Sanguis in Animalibus*.[37] Their common investment in natural cycles notwithstanding, the two texts differ insofar as *De Motu* uses anatomy then logic to resolve a longstanding mystery and *De Generatione* converts anatomical studies into analogies evocative of a mystery, with the human imagination its linchpin. As Whitteridge explains, Harvey's search for the cause of generation and the sequence of gestation is at once more reverential and uncertain than the airtight argument of *De Motu*. Appealing to contagion and mental conception as comparable cases, Harvey's main dilemma is that for all the care taken in his anatomies of chickens and deer, he can find no material vestige that might be said to generate life at all, not to mention a body resembling the parent.

This is not to say that Harvey's study is purely fideism and fancy. Far from it, he insists on the veracity of his method and promulgates a respectably Aristotelian theory: epigenesis. All the same, prominent mysteries of religious circumstance – the heredity of persons, the operation of fancy, the complex relationships between natural and supernatural agencies – converge in Harvey's investigation of embryos and fetuses, with his patron and witness none other than the dedicatee of Bacon's natural histories, Charles I.

According to its Aristotelian paradigm, Harvey's method abstracts universals from particulars and singulars. But as it turns out in the course of *De Generatione*, mental conception participates in the very mysteries of agency that beleaguer the student of procreation or, more urgently, of plague. From the very beginning, Harvey allows that even perception is unstable: following their imaginations, painters and poets are often singular in their descriptions, he reminds us, while once an object is removed, ordinary human beings must struggle to sustain its picture in the imagination that abstracts it or in the memory that stores it. Fundamental as sensation is to the anatomist, it must be repeated and methodized with "the right verdict of the senses controlled by frequent observations and valid experience" (*De Generatione*, 13), otherwise our conceptions will prove vain, fleeting, and unmoored. Harvey's basic inductive sequence might be Aristotle's – sense impressions stored, multiplied and abstracted into axioms – but his formulation of imagination's idolatrous other, "fancy," is Baconian: those who gather their knowledge about nature from books alone "do not conceive in their own minds aught but deceitful eidola and vain fancies and never true Ideas" (16).

Eventually, imagination serves as a model for the mysteries of uterine conception and heredity. But first those mysteries must be posed. As he puts the question early on and then repeatedly, Harvey seeks to trace animals to their beginnings, to uncover "out of what primordial matter, by what effective principle" they came "and how from out of these the capacity for formation and growth proceeds, as well as the processes which Nature follows in this work" (17). Scholars agree that Harvey's focus has shifted in this work from any one organ to blood and spirit, and that his metaphysics is largely monistic, even vitalistic.[38]

But if natural spirit accrues a heightened and at times an endogenous agency in *De Generatione*, Harvey's monism keeps alive the provocative query of just how divine and material causes interrelate – of whether God is ultimately mundanized or matter subsumed by an all-in-all God. The wisdom of providence is touted in the rhetoric of the text, at times decidedly Christian, at times variously pneumatic. Epigenesis – or the theory that life forms evolve bit by bit in the egg or uterus rather than simply expand from some intact and preformed whole – is suggestive either of remarkably vigilant providence or of natural forces prudently and energetically in charge of themselves. Harvey is confident about epigenesis – his anatomies showcase embryonic or fetal development from stage to stage – but he comes up empty on the trace of beginnings, a failure all the more significant because he plans to extrapolate from hens and deer to other, even human, animals.

No matter how coarse or quaint the experiment, Harvey's questions about agency are incessant. In attempting to decide whether a rooster's voice fecundates the hen, he will venture a dogmatic repudiation of atomic or particulate theories of matter. Even though atomism gains legitimacy during the very decades in which Harvey flourishes, atomic theory and its siblings disappoint him on both physical and religious grounds. Atomists "seek the causes of the diversity of the parts from the diversity of the material from which they were framed," whereas Harvey contends that generation is not a collection of the diverse but an evolution from the homogeneous (65). Moreover, materialist philosophies elevate chance and so erase "the existence of the divine Agent and the deity of Nature whose works are guided with the highest skill, foresight and wisdom, and who performs all things to some certain end or for the sake of some certain good." The good doctor will not permit the modernist embroilment in secondary causes to "derogate from the honour of the divine Architect, who made the shell to be the guardian of the egg with no less skill and foresight than he composed all the other parts of the egg out of the same material and through the same formative power" (65). As Walter Pagel has emphasized, the "religious motives" of Harvey's work often manifest themselves hieroglyphically; that is, if Browne is predisposed to imagine quincunxes in the garden of the world, Harvey traces those circles in which Nature operates and through which all things are enlivened and preserved.[39] But the "endless revolutions" so important to Harvey ironically exaggerate the difficulty of reaching "the inmost secrets of generation and its hidden beginnings," not least because no conceptual material is ever clearly in evidence during Harvey's inspections.[40] The anatomist is left to ponder whether the divinity of nature creates now, as in the beginning, *ex nihilo*.

Harvey's terminology for the creative, preservative, augmentative, and regulatory power of providence makes it only more mysterious, at times seemingly endogenous to a vital nature, at other times more orthodox as an external, supernatural cause, a divine mind as much as a pervasive spirit. He delights in theological paradox – for example, "that the omnipotent Creator should wish to appear at his greatest from the smallest beginnings" – this, in an age when atoms are frequently spiritualized, Platonized, and metaphorized (188–89).

But Harvey is also committed to solving the mystery of generation, this in an age when with Bacon, spirit can be detheologized. Thus the immediate cause of generation – "the mere touch of coition" – is every bit as mysterious as the artificial divinity "that assists and lends his aid to so great a work." But unlike God and like the weapon salve, magnetism, imagination, or winds, the "thing . . . derived from the male into the female, from the female into the egg, from the egg into the chick" can be featured in a natural (if nameless) history. This history has questions: "What is this thing thus handed on, that cannot be found either remaining, or touching, or perceptibly contained, yet performs its office with consummate wisdom and foresight, beyond all the bounds of art, and which even when it has departed and vanished makes the egg fertile, not because it now touches it but because it once touched it" (189). Harvey's is a history with observations and dissections, but also with hosannas amid the circumstances of familiar and frequent conversation with nature.

Between question and observation, however, Harvey interjects analogies linking one wonder to another and, therefore, persists in taking stock of the mysteries that he exalts. It is easy enough to imagine how Harvey's contemporaries might superimpose questions of biological heredity on those of genealogy, just as easy to suppose how they might convert the contrast between epigenesis and preformation into the alternatives of Arminianism and Calvinism. For Harvey such metaphors and transfers must remain inexact or irregular: after all, preformation can involve more chance than does epigenesis, which seems to require only that a chick make itself but which ultimately showcases God's art. Whatever its loose and flexible sense, however, analogy constitutes the principal figural translation for Harvey's most pressing question: what is the efficient cause of generation, what Aristotle calls "the changer of that which is changed" (209)? So it is that generation merges with contagion, and both in turn with imagination.

Harvey admits that his analogies are as enigmatic as each member of the analogy is obscure. Indeed, with magic under reinvestigation by Bacon, imagination is even more of a litmus test for natural studies than plague. In bringing all three together – generation, imagination, and plague – it is Harvey's hope that their shared patterns of transmission might illuminate and not simply compound the mystery of cause.

If it resembles contagion, generation also approximates mental conception: both have a certain immateriality; produce actions in the body; include desire for an external object; have similar vessels in the uterus and brain; and convey ideas whether in the case of heredity or in the case of art. Harvey tends to elevate nature over art and his analogies between the two can be rough and inexact. But mental conception helps to explain how heredity might occur and, more importantly, to articulate the enigmas of generation. Thus in the end Harvey returns to the problem with which he began in his prefatory remarks on method, namely, the challenge of fashioning then sustaining an accurate image in one's mind. That painters can render so skillfully those objects seen so long ago is a commonplace marvel, but hardly a match for those caged birds able to remember old songs or to build a nest "never having seen its model, and so not from memory or habit but only from imagination, and also how the little spider without either a model or brain, weaves its webs by the help of imagination only" (447). Just so, women are impregnated or touched by hereditary ideas, with no clearly defined or observed efficient cause of their uterine fancy.

Anticipating that his readers will laugh at his hypothesis, Harvey reminds them that the advancement of learning itself depends on imagination, that "indeed all those opinions which we now cry up were in the beginning pure figments of the mind and the imagination, until they were proved by experiments whose validity could be perceived by the senses and confirmed by the knowledge of their necessary causes, and so received fuller credence" (447). In trying to decipher how ideas are transmitted from mind to mind – how Democritus fertilized the brain of Epicurus – and how wombs conceptualize posterity, Harvey triangulates imagination, wonder, and induction ("sensation and experience") in an effort to move natural philosophy beyond its "stand-still": that is, in the hope that what at first sight may seem a fiction and fable might provoke others to reconsider and perhaps discard their atomic effluvia, angels and demiurge spirits (448–49).

The mystery of the efficient cause is responsible for a basic dilemma in Harvey's study of generation. A demotion of reason is Harvey's quasi-Baconian way of provoking his readers to disenfranchise their ordinary and narcissistic contention that nature must always function precisely as human reason is convinced it must and should. The powers and operations of nature depend on no faculty or discursive system, but act intuitively as if according to "some order or mandate" – part vegetative, part divine – so that generation is like spiders spinning webs, birds building nests, or bees and ants gathering food and fashioning homes: all more wonderful than "art" understood as rational "prudence" or "foresight, discipline or judgement" (236–37).

But Harvey's Baconian efforts to challenge man as the measure of all things are accompanied by two ironies. One is that Harvey betrays considerable conflict over whether the dethroning of reason is better served by the cultivation of religious wonder in natural philosophy. If his chief agents – especially blood or spirit – all share in a naturalized, pneumatic Christology whereby they are part soul and part body, partly visitors from another world yet also inhabitants of the mundane, it is nonetheless the case that Harvey faults the human love of lofty, magical names for the confusion plaguing anatomy: thus human beings rhapsodize when they hear "spirits and innate heat" but yawn when they hear "blood."

The more dogged irony, however, is the anthropocentrism of Harvey's analogies: like Fludd's study of the little and big worlds and his depiction of art as the ape of nature; like the tendency of Hakewill to interweave cultural and natural histories; like the insistence of such poets as Herrick and Denham that nature is framed by or inscribed with human significance: like all these, Harvey can take the Baconian challenge in an entirely humanized fashion, always pressing the question of how the study of nature can be illuminated by analogies to human faculties and practices, and anatomizing the bodies of a wider range of creatures so as to gain a better understanding of the human body itself. What is more, Harvey's work on generation would understand nature in terms comprehensible to human artists – hence the analogies to painters and sculptors – and where not comprehensible, then numinous and rapturous: hence the emphasis on imagination and divinity, to the exact names of which Harvey, like Lord Herbert, shows an indifference.

Between the time that he worked on the circulation of the blood (almost entirely in the Jacobean period) and the time that he conducted his work on generation, Harvey underwent a major change in the way in which he approached the study of nature. In the later work, he accounted for the religious implications of his research, heightened its awareness of doubt, faith, and imagination; and situated his experiments in the circumstantial domain of English history. Charles and Henrietta Maria are the presiding daimons in the providential cosmos of *De Generatione*, and the mysteries of nature are offered to them as magical and imaginative spectacles for a beleaguered, once heroic and decorous court. In consecrating and mystifying nature, Harvey is intent on expanding the presence of the sacred in England at the very moment in history when, in his view and Browne's, the sacred might be intent on abandoning England.

CHAPTER 7

Nature (II): church and cosmos

Browne's *Religio Medici* and Harvey's *De Generatione* epitomize how complex and exploratory the calibration of natural theology becomes in Caroline England. In their framing of religious circumstances with problems in natural theology, Browne and Harvey were the fruition of an English religious culture in the 1620s and 30s that featured such conflicted texts as Donne's *Devotions* of 1624. Throughout his career, Donne sustains no consistent attitude toward the "new philosophy," but in the *Devotions*, he struggles to interweave a theory of natural plenism and holism with his belief in the ceremonial unity of the church. This fusion is meant to counter the frightening possibility that community and correspondence can no longer protect the witty self from isolation and singularity. Writing in the years of Bacon's Great Instauration, that is, Donne struggles against those compelling models of the mind and of nature that threaten to destroy his argument for holism, plenism, and plurality.[1] Defined both as cosmic correspondence and ritual context, the network of circumstances in *"Natures nest of Boxes"* extends the pneumatic spirit of imagination outward from the isolated patient to the world at large, especially by way of analogies. Far from resting assured in the holism of church and cosmos, however, Donne equivocates about whether the thoughts and intentions of the solitary wit necessarily remain within the nest.

Indeed, some natural philosophers attempt to introduce a simplicity, stability, or system to the circumstances of English Protestantism, even if this aim requires that they boldly remove a previously vital and orthodox component. For instance, Lord Herbert attempts to systematize knowledge, nature, and redemption but at the expense of the church. For the church is his evidence for the tendency of unruly circumstance to subvert the peace and harmony of true religion.

I

Herbert wants to guarantee the unity of religion in terms of a rational and natural law, and in a systematic way that nonetheless flexes in response to individual experience. But his bold move toward unifying Christendom in terms of the natural principles of religion is to excise the church from the construct – to jettison the circumstances of religious culture that (he believes) produced the Thirty Years War, the polemical battles of the ceremonialists and iconoclasts, the insoluble contentions over the pedigrees of salvation and church tradition, and eventually the English Civil War. Herbert's religion of common notions rewrites Hooker's conformist enterprise but without the prelatical church and with a heightened sense that skepticism and induction have raised the stakes and altered the criteria for a scholasticism of circumstance.

Edward Herbert's work on the common notions of religion first appeared as *De Veritate* in the Parisian edition of 1624, the same year as Donne's *Devotions*, then in English editions dated 1633 and 1645. Later works – *De Religione Gentilium* and *Religio Laici* – show that Herbert continued to refine his argument for the natural theology of common notions and to elaborate its implications for pagan magic.[2] *De Veritate*'s opening eight sections – about human faculties of perception and thought – corroborate the shift from Hooker to Browne, namely, that skepticism has moved natural theology inside the web of circumstance and has accentuated the need for a criterion according to which religious truth can be known whatever the circumstances.

For all its concessions to special revelation and useful ceremony, Herbert's theology is shorn of rituals and priests, of canon laws, subtle genealogies of divine decrees, and eschatology. Herbert's is the church of the naturally instinctive notions whose mental hegemony can, he implies, advance Christianity beyond discord and uncertainty. But this natural church is as embedded in the conditions of human perception as it is responsible for overseeing and governing those circumstances, and therefore it is divided between a heavenly tranquillity and an earthly militancy, apart from but also fully interactive with the internal and external senses, the body, and discursive reason.

In *De Veritate*, Herbert comes to religion and the church last. First he lays the groundwork of the common notions in general and of their epistemological purchase and charge in particular. Aiming to foreclose sectarian controversy, priestly craft, and fanciful subjectivity, Herbert promises to ground his understanding of universal truths in a carefully rendered notion of Nature, a general providence separate from yet harmonious with the specific providence of grace. Attacking extreme skeptics, confident dogmatists, and irrational fideists alike, Herbert himself is not blindly committed to human rationality, for discursive reason is the source of so much error in human thought. Rather, he argues that general providence has instilled in all human beings, in all cultures and at all times, a natural instinct instantiated in common notions, the substance, system, and application of which it is incumbent on conscience freely to decipher amid the tumult of emotions, sensations, and thought processes.

In simplest terms, the common notions instill in us the desirability of self-preservation, both spiritual and physical. But theirs is the authority of a universal consent that only madmen or perverse sinners deny and which directs us beyond the mutually condemnatory theologies and philosophies of the present age. The common notions make human nature intimate with the dispensations of grace, border on the revelations from which they nonetheless differ, and "ought to be completely trusted even when no reason for following [them] can be perceived" (*De Veritate*, 77).

But while this "voice of nature" can (if we choose to heed it) provide us with truth and so with peace, charity, and hope, there is no getting around the fact that this voice must be heard or perceived, and that Herbert must somehow guarantee the processes of the reception of instinct in the human frame. Whereas, then, the reductive common notions recur throughout *De Veritate*, the bulk of the discussion is given over to an expandable and elusive topic, namely, our God-given faculties, their objects, the conditions of conformity between faculties and objects, and the sources of error. Lord Herbert implies that he is normative man but it is just as important that each one of us freely experience the blessed recovery of the guiding instinct in ourselves.

The tranquillity of a few common notions ensuring the true and blessed conformity between faculties and objects must contend with the struggle for the "right conditions" in which "the intellect cannot deceive, even in dreams" (106–07). If a reliance on the common notions reduces the circumstances of faith, Herbert's analysis of faculties multiplies them, for "Man is an animal of complex structure and endowed with diverse and marvellous faculties, external and internal, so that I find it a difficult task to classify them" (115). There are four basic epistemological groups – natural instinct (or the common notions), internal senses, external senses, and discursive thought – and the four are studied thus in order of descending importance and reliability. But the senses and discursivity transfer the plague of variable circumstance to the conscientious work of the instinct that must inform these faculties and establish their several conformities to their respective objects in their various domains.

To make matters worse, the institutional church and dominant theologies are unprecedented in the pressure they exert and the confusion they impose on attempts at epistemological conformity. Preachers exhort their audiences to embrace some biased dogma or be damned, leaving the multitude of Christians with "no refuge, unless some immovable foundations of truth resting on universal consent are established, to which they can turn amid the doubts of theology or of philosophy." With complexity within and persecution without, feeble human beings find themselves "incapable of using their own faculties," let alone of exerting their free will in making their notions and faculties conform to the attributes of God – a conformity that weds instinct and faith in the widely dispensed but too often mistaken beatitude of salvation (117).

Thus, even if the common notions retain a self-evidence that tends to supplant scripture in his philosophical religion, Herbert posits conflictive models of this redemptive epistemology in which one's conscientious inner vigilance is an integral part of God's providence and preparatory to God's grace. Our humors and drives, our fears, melancholy, nightmares, itches, apathy, hunger and thirst, our laughs and yawns are irksome and clamoring, even savage or stormy. As often as not, medicine can aid us against this violence as much as morality; one should not, he warns, confuse a humoral problem with a spiritual one, but Herbert's apologies for human nature entail that redemption from sin, while accessible, must still be sought by conscientious Christians in their own perceptual processes and the choices that lead to and issue from these processes.

In what is his boldest stroke, Herbert argues that his philosophy can do more for conformity in an amorphous church than the church can for his philosophy. Herbert charges conscience with overseeing perception and with organizing the inner senses into forces of moral beatitude according to the common notions; but to this end, conscience takes its critical place not in an ecclesiastical hierarchy but in an epistemological system. Conscience is an inner court for the moral trials of the most nitty-gritty human experience, magisterial like the common notions yet not so Edenic in its sites. The pulpits, despite their recourse to terror, have done a better job of clarifying the value of conscience and the need for its reformation but all the same conscience can grow too delicate

or callous and so requires our instinctive and prayerful attention "as a
sacred bond linking the higher order to the lower" (188).

Herbert insists that discursive reason in particular traps human beings
in their biases, vanities, and errors; it lacks discipline or resolution but
enslaves the man who fails to think "with freedom and candour" or
to listen "with humble heart to the voice within him." But the church
and its canons often collude with the various other products of discursive
reason – as unreliable as ever fancy was – so that the human obligation to
the laws of nature is abandoned for civil and religious laws, and eventually
for "the rule of his own caprice" (233–34). For all the expansive freedom
that Herbert bestows on human agency, his common notions are severe
and demanding. After all, they internalize the conformity that Laudian
divines would ritualize. According to Herbert, however, the church must
adhere to the notions – that there is a supreme god; that this deity should
be worshiped virtuously and piously; that the human mind is horrified
by its own wickedness and hungers for expiation; that there are reward
and punishment in the afterlife – and not notions to the church. So too
in the later manifestations of Herbert's church of natural instinct – in *De
Religione Laici* and *De Religione Gentilium* – Christianity is worthy to the
extent to which it shares in the common notions with the pagan religions
of past and present – belief in God to be worshiped with piety and virtue,
with repentance, and with reward and punishment in the afterlife. All
in all, Herbert's rational faith attempts to naturalize the circumstances
of religious knowledge, but this end can be achieved in Herbert's view
only if the genealogical and ecclesiastical respects of salvation are almost
wholly ignored.

II

Other Caroline writers were attracted to the attempt of making "an
account of religion by reason," as John Suckling labeled it. In most
cases, natural theology affords the Caroline writer new ways of situating
the English church among all the inner and outer circumstances in which
a Christian's life is carried out.

For Caroline natural theologians, the most perilous slope ending in
atheism is the newly prominent philosophy of the Epicureans, whose
atomism and ethics of pleasure undergo a revival in Caroline England
yet whose anti-providential theology and subjection of all spiritual phenomena to atomic analysis are anathema. For nascent atomists, the fortuitous theology of the Epicureans – according to which the gods have

no interest or involvement in the affairs of the world – must be defended on the merits of free will or simply filtered out.[3] This question of how much free will to allow in the *ordo salutis* was reckoned alongside assessments of the levels of chance and vacuity in the universe. Together these preoccupations illustrate how in the 1620s and 30s natural philosophy heightens religious controversy as much as it pacifies the same. One can find the resurgent views of Epicureanism in many Stuart texts, Bacon's and Burton's among them, but one Biblical question that well illustrates the search for the proper understanding of contingency is the casting of lots.

Thomas Gataker's *Of the Nature and Use of Lots: A Treatise Historicall and Theologicall*, published first in 1619, was enlarged for its 1627 edition. Its inception in the Jacobean period was stimulated by the Book of Sports, for one of its principal (if not immediately apparent) aims is to defend the honest, even pious uses of recreation. But between 1619 and 1627, its other principal goal – a proper evaluation of chance and contingency in a Protestant theology – accrued considerably greater import after Dort and in the heyday of the Montagu brouhaha over England's relationship to the ceremony, tradition, and free will doctrine of Rome.

Gataker divides putatively indifferent and "natural" lots from those Biblical lots with claims on divine inspiration as a means of defending the innocence and piety to be found within the circumstances of everyday chances. His *homo ludens* encounters so many occasions of "make-sport" as surely as life is filled with the happenstance of hats blown in the wind or of animals racing across his way. If joy might be prompted by the curvature of waves, why not by surprises in lots, oratory, or "the other circumstances" that the Bible has "left to mans discretion and wisdome"?[4] Gataker strengthens his position in placing this discretion under the composite guidance of nature, magistrates, and "the generall rules of Gods word concerning the same" (173). Prohibit sports, Gataker warns, and one might as well censor what people have in their pockets, for their lunches, or in their dreams. Some dreams, he adds, have been sacred, but many more have not, and at long last the oracular days have passed.

Through his careful analysis of the role of chance in everyday life, Gataker opposes those zealots who look for a virtually fatalistic providence in all life's affairs. In 1639, by contrast, William Ames offers his own account of what makes a decisive lot holy and lawful, tipping the balance from fortuity to providence again, and dismissing playful lots together with any appeal to casualty or contingency in the making of

serious decisions.[5] Ames understands that the position a divine takes on
lots – or on sports – is not simply a factor of his presuppositions about
the natural order; for, Ames believes, one's position on the role of chance
in Protestant living is ultimately symptomatic of the views one takes on
church ceremony, human agency, and divine providence in the processes
and genealogy of redemption. Gataker is too focused on sports to defend
divine providence as it works through nature to harmonize the circumstances of Protestant faith. That lot falls to George Hakewill, who differs
from Lord Herbert in insisting on finding a place for the church in the
natural order of divine providence. That place, however, is singularly
hard to find.

III

If one Baconian directive was that nature be cleared of human projec-
tions and reread in its own alphabet, Caroline writers responded with
a new conceptual landscaping of the divine creation vis-a-vis human
history and heroism, politics and art, and, framing all, religion. The
magisterial instance of such Caroline recontextualizations of nature is
George Hakewill's apology for providence in answer to the many and
popular arguments for natural decay. But there is also poetic and pic-
torial evidence, some of it quite secular, that indicates a Caroline drive
to retrace the interstices of art, faith, and nature, to re-imagine the human situation in nature and the place of nature in human life – a drive
as powerful as the one to locate the mind at some remove from nature
and withal to work at breaking those idols that have imposed inventive
imagination, rational systems, or unreliable language on God's creatures,
their structures, constituents, and motions. In Caroline religious culture,
moreover, the question of human invention's role in the conception of
the cosmos is linked to, though not at all equal with, the debate over the
role of human fancy in the services of worship.

The recontextualization of nature emerges together with landscape
painting and poetry. In *English Taste in Landscape in the Seventeenth Century*,
Henry V. S. and Margaret Ogden use Edward Norgate's manuscript
treatise on limning as a springboard for their argument that the Caroline
decades testify to a deepening interest in and sophistication about landscape. Written around 1625 and enlarged in a 1649 version, Norgate's
treatise not only promotes the genre's recent rise to prominence, but also
speaks to the techniques with which one can bestow unity and perspective
on a pleasing, contrastive variety of natural and artificial components.[6]

As the Ogdens point out, such enthusiasm coincides with habits of collecting paintings in the 1620s and 30s which manifest a growing preference for landscape. As proponents of landscape often note, the variety of the genre is especially stimulating to fancy, a point made by Denham in "Cooper's Hill" but also by the Earl of Arundel's librarian, Francis Junius, in remarking that perceptive viewers are "studying always to enrich their Phantasie with lively impressions of all manner of things" (37). Caroline landscape also has a heroic dimension, from paintings of Charles as St. George to Denham's treatment of Windsor's natural setting. In such cases, as Vaughan Hart has discussed, heroism is royal and magical, for the Stuart monarchy is credited with the recovery of ancient languages and symbologies that allow kings to tame nature as well as to sympathize with its profound order.[7] Such hieroglyphics can be found in gardens, architecture, and masques but also in heraldry, linking the genealogies of persons and natural magic.

Building on the work of the Ogdens but focusing on poetry, James Turner corroborates the growing richness and frequency of landscape in Caroline culture, but argues in addition that this vogue has complex and ironic resonance for human "geography," including social, political, emotional, and epistemological respects. For one thing, there is a marked ambivalence about whether landscape yields truth or trickery; for another, landscape figures centrally in the ironic use of rural verse as a sign of courtly urbanity, an appropriation that involves the "contradiction and suppression" of, but also certain disdain for, the material realities of labor. In sum, landscape poetry flourished in this period; it matured in the qualities of variety and structure, in "wild civility," in perspective, and in contrastive composition. Students of landscape were self-conscious about such matters as the proper mean between clutter and bleakness, and this concern also entailed an interest in the reticulation of reason and fancy.[8]

For Turner, then, there is a world of difference between Jacobean landscape poets and their Caroline successors, with the latter joining amplitude and plenitude. But together with the heightened facility and attention come larger questions about the human contexts of landscape, not least the religious query about whether landscape embodies profound and total knowledge or impressive, mysterious deceit. Thus Turner:

Landscape was a new found land. It made unfamiliar demands on the viewer's emotions and sense of reality. John Barclay, enthralled by the view from Greenwich hill, asks himself "What should it bee, that thus unawares had ravished mee? Why should this prospect soe wonderfully please? What hidden force or reason had thus wrought upon my minde?" (34–35)

As Turner explains, Barclay's contemporaries answer his question variously, sometimes attributing beneficence and veracity to the spirit of landscape, at other times distortion and "pernicious fantasy, dangerously beautiful" (47). And Turner is not alone in his argument that the vogue of landscape raises larger human questions in the Caroline period. In the 1620s and 30s, Ronald Hutton has recently shown, poets and other writers were engaged in a full-scale battle over those pastimes that epitomized a fundamental controversy over how natural, social, and ecclesiastical respects pertain to one another.[9] The poetry of Robert Herrick is a clear example of how these three respects converge in a contest against the denuding of a mythic cosmos, festive society, and ceremonial church.

The conflict over pastimes was not always neat and simple but often produced complex and ironic results, not least the poetry of Robert Herrick which conflated "royalism, classicism, elitism, social benevolence, sensuality, intense love of ritual, Christian piety, and a deeply ambivalent attitude towards the countryside."[10] Herrick stands as a monument to the new contextualization of nature after Bacon: in his poetry, nature is meaningless apart from human fancy, desire, social relations, and religious worship. Even the microscopic world reveals to the imagination a fairy society dining on atoms but not Democritean particles or even a Baconian *pneuma* freed from the idols of human wit.[11]

Herrick is neither Fluddean nor Baconian: his is a nature framed and given value by the circumstances of church ceremony, fancy, and social respects. In this regard, the natural philosophy most closely allied with Herrick's orientation, though very different from Herrick's specific strategies and images, is George Hakewill's apology for providence and its natural economy in the historical context of human manners, heroism, learning, and religion. But context proves as problematic for Hakewill's natural philosophy as it is crucial.

On occasion, Hakewill cites Richard Hooker's *Laws* as evidence – from its arguments but also from the modernity of its gifted author – for the natural economy that the *Apologie* promotes.[12] Quoting Hooker's great paean for the natural law sustaining the courses of cosmic design, he in some measure diverts the momentum of the *Laws* itself; for while Hakewill aims to explain the relationship between the course of nature and the status of the church, that explanation is far less consistently clear or even valuable to Hakewill than the exposition of nature's circular vicissitude.

Circular vicissitude means first that there is variation – commonly cyclical – in the quantity and quality of any natural resource found at any one time or in any one place; but second that a survey of all places and times – a natural history of the world conducted by a citizen of the world – reveals a fundamental sameness in the vitality, welfare, and magnitude of nature. If there is a modern wane in one thing (say, fish), or if a thing wanes in a particular place (say, Yarmouth), then modernity will bear witness to an increase in some other thing (say, fowl) or the decline of fish in one place will be reciprocated by an increase in fowl in that same place accompanied by an increase of fish elsewhere, say in Holland. Other factors – some accidental (fishing practices), some willful, some divine – can help explain variations, but nature's waxes and wanes, far from impugning regularity, paradoxically ensure it.

At face value, the factors of will and the supernatural are simple enough for Hakewill, who argues that if there is any extraordinary decline in human affairs, it can be chalked up to the sins of free will, while if there is any extraordinary interruption of the natural course – in weather or longevity, for example – it can be attributed to a special divine dispensation. Although this latter distinction – between God's grace and the ordinary providence of nature – is eventually blurred in Hakewill's discussion of the Reformation, it is crucial nonetheless for his supernatural conception of the creation and the apocalypse. And it allows him to mount a defense of ordinary providence according to those attributes of God – justice, mercy, ubiquity, and power – that guarantee sameness and balance, uniformity and circulation, or "compensative renewing" in what he characterizes as the ceaseless and various river of mutability (*Apologie*, 13).

As Hakewill sees it, the fall of man has not significantly marred the creatures, nor will the redemption of man save them. In response to those arguments that nature declines until the apocalypse renovates it, Hakewill maintains that there is no continuous degeneration and thus no renewal but a fiery annihilation for the good of the whole – one executed by God's special providence. If there is spiritual decline, nature is no more responsible for it than nature was for the fall, and indeed the theory of decay serves only as excuse for a lazy, wasteful kind of living. Hakewillian nature has made the moderns neither dwarves nor giants, though his position on modernity's relationship to heroism proves less neutral than that claim promises.

As Victor Harris has shown, the arguments against decay reveal Hakewill's tendency to read the universe from the guarantee of the planets downward to earth and so to resist the decayist's view that human decline must be read outward to the macrocosm.[13] It is true that, as in

Bacon's works, Hakewill's criticisms of the macro-microcosmic analogies indicate a complex understanding of how human and natural histories converge. But Hakewill's overall commitment to analogy is clear. Given the sidereal influences on the earth and its elements, an argument for natural decay is forestalled by the conclusion that the quality and quantity of the heavens are preserved over time.

From scripture and experience alike come various objections to the astral premise, but Hakewill is ready with answers: the fact that Galileo can see spots on the sun hardly means that those spots are new, while decidedly novel phenomena – the star of 1572, for instance – are forecasts or memorials of God's judgments. Hooker is invoked in support of the commonplace that angelic ministers guarantee the regularity and uniformity of the heavens. But given those ministers' freedom to sin, this point receives less attention than the attributes of preservation as they characterize the substance, motion, light, warmth, and influence of the heavens – this, despite recently urgent predictions of the apocalypse, "a *curious inquisition*" that supplants the proper focus on sinfulness (114).

From Hakewill's view of constancy in the heavens, it is but an easy leap to a "reciprocall vicissitude" in the elements below, where all species can be found "running the same race, and incessantly travailing up and downe by the same path" (120). If weather is no better than it was for the ancients, then it is no worse and indeed if there is any linear momentum in Hakewill's economy at all, it favors improvement, generation, and refinement – an incommensurable tendency once it is extended to the manners, arms, and arts of nature's human faction.

Not only, then, does Hakewill oppose any notion of the earth's decay – witness, he notes, the fertility of 1634 – but he also maintains that husbandmen in general are better off than they used to be. And while all mixed bodies cycle through birth, growth, dissolution, and rebirth, there may well be some metals and stones that last virtually forever, and there is practically no species that simply disappears. For Hakewill, decay is natural in the "mutuall traffique and interchange" of the elements, but only God can devour a species: time is a toothless measure of motion, and nature – that "most indulgent mother" – always "by succession paies home her losses with an equivalent compensation" – at least until God decides otherwise (5.7, 14).

The methodological requirements of Hakewill's argument are as daunting as they are critical for getting beyond skeptical impasse, and his method combines the attractions of Lord Herbert's deduction and of Bacon's induction with the pitfalls and challenges of each. To the charge made by Godfrey Goodman that his apology relies too much on "Instances," too little on axioms, Hakewill responds that his instances "are deductions or branches drawne out for the better illustration and strengthening of the rule, all rules being first grounded and built upon the observation and induction of many instances, and then the instances serve to add both light and life unto them" (5.57). But all the same, Bacon's method and natural history have a complicated relationship to the apology.

For example, Hakewill exhorts all students of nature to operate as citizens of the world. In the preface, however, he admits that he "staggered in [his] opinion, whether [he] were in the right or no" until he cast aside his own personal circumstances: "perchance the state of my body, and present condition, in regard of those faire hopes I sometimes had, served as false perspective glasses to looke through." Divested of his own person, he could mount a "higher pitch" and uncover the providential balance in all times and places (preface). For if one focuses on a nation, person, family, or phenomenon, one knows only the corner of a huge tapestry, "whereas hee that as a Citizen of the world, and a part of mankind in generall, takes a view of the Universall, and compares person with person, family with family, nation with nation," learns to question the evidence for decay until contrary evidence shows clearly the "*Periodicall Revolutions* fully restored" in the universal economy (109).

The citizen of the world might require an imaginary perspective, the kind that Burton associates with fictional flyers, that neoclassicists trace back to the Epicurean sage on the hill overlooking the world of man, and that Lord Herbert desired in his embrace of that natural faculty that united all religions under five common notions. This orientation is in keeping with Goodman's charge that Hakewill relies too heavily on poesies, to which the latter retorts with a host of theological, historical, and philosophical texts, but also with those many modern, cutting-edge scholars with whom he consults.

When he seeks to compare modern to ancient weather, Hakewill recommends a study of the "*Generall History* of the World at large, or the severall *Chronicles* of particular nations," and he appears to afford the term "History" its two Baconian meanings: inquiry into phenomena and a survey of past accomplishments (124). But Hakewill's appraisal of Bacon's works is decidedly mixed, and any heavy appeal to experience troubles the apologist as much as the reliance on poesies. Thus when he comes to the question of whether the waters and their inhabitants decline, Hakewill confesses his inability to find out for himself and, regarding the status of rocks, he chides Goodman for his dogmatism when one has no way of observing the same in all places at all times. Hakewill erects enormous standards of inclusion for his history but can posit no method that does not require a special dispensation from God over and above that awarded those patriarchs charged with populating the world and with instituting the "Arts and Sciences."

In his case for natural inalterability, Hakewill at times anticipates the most knotty problem of his apology, namely, an exact and cogent account of how the economy of nature is modified by its human constituents, from the art of husbandry to the education of scholars, and from civil manners to heroic aspirations, the greatest of which are spiritual and ecclesiastical. Hakewill's natural economy and its separate yet complementary supernatural order are unsettled whenever he measures the contribution of human thought and effort in either domain. That is, the specifically human circumstances in Hakewill's apology are firmly embedded in critical debates and uncertainties over the personal agency of salvation, the invented ceremonies of the church, the heroic stature and traditional pedigree of English Protestantism; and this context provokes him to insist on factoring humanity into his economy even as it renders him unsure about just how to do it.

The question of Protestant heroism is a good example of Hakewill's resilience and inconsistency in his treatment of circumstances. Wanting to prove that the moderns can attain the strength of those giants supposed to have lived in the past, he also wants to advance a heroic spirit in modern learning and in the church. A key to this assertion will be imagination and hope, but long before that line of thought unfolds, the volume testifies to the important but tricky movement from body to mind in the argument. In his commendatory blurb, Henry Briggs is right to emphasize Hakewill's thesis that "neither the mindes nor the bodies of men have suffered any generall decay" (C1v). But it is the assessment of mind, manners, and learning, that begins to obscure the outlines of the natural economy – an equivocation carried further still in the treatment of religion.

In opposing the decay of arts and manners, Hakewill prefaces his arguments with a division he has already drawn between natural and free agencies. In addition to God's "secret counsell," free will renders us enormously uneven and unpredictable as we swerve wildly from virtue to vice and alternate between civility and barbarity or between laziness and industry. Just so, at one point he resists analogies between "naturall endowments" or laws and any one civil arrangement for inheritance.

But, he insists, changes in manners are not progressively downward and, what is more, such variation can be worked into the cycle of proclivities that Hakewill extends from mixed bodies to cultures and minds. On occasion, he even attempts to explicate the network linking bodies to minds and manners and eventually to souls.

Thus, whereas art and wit are associated with stature, strength, and longevity, virtues and vices are subject to cycles of regeneration and decline, and are founded on and inextricable from the temper of the body:

Such is the neare affinitie and mutuall connexion betwixt these foure, *Age, Strength, Wit, & Manners*, that as the *three* former ordinarily follow the temper & complexion of the body, so for the most part doth the *fourth* too; though I must confesse that by the freedome of the will in *morall* matters, wee are more masters of the *fourth* then of the other *three*, which are more naturall, and consequently lesse in our power to alter or command; as *strength* then is the comfort of *age*, and *wit* the grace of *strength*, and *vertue* the guide of *wit*: so *age* without *strength* is tedious, *strength* without *wit* dangerous, *wit* without *vertue* hurtfull and pernicious. If then having matched men of *latter ages* with those of the *former*, in regard of *age, strength*, and *wit*, they should not likewise prove matchable in regard of *vertue*, it were a blemish rather then an ornament, a discommendation then a praise. (331)

Manners, then, stride the boundary between natural economy and voluntary morality; more than longevity, wit, or strength, they transcend that economy. But a large part of Hakewill's argument is given over to compiling evidence that manners have their cycles and overall sameness too. The picture is complicated, however, by his tendency to extol the advances of modernity – in warfare, learning, and virtue alike – and some but not all of these advances require a religious explanation. But the church itself, like manners and poetic fancy, at times appears to fit Hakewill's natural economy.

Like Bacon, Hakewill protests that he would give the ancients their due in matters of learning; and as Tuveson has remarked, like Hakewill, Bacon has some interest in "a kinde of *circular* progresse" in history, with births, growths, maturation, decline, then rebirth.[14] The section of the apology concerning letters, however, is most like Bacon's understanding of how the "restauration of good letters" requires "*Heroicall* spirits" and can amount to a modern advancement of learning that fulfills prophecies found in Daniel and Seneca alike (260). Over and over again, and in the guise of illustrating vicissitude, Hakewill lauds "the great Heroes and miracles for all kinde of learning" in his own day.

Hakewill reminds his readers that learning fits into a natural economy whereby "the ballance of humane affaires," of, for instance, barbarous masculinity and cultural effeminacy, is always "kept upright" (58). Even so, his survey continues loosely to follow Bacon's *Advancement* in scope and agenda, including praise for modern topography and chronology. The more he moves away from cycles into advancement, however, the more Hakewill is inclined to invoke "*Gods* blessings toward this age," keeping on the margins of his discourse the question of just how the natural economy and the millennial finale interrelate (278).

The history of fancy is considered too. The main point is that poetic imagination is as little decayed as the sun, with the corollary that poetic wit, like the rest of learning, has blossomed of late. The modern accomplishments begin to mount: navigation, horsemanship, poesy, heraldry, agriculture, architecture, painting, sermons, and of course natural philosophy and mathematics. With Henry Briggs testifying to the successes in mathematics, Bacon figures centrally in the praises for natural philosophy, not least for that "noble and worthy endeavour of my Lord of S. *Albanes*, so to mix and temper practice & speculation together, that they may march hand in hand, and mutually embrace and assist each other" (302). It is a paean enlarged by Hakewill's plagiarist-cum-condenser, John Jonston of Poland, who lists the major Baconian works of the 1620s.[15]

But Hakewill's Baconianism is also severely qualified, and not just methodologically. The author of the *Apologie* can sound very much like Bacon, for example, in his assessment of alchemy, and he supports the modern age in its rectification of so many arts and sciences – among them, the study of "*immateriall substances*" – but also of porcelain, beer, hats, and waterworks. Yet Hakewill quotes a letter by Sir Thomas Bodley to Bacon in critique of *The Advancement of Learning*. The upshot of the letter is that there is nothing new under the sun, that only vicissitude rules in deeds and words.[16] Returning to the cycles of nature, that is, Hakewill would keep learning, fancy, manners, heroism, and technology together with mixed bodies in the economy of holism and sameness. But respect to manners, to imagination, heroism, and even persons, is hard to liberate from a theology of grace designed for these latter days.

Despite Hakewill's basic premise that human art and will are unable to damage, improve, or alter natural law in any fundamental way, his apology for natural revolutions is concerned as much with the stimulation of hope as it is with the recovery of truth. In turn, hope is linked to the heroic imagination. Hakewill revels in modern examples of extraordinary abstinence and fasting as well as strength or naval prowess, and he links the former cases to the greatness of reformed religion. Indeed, Gustavus Adolphus is featured among those moderns enduring the oppressive hardships of battle. But Hakewill's is an apology for heroism that the Ferrars could not believe, even as they would hope to embody it.

The revival of a heroism made possible by hope and fancy amounts to Hakewill's Baconian answer to the kind of malaise and skepticism voiced at Little Gidding. At times modern heroism participates in a circular logic that as with all natural things, so too with "the ancient *Heroes*," what goes around comes around (489). But the apologist for nature defines the heroic imagination with as much respect to free will as to natural regeneration. Heroic hope must be cultivated carefully and imaginatively in the magical sense that Bacon finds so engaging if also suspect: that one's imagining a thing to be so can end up making it so. The key project of the *Apologie* is fanciful: truth matters to Hakewill, but imagination almost matters more, for it can heroically serve, even conjure the truth to which a faith in God's providence compels the historian of nature.

Hakewill ventures so far as to assert that "the force of imagination is wonderfull, either to beget in us an abilitie for the doing of that which wee aprehend we can do, or a disabilitie for the not doing of that which wee conceive wee cannot do: which was the reason that the *Wisards* and *Oracles* of the *Gentiles* being consulted, they either returned an hopefull answer, or an ambiguous, such as by a favourable construction, might either include or at leastwise not utterly exclude hope." The point is so important that Hakewill repeats it, with English examples: explaining "the admirable efficacie of the *Imagination*, either for the elevating or depressing of the minde, for the making of it more abject and base, or more active and generous," he argues that one's theory of nature can have a considerable impact on the prosperity or decline of a culture, with all its "*Civill*, *Charitable*, or *Pious* uses" (20–23).

At some level, then, Hakewill allows for the value of fictionalizing in theories of nature. At another level, only his view of nature is posited as true to a Christian's conviction that "Gods grace and our own endeavours concurring, there is a possibilitie wee should rise to the same degree of worth" as our predecessors. But the heroic imagination is a contingency – hardly so compelled as natural cycles, though no doubt made possible by a level historical-cosmic field – and so it is fortunate that human beings can dream their own immortal destiny in the afterlife but also their own noble heritage. For personal pedigree figures into the heroic imagination too: "To like purpose was that custome among the Heathen of deriving the pedegree of valiant men from the Gods, as *Varro* the most learned of the *Romanes* hath well observed" (17–23).

The whole of Hakewill's apology treats natural regularity as mankind's reliable pedigree, arguing for a basic sameness in the identity of both species and individuals, no matter what the apparent and ongoing vicissitudes. But imagination, like free will, can produce the very advancement or decay that nature would appear to rule out, and one way that human beings have prevented the decay is by cultivating family respect.

Hakewill's apology for God's providence, then, would unite and resolve the several critical questions haunting Caroline religious thought – questions about fancy and knowledge, persons, nature, and the heroic past. But at long last he must come to terms with the apocalyptic future of the church, and to assess the relationship between this future and the economy of nature. That assessment is both more and less simple than the convergence of the other circumstances in Hakewill's scheme: more simple, insofar as aggressively apocalyptic Protestants are intent on locking natural economy into a more calculable future and specific pedigree for the church militant; less simple, because Hakewill resembles Lord Herbert in resisting an engagement with the polemical religious culture in which those calculations and specifics are hammered out.

From start to finish, Hakewill's apology pursues an expressly religious argument – one that can be generally linked to other defenses of providence launched against those Neoepicureans with whom Hakewill loosely and ironically lumps the decayists. There are relatively random comments about the Christian church: its aids to virtue are likened to the arts of printing and navigation with their respective advances, while the ideal church is characterized as avoiding the extremes of papist superstition and Puritan singularity. But the overall argument is much more systematic, namely, that Hakewill's economy of nature testifies to the mercy, justice, strength, wisdom, bounty, and ubiquity of God much more cogently than the theory of decay. What remains obscure is the place of the progress of the church within that economy.

Hakewill urges readers to consult histories in order to determine whether the ideal church can be found throughout the course of time. The reformed church has reemerged together with "the reviving of the *Arts* and *Languages*" (epistle) and contributes to manners; as far as divinity goes, "Our silliest women now better understand the deepest mysteries worthy or needefull to bee knowne, then the profoundest Philosophers then did" (262). But this testimony again leaves unclear how natural cycles, in addition to "the *redeeming of a captivated truth*, the *vindicating of Gods glory*, [and] the *advancement of learning*" should also magnify "*the honour of the Christian & reformed Religion*," especially given what was no doubt the exceeding rarity of modern European claims that Christ had brought with him the decay of nature (preface).

At times, Hakewill's balanced characteristics for nature – constancy and vicissitude – are divided among the various manifestations of the church. Whereas the church triumphant is as constant as the heavens, the church militant resembles the moon, all mixed bodies, and all kingdoms in its cycles of change, with the overall result "that no man might either too confidently presume, because they are subject to continuall alteration; or cast away all hope, & fall to despaire, because they have their seasons and appointed times of returning againe" (preface). Hakewill believes that his view of nature cultivates the right spiritual qualities – humility, piety, charity, and hope – in contrast to the notion of decay that only apparently springs from humility. But he also posits that the modern age is blessed above the past, though there is some slippage on whether this age is the Christian era itself or a "latter age" more exclusive to the seventeenth century.

At times, this special dispensation is easily relegated to the domain of grace, much as sin is voluntary and not natural per se, and much as the end of the world will be supernaturally rendered. But Hakewill returns to a triangulation between art, nature, and grace that fits all three into his opposition to decay. For instance, responding to the axiom that the further a thing moves away from its origin, the more corrupt the thing becomes, he maintains that "whether wee behold the workes of *Art*, or *Nature*, or *Grace*, wee shall finde that they all proceed by certaine steps from a more imperfect & unpolished beeing, to that which is more absolute and perfect" (57). Perhaps the providence involved in this procession is different in each case, but the course of each appears to be joined nonetheless in what Bacon would call a prime philosophy. To make matters more slippery, his examples are at times individuated – one Christian's faith, one painting, the growth of one tree – again leaving unclear how the history of the three providences compare; but at times they center on species, suggesting the progress of nature, art, and the church over time.

At times, he stretches the analogy quite far from its emphasis on the distinction between natural and supernatural providence. Building on

the received opinion that soldiers, orators, poets, philosophers, historians, and politicians were excellent around the birth of Christ, Hakewill
extends this coincidence to nature:

> that *Nature* was at this time rather *strengthened* then *enfeebled*, in as much as both
> Art and Grace are built upon *Nature*, I meane the *naturall faculties* of the soule,
> which commonly follow the temper of the body, and the more vigorous they
> are, the more happily are both *Art* and *Grace* exercised by them. (58)

The magnification of art and grace is founded in nature, which proves
to be the soul that turns out to follow the body. How, then, an argument
for the regulated economy of mixed bodies and of nature would account
for changes in grace, set aside manners, is no clearer than how grace
can improve nature in an economy that insists on constancy in nature.
The main point is simple – distance from the origin is not the same
thing as decline – but Hakewill's argument about how nature – if there is
no violence – will grow stronger thanks to God's motivating hand fits
uneasily in the apology.

On a number of occasions, Hakewill assesses the history of the church
vis-a-vis his theory of nature. His explanation of Cyprian's defense of decay is contextual: the saint was dejected by the contemporary difficulties
of the church, whereas – in *prosopopeia* – we hear how Cyprian would have
changed his tune had he lived until the conversion of Constantine. By
implication, Cyprian's would-be analogies between the renewed vitali-
ties of Christianity and of earth are not grounded in nature itself, though
Hakewill posits that the influence of Christian renewal on nature and
art is a "more likely and certaine cause" than that held by the view that
Christianity led to the world's decline, the charge answered famously by
Arnobius (65).

But Hakewill also includes a century-by-century history of the church
with those surveys of law and medicine in the section of the apology that
employs the evidence of the arts to demonstrate the cycles of nature.
In this respect, the heyday of sermons, casuistry, and devotion in and
after Elizabethan literature would seem to argue for latter day grace.
Hakewill, however, compares the evidence of his ecclesiastical history to
the uneven brightness of stars in the sky. Each age has its incandescence,
while overall the church progresses from better to worse, then back to
better again. In this sense, the vicissitudes of the church are little different
from those of poetry or the fish supply, though when Hakewill claims a
"naturall . . . union" between Christianity and the virtues, he implies that

the economy of nature has been subsumed and transformed by grace. And this metamorphosis includes the virtue of heroic fortitude, active and passive, that Machiavelli has denied to Christians. Even so, Hakewill allows that modern day Saracens are also more heroic than the ancient Romans – so that Christendom is part of a natural loop of manners rather than the other way around.

Hakewill stays with the case of "heroicall" valor over a sizable space, as if it were a critical touchstone for the debate. Paul Paruta is quoted in praise of Charles V, Francis I, and Sultan Solyman, this last soliciting Paruta's concession that he has set religious matters aside and focused on "the gifts of nature and fortune" (525). His principal point – that modern advances in artillery and fortification heighten courage – supports this focus too. But there is a persistent spiritual and millenarian dimension to Hakewill's defenses of modern heroism. At the level of personal spirituality, he argues, the case for decay can double as a physics of chance and so evacuate any aspiration or endeavor along with anxiety.

According to Hakewill, nature sharpens our sense of God's grandeur and compassion, and it inspires our own duty to care more for one another and for public welfare, to bear misfortune with patience, serve God, and humble ourselves to our vocations. The apocalyptic dimension of Hakewill's apology is in part linked to this optimism: one chapter aims to show "that the Church of Christ before the consummation of the world, shall enjoy a more peaceable and flourishing estate then at any time hitherto it hath," as if the cycles of the militant church were ending at an apex (546). Hakewill still poses the case of horrific last times, only to point out that such a state of affairs could agree with the vicissitude of manners: the whole point, he admits, is exceedingly difficult. Yet he insists that before the end of the world, the Antichrist will be undone by a "great heroicall spirit," the Jews and pagans converted, and also that the Antichrist has been at work in the world for a long time (557).

At the very least, then, apocalypse can lend no support to natural decay. But does it advocate for Hakewill's own natural philosophy? Hakewill's overriding answer to this question is no: a major contention of his opus is that the final, fiery consummation is an article of faith in a supernatural act carried out according to God's mysterious prerogative, in short, that its status is fundamentally different from that of nature and that "naturall discourse" can make no sense of it or, for that matter, of any Christian mystery. "A beast is guided by his sense," Hakewill concludes, "a man by his reason, a Christian by religion," and so a faithful Christian should know that the final consummation will "depend not upon the law of *Nature*, or chance of second Causes, but upon his will and pleasure, who as he made the World by his word, so by his becke can and will unmake it againe." As Goodman, his chief opponent, points out, Hakewill bifurcates divine means into ordinary and extraordinary kinds, a move that (the critic adds) teeters on the brink of divided truths about God, a danger putatively avoided by the theory of decay. Yet Hakewill urges a "religious ignorance" in these matters, chides those wits that would calculate the end, and rebukes Goodman for mixing up religious and natural arguments and proofs (24–25, 95).

Goodman reverses the charge in declaring that Hakewill is to blame for the contamination of arguments: he questions the apologist's use of Christian history against decay, noting that "religion is not inbred and naturall unto us, but revealed" – this, in the process of making the supposed decline of the Church of England evidence for natural decay. Hakewill retorts that it was not he who initiated a study of religion in the context of natural philosophy; rather, he sought only to save his theory of nature from the ill repute of impugning Christianity – this, in the process of opining "that hee who stands for modernitie, must consequently stand for the honour of religion; so as whither it bee naturall or revealed, it is not at all materiall, it carrying the same relation to the time in which it was first instituted, whither it be the one or the other" (5.120–21).

At times nature does seem germane, if variously so, in Hakewill's hope for the latter day church. Sometimes the church is said to have its cycles: "The Christian Church and religion have in all ages in somethings gotten somewhat, and lost in others: When it got in knowledge, it lost in zeale, and when it got both buildings and revenues, it lost in zeale and knowledge" (5.122). At other times, he strangely prohibits the possibility of miracles in the final consummation. Arguing that all the brute creatures will be destroyed in the fire, Hakewill reasons that their redemption would require some miracle and some mysterious choice on God's part, possibilities ruled out in favor of the dictates of those creatures' "primitive natures" (568). Hakewill is so hard pressed on this point that he is willing to leave Romans 8 at a skeptical impasse, despite his claim (as a critical friend points out) that God has blessed the moderns with wit and industry enough to see the scriptures anew and might well bless the creatures with redemption.

Nature and the church simply will not part ways in Hakewill's reconstruction of the religious heroic imagination. He argues that his apology for providence in natural affairs bodes well for the ongoing survival of the church, and in an elaborate conceit he compares the church militant once again to the cyclical moon. At the same time, however, and for all his protest that the final consummation is an article of faith, Hakewill would join Lord Herbert in finding the same idea in the rational discourse of the pagans, mental sameness-in-vicissitude discovered via comparative religion. The church will not go away in Hakewill's economy but it will not give way to polemics either. For all his skeptical caution about recent attempts to calculate the world's end, Hakewill clearly admires Joseph Mede as a heroic spirit of the latter day. But his use of Mede's work on the key to the apocalypse bears little resemblance to the image of a pugnacious radical that nonconformists and sectarians made of Mede through the 1640s.

Mede, who has his share of humble skepticism about the specific conclusions of his own calculations nonetheless aims to free interpretations of prophecy from the clutches of amorphous fancy and radical skepticism, and thus to clear a way for the triumphant future of the church. First setting forth his *Clavis Apocalyptica* in 1627, the year of Hakewill's first edition, Mede seeks to methodize prophecy. But his tentative, controversial speculation about the crucial place of Gustavus Adolphus in the sequence – as the fourth vial in Revelation – suggests that the key to the apocalypse, for all its famous reliance on the advancement of learning, joins its understanding of history, nature, and imaginative language together in an advancement of the church through troubled times.

Hakewill applauds two characteristics of Mede's *Clavis*: the precision of its synchronisms and its conclusion that the millennium is just ahead, with Satan about to be bound and the church poised on the brink of paradise. But Hakewill's imitator, John Jonston, is so eager to know these things for certain that he is bursting with those questions that method cannot finally answer: will Satan be completely undone? Will the troubles of the church cease altogether? Is such a hope itself a heretical dream of glory, the very kind of heroic fancy that method might either newly legitimize or finally explode? Hakewill offers a magisterial defense of providence as it operates in the natural, human, and ecclesiastical circumstances of English Protestant culture, but the whole point of that defense is to remove English Protestant culture from its own circumstances, to resituate it in a grand perspective of all the cosmos and of a universal, disembodied church. By contrast, Mede's apocalyptic focus entails that his sweeping interpretation of nature and human history is ripe for the picking by partisan English Protestants of various affiliations.

IV

After his death, Mede's more orthodox admirers liked to emphasi e his vast learning. Having died in 1638, the great scholar left most f his work in manuscript, no doubt in response to trouble from the Ca oline censors who would not have been impressed by Mede's announcement that his readings of prophetic characters observed the principles of natural decorum. But his first editor and biographer, John Worthington, minimizes the importance of Mede's occasional errors, and celebrates the method according to which the scholar assembled historical order from synchronized passages of Revelation.

The editor extols Mede's knowledge of ancient customs, oriental languages and symbols, but also of anatomy, mathematics, logic, and philosophy, all in an effort (as Katharine Firth explains) "to disentangle the thought of Joseph Mede from his reputation as a prophet of the Revolution." Firth concludes that Worthington sought to preserve the authority of Mede's method, itself the guarantee that Protestant historical exegesis would survive whatever the wildly fanciful course it had taken in the 1640s. Worthington believes, that is, that the radical appropriation of Mede's work "would threaten the very existence of the Protestant faith."[17]

Whereas Worthington would save Mede from his image as a fanciful civil war chiliast, Mede himself gave readers in the 1630s and 40s ample reason to believe that he was no timorous scholar either. Mede understood that Revelation treated not the remote and largely irrelevant past but the imagined and imminent future. As Firth argues, Mede's exacting scrutiny of history was aimed at resolving its problems once and for all and then at looking toward the future, for only "then the real questions could be raised: when was the millennium coming, what remained to be done before it could come, and what would it be like?" (240). If considerations of the past were merely instrumental in imagining the future, considerations of nature were more integral to the utopian vision. It is not surprising that another Cambridge man, the author of "Lycidas," wrote apocalyptic pastoral, for in the age of Hakewill, Bacon, the Rosicross, Comenius, and Mede, the end of the world entailed an entirely new understanding – and state – of nature. In opposition to those Laudian prelates whose natural world is holistic and whose ceremonies are conformist, Milton imagines a diseased and jangled natural world, together with a carnal church ceremony that must be repaired by the sudden violence of divine agency.

But if Mede's work was the end of the line for historical apocalypticism, it studied history with a vengeance: it offered a genealogy of the world, together with assessments of dreams, heroic events, and natural signs from the past. In a 1634 letter to Mede, Dr. Twisse concurs with the decision not to publish this volatile scholarship in what Twisse considers troubled times, all the while pressing Mede to retract his view that English plantations in the New World could never host a New Jerusalem.[18] Mede sees virtually no hope for the conversion of the pagans and lambastes the New World as a place where the devil has lately set up shop.

Still, he wishes the colonists well, even as he offers to return to his methodical analysis, to leave that "fancy" or those "mere conjectures" about the New World that Twisse regards as "*sage conceits*" (809). In 1635, it is Mede who writes to Twisse that they must patiently wait and see if the apocalypse is happening in Europe – if the Habsburgs will be undone and if the guardian angel Michael can indeed look homeward to a recovered paradise. But in the same year Mede is writing to Hartlib that the German war "is an intricate business, so full of windings and turnings, that no man can yet guess what is the way that Providence aims at to accomplish its end." For its part, the Church of England seems increasingly and tragically in love with its own "Form, Rites and Discipline," with its own genealogy too, for there to be any reconciliation between it and the Continental Protestants (865).

Like the world itself according to Mede's early bout with skepticism, so with the specific versions of the apocalyptic dream in the 1630s: whatever the new methods, the chief methodist cannot help wondering aloud if the church heroic "were any more than a mere Phantasm or Imagination."[19] Mede's synchronisms hold little truck with the Laudian censor but they can never be happy with the sectarian dreamer either. In the 1620s and 30s, that search for method prompted by natural philosophy would free truth from those human circumstances that corrupt or constrict it, but a truth so freed also bears the promise of transforming the circumstances of human faith – heroic, epistemological, social, natural, and cultic – beyond recall.

In the 1620s and 30s, and throughout all of Europe, the religious stakes of natural philosophy had never been higher and never more conflictive. In a time of what Firth calls "a new spirit of millenarianism,"[20] there arose a heightened sense that students of nature and of religion stood together at a crossroads, and that they were forced to decide on the future of God's children once and for all. Not surprisingly, Johann Valentine Andreae placed civil and church history together with natural philosophy in his *Christianopolis* (1619), a utopia that represents a growing tendency to treat natural philosophy – however empirical or platonic, magical or mechanical – as the linchpin of general and programmatic reform – of religion, learning, and civil life.[21]

This utopian trend in natural philosophy was both intensified and undercut by the confessional morass of the Thirty Years War. It spanned a wide range of religious orientations, from the Catholic Tommaso Campanella whose Telesian magic, astrology, and admiration for Galileo figured into a vision of what John Headley has called the "transformation of the world" under Spanish rule and the Pope; to the ephemeral links between Rosicrucianism and the great Protestant hopes, Frederick and Elizabeth.[22] Conflict over such dreams is illustrated by the split in European opinion over whether the Rosicrucians were real or illusory, serious or quixotic. And the same conflict emerged after 1614 over the natural religion derived from the "ancient theologians": once Casaubon had finally exposed the previously suspect Hermes as an invention of late antiquity, then his learned audience had a choice to make between crediting the legendary basis of a universal religion whose attractions are culled in the work of Edward Herbert, and admitting that "natural religion" might well be history's most extended and fanciful masque.

Whatever their dreams of transmuting the world, English intellectuals in the second quarter of the seventeenth century participated in an extraordinary transformation of natural philosophy. For many, this crucial moment was defined by an uncommonly strong intimacy between theology, the church, epistemology, the social order, and natural philosophy, in part as a resistance to powerful pressures to pry nature apart from everything human. As a consequence, inquiries were combined in new ways yet also newly divided in their jurisdictions.

As Owen Hannaway and Brian Vickers among others have maintained, occult magic and a natural philosophy critical of magic finally parted ways in the first half of the seventeenth century.[23] But it was a long and complicated farewell. There was cross-fertilization as well as segregation, and the alliances of each shifted with alarming frequency. Everything was affected by these shifts: notions of human language and society, of landscape, of the relationship between little world and large, between human beings and the creatures, and, framing all, assessments of the circumstances of faith deep into the Protestant Reformation. But when the smoke of civil war had cleared and the whirlwind of the 1650s had dispersed, the religious imagination of science had narrowed, not entirely but noticeably.

In the years 1626 to 1660, Charles Webster has argued, Europe "was distinguished by a spectacular phase of creative work in experimental science, the rapid development of scientific organisation, and a major philosophical reorientation. It is not an exaggeration to claim that between 1626 and 1660, a philosophical revolution was accomplished in England."[24] That modern scholars can debate the confessional accents and orientations of this revolution demonstrates just how complex the theology of nature was in these years – but also how contested in what Vickers has called "high-level intellectual pugilism."[25] So it is that from 1621 to 1638, successive editions of Burton's *Anatomy of Melancholy* purvey a deepening involvement with the new atomic philosophy and its attractive but dangerous legacies.[26] Burton sometimes repudiates these legacies in behalf of providence and its plenistic-elemental cosmos, sometimes embraces them as a liberating hypothesis. But he is just as active in conceiving a theological warrant for heliocentrism, an infinite universe, and neo-atomism. In "The Digression of the Air" alone, he rehearses the Christian justifications for these hypotheses; sums up the argument for Biblical accommodation as a solution to the oppression of natural philosophy by the church; captures the non-monolithic status of both the church and philosophy in debates over the two world systems; and exposes their equally fraudulent fictions invented at the expense of one another, with the Epicurean theological extrapolations from atomic physics no better and no worse than the "*Dedalaen* heads" who perform the dirty mathematical work of those church leaders who believe that God would require us to lie about the universe.[27]

In the 1650s, magical and mechanical interests could still very much cohabit in the minds of such intellectuals as Sir Kenelm Digby. But the words of Seth Ward represent the desire to get beyond any such philosophical mess as "The Digression of the Air" or as that found in the works of his opponent, John Webster: "there are not two waies in the whole World more opposite, then those of L. *Verulam* and D. *Fludd*, the one founded upon experiment, the other upon mysticall Ideal reasons; even now he [Webster] was for him, now he is for this, and all this in the twinckling of an eye, O the celerity of the change and motion of the Wind."[28] With dazzling "celerity," the years of Bacon's Great Instauration and of Fludd's great correspondences wrought new intimacy and discord, new certainties and new doubts, about how God wants us to read nature and about how nature instructs us to imagine God.

Conclusion: Rome, Massachusetts, and the Caroline Protestant imagination

In his celebrations of the Church of England, Thomas Browne often draws circles. Sometimes he envisions that the faithful children of that church follow its "great wheele," Browne's version of hunkering down behind what Laud called the hedge and George Herbert the double moat of the *ecclesia anglicana*.[1] According to Browne, Laud, and Herbert alike, outside the privileged temple crouch heresy, schism, and insubordination, three enemies just waiting for an opportune gap. But as Anthony Milton has recently written of this collectively but variously imagined circle in early Stuart religious culture, the dynamic and ambiguous struggle to determine the identity of the Church of England became increasingly divisive – or at least more openly and aggressively fractious – in the 1620s and 30s, reason enough for Laud to heighten the hedge and for Herbert to double the moat.[2] For Browne, however, the loyal child of the mother church also explores the vast space outside a circle, singularly pursuing those "many things untouch'd, unimagin'd, wherein the libertie of an honest reason may play and expatiate with security and farre without the circle of an heresie."[3] If the safer Church of England relegates recusants and nonconformists to the jurisdiction of circumstance – standing around orthodoxy – Browne's re-conception of the theological cosmos applauds the same church for boldly and fervidly wayfaring in that extra-circular area.

I have argued that the Caroline expatiation in the circumstances of faith accounts for the stocktaking complexity and exploratory richness of its religious discourse. But it also opened English Protestantism to heightened critiques from recusants and nonconformists. Both sets of critics attack the English church for its compromise by or degeneration into matters of circumstance, the Catholics for the skeptical impasse loosening the English hold on truth, the Massachusetts pilgrims for those worldly respects impeding divine love and its "faire and easie way to heaven." Around 1637, however, both sets of critics are compelled into an engagement with the circumstances of their own faith, the Catholics with a charity that might contaminate their truth, the New World nonconformists with a truth that might mundanize their love. The main catalysts of these dramatic yet disenchanted episodes are William Chillingworth and Anne Hutchinson.

Chillingworth's *Religion of Protestants* was the climactic, if by no means final, sally in the "charity debate" of the 1630s. In the late Jacobean years, animated no doubt by the comprehensive brilliance of Bellarmine, by the turning tide of events in wartime Europe, and by the Arminian brouhaha in England, the recusant assault on the *ecclesia anglicana* was bolder than it had been in recent memory. It sought to reclaim such Protestant mainstays as the Bible and Augustine,[4] and it asserted that its hold on divine truth was secure beyond or above the casuistical negotiations and affective accidents of the failing English schismatics. Protestant response was doubly pronged: it argued, first, that of course the human pursuit of religious truth was implicated in natural, social, ecclesiastical, and epistemological circumstances, a matter of course to God as well; and second, that Catholic claims on infallibility, aside from their blindness to the human element in their own traditions, violated the spirit of charity that also involves the church militant in the complexities and imperfections of circumstance.

In *A Conference with a Lady about Choice of Religion* (1638), Sir Kenelm Digby contrasts the Roman "precise a[n]d determinate rule of faith" with "that pretend reformation", which cannot honestly claim a "certaine and common rule of faith, but euery particular man gouerning himselfe in this matter by the collections of his owne braine."[5] Again, the reformed church possesses "noe generall and certayne rule; but leauing euery man to the Dictamens of his owne priuate iudgement, according to the seuerall tempers and circumstances (as we sayd before) that sway euery single man in particular, there must result (which we see by experience) as great a variety of opinions as those are different" (76–77).

Roman infallibility means that no circumstance can shake truth from the form of the church or the grasp of its ministers, "for we haue proued that no meanes or circumsta[n]ce, ether morall, naturall or supernaturall, is wanting in it to begett infallibility in matters of faith" (78). This claim amounts to saying that universal religion pervades all time, persons, and places – or historical, social, and material circumstances – so thoroughly and definitively as to remain invulnerable to their compromises and contingencies. By contrast, the reformers are riddled by those circumstances in the course of knowledge explored by the skeptic, and therefore they must "floate allwayes in a greate deale of incertitude and anxious apprehension and feare of error" (79). But, as John Fisher (alias Percy) never tires of repeating in *The Answere unto the Nine Points of Controversy . . .* (1626), the true church must "adhere vnto an infallible externall ground of assurance" while any church reliant mainly on internal means is recklessly, hopelessly imperfect. What is more, Fisher argues, any disobedience to Catholic doctrine is absurdly obsessed with "the accidentall circumstances of institutions, Sacraments, precepts, primitiue Customes being variable according to the variable disposition of thinges vnto which the Church militant in this life is subiect."[6] The truth infallibly owned by Rome is substantial, then, not accidental, but disobedience in a matter of circumstance is substantially transgressive.

At times, Catholic polemic mocks those Protestants whose historical arguments tracing church pedigree are unable to offer the specific circumstances of either Catholic degeneration or Protestant emergence. Thus, in *Via Vere Tuta. Or the Truly Safe Way* (1631), John Heigham taunts his Protestant foes with the dearth of "all these circumstances" in their church pedigrees, the when, where, and who in the formation of their church. In *The Converted Jew* (1630), John Clare also accuses Protestant polemicists of failing to present circumstantial genealogies of time, place, and persons, a charge that owes much to Bellarmine.[7] Such an argument avers that Protestants care too much about doctrine, not enough about the specific lines of succession in the faith. A similar argument is central to John Floyd's *A Paire of Spectacles* and in *Maria Triumphans* (1635), the author of which (N. N.) legitimizes miracles by claiming that "they are circumstanced with all particularities of Truth: As expressing the *Names* of the Persons there cured; the *Diseases* of which, and the *Tyme* when they were cured, with many witnesses thereof."[8] Despite claims made by critics that romances comprise just as many accidental details as miraculous reports, N. N. is interested in "particularly registring all the Circumstances of ech of them, and the approbation of the Magistrates of them by Witnesses" (259).

But if Catholicism claims an extensive and particularized pedigree, this is not to admit that apostolic circumstance risks the same uncertainties and instabilities as Protestant respects. Heigham is committed to stabilizing his church as "*the Ground and Pillar of truth*" set forth in 1 Timothy 3:15, and to protecting the church by placing it where Winthrop would situate Boston, a "*Citie built vpon a hill*, which can not be hid or couered with any cloud of error."[9] Just so, in 1631, Richard Smith assails the Protestant fortress at its most complacently held portal, scriptural warrant, by contrasting Catholicism's infallible traditions with Protestantism's

"Pondering of circumstances, of the stile and Phrase of Scripture, conference of places, recurring to the Hebrew and Greek text, praier, and the like," all of which means remain fallibly "humane, for they be our pondering, our conference, our recurring, our praier."[10] In *The Triall of the Protestant Spirit* (1630), James Sharpe indicts the fanciful warrant of "private spirit" in similar terms, for such a spirit is too various, unstable, and uncertain to judge controversies. Like the moon, it changes "in euery place, tyme, and person."[11]

More than anything else, however, it is Chillingworth's heroic skepticism and fallible but righteous probabilities which ignite the charges of compromising circumstance. In *Christianity Maintained* (1638), Matthew Wilson finds in Chillingworth's church more motivation than ever before to assert "the absolute Certainty of Christian Fayth; against an Aduersary, who seeketh to turne the *diuine beliefe* of Christians into *humane Opinion*."[12] If we are to credit Chillingworth, the dedicatory epistle warns King Charles, Corinthians is no more reliable than Caesarian history. Now more than ever, Charles I should protect English religion from that Socinianism that invades "*this Kingdome vnder the shrowde of* Naturall Reason" (5). Much the same emphasis governs *The Judgement of an University Man Concerning M. William Chillingworth* (1639) and John Floyd's *The Church Conquerent over Humane Wit* (1639?). Both texts conflate Chillingworth's alleged Socinianism with an insincere brand of skepticism so that the wit behind *The Religion of Protestants* becomes that of a doubting Pilate not staying for the recusant's definitive answer. No wonder, this argument goes, that Chillingworth metamorphoses through any number of religious shapes, for he never directly experiences anything. For the Socinian skeptic, all experience is lived *quasi*: he sees as though he saw and believes as though he believed. His addiction to the circumstances of knowledge entails that he must remain suspended in a mist, protean in "many and many a Metamorphosis" and contentious in the position that "life and religion is nothing else but dispute."[13] "So *Fayth* then with such men is but a *Fancy*," the "University Man" concludes, "as the obiect that beget's it but a phantome, a thing not so, but only seeming so" (74).

The circumstantial "as if" of skeptical Socinianism is said to undermine "euen Protestancy it selfe, and all Religion," but chiefly the malleable Caroline church which Chillingworth purports to epitomize (101). According to the "University Man," one can easily understand Chillingworth's motivation, for a circumstantial religion allows the impersonation of any religious orthodoxy – Arminian, Calvinist, what have you – that the state prefers and prescribes: "For who can question the

aduantage which he hath ouer a Religion-bound Conscience, who himselfe hath either none, or a *Socinian* one, which is so flexible & changing
with euery turne of fancy or affection, varying with euery variety of
occasion?" (149). Far from being a Puritan bogey for the Caroline and
Laudian church, fancy is credited by the "University Man" with being
the skeptical-circumstantial Socinian's means of survival in the mutable
political course of the English church.

In *The Church Conquerent over Humane Wit*, Floyd is less concerned
with the politics of the Socinian than with the argumentative labyrinth
in which the once proud wit invariably traps itself. In Floyd's view,
Chillingworth refuses to attribute self-evident certainty to tradition; cares
little about who it is – it might be Satan – that articulates a probable
truth, so long as it is probable; urges individuals to rely on their own
wits, only to dispute with other Protestants over the strangely hybrid
orthodoxy that must supplement and mediate between those wits; and
refuses to write out fundamentals, so committed is he to teasing out
the circumstances of Christian faith and practice. But if Chillingworth
finds himself always in the labyrinth of circumstances, it is a clueless
trap of his own making, for his authority – the "dictats of human reason" – is necessarily and bemusingly "variable according to the diuersity
of tymes, places, persons, customes."[14] To make matters worse, Floyd
scoffs, Chillingworth is confused about the status of circumstantial points
in belief: he leads Protestants to think that they need worry only about
faith in and obedience to fundamentals; then in homage to circumstance refuses to list them; and consequently fails to understand that
disobedience to the church in accidental matters is a fundamental transgression – setting aside for the moment Laud's point that circumstances
and fundamentals are often reticulated.[15]

But in 1639, Floyd still responds defensively to the charge accumulat-
ing over the course of the 1630s that Catholic claims on truth are subverted by the evacuation of charity from the strategies of those claims.
So it is that Floyd reminds himself to temper his critique with charity,
and he protests in an increasingly commonplace fashion that his critique
is charitable. On the one hand, Chillingworth's probabilities have revived enthusiasm among recusants that their traditions are beyond the
circumstantial "as if," politic impersonation, and ceaseless transmutabil-
ity. On the other, he has elaborated the case that without commitment
to being all things to all people, without the offices of casuistry and
compromise, the Catholic way lacks the most redemptive theological
virtue of them all, love. For the Chillingworth hero, safety follows from

the love of truth and of its saving effects on human souls, not from the isolationist arrogance attending those ever more shrill suppositions of infallibility.

The Caroline charity debate commenced in the 1630s with an anonymous work now attributed to Sir Tobie Matthew, *Charity Mistaken, with the Want Whereof, Catholickes are Vniustly Charged*. Three years later, this work was answered by Christopher Potter, chaplain to Charles I, in *Want of Charitie Iustly charged . . .* , a defense of the *ecclesia anglicana* revised in 1634 and prompted by Laud himself.[16] Also in 1634, the recusant side found in Matthew Wilson's *Mercy & Truth. Or Charity Maintayned by Catholics*, a champion who would provoke Chillingworth to defend the redemptive fallibilities of a properly conceived Protestantism. Wilson's text was, moreover, dedicated to King Charles, its main point being that separation from the one and only true church is damnable, no matter whether in circumstantial points and no matter what the circumstances. As Wilson puts it, we are not allowed to "disbelieue any one truth witnessed by almighty God, though the thing be not in it self of any great consequence, or moment."[17] Thus the Protestant construction of a world of difference between fundamentals and *adiaphora* is a self-serving fantasy that distracts the likes of Potter "from questions which concerne things as they are considered in their owne nature, to accidentall, or rare circumstances of ignorance, incapacity, want of meanes to be instructed, erroneous co[n]science, and the like, which being very various and different, cannot be well comprehended vnder any generall Rule." According to Wilson, Potter spends too much time worrying about exceptional cases, for "in deliuering generall doctrines we must consider things as they be *ex natura rei*, or *per se loquendo* (as Deuines speake) that is, according to their natures, if all circumstances concurre proportionable thereunto" (18–19). Whereas Potter obscures doctrine like a theologian, that is, he needs to simplify it like a preacher. To Wilson's mind, it is worse still that the Laudian divine misses the paradox of obedience according to which we might not always expressly believe or completely comprehend the various points of our religion, but we must never actively disbelieve what God has authorized and enabled the church to inform us. Thus, while God might release us from some positive beliefs, God will never permit us to disavow what he has promulgated as truth.

But Wilson admits that in practice, it is difficult to maintain a proper measure of charity, to resist the liabilities of too little and the compromise of too much (150). Thus in the 1630s charity becomes a volatile, contradictory value for Catholics who seek to criticize the English church and its warrants. For while Laudians like Robert Shelford are indicting Puritanism for drying the well of charity so abundant in Catholicism, the advocates of the Church of England opt to assail recusants for the lack of their standard warrant, charity, but in such a way as to save the Roman church from its metaphysical cloister by means of an engagement with English Protestantism that just might mire Rome in skeptical circumstance.

In *Want of Charitie*, Potter claims that the English church is uncommonly charitable "after all imaginable sorts," diffusive in both the external and spiritual means of charity.[18] Arguing that diversity of opinion, if lovingly bound together, is congruent with the unity of the faith, he reminds his readers that Protestants have repudiated not the universal church but its papist corruptions. As with Thomas Browne, Potter believes that the "peaceable and modest" Christian is "teachable and tractable," "soft and flexible" but also capable of disagreeing with (while still loving) a fellow wayfaring Christian (120). Each of us must recognize that no church on earth is infallible or absolute, and that "many truthes lie unrevealed in the infinite treasurie of Gods wisdome, wherewith the Church is not acquainted" (19).

Aside from investments in peace and unity among Christians, a major part of the Caroline impetus for diffusive, unbounded charity is the deepening of inquiry according to a humble skepticism. Skepticism can offer both subtle and powerful support of Catholic authority, as it does in the great legacy of Erasmus, Montaigne, and Charron. But the vulnerable circumstances of a skeptical church – those ridiculed as Socinian in Chillingworth's persona – appear in bold and complex guises in the Catholic theology of the 1630s. Some recusants undertake an intellectual engagement with skepticism in order to preserve Roman authority without diffusing its integrity by way of love. The English writer who most powerfully resituates traditional assertions of infallible authority within the skeptically inflected circumstances of faith is William Rushworth in his *Dialogues* (1640).

With his three quasi-Socratic dialogues between an uncle and his nephew, Rushworth employs a closet version of the kind of conversations staged at Little Gidding. But he aims to defend Catholic tradition, not so much as beyond a skepticism about circumstance but as the unanimous and invulnerable constant among the variables of circumstance. By itself, and for all the fixity of its written words, scripture will always provoke controversy or at least variation according to circumstances: it will always be a "vagabonde in particulars." By contrast, Rushworth argues, oral tradition "is grounded vpon *that* which all men agree in, and vpon *that* which is common to all ages, all nations, all conditio[n]s."[19] To make oral matters better, tradition is blessed in its flexibility of expression, for this quality permits the suasive transmission of the unanimous "in diverse countries and circumstances."[20]

Scripture belongs, then, within tradition but "Scripture remains particular: it is the local formulation of the universal doctrine." As John Belson rephrases the argument in 1662, scripture comprises truth but as for those readers who seek it, it is doubtful "that this truth will be enough to serve all the exigencies of all mankind in all circumstances." The question is not whether man can be saved by scripture but "whether it be sufficient for the conduct of all dispositions found in mankind, through all circumstances the Church will be in from the Resurrection to the day of Judgement."[21]

In an epistemological vein, the uncle seeks to assert Catholicism's transcendence over corrosive and compromising circumstance, but without the naivete of the dogmatist who ignores the structures and processes of religious belief and thought. For Rushworth, love tempts us from truth, even if questions of truth falter in their escape from circumstance. Love involves diffusive expenditure and a willingness to compromise with the foe – this, despite Rushworth's own version of knowledge as a soft and flexible sense that unites all human beings in the very nature of things. In the wake of the 1630s, however, at least one poet advocates for the Catholic church against his onetime fellow English Protestants by diffusing throughout his verse the images of a divine love that transgresses all the boundaries of being, experience, and language. The Ferrars' friend, Richard Crashaw, is carried away by a mystical love that on the one hand offers a transcendence of skepticism and controversy, but on the other crosses so many boundaries that any defensive doctrine or protective discipline is perforce undone, its rigors blunted and its purity contaminated. For Crashaw, divine love is witty in overcoming experiential boundaries, in transposing grammatical and aesthetic expectations, and in merging rival spiritual styles. Defending his hymn to Teresa of Avila, he moves from love's eloquence to its power and legitimizes a spiritual match between Spain and England.[22] As in Browne's *Religio*, Crashaw's notion of sacramental charity merges modes of piety that are otherwise nationally delimited: thus Browne's claim that he can digest all ceremonies (as well as all cuisines), and Crashaw's reversed transubstantiation of Christ's body into a strong poetic wine that Catholics and Protestants alike can consume.[23] Souls most properly speak the dialect of heaven, not of Spain, but for Crashaw this better language thrives on transposition and mixture.

Throughout Crashaw's verse, divine love transposes England and Spain, actives and passives, life and death, divinity and self, aggressor and victim, mystical annihilation and sensuousness, male and female, angel and human. Love knows no impossibilities or boundaries; or rather its logic is that of certainty-in- impossibility. More often than it seeks transcendence, this wit of love offers to agitate, overflow, and intermix. It is not surprising that Crashaw prefers those Caroline embodiments of devotion that lend themselves to hybrid reception: Herbert's poetry, Shelford's treatises, and Little Gidding heroics.[24]

But the absolute invulnerability of love is more decidedly the clarion call of the so-called Antinomians in Massachusetts. Crashaw's is a poetics of divine love that seeks to re-conceive Catholic spirituality as wondrously traversing rather than escaping the normative bounds and grammars of religious faith. "Amorous languishments" involve the Crashavian weeper in a "wit of love" that mixes cosmic realms, poetic metaphors, and domains of experience in declaring that "All places, Times, and objects be / Thy teare's sweet opportunity" (*Complete Poems*, 133). Love is no release from, it is rather a new lease on, the agitated and often indecorous humanity of Christian worship.

From his quarters in the Arbella, John Winthrop wrote letters of urgent business, but just as often he wrote letters of love. In letters to his family and friends, in letters praising God or consoling his wife, he promises to "rest in thy Loue" and envisions a hilltop city in which God's love as it is instantiated in human affairs will escape as well as illuminate an England mired in legal, social, political, moral, and – subsuming all – religious circumstances.[25] Always short of rhapsody yet full of emotion, Winthrop's letters sometimes privatize this love as the magical and secret conveyance of thoughts between a husband and wife. In his famous sermon on the voyage over in 1630, however, Winthrop's discourse on charity may retain a significant residue of social circumstance, but its celebration of a love appropriate for "extraordinary times and occasions" anticipates a community "all knitt more nearly together in the Bond of brotherly affeccion" (2.283).

Throughout its history, Winthrop claims, the Christian church has been distinguished by "the sweete Sympathie of affeccions which was in the members of this body one towardes another." But in the "great migration" of the 1630s, it is only by revitalizing Christian love that the colonists can perfect their own congregational church, "for to loue and liue beloued is the soules paradice, both heare and in heaven" (2.290–92). In sum, the bond of love must be powerful enough to unify the hilltop city in spirit, in good times and bad. One of its worst contaminants is held to be self-interest at the expense of duty toward and affection for the whole, the prevention of which is abetted by a nonconformist polity that keeps its distance from those ungrateful separatists scornful of the mother church.

Whatever the various motives of the 21,000 emigrants from Caroline England to the New World, the size of the group testifies to the pervasiveness of Winthrop's desire to sail and rebuild beyond what Andrew Delbanco has described as an England sullied by "casuistical compromise."[26] But for the affiliates of Hutchinson, Winthrop himself embodied such a compromise corroding the heart of New England. Even a cursory study of his papers reveals that like Thomas Shepard, John Cotton, and John Davenport, Winthrop faced what scholars have variously named an "ordeal" or "dilemma," not least in the realization that the demands of colonial living and day-to-day struggle for grace prompted, even compelled, a search for the truth in love, an inquiry that could not be pursued outside the network of human circumstance.[27]

In her modification of Perry Miller's seminal study of the covenantal and preparationist components of the "New England mind," Janice Knight restores to prominence a rival New England orthodoxy that accentuated love. This, the orthodoxy of the so-called Spiritual Brotherhood, prevails in such colonists as Cotton, Davenport, and Henry Vane, and derives from Sibbes and Preston in the homeland. It stresses an emotive mysticism, a boundlessly benevolent God, a consuming "transformation of the heart," and a rhapsodic, lyrical style. It de-emphasizes "the *ordo salutis* as a sermonic plot," with that plot's gradations, covenants, preparatory processes, and created means of dispensing grace.[28]

In England, Knight argues, the Spiritual Brotherhood valued preaching so highly that its members were willing to compromise the supposed purity of congregationalism, a predilection that allowed them to gain influence and presence even at court. In Massachusetts, however, they were active, even aggressive contestants in the explosive battle and complex negotiation over orthodoxy that unfolded from 1635 to 1638. Their rivals, the so-called Intellectual Fathers, countered the orthodoxy of God's love with an orthodoxy of God's power, its corollaries emphasizing the *ordo salutis*, preparation as a "protracted process," covenant, created means, congregationalism, measure rather than boundlessness, print rather than pulpit, logical or incremental discourse rather than lyrical rhapsody, and "the functional application not the indwelling of Christ" (78). The Intellectual Fathers prescribed the strenuous, ongoing struggle with the "conditionality" of God's grace, a term which according to the *Oxford English Dictionary* often entails a careful and fervent inspection of circumstance (89–95).

By contrast, the Spiritual Brothers celebrate God's absolute promise, limitless mercy, preemptive union with a soul prior to any faith or sanctification, and warm divine breath on (rather than violent strikes against) the human heart. Whereas the Spiritual Brothers marvel at God's expansive love, the Intellectual Fathers examine love in terms of the circumstances of covenantal and casuistic obligation. As Knight puts it, Ames's characteristic analysis of love "hinges on the force of rule and the trope of measuring. Just as their sermons unfold in measured units, and just as the *ordo salutis* insists on a measured progression, so too love is quite literally to be divided and weighed. Ames sets out rules for those times 'when we cannot exercise our love actively towards all,' a contingency that Sibbes and Cotton prefer not to consider. Ames, however, spends his energy on precisely this circumstance" (169).

Indeed, the preparationists are multiply invested in the rigorous examination of circumstance. The individual sinner is commanded to perambulate through what Thomas Hooker calls "all these sinfull circumstances"; to persist in this spiritual journey until the "heart [has] sunke vnder these circumstances thus gathered together"; and to taxonomize the conditions or "five generall circumstances of preparation."[29] In turn, circumstantial preparation has its objective correlatives in church and society. As Edmund Morgan has shown, conversion narratives became increasingly critical in the 1630s for membership in the congregational polity, a criterion even dubbed "the Circumstantial manner of joyning to the church."[30] If this entrance narrative had to be compelling in its details and plots, Congregationalists also argued that their polity afforded a "precise practique knowledge of the fact and frame of spirit in the person transgressing," that is, "into the circumstantiation of the fact, and person."[31]

In addition to the redemptive process and its narrative, the Preparationists confront ecclesiastical circumstance in their sifting of "all known means" of grace in the ordinances of God, and in their Amesian casuistry of worship, social practices, and works.[32] Ames's *Marrow of Theology* can be fairly said at various points to harp on circumstance, from "All the circumstances [that] must be good to make the shape or the mode [of actions] good," to "the circumstances of worship to be especially observed," inward and outward and, among the former, the "antecedent, concomitant, or consequent."[33]

As Knight concedes and Delbanco italicizes, the plurality of orthodoxies in Massachusetts was not a simply or neatly divided polemical campaign. Rather, it suspended such mediators as Cotton, Davenport, and Shepard between their overwhelming desire for God's merciful love and an equally formidable respect for God's just power. Boston itself hung in the balance between a *locus amoenus* of loving spiritual siblings and a regulated polity of laws and obligations.[34]

Some of the most poignant reports from Massachusetts testify to the all- too-soon and utterly demoralizing deflation of great love in the New World. Among others, Thomas Shepard illustrates how complex and plaintive this struggle between love and circumstance could become. In *The Parable of the Ten Virgins Unfolded*, he distances himself from – and repeatedly indicts – the Antinomians' denigration of God's created ordinances in their "golden dreams of grace."[35] But his other choral refrain – one that betrays his onetime affiliation with Antinomian strains of piety – laments the decay of love in New England, a decline which he tries to remedy with a return to those ordinances that Anne Hutchinson despises as the acid corroding love. It is for good reason, then, that Shepard quotes 2 Thessalonians 2.10, "They receive not the truth in love," for it is Winthrop's attempt to legislate the reception of love in truth that epitomizes the irreparable breach in the New England projection of a city on the hill.[36]

For Winthrop, the England of 1629 was a world inhabited by hollow men. Of a friend he asked, "why meet we so many wandering ghostes in shape of men, so many spectacles of misery in all our streets, our houses full of victuals, and our entryes of hunger-starved Christians?"[37] His decision to emigrate appears to have been a sudden one, following his disenchantment with the Court of Wards and with a king who maltreated his parliaments.[38] In its wake, he fixated on a casuistry of colonization. No doubt his own prudent, legal, and covenantal mind had a penchant for such analysis, but his correspondents and friends compelled him to that casuistry all the same. One associate stands out in this regard: Robert Ryece. Ryece cautions Winthrop about "vayne hopes with many difficulties and vncertaynties" concealed behind the fancied perfections of the Massachusetts dream; and he urges Winthrop to fulfill his vocation by helping to repair what the latter himself calls "euill and declininge tymes" in England.[39]

In turn, Winthrop labors to convince Ryece and others of the legitimacy of his involvement in New England. In several drafts, he spells out his justifications in "arguments for the plantation": its service to the mother church, its rejection of England's pervasive dishonesty and corruption, its answer to demoralization and malaise, the justice of colonial occupation, and the advantage of gentle and experienced occupants, the imminence of divine judgment against England, and the various benefits of New England, whether that place be understood as a paradise or simply as a hiding place from which those abdicated European dangers can be held in contempt (2.111–13).

But even when Ryece has accepted Winthrop's reasoning, he presses the soon-to-be governor for an analysis of "all necessary circumstances" (2.127). And even conceding this much legality to the enterprise, Ryece continues to remind Winthrop of how much the church at home needs his leadership and attention, for "the furtherance of a particular church is not so to be preferred, before the betteringe of some smalle parte of a church allredy setled, that by absence of wonted care and respecte, the same maye suffer a defecte and diminution in recession" (2.128). With a sense of what is lost at home, Ryece encourages Winthrop to be ever vigilant, even fearful of failure in the New World, for fear occasions policy and policy preempts or at least mitigates religious factions, political incompetence, economic vicissitudes, social tensions, and ruination by disease, war, and mutiny.

It is Anne Hutchinson's challenge to civil, male, and ecclesiastical authority that stimulates Winthrop to veer away from "familistical" fancies in the direction of the circumstances of truth. With the emergence of Hutchinson in the middle part of the decade, Winthrop is compelled to combat her rhetorically powerful, socially legitimate, and spiritually authoritative critiques of church ordinances, of preachers, and of the civil and soteriological conceptions of personhood. One recourse for Winthrop, not a very viable one, is to quash the debate; in this spirit "it was earnestly desired, that the word person might be forborn, being a term of human invention, and tending to doubtful disputation in this case." Others, especially Cotton, seek to discover and stabilize the crux of a theological squabble that to many bystanders seems airy thin and elusive. As Cotton ventures the point, the controversy is all "about magnifying the grace of God; one party seeking to advance the grace of God within us, and the other to advance the grace of God towards us."[40] This much is clear: that the so-called Antinomians want a faith generated exclusively by the Holy Spirit's preemptive unification with and transformation of the self; and that such an absolute promise obviates any conditional concerns for an actively justifying faith, the created means for dispensing grace, the evidence of sanctification, and the casuistry of worship and duty in the face of doubt.[41]

Sometimes, ironically, Hutchinson evades her examiners by equivocating "with such explanations and circumstances as gave no satisfaction to the church."[42] But as her impolitic claims on the immediate inspiration of the Holy Spirit let on, she seeks to remove all circumstance – all naturalness and humanness – from the consuming unification of the self with divinity, a desire that re-creates the Family of Love's allegations of being "godded with God."[43] Winthrop's own repudiation of "rank familist[s]" and of monstrously "familistical opinions" spells the subjection of fanciful love to rational circumstance in his orthodoxy; it announces an emphasis on law, government, social decorum and hierarchy, religious conformity, and spiritual preparation, all deeply involved in mapping, anatomizing, and controlling circumstance.[44] For Hutchinson and her loyal followers, this turn begins New England's descent into what William Stoever glosses as "the moral ambiguities of creaturely existence . . . the canons of 'common,' 'earthly,' merely 'legal' morality."[45]

In condemning John Wheelwright's provocative Fast-Day sermon – that sermon in which the preacher appears in the eyes of Hutchinson's critics to recommend insurrection and to tar virtually all authorized preachers with the brush of "legalism" – Winthrop reproves the Antinomians for their naivete regarding the circumstances of faith. In one instance, he chides Wheelwright for his satirical sleights of hand, remarking "that he who designes a man by such circumstances, as doe note him out to common intendments, doth as much as if he named the party."[46]

But more elaborately than this lesson in pulpit oratory, Winthrop justifies the censorial practices of the civil court with an elementary lesson in the decorum that modifies truth, "so the difference of persons and places, made a difference in the season of the doctrine."[47] A proper study of the appropriate texts in the Bible would, Winthrop concludes, no doubt have informed Wheelwright "that the Spirit of God doth teach his servants to discern of seasons, as well as of truths; for if there be such a point in wisdom, as men call discretion, sure, Religion (which maketh truely wise) doth not deprive the servants of God of the right use thereof" (295–96). To find the truth in love means in Winthrop's critique to resituate God's love within the economies of nature, society, and interiority from which the desire to escape is a vain impious fancy.

In 1637, Peter Bulkeley sent a letter to John Cotton in which he laments the dearth of love in the city on a hill: "I doe confesse I haue found as little [love] toward myselfe here, as euer I did in any place that god brought me vnto. It is the place that I haue desired to shew loue vnto . . . and yett haue I found soe much strangenes, alienation, and soe much neglect from some whoe would sometimes haue visited me with diverse myles going."[48] As Delbanco argues, the colonists had always been fearful of becoming or remaining the creatures of the self-interest, casuistic adjustments, worldly duties, and spiritual brokerage that were eviscerating the church flocks back in England. For those in search of a love beyond chronic doubt, personal respects, and ambiguous spiritual processes, the ghosts of London appeared to have come over on the Arbella with them, with sin following the church just as Herbert's "Church Militant" predicts. "In America," Delbanco writes, "the language of ecstasy gave way in Shepard's mind to a language of discipline," and all around the colony, in Winthrop as well as Shepard and Cotton, the failure of the people to let the spirit of love annihilate circumstance was experienced as "a sense . . . of grievous imaginative loss."[49]

In complex and dynamic ways, advocates of the Stuart Church of England secured their imaginative, spiritual, and intellectual territory apart from papists and separatists.[50] But security was always situated within a fluctuating boundary. Most intensely during the reign of Charles Stuart, the Church of England was bolstered and subverted by an extraordinary survey of the ordinary conditions that characterized the conceptual landscape of English Protestantism. Variously hopeful and beleaguered, inventors of Caroline orthodoxy attempted to convert the vexations of circumstantial compromise into a code of valor, a boon to the fancy, a genealogy of religious truths, a decorum of holiness, and a natural philosophy. But for the children of Rome or for the sojourners to Boston, the criteria of love and truth – of "kind pity" and "brave scorn," as Donne once wrote – wakened dreams of perfection with the chill of creature discomfort. Circumstance was the scourge and the minister of their cities on the hill.

Notes

INTRODUCTION

1 C. A. Patrides, ed., *Sir Thomas Browne: The Major Works* (New York: Penguin Books, 1977), 148.

2 Achsah Guibbory, *Ceremony and Community from Herbert to Milton: Literature, Religion and Cultural Conflict in Seventeenth-Century England* (New York: Cambridge University Press, 1998); and Kevin Sharpe, *Remapping Early Modern England: The Culture of Seventeenth-Century Politics* (New York: Cambridge University Press, 2000).

3 William Laud, *The Works*, 7 vols., ed. William Scott and James Bliss (Oxford: John Henry Parker, 1847–60), 4.336.

4 Julian Davies, *The Caroline Captivity of the Church: Charles I and the Remoulding of Anglicanism, 1625–1641* (Oxford: Clarendon Press, 1992), 3. Further references will be made parenthetically to this text and to H. R. McAdoo, *The Structure of Caroline Moral Theology* (New York: Longmans, Green and Co., 1949); McAdoo's *The Spirit of Anglicanism: A Survey of Anglican Theological Method in the Seventeenth Century* (London: Adam & Charles Black, 1965); and Paul Elmer More and Frank Leslie Cross, *Anglicanism: The Thought and Practice of the Church of England, Illustrated from the Religious Literature of the Seventeenth Century* (Milwaukee, Wisconsin: Morehouse Publishing Co., 1935).

5 McAdoo, *Spirit*, 30.

6 Kevin Sharpe, *The Personal Rule of Charles I* (New Haven: Yale University Press, 1992).

7 Patrides, ed., *Sir Thomas Browne*, 61.

8 Joseph Mede, *The Works* (London, 1677), 15, 742, 823.

9 *The Oxford English Dictionary* (Oxford: Clarendon Press, 1989).

10 *Othello*, III.iii.370, in David Bevington, ed., *The Complete Works of William Shakespeare*, 4th edition (New York: Harper Collins, 1992), 1146.

11 *The Winter's Tale*, V.i.90–92, in Bevington, ed., *Complete Works of William Shakespeare*, 1519.

12 *Hamlet*, III.iii.83, in Bevington, ed., *Complete Works of William Shakespeare*, 1095.

13 Laud, *Works*, 2.xii–xvi. George Herbert, "The British Church," in Louis L. Martz, ed., *George Herbert and Henry Vaughan* (New York: Oxford University Press, 1986), 97.

14 Guibbory, *Ceremony*, 4.
15 John Donne, *Biathanatos*, III.iii.3, in Neil Rhodes, ed., *John Donne: Selected Prose* (New York: Penguin Books, 1987), 78.
16 George Parfitt, ed., *Ben Jonson, The Complete Poems* (Baltimore: Penguin Books, 1975), 434–35.
17 Seneca, *Naturales Quaestiones*, trans. Thomas H. Corcoran (Cambridge, Mass.: Harvard University Press, 1971), 111. For Bacon, see *The "Instauratio Magna": Last Writings*, ed. Graham Rees (Oxford: Clarendon Press, 2000), 212–13.
18 *Outlines of Pyrrhonism*, in *Sextus Empiricus*, 3 vols., trans. R. G. Bury (New York: G. P. Putnam's Sons, 1933), 1.61.
19 Laud, *Works*, 4.336–38.
20 Hugh Trevor-Roper, "Three Foreigners: The Philosophers of the Puritan Revolution," in *Religion, the Reformation and Social Change, and Other Essays*, rev. 3rd edition (London: Secker & Warburg, 1984), 246.
21 For Charles's theological dyslexia, see Davies, *Caroline Captivity*, 12.
22 John Stachniewski, *The Persecutory Imagination: English Puritanism and the Literature of Religious Despair* (Oxford: Clarendon Press, 1991).
23 Thomas Carew, "An Elegie upon . . . Dr. Iohn Donne," in Rhodes Dunlap, ed., *The Poems of Thomas Carew, with His Masque "Coelum Britannicum"* (Oxford: Clarendon Press, 1949), 73.
24 *Hamlet*, I.iii.103, in Bevington, ed., *Complete Works of William Shakespeare*, 1073.

1 THE CHURCH HEROIC: CHARLES, LAUD, AND LITTLE GIDDING

1 Achsah Guibbory, *Ceremony and Community from Herbert to Milton: Literature, Religion and Cultural Conflict in Seventeenth-Century England* (New York: Cambridge University Press, 1998), 4.
2 Philip Nichols, *Sir Francis Drake Reuiued* (London, 1626), title page.
3 Christopher Hodgkins, "Stooping to Conquer: Heathen Idolatry and Protestant Humility in the Imperial Legend of Sir Francis Drake," *Studies in Philology*, 94 (1997): 428–64, quotation on 433.
4 Mervyn James, "English Politics and the Concept of Honour, 1485–1642," *Past & Present*, Supplement 3 (1978): 1–92, quotation on 72.
5 *Vox Coeli*, in Thomas Scot, *Works* (Utrecht, 1624), separately paginated, 36.
6 *The Second Part of Vox Populi*, in Scot, *Works*, separately paginated, 26.
7 Thus a Tuscan ambassador, quoted in R. Malcolm Smuts, *Court Culture and the Origins of a Royalist Tradition in Early Stuart England* (Philadelphia: University of Pennsylvania Press, 1987), 37.
8 Smuts, *Court Culture*, 21.
9 Kevin Sharpe, *The Personal Rule of Charles I* (New Haven: Yale University Press, 1992), 45.
10 J. S. A. Adamson, "Chivalry and Political Culture in Caroline England," in *Culture and Politics in Early Stuart England*, ed. Kevin Sharpe and Peter Lake (Stanford University Press, 1993), 161–97; and Marlin E. Blaine, "Epic,

Romance, and History in Davenant's 'Madagascar'," *Studies in Philology*, 95 (1998): 293–319.

11 Stephen Orgel and Roy Strong, *Inigo Jones: The Theatre of the Stuart Court*, 2 vols. (Berkeley: University of California Press, 1973), 668.

12 *The Decayes of the Cathedral Church of St. Paul* (London, 1631), 17. For the classical model, see Graham Parry, *The Golden Age Restor'd: The Culture of the Stuart Court, 1603–42* (New York: St. Martin's Press, 1981), 261.

13 Lancelot Andrewes, *A Discourse of Ceremonies Retained and Used in Christian Churches*, in *The Works of Lancelot Andrewes*, 11 vols. (Oxford: John Henry Parker, 1854), 6.365–92. The authorship of this text, which was first published in 1653, has been questioned.

14 Peter Heylyn, *Antidotum Lincolniense* (London, 1637), 2.80.

15 Quoted in George Ornsby, ed., *The Correspondence of John Cosin, Publications of the Surtees Society*, 52 (1869): 166–67.

16 On Williams and the altar policy, see Sharpe, *Personal Rule*, 337–38; and Julian Davies, *The Caroline Captivity of the Church: Charles I and the Remoulding of Anglicanism, 1625–1641* (Oxford: Clarendon Press, 1992), chap. 6.

17 John Williams, *The Holy Table Name and Thing* (Printed for the Diocese of Lincoln, 1637), 233.

18 On the ceiling, see Per Palme, *The Triumph of Peace: A Study of the Whitehall Banqueting House* (Stockholm: Almqvist & Wiksell, 1956); D. J. Gordon, *The Renaissance Imagination*, ed. Stephen Orgel (Berkeley: University of California Press, 1975), 24–50; and Roy Strong, *Britannia Triumphans: Inigo Jones, Rubens and Whitehall Palace* (New York: Thames & Hudson, 1981).

19 Parry, *Golden Age Restor'd*, 184.

20 For the masque and ship money, see Strong, *Britannia Triumphans*, 7.

21 Orgel and Strong, *Inigo Jones*, 663, 666.

22 Orgel and Strong, *Inigo Jones*, 600–01. Cf. Parry, *Golden Age Restor'd*, 196: "the Queen was fabled to be of Indian origin."

23 Hugo Grotius, *True Religion* (London, 1632), Book 4: the book is interested in the conversion of East Indians in particular; and Thomas Morton, *New English Canaan or New Canaan* (1637), 20–22.

24 For Charles, Laud and the "church abroad," see Hugh Trevor-Roper, *Archbishop Laud, 1573–1645*, 3rd edition (London: Macmillan, 1988), 258–61.

25 Rhodes Dunlap, ed., *The Poems of Thomas Carew, with His Masque "Coelum Britannicum"* (Oxford: Clarendon Press, 1949), 280.

26 Orgel and Strong, *Inigo Jones*, 574.

27 Sharpe, *Personal Rule*, 222.

28 James, "English Politics and the Concept of Honour," 73–74.

29 For Markham and Lord Brooke, see James, "English Politics and the Concept of Honour." For the legacy of Foxe, see John R. Knott, *Discourses of Martyrdom in English Literature, 1563–1694* (New York: Cambridge University Press, 1993); and William Lamont, *Godly Rule: Politics and Religion, 1603–60* (New York: St. Martin's Press, 1969).

30 William Laud, *The Works*, 7 vols., ed. William Scott and James Bliss (Oxford: John Henry Parker, 1847–60), 6.460 and 7.351.

31 For Laud on the "laberinth," see *Works*, 7.367. For the "hedge," see *Works*, 2.xii–xvi. For Finet, see Albert J. Loomie, ed., *Ceremonies of Charles I: The Note Books of John Finet, 1628–1641* (New York: Fordham University Press, 1987), 15–19. For Sydenham, see Kenneth Fincham, "Episcopal Government, 1603–1642," in *The Early Stuart Church, 1603–1642*, ed. Kenneth Fincham (Stanford University Press, 1993), 71–91, quotation on 91.

32 Peter Heylyn, *The History of . . . St. George*, 2nd edition (London, 1633), 58.

33 Henry Burton, *For God, and the King* (1636), 30.

34 Parry, *Golden Age Restor'd*, 267.

35 Ornsby, ed., *Correspondence of John Cosin*, 21, 85, 97.

36 Trevor-Roper, *Archbishop Laud*, 74, mentions Montagu's favorite quotation.

37 A. L. Maycock, *Nicholas Ferrar of Little Gidding* (Grand Rapids, Michigan: William B. Eerdmans Publishing Co., 1980), 109.

38 Maycock, *Nicholas Ferrar*, 109.

39 *The Story Books of Little Gidding, Being the Religious Dialogues Recited in the Great Room, 1631–2*, ed. and intro. E. Cruwys Sharland (London: Seeley and Co., 1899), xliv.

40 Louis L. Martz, ed., *George Herbert and Henry Vaughan* (New York: Oxford University Press, 1986), 203.

41 On Foxe, see Knott, *Discourses of Martyrdom*, chap. 2. For Nicholas Ferrar's love of Foxe, see *The Ferrar Papers*, ed. B. Blackstone (Cambridge University Press, 1938), 10; and J. E. B. Mayor, ed., *Cambridge in the Seventeenth Century: Nicholas Ferrar: Two Lives by His Brother John and by Dr. Jebb* (Cambridge: Macmillan, 1855). The Gidding interest in historical narratives is well documented; see Blackstone, ed., *Ferrar Papers*, 46–48. For a brief discussion of Gidding interest in "Christian heroism," see Pamela Tudor-Craig, "Charles I and Little Gidding," in *For Veronica Wedgwood These: Studies in Seventeenth-Century History*, ed. Richard Ollard and Pamela Tudor-Craig (London: Collins, 1986), 174–87.

42 The quotation from Foxe is taken from *The Acts and Monuments of John Foxe*, 4th edition, revised and corrected by Josiah Pratt, 8 vols. (London: Religious Tract Society, 1887), 1.xxvi.

43 Quoted by Maycock, *Nicholas Ferrar*, 308; cf. Mayor, *Cambridge in the Seventeenth Century*, 72.

44 Elizabeth Clarke, "George Herbert's *The Temple*: The Genius of Anglicanism and the Inspiration of Poetry," in *The English Religious Tradition and the Genius of Anglicanism*, ed. Geoffrey Rowell (Wantage: IKON, 1992), 127–44, quotation on 135.

45 For a revision of the Little Gidding relationship with Charles I, see Robert Van der Weyer, "Nicholas Ferrar and Little Gidding: A Reappraisal," in *For Veronica Wedgwood These*, ed. Ollard and Tudor-Craig, 152–72. Thomas Fuller mentions the "causeless cavil" over Little Gidding (see Mayor, ed., *Cambridge in the Seventeenth Century*, 75–76).

46 See Blackstone, ed., *Ferrar Papers*, 74. Edward Lenton's letter describing his visit to Little Gidding appears in Mayor, *Cambridge in the Seventeenth Century*, xxiii–xxvi.

47 For the Little Academy, there are three main sources: Sharland, ed., *Story Books*; Blackstone, ed., *Ferrar Papers*; and A. N. Williams, ed., *Conversations at Little Gidding* (New York: Cambridge University Press, 1970).

48 For the critique of "opinions," see Sharland, ed., *Story Books*, 1–2; for the priest of Antioch, 23–28; for King Henry, 33; for Katherine, 36–37.

49 Martz, ed., *George Herbert and Henry Vaughan*, 59.

50 Karl Brandi, *The Emperor Charles V: The Growth and Destiny of a Man and of a World-Empire*, trans. C. V. Wedgwood (London: Jonathan Cape, 1939), 13.

51 Williams, ed., *Conversations*, 29.

52 David Ransome, intro., *The Ferrar Papers, 1590–1790, in Magdalene College, Cambridge* (East Ardsley, England: Microform Academic Publishers, 1992), Reel 3.

53 *Ferrar Papers, 1590–1790*, intro. Ransome, Reel 3.

54 Samuel Purchas, *Hakluytus Posthumus*, 20 vols. (New York: AMS, 1965), 1.20.

55 *Ferrar Papers, 1590–1790*, intro. Ransome, Reels 1–3.

56 See John Watkins, *The Specter of Dido: Spenser and Virgilian Epic* (New Haven: Yale University Press, 1995).

57 For the Ferrars and the Virginia Company, see D. R. Ransome, ed. and intro., *Sir Thomas Smith's Misgovernment of the Virginia Company by Nicholas Ferrar* (Cambridge: Roxburghe Club, 1990), xi–xxii.

58 See Martz, ed., *George Herbert and Henry Vaughan*, 178. For the poem as an epic, see Raymond Anselment, "'The Church Militant': George Herbert and the Metamorphosis of Christian History," *Huntington Library Quarterly*, 41 (1978): 299–316. For the poem's argument, see Kenneth Alan Hovey, "'Wheel'd about . . . into Amen': 'The Church Militant' on Its Own Terms," *George Herbert Journal*, 10 (1986–87): 71–84.

59 Anselment, "'The Church Militant,'" 313.

60 Colin Burrow, *Epic Romance: Homer to Milton* (New York: Oxford University Press, 1993), 222–32.

61 A. B. Chambers, "'Good Friday, 1613. Riding Westward': The Poem and the Tradition," *English Literary History*, 28 (1961): 31–53, see 52.

62 Williams, ed., *Conversations*, 68–69.

63 Blackstone, ed., *Ferrar Papers*, 119.

64 Sharland, ed., *Story Books*, 192.

65 Williams, ed., *Conversations*, 81, 88.

66 For Nicholas's iconoclasm, see Blackstone, ed., *Ferrar Papers*, 75.

67 On the bonfire, which took place 28 November 1637, see Blackstone, ed., *Ferrar Papers*, 63.

68 Sharland, ed., *Story Books*, 120.

69 For Nicholas's travels, see Maycock, *Nicholas Ferrar*, 35–61; and Mayor, *Cambridge in the Seventeenth Century*.

70 Blackstone, ed., *Ferrar Papers*, 127.

71 Blackstone, ed., *Ferrar Papers*, 144–45.

72 Williams, ed., *Conversations*, 172. For the struggle at Little Gidding with the lack of an "adequate tradition of spiritual teaching," see Maycock, *Nicholas Ferrar*, 7.

73 Williams, ed., *Conversations*, 172.

2 GREAT TEW AND THE SKEPTICAL HERO

1 George Parfitt, ed., *Ben Jonson, The Complete Poems* (Baltimore: Penguin Books, 1975), 212.

2 For the notion that Lucius Cary always felt compelled to "pass for a hero," see Kenneth B. Murdock, *The Sun at Noon: Three Biographical Sketches* (New York: Macmillan, 1939), 61–70. Other biographical sources cited below include Kurt Weber, *Lucius Cary, Second Viscount Falkland* (New York: Columbia University Press, 1940); J. A. R. Marriott, *The Life and Times of Lucius Cary, Viscount Falkland* (New York: G. P. Putnam's Sons, 1907); and Irene Coltman, *Private Men and Public Causes: Philosophy and Politics in the English Civil War* (London: Faber & Faber, 1962).

3 For the Graces, see Richard Bagwell, *Ireland under the Stuarts and during the Interregnum*, 3 vols. (London: Holland Press, 1963), 1.180–85; and Aidan Clarke, *The Graces, 1625–41*, Irish History Series, 8 (1968).

4 "To Sir Henry Cary," in Parfitt, ed., *Ben Jonson, The Complete Poems*, 55.

5 Edward Hyde, Earl of Clarendon, *The History of the Rebellion and Civil Wars in England begun in the year 1641*, 6 vols., ed. W. Dunn Macray (Oxford: Clarendon Press, 1888), 3.187–89; and *The Life of Edward Earl of Clarendon . . . written by himself*, 2 vols. (Oxford: Clarendon Press, 1827), 1.44.

6 Christopher Hodgkins, "Stooping to Conquer: Heathen Idolatry and Protestant Humility in the Imperial Legend of Sir Francis Drake," *Studies in Philology*, 94 (1997): 433.

7 Barry Weller and Margaret W. Ferguson, eds., *Elizabeth Cary the Lady Falkland: "The Tragedy of Miriam the Fair Queen of Jewry"* (Berkeley: University of California, 1994), 12–17.

8 *The History of the Life, Reign, and Death of Edward II* (London, 1680), 8.

9 Weber, *Lucius Cary*, 283.

10 *The Poems of Lucius Carey, Viscount Falkland*, ed. Alexander B. Grosart, Miscellanies of the Fuller Worthies' Library (London, 1871), 422–23.

11 For this dilemma over duty in the Falkland circle, see J. C. Hayward, "New Directions in Studies of the Falkland Circle," *The Seventeenth Century*, 2 (1987): 19–48.

12 Rhodes Dunlap, ed., *The Poems of Thomas Carew, with His Masque "Coelum Britannicum"* (Oxford: Clarendon Press, 1949), 74–77.

13 Parfitt, ed., *Ben Jonson, The Complete Poems*, 193.

14 For Cary's admiration of *Coelum Britannicum*, see Weber, *Lucius Cary*, 63. For the gift of Synesius to Robert Cresswell, see Hayward, "New Directions," 23–24.

15 Sir John Suckling, "A Session of the Poets," in Thomas Clayton, ed., *Sir John Suckling: The Non-Dramatic Works* (Oxford: Clarendon Press, 1971), 75.

16 Clarendon, *The Life*, 1.47.

17 Aside from Proclus's commentary on Plato's *Cratylus*, the key text is Iamblichus of Chalcis, *On the Mysteries, De Mysteriis Aegyptiorum*, ed. Stephen Ronan, with the translations of Thomas Taylor and Alexander Wilder (Hastings, England: Chthonius Books, 1989). Gregory Shaw's discussion is in *Theurgy and the Soul: The Neoplatonism of Iamblichus* (University Park: Penn State University Press, 1995), 132–33.

18 Iamblichus, *On the Mysteries*, 50, 52.

19 Hans Lewy, *Chaldaean Oracles and Theurgy* (Paris: Etudes Augustiniennes, 1978), 195; Shaw, *Theurgy and the Soul*, 79.

20 Leone Ebreo, *Dialoghi D'Amore*, trans. F. Friedebert and Jean H. Barnes, intro. Cecil Roth (London: The Soncino Press, 1937). For the etymological conflation, see Mark Rose, *Heroic Love: Studies in Sidney and Spenser* (Cambridge, Mass.: Harvard University Press, 1968), 11.

21 Bruno, *The Heroic Frenzies*, trans. Paul Eugene Memmo, Jr. (Chapel Hill: University of North Carolina, 1964), 17. For the diseased version of heroic love, see Burton's *Anatomy of Melancholy*, 6 vols., ed. Thomas C. Faulkner et al. (Oxford: Clarendon Press, 1989–2000), 3.39–65.

22 Bruno, *Heroic Frenzies*, 99.

23 See Torquato Tasso, *Discourses on the Heroic Poem*, trans. Mariella Cavalchini and Irene Samuel (Oxford: Clarendon Press, 1973), 16, 47–49; and Michael Drayton, *Englands Heroicall Epistles*, in *The Works of Michael Drayton*, 5 vols., ed. J. William Hebel (Oxford: Basil Blackwell, 1961), 2.130.

24 Eusebius, *Preparation for the Gospel*, 2 parts, trans. Edwin Hamilton Gifford (Grand Rapids, Michigan: Baker Book House, 1981), 1.80–141. For Augustine's critique, see *City of God*, ed. David Knowles, trans. Henry Bettensen (New York: Penguin, 1972), Book 9. Joseph Mede, *The Works* (London, 1677), 631–32; Gerhardus Vossius, *De Theologia Gentili* (1641), 296.

25 Edward Herbert, *Pagan Religion: A Translation of De Religione Gentilium*, trans. John Anthony Butler (Binghamton, NY: Medieval and Renaissance Texts, 1996), 191.

26 Herbert, *Pagan Religion*, 201n, 203; chap. 15.

27 C. A. Patrides, ed., *The Cambridge Platonists* (Cambridge, Mass.: Harvard University Press, 1970), 164.

28 Hutton's argument appears in Anna Baldwin and Sarah Hutton, eds., *Platonism and the English Imagination* (New York: Cambridge University Press, 1994), 72.

29 Henry More, *A Platonick Song of the Soul*, ed. Alexander Jacob (Lewisburg: Bucknell University Press, 1998), 160.

30 Plutarch, *Moralia*, trans. Frank Cole Babbitt (Cambridge, Mass.: Harvard University Press, 1936), 5.379–87.

31 Hayward, "New Directions," 28.

32 Hayward, "New Directions," 24.

33 For Synesius and Neoplatonic heroes, see Alan Cameron et al., *Barbarians and Politics at the Court of Arcadius* (Berkeley: University of California Press, 1993), 353–54.

34 George Sandys, *Ovid's Metamorphoses* (Oxford, 1632), 393.

35 *Poems of Lucius Carey*, ed. Grosart, 383–84.

36 John Klause, "Hope's Gambit: The Jesuitical, Protestant, Skeptical Origins of Donne's Heroic Ideal," *Studies in Philology*, 91 (1994), 181–215.

37 Richard H. Popkin, *The History of Scepticism from Erasmus to Spinoza* (Berkeley: University of California Press, 1979).

38 John Donne, *The Complete English Poems*, ed. A. J. Smith (New York: Penguin Books, 1971), 163.

39 For rational theology, Falkland, and Erasmus, see John Tulloch, *Rational Theology and Christian Philosophy in England in the Seventeenth Century*, 2 vols. (London: William Blackwood and Sons, 1874), vol. 1; B. H. G. Wormald, *Clarendon: Politics, History, and Religion, 1640–1660* (University of Chicago Press, 1976), 257–59; and Hugh Trevor-Roper, *Catholics, Anglicans and Puritans: Seventeenth Century Essays* (University of Chicago Press, 1988), 170–230.

40 Charron, *Of Wisdom* (London, trans. before 1612), 11.

41 See Triplet's dedication of the 2nd edition of *A Discourse of Infallibility* to Henry Lord Viscount Falkland; and Clarendon's *Life*, 1.47.

42 Erasmus, "The Godly Feast," in *Ten Colloquies*, trans. Craig R. Thompson (New York: Liberal Arts Press, 1957), 172.

43 Trevor-Roper, *Catholics, Anglicans and Puritans*, 199–200.

44 Wormald, *Clarendon*, 247.

45 Trevor-Roper, *Catholics, Anglicans and Puritans*, 170, 208, 230.

46 Falkland, *A Discourse of Infallibility* (London, 1660), ci v.

47 Falkland, *Reply to Thomas White*, in *A Discourse of Infallibility*, 138–39.

48 Falkland, *Reply to Thomas White*, 221–23 (mistakenly numbered 221–31).

49 Samuel Parker, *A Free and Impartial Censure of the Platonick Philosophie* (New York: AMS, 1985), 22.

50 Wormald, *Clarendon*, 246.

51 Quoted by Wormald, *Clarendon*, 258–59.

52 William Chillingworth, *Religion of Protestants* (Oxford, 1638), preface, paragraph 20.

53 John Earle, *Microcosmography*, ed. Harold Osborne (London: University Tutorial Press, n.d.), 74–75. Cf. Aubrey's view that Chillingworth "much delighted in Sextus Empeiricus" (in Oliver Lawson Dick, ed., *Aubrey's Brief Lives* (London: Mandarin, 1992), 64.

54 Chillingworth, *Religion of Protestants*, 8. On Chillingworth's philosophy of religion, see Robert R. Orr, *Reason and Authority: The Thought of William Chillingworth* (Oxford University Press, 1967).

55 William Laud, *The Works*, 7 vols., ed. William Scott and James Bliss (Oxford: John Henry Parker, 1847–60), 2.173.

56 For Sandys and the New World, see Richard Beale Davis, *George Sandys, Poet-Adventurer: A Study in Anglo-American Culture in the Seventeenth Century* (New York: Columbia University Press, 1955).

57 Clarendon, *The Life*, 1.49.

58 See David J. Hill's introduction to A. C. Campbell's translation of *De Iure Belli ac Pacis* (New York: M. Walter Dunne, 1901). For Chillingworth and Grotius, see Weber, *Lucius Cary*, 187.

59 Richard Tuck, *Natural Rights Theories: Their Origin and Development* (New York: Cambridge University Press, 1979), chap. 3.

60 Grotius, *De Iure Belli ac Pacis*, 271–73.

61 The metaphor of passing is Murdock's, *The Sun at Noon*, 144.

62 For Cary and ship money, see Marriott, *Life and Times*, 129.

63 Quoted in Weber, *Lucius Cary*, 121.

64 Marriott, *Life and Times*, 177.

65 Marriott, *Life and Times*, 181–82.

66 For Clarendon on the church, see Wormald, *Clarendon*, 242–88. Cf. Clarendon, *The Life*, 1.61.

67 Morley's remark to an interlocutor's query about what positions the Arminians "hold" – the interlocutor is asking about doctrine – was that they hold all the best livings in England.

68 See Marriott, *Life and Times*, 226.

69 For a summary of the critique, see Marriott, *Life and Times*, 1–55.

70 Cf. Clarendon, *The History*, 3.189.

71 Clarendon, *The History*, 3.189.

72 Coltman, *Private Men*, 11.

73 Thomas Hobbes, trans., *Thucydides, The Peloponnesian War*, ed. David Grene (University of Chicago Press, 1989), xx. For Clarendon and his epic conventions, see George Miller, *Edward Hyde, Earl of Clarendon* (Boston: Twayne, 1983), 74–76.

74 Tacitus's *Agricola*, trans. H. Mattingly, rev. S. A. Handford (New York: Penguin Books, 1970), 51.

75 Tacitus, *Agricola*, 55–95.

76 Clarendon, *The Life*, 1.62.

77 Milton discusses his epic plans in the preface to the second book of *The Reason of Church Government*; for Hobbes's later views of heroism, see the prefatory matter to his translation of Homer.

78 Sir William Davenant, *Preface to Gondibert, An Heroick Poem*, in J. E. Spingarn, ed., *Critical Essays of the Seventeenth Century*, 3 vols. (Oxford: Clarendon Press, 1908), 2.1.

79 Hobbes, *Answer to Davenant*, in Spingarn, 2.60.

80 In addition to Suckling's account (*Non-Dramatic Works*, ed. Clayton, 75), see Clarendon, *The History*, 3.179–80, and *The Life*, 1.47.

81 William Alexander, *An Encouragement to Colonies* (London, 1624); Richard Eburne, *A Plaine Path-way to Plantations* (London, 1624); and Thomas Morton,

New English Canaan (Amsterdam); the quotations are taken from Alexander, A3v and Eburne, 7. The commonplace is discussed in Raymond Anselment, "'The Church Militant,' George Herbert and the Metamorphosis of Christian History" *Huntington Library Quarterly*, 41 (1978): 302; and in Dwight Levang, "George Herbert's 'The Church Militant' and the Chances of History," *Philological Quarterly*, 36 (1957): 265–68.

82 Quoted in Louis B. Wright, *Religion and Empire: The Alliance Between Piety and Commerce in English Expansion, 1558–1625* (Chapel Hill: University of North Carolina, 1943), 149.

83 Edwin Sandys, *Europae Speculum* (London, 1605), 205.

84 George Wither, *A Collection of Emblems* (1635) (Menston, England: Scolar Press, 1968), 30. For the marriage between power and wisdom, see 80, 103, 137, 163, and 238. Cf. Quarles's appeal to "heroick fire" in *Emblemes* (1635), 1 (text paginated separately). See also 18, 23, and 37. For the Order of the Bugle, see John Kerrigan, "Thomas Carew" in *Proceedings of the British Academy*, 74 (1988): 311–50; for the Order of the Fancy, see Timothy Raylor, *Cavaliers, Clubs, and Literary Culture: Sir John Mennes, James Smith, and the Order of the Fancy* (Newark: University of Delaware Press, 1994).

85 Quoted in Weber, *Lucius Cary*, 283.

86 Quoted in Davis, *George Sandys*, 46.

87 For the lotos eaters and the Queen of Bohemia, see Richard Beale Davis, "George Sandys and Two 'Uncollected' Poems," *Huntington Library Quarterly*, 12 (1948–49): 107. The quotations from Sandys's Ovid are taken from the 1632 Oxford edition, "the Minde of the Frontispeece" and 392–93.

88 Sandys's Ovid, dedication to the King.

89 For analogies, see Sandys's Ovid, 65, 253, and 454. Sandys's glosses are filled with commentary on "heroic" virtue (for instance, 187–90, 197, 329, 420, 426, 447, 475, and 478). In a poem on Sandys, Lucius Cary compares him favorably to Homer, Odysseus, and Grotius, for Sandys is at once an epic poet, adventurer, and missionary. See *The Poems of Lucius Carey*, ed. Grosart, 423–25.

90 For the church in lunar terms, see Laud, *Works*, 2.226 (with reference to Augustine's epistle cxix, cap. 6; and Wither, *A Collection of Emblemes*, 111.

91 Sandys's Ovid, 261.

92 Kenneth Murdock, *Literature and Theology in Colonial New England* (Cambridge, Mass.: Harvard University Press, 1949), 61.

93 Richard Beale Davis, "Two New Manuscript Items for a George Sandys Bibliography," *Publications of the Bibliographical Society of America*, 37 (1943): 221.

94 For Richard Norwood, see *The Journal of Richard Norwood*, intro. Wesley Frank Craven and Walter B. Hayward (New York: Scholars' Facsimiles and Reprints, 1945).

95 Nigel Smith, *Literature and Revolution in England, 1640–1660* (New Haven: Yale University Press, 1994), 203 and chap. 7.

3 BETWEEN LITURGY AND DREAMS

1 Achsah Guibbory, *Ceremony and Community from Herbert to Milton: Literature, Religion and Cultural Conflict in Seventeenth-Century England* (New York: Cambridge University Press, 1998), 8.

2 H-57, in Robert Herrick, *The Complete Poetry*, ed. J. Max Patrick (New York: Anchor, 1963), 31. Patrick cites Plutarch's *Moralia*, trans. Philemon Holland (1657), 215.

3 N-128, in Herrick, *Complete Poetry*, 497.

4 William Prynne, *A Breviate of the Life of William Laud, Arch-Bishop of Canterbury* (London, 1644), 33.

5 William Laud, *The Works*, 7 vols., ed. William Scott and James Bliss (Oxford: John Henry Parker, 1847–60), 4.365.

6 Laud, *Works*, 3.264. For dream lore, see Manfred Weidhorn, *Dreams in Seventeenth-Century English Literature* (The Hague: Mouton, 1970).

7 For a psychological treatment of the dreams, see Charles Carlton, *Archbishop William Laud* (New York: Routledge, 1987), 40, 52–53, 56, 64, 144–53.

8 For the status of imagination in the period, see William Rossky, "Imagination in the English Renaissance: Psychology and Poetic," *Studies in the Renaissance*, 5 (1958): 49–73.

9 See especially Julian Davies, *The Caroline Captivity of the Church: Charles I and the Remoulding of Anglicanism 1625–1641* (Oxford: Clarendon Press, 1992), chap. 2; and Kevin Sharpe, *The Personal Rule of Charles I* (New Haven: Yale University Press, 1992), 275–402.

10 Quoted in G. J. Cuming, *A History of Anglican Liturgy*, 2nd edition (London: Macmillan, 1982), 102.

11 William Lamont, *Marginal Prynne, 1600–1669* (London: Routledge & Kegan Paul, 1963); and Gerald R. Cragg, *Freedom and Authority: A Study of English Thought in the Early Seventeenth Century* (Philadelphia: Westminster, 1978), 115–18.

12 Ambrose Fisher, *A Defence of the Liturgie of the Church of England, or Booke of Common Prayer* (London, 1630), 148; Peter Heylyn, *The History of . . . St. George*, 2nd edition (London, 1633), 67, 74–75; Heylyn, *A Briefe and Moderate Answer, to . . . Henry Burton* (London, 1637), 124.

13 See Cosin, *The Works of the Right Reverend Father in God John Cosin, Lord Bishop of Durham*, 5 vols., ed. J. Sansom and James Bliss (Oxford: John Henry Parker, 1843–55), 1.96–124, quotation on 124.

14 *The Book of Common Prayer . . . for Scotland*, intro. James Cooper (London: W. Blackwood, 1904), 9, quoted by John Morrill in "A British Patriarchy?: Ecclesiastical Imperialism under the Early Stuarts," in Peter Roberts and Anthony Fletcher, eds., *Religion, Culture and Society in Early Modern Britain: Essays in Honour of Patrick Collinson* (New York: Cambridge University Press, 1994), 209–37, quotation on 235.

15 Richard Montagu, *A Gagg for the New Gospell? No; A New Gagg for an Old Goose* (1624) (Norwood, NJ: Walter J. Johnson, 1975), 74; and Montagu,

Appello Caesarem (1625) (New York: De Capo, 1972). References are made parenthetically in the text.

16 Thomas Fuller, *The Holy State and the Profane State*, 2 vols., ed. Maximilian Graff Walten (New York: Columbia University Press, 1938), 2.177.

17 Michael MacDonald, *Mystical Bedlam: Madness, Anxiety, and Healing in Seventeenth-Century England* (New York: Cambridge University Press, 1981), 157.

18 Quoted in MacDonald, *Mystical Bedlam*, 218–19.

19 John Stachniewski, *The Persecutory Imagination: English Puritanism and the Literature of Religious Despair* (Oxford: Clarendon Press, 1991) 25–27.

20 *Journal of Richard Norwood*, intro. Craven and Hayward, 26–27; *The Diary of Ralph Josselin, 1616–1683*, ed. Alan Macfarlane, *Records of Social and Economic History*, n.s. 3 (London: British Academy, 1976), 334–39.

21 Quoted in Stachniewski, *Persecutory Imagination*, 115.

22 Nigel Smith, *Perfection Proclaimed: Language and Literature in English Radical Religion, 1640–1660* (Oxford: Clarendon Press, 1989), 102.

23 See Gerrard Winstanley's *Works*, ed. George H. Sabine (New York: Russell & Russell, 1965), 569.

24 Lady Eleanor Davies, *Appeal . . . to Mr. Mace* (1646), 4–7.

25 Davies, *Appeal*, 20–21.

26 Quoted in George Ballard, *Memoirs of Several Ladies of Great Britain*, ed. Ruth Perry (Detroit: Wayne State, 1985), 261, from Heylyn's life of Laud, part 2, 266.

27 Ballard, *Memoirs*, 261–62. For "fleeting things," see Gerald Hammond, *Fleeting Things: English Poets and Poems, 1616–1660* (Cambridge, Mass.: Harvard University Press, 1990).

28 See *Cal. State Papers, Dom.*, January, 1637–38; and Laud, *Works*, 5.346.

29 Esther S. Cope, *Handmaid of the Holy Spirit: Dame Eleanor Davies Never Soe Mad a Ladie* (Ann Arbor: University of Michigan Press, 1992), 84.

30 Quoted in Kenneth Murdock, *Literature and Theology in Colonial New England* (Cambridge, Mass., Harvard University Press, 1949), 50, from *The Complete Works of Richard Sibbes*, 7 vols., ed. Alexander B. Grosart (London: James Nisbett, 1862), 1. ci.

31 Winstanley, *Works*, 260.

32 Thomas Edwards, *Gangraena*, intro. M. M. Goldsmith and Ivan Roots (Exeter: The Rota, 1977), 31.

33 Smith, *Perfection Proclaimed*, 73–103.

34 *Complete Works of Richard Sibbes*, ed. Grosart, 1.1.84.

35 Janice Knight, *Orthodoxies in Massachusetts: Rereading American Puritanism* (Cambridge, Mass.: Harvard University Press, 1994), 114–19.

36 Rossky, "Imagination in the English Renaissance," 49–73.

37 See Marsilio Ficino, *Three Books on Life*, trans. Carol V. Kaske and John R. Clark (Binghamton, NY: Medieval & Renaissance Texts & Studies, 1989), Book 3.

38 See Leonardus Lessius, *Hygiasticon* (Cambridge, 1634), 154–55.

39 Thomas Goodwin, *The Vanity of Thoughts Discovered with their Danger and Cure* (London, 1638), 1–2.

40 Lancelot Andrewes, *A Pattern of Catechistical Doctrine*, in *The Works of Lancelot Andrewes*, 11 vols. (Oxford: John Henry Parker, 1854), 6.82.

41 Francis Bacon, *De Augmentis Scientiarum*, book 5, chap. 1, in John M. Robertson, ed., *The Philosophical Works of Francis Bacon* (New York: E. P. Dutton, 1905), 499.

42 Fuller, *Holy State*, 2.177.

43 See John B. Payne, *Erasmus: His Theology of the Sacrament* (Richmond, Virginia: John Knox, 1970), 133–35; and Erasmus, *The Enchiridion*, trans. Raymond Himelick (Bloomington: Indiana University Press, 1963), especially Rule 5, chapter 14.

44 Edwin Sandys, *Europae Speculum* (London, 1605), 8–10.

45 Henry Burton, *For God, and the King* (1636), 34–35.

46 John Williams, *The Holy Table Name and Thing* (Printed for the Diocese of Lincoln, 1637), 198, 142.

47 Peter Heylyn, *Antidotum Lincolniense* (London, 1637), section 3, 36–37. For defenses of liturgy and ceremony, see Richard Hooker, *Of the Laws of Ecclesiastical Polity*, in The Folger Library Edition of the *Works of Richard Hooker*, 4 vols., ed. W. Speed Hill (Cambridge, Mass.: Harvard University Press, 1977–81); John Cosin, *A Collection of Private Devotions*, ed. P. G. Stanwood (Oxford: Clarendon Press, 1967), the preface; Jeremy Taylor, *An Apology for Authorized and Set Forms of Liturgy, against the Pretense of the Spirit*, in *Works*, 15 vols., ed. Reginald Heber (London: Longman, 1839), vol. 7; Taylor, *A Discourse of Prophesying*, in *Works*, vols. 7, 8; and Ambrose Fisher, *A Defense of the Liturgie*. For a summary of these matters, see Horton Davies, *Worship and Theology from Andrewes to Baxter and Fox, 1603–1690* (Princeton University Press, 1975), chap. 5.

48 Joseph Glanvill, *Some Discourses* (London, 1681), 80; cf. 3–4, 8–9, 39–40, 178–79, for discussions of fancy and dreams.

49 Taylor, *Works*, 8.212–13, 7.310.

50 Taylor, *Works*, 7.ccccxvi–ccccxvii.

51 Donne, quoted in Davies, *Worship and Theology*, 68; cf. 83.

52 Davies, *Worship and Theology*, 17.

53 Louis L. Martz, ed., *George Herbert and Henry Vaughan* (New York: Oxford University Press, 1986), 160–61.

54 Andrewes, *Works*, 5.60.

55 Davies, *Worship and Theology*, 204–05, 210, 260.

56 Barten Holyday, *Three Sermons* (London, 1625), 82.

57 Thomas Lawrence, *A Sermon Preached Before the Kings Maiestie at White-Hall, the VII. Of February, 1636*, 2nd edition (London, 1637), 2.

58 Thomas Lawrence, *Two Sermons* (Oxford, 1635), 34.

59 Foulke Robartes, *Gods Holy House and Service* (London, 1639), 88.

60 For the paganism of ceremony, see Andrewes, *Discourse of Ceremonies*, *Works*, 6.365–92; John Aubrey, *Remaines of Gentilisme and Judaisme*, in *Three Prose Works*,

ed. John Buchanan-Brown (Carbondale, Ill.: University of Illinois Press, 1972); and Thomas Fuller, *Church History of Britain*, ed. J. S. Brewer (Oxford University Press, 1845), vol. 1. On play and ritual, see Johan Huizinga, *Homo Ludens: A Study of the Play Element in Culture* (Boston: Beacon, 1950). For Prynne, in addition to *Histriomastix* (discussed in chap. 5 below), see *Documents Relating to the Proceedings against William Prynne, in 1634 and 1637*, ed. Samuel Rawson Gardiner (Westminster: Camden Society, 1877), 2–3.

61 *Documents Relating to . . . Prynne*, ed. Gardiner, 2–3.

62 *A Book of Masques in Honour of Allardyce Nicoll*, ed. T. J. B. Spencer and Stanley Wells (New York: Cambridge University Press, 1967), figs. 25–28; text on 358.

63 R. Malcolm Smuts, *Court Culture and the Origins of a Royalist Tradition in Early Stuart England* (Philadelphia: University of Pennsylvania Press, 1987), 237; see also Davies, *Worship and Theology*, 203, 213.

64 Ben Jonson, *Selected Masques*, ed. Stephen Orgel (New Haven: Yale University Press, 1970), 47–48.

65 *Book of Masques*, ed. Spencer and Wells, 277, 285.

66 Stephen Orgel and Roy Strong, *Inigo Jones: The Theatre of the Stuart Court*, 2 vols. (Berkeley: University of California Press, 1973), 480; cf. 662–63.

67 *Book of Masques*, ed. Spencer and Wells, 301.

68 *The King and Queenes Entertainement at Richmond* (Oxford, 1636), 6.

69 Michael Neill, "'Wit's Most Accomplished Senate': The Audience of the Caroline Private Theaters," *Studies in English Literature*, 18 (1978), 341–60, quotation on 357.

70 The play was Strode's *The Floating Isle*. For Laud's commission, see Carlton, *Archbishop William Laud*, 138.

71 *Book of Masques*, ed. Spencer and Wells, 304.

72 Orgel and Strong, *Inigo Jones*, 544. For Cosin, see *Collection of Private Devotions*, ed. Stanwood; for Feltham's private liturgy for a family, see Ted- Larry Pebworth, "An Anglican Family Worship Service of the Interregnum: A Canceled Early Text and a New Edition of Owen Feltham's 'A Form of Prayer,'" *English Literary Renaissance*, 16 (1986), 206–33.

73 Weidhorn, *Dreams in Seventeenth-Century English Literature*.

74 Milton, "On the Morning of Christ's Nativity," in *John Milton: Complete Poems and Major Prose*, ed. Merritt Y. Hughes (New York: Odyssey, 1957), 46.

75 C. A. Patrides, ed., *Sir Thomas Browne: The Major Works* (New York: Penguin Books, 1977), 154–55.

76 For the transitory splendor of the masque, see Jonson's introduction to *Hymenaei* in *Selected Masques*, ed. Orgel, 47–48.

77 Patrides, ed., *Sir Thomas Browne*, 63.

4 RESPECTING PERSONS

1 Achsah Guibbory, *Ceremony and Community from Herbert to Milton: Literature, Religion and Cultural Conflict in Seventeenth-Century England* (New York: Cambridge University Press, 1998), 19–21.

2 John Donne, *The Sermons*, 10 vols., ed. George Potter and Evelyn Simpson (Berkeley: University of California Press, 1953–62), 8.292.

3 Key Biblical passages include the following: Deuteronomy 1.17, 10.17; Leviticus, 19.15; II Samuel 2.14; II Chronicles 2.19; Job 32.21, 34.19; Proverbs, 18.5, 28.21; Malachi, 1.8; Psalms, 82.2; Lamentations 4.16; Matthew 12.13, 22.16–17; Acts 10.34–35; Romans 2.8–11; Ephesians 6.9; Colossians 3.25; Galatians 2.6; James 2.1; Jude 16; and I Peter 1.17.

4 For the "multiplex" *person* in the Renaissance, see Debora Kuller Shuger, *Habits of Thought in the English Renaissance: Religion, Politics, and the Dominant Culture* (Berkeley: University of California Press, 1990), 94–102.

5 Antony Fawkner, EIRENOGONIA; *or The Pedegree of Peace* (London, 1630), 4.

6 *The Works of Robert Sanderson*, 6 vols., ed. William Jacobson (Oxford University Press, 1854); unless otherwise noted, this edition is cited parenthetically in the text.

7 Peter du Moulin, *The Anatomy of Arminianisme* (1620) (Norwood, NJ: Walter J. Johnson, 1976), 88.

8 Richard Montagu, *A Gagg for the New Gospell? No; A New Gagg for an Old Goose* (1624) (Norwood, NJ: Walter J. Johnson, 1975), 167.

9 Richard Montagu, *Appello Caesarem* (1625) (New York: De Capo, 1972), 164.

10 *Sapientia Clamitans, Wisdome Crying Out to Sinners to Returne from Their Evile Wayes*, compiled by William Milbourne (London, 1638), 178.

11 See, for example, Thomas Jackson, *The Works*, 12 vols. (Oxford University Press, 1844), 5.150.

12 On pedigree, see Jackson, *Works*, 3.19–21.

13 For this conflict over pedigrees, see Anthony Milton, *Catholic and Reformed: The Roman and Protestant Churches in English Protestant Thought, 1600–1640* (New York: Cambridge University Press, 1995), chap. 6.

14 Milton, *Catholic and Reformed*, chap. 6.

15 *Table Talk of John Selden*, ed. Sir Frederick Pollock (London: Quaritch, 1927), 91.

16 James Bulman, "Caroline Drama," in *The Cambridge Companion to English Renaissance Drama* (New York: Cambridge University Press, 1990), 363–64.

17 For Sanderson's sermon, see *Works*, 3.153.

18 Selden, *Table Talk*, 81.

19 Milton, *Catholic and Reformed*, 305.

20 William Hardwick, *Conformity with Piety, requisite in Gods Service* (London, 1638), 5.

21 William Laud, *The Works*, 7 vols., ed William Scott and James Bliss (Oxford: John Henry Parker, 1847–60), 6.20.

22 George Herbert, *Country Parson*, in John Wall, ed., *George Herbert: The Country Parson, The Temple* (New York: Paulist Press, 1981), 95–96.

23 James Hyatt, *The Preachers President, or the Master and Scholler* (London, 1625), 19.

24 Jonas Barish, *The Antitheatrical Prejudice* (Berkeley: University of California Press, 1981), 58–59.

25 Thomas Fuller, *Ioseph's Party-Coloured Coat* (London, 1640); and Sanderson, *Sermon ad aulam*, in *Works*, 1.292. See also James Ussher, *A Sermon Preached before the King, at Greenwich, Sunday, June 25, 1627*, in *The Whole Works of James Ussher*, 17 vols., ed. C. R. Elrington and J. H. Todd (Dublin: Hodges and Smith, 1847–64), 13.343–46.

26 Robert Shelford, *Five Pious and Learned Discourses* (Cambridge, 1635), especially sermon 2.

27 See G. M. Story, ed., *Lancelot Andrewes: Sermons* (Oxford: Clarendon Press, 1967), xiv.

28 See Trevor A. Owen, *Lancelot Andrewes* (Boston: G. K. Hall, 1981), 61–73; Maurice F. Reidy, S. J., *Bishop Lancelot Andrewes, Jacobean Court Preacher: A Study in Early Seventeenth-Century Religious Thought* (Chicago: Loyola University Press, 1955), 26–29; Nicholas Lossky, *Lancelot Andrewes the Preacher (1555–1626): The Origins of the Mystical Theology of the Church of England*, trans. Andrew Louth (Oxford: Clarendon Press, 1991), 117–18, 259; and *The Works of Lancelot Andrewes*, 11 vols. (Oxford: John Henry Parker, 1854), 1.406–09.

29 See Barish, *Antitheatrical Prejudice*, 22–23, 158.

30 See Gordon Braden, "James Shirley," in *Jacobean and Caroline Dramatists*, ed. Fredson Bowers, *Dictionary of Literary Biography*, 58 (1987): 249–66, especially 256.

31 Lossky, *Lancelot Andrewes*, 64, 78, 117–18.

32 For imitators of Andrewes, see Owen, *Lancelot Andrewes*, 114; and W. Fraser Mitchell, *English Pulpit Oratory from Andrewes to Tillotson* (New York: Macmillan, 1932), 160.

33 Quoted in Paul A. Welsby, *Lancelot Andrewes: 1555–1626* (London: SPCK, 1958), 192; cf. Story, ed., *Lancelot Andrewes*, lxvii.

34 *The Country Parson*, ed. Wall, chap. 7. For the Scottish lord, see Owen, *Lancelot Andrewes*, 145.

35 For a commonplace example, see Niels Hemmingsen (Nicholas Hemminge), *The Preacher, or Methode of Preaching*, trans. John Horsfall, 2nd edition (1576), 19r–20r.

36 William Laud and John Buckeridge, dedication to Charles of an edition of Andrewes's sermons; see Andrewes, *Works*, 1.xvii–xviii.

37 Buckeridge, in Andrewes, *Works*, 5.291, 295. Cf. Anthony Milton, *Catholic and Reformed*, chap. 6.

38 See Irvonwy Morgan, *Prince Charles's Puritan Chaplain* (London: George Allen & Unwin, 1957); Kevin Sharpe, *The Personal Rule of Charles I* (New Haven: Yale University Press, 1992), 363–64; and Sheila Lambert, "Richard Montagu, Arminianism and Censorship," *Past & Present*, 124 (1989): 36–68.

39 Julian Davies, *The Caroline Captivity of the Church: Charles I and the Remoulding of Anglicanism, 1625–1641* (Oxford: Clarendon Press, 1992), chap. 4; Patrick Collinson, *Godly People: Essays on English Protestantism and Puritanism* (London: Hambledon, 1983), 491–98.

40 For Elizabeth, see Alan Fager Herr, *The Elizabethan Sermon: A Survey and a Bibliography* (Philadelphia: University of Pennsylvania, 1940); for James,

see Kenneth Fincham, *Prelate as Pastor: The Episcopate of James I* (Oxford: Clarendon Press, 1990), 245.

41 Fincham, *Prelate as Pastor*, 277.

42 Quoted by Fincham, *Prelate as Pastor*, 266.

43 John Cosin, *The Works of the Right Reverend Father in God John Cosin, Lord Bishop of Durham*, 5 vols. (Oxford: John Henry Parker, 1843–55), ed. J. Sansom and James Bliss, 1.96.

44 Richard Tedder, *A Sermon Preached at Wimondham . . . at the Primary Visitation of. . . Matthew (Wren)* (1637), 9, 12.

45 John Broughton, *Concerning Publike Prayer and the Fasts of the Church* (1636), 49.

46 Humphrey Sydenham, *Sermons upon Solemne Occasions: Preached in Severall Auditories* (London, 1637), 227.

47 Davies, *Caroline Captivity*, chap. 4; Collinson, *Godly People*, 469.

48 Quoted in Paul S. Seaver, *The Puritan Lectureships: The Politics of Religious Dissent, 1560–1662* (Stanford University Press, 1970), 86.

49 John Hales, "On Dealing with Erring Christians," in *The English Sermon, 1550–1650*, ed. Martin Seymour-Smith (Cheadle, England: Carcanet, 1976), 397.

50 Ussher, *Works*, 13.563. Falkland's remark is quoted in Fincham, *Prelate as Pastor*, 91; Fuller is quoted on 110–11.

51 Geoffrey Nuttall, *The Holy Spirit in Puritan Faith and Experience*, intro. Peter Lake (University of Chicago Press, 1992), 171.

52 Nuttall, *Holy Spirit*, 171.

53 Sanderson, *Works*, 3.87. Featley is quoted in Caroline Frances Richardson, *English Preachers and Preaching, 1640–1670* (New York: Macmillan, 1928), 304.

54 Lake, introduction to Nuttall, *Holy Spirit*, xxii– xxiii.

55 Seaver, *Puritan Lectureships*; and Isabel M. Calder, *Activities of the Puritan Faction of the Church of England, 1625–33* (London: SPCK, 1957).

56 Quoted in Seaver, *Puritan Lectureships*, 22.

57 William Haller, *The Rise of Puritanism* (New York: Harper, 1938); and Seaver, *Puritan Lectureships*, 43.

58 *The Complete Works of Richard Sibbes*, 7 vols., ed. Alexander B. Grosart (London: James Nisbett, 1862), 7.188.

59 Grosart's introduction to Sibbes's *Works*, 1.xxxviii.

60 For "singular" holiness, see William Ames, *Conscience with the Power and Cases Thereof* (Leyden and London, 1639), 4th book, 64–65.

5 DECORUM AND REDEMPTION IN THE THEATER OF THE PERSON

1 William Haller, *The Rise of Puritanism* (New York: Harper, 1938), 86.

2 See J. T. Cliffe, *The Puritan Gentry: The Great Puritan Families of Early Stuart England* (Boston: Routledge & Kegan Paul, 1984), 137–38.

3 Cliffe, *Puritan Gentry*, 10–11.

4 See Cliffe, *Puritan Gentry*, 9, 15–16, 21.

5 Cliffe, *Puritan Gentry*, 192.

6 John Mayer, *Praxis Theologica* (London, 1629), 7.

7 William Ames, *Conscience with the Power and Cases Thereof* (Leyden and London, 1639), 5th book, 123.

8 Thomas Wilson, *A Christian Dictionary*, 4th edition, (1635), MM2r; Richard Braithwait, *The English Gentleman* (1630) (Norwood, NJ: Walter J. Johnson, 1975).

9 Martha Tuck Rozett, *The Doctrine of Election and the Emergence of Elizabethan Tragedy* (Princeton University Press, 1984), 21; and Bryan Crockett, *The Play of Paradox: Stage and Sermon in Renaissance England* (Philadelphia: University of Pennsylvania Press, 1995), 6–7. See also Horton Davies, *Like Angels from a Cloud: The English Metaphysical Preachers, 1588–1645* (San Marino, California: Huntington Library, 1986), 112, 235.

10 William Prynne, *Histriomastix* (1633), intro. Arthur Freeman (New York: Garland, 1974), 793.

11 Jonas Barish, *The Antitheatrical Prejudice* (Berkeley: University of California Press, 1981), 87. Cf. Elbert N. S. Thompson, *The Controversy between Puritans and the Stage* (New York: Henry Holt, 1903).

12 Prynne, *Histriomastix*, 987.

13 Barish uses the term "Puritan" but acknowledges its problems (*Antitheatrical Prejudice*, 87). For Prynne's establishmentarian tendencies, see William Lamont, *Marginal Prynne, 1600–1669* (London: Routledge & Kegan Paul, 1963). For drama censorship in the reign of Charles I, see N. W. Bawcutt, ed., *The Control and Censorship of Caroline Drama: The Records of Sir Henry Herbert, Master of the Revels, 1623–73* (Oxford: Clarendon Press, 1996).

14 Barish, *Antitheatrical Prejudice*, 158. For Lucy Hutchinson, see *Memoirs of the Life of Colonel Hutchinson*, ed. James Sutherland (New York: Oxford University Press, 1973), 44. For Ussher, see Caroline Frances Richardson, *English Preachers and Preaching, 1640–1670* (New York: Macmillan, 1928), 63.

15 Henry Leslie, *A Full Confutation of the Covenant* (London, 1639), 4. For Chillingworth and Hobbes, see Richardson, *English Preachers*, 63–64; for Hammond, see Crockett, *Play of Paradox*, 56. Richard Bernard, *The Faithfull Shephearde* (1st edition, 1607; revised 3rd edition, 1621), 38–39; cf. Sister Jean Carmel Cavanaugh, ed., *"Technogamia" by Barten Holyday: A Critical Edition* (Washington, DC: Catholic University Press, 1942), xli; and Laurens J. Mills, *Peter Hausted: Playwright, Poet, and Preacher* (Bloomington: Indiana University Publications, Humanities Series, no. 12, 1944).

16 *Table Talk of John Selden*, ed., Sir Frederick Pollock (London: Quaritch, 1927), 94–96, 105–07. Cf. John Tombes, *Anthropolatria* (London, 1645).

17 Feltham is quoted in Richardson, *English Preachers*, 63–64. For Gomersall, see *Poems* (London, 1633), dedicatory epistle to Francis Hide for *The Tragedy of Sforza*.

18 Abraham Wright, *Five Sermons, in Five Several Styles; or Waies of Preaching* (London, 1656), A3v.

19 Barish, *Antitheatrical Prejudice*, 107, 158.

20 Sir Richard Baker, *Theatrum Redivivum, or The Theatre Vindicated* (1662, written in 1630s) intro. Arthur Freeman (New York: Garland, 1977), 131.

21 Bawcutt, ed., *Control and Censorship*.

22 For Brinsely and Ames, see Thompson, *Controversy Between Puritans and the Stage*, 155–56.

23 William Haller, *The Rise of Puritanism* (New York: Harper, 1938), 32–33; cf. Barish, *Antitheatrical Prejudice*, 114.

24 Cliffe, *Puritan Gentry*, 142–43. Margot Heinemann, *Puritanism and Theatre: Thomas Middleton and Opposition Drama Under the Early Stuarts* (New York: Cambridge University Press, 1980); and Martin Butler, *Theatre and Crisis, 1632–1642* (New York: Cambridge University Press, 1984).

25 James Bulman, "Caroline Drama," in *The Cambridge Companion to English Renaissance Drama* (New York: Cambridge University Press, 1990), 363–64.

26 Jonas Barish, "Three Caroline 'Defenses' of the Stage," in A. R. Braunmuller and J. C. Bulman, ed., *Comedy from Shakespeare to Sheridan: Change and Continuity in the English and European Dramatic Tradition: Essays in Honor of Eugene M. Waith* (Newark: University of Delaware Press, 1986), 194–212; reference on 203.

27 Thomas Randolph, "To His Dear Friend, Thomas Riley," in *Poetical and Dramatic Works*, 2 vols., ed. W. Carew Hazlitt (London: Reeves and Turner, 1875), 1.61.

28 Randolph, *Poetical and Dramatic Works*, 1.258–59.

29 Jackson I. Cope, *The Theater and the Dream: From Metaphor to Form in Renaissance Drama* (Baltimore: Johns Hopkins University Press, 1973), 125–26.

30 *The Dramatic Works of Richard Brome*, 3 vols. (London: John Pearson, 1873), 2.87 (play separately paginated). Cf. Massinger's *The Bondman* and *Maid of Honour*; and Cartwright's *The Royal Slave*.

31 Kevin Sharpe, *Politics and Ideas in Early Stuart England: Essays and Studies* (New York: Pinter, 1989), 106.

32 Glenn Burgess, *The Politics of the Ancient Constitution: An Introduction to English Political Thought, 1603–1642* (University Park, PA: Penn State Press, 1992), 181–93, 200–01.

33 Anthony Milton, *Catholic and Reformed: The Roman and Protestant Churches in English Protestant Thought, 1600–1640* (New York: Cambridge University Press, 1995), 538–39. Milton modifies Burgess's position.

34 Lisa Hopkins, *John Ford's Political Theatre* (Manchester University Press, 1994), 45–46.

35 Lawrence Stone, *The Crisis of the Aristocracy, 1558–1641* (Oxford: Clarendon Press, 1965), 23–25.

36 D. H. Craig, ed., *Ben Jonson: The Critical Heritage, 1599–1798* (New York: Routledge, 1990), 141.

37 Craig, ed., *Ben Jonson: The Critical Heritage*, 207, 194.

38 Butler, *Theatre and Crisis*, 111.

39 Bawcutt, ed., *Control and Censorship*, 180, 75.

40 Ira Clark, *Professional Playwrights: Massinger, Ford, Shirley & Brome* (Lexington: University of Kentucky Press, 1992), 112.

41 Richard Morton, "Deception and Social Dislocation: An Aspect of James Shirley's Drama," *Renaissance Drama*, 9 (1966): 227–45, quotation on 228.

42 Gordon Braden, "James Shirley," in *Jacobean and Caroline Dramatists*, ed. Fredson Bowers, *Dictionary of Literary Biography*, 58 (1987): 256.

43 See *The Dramatic Works and Poems of James Shirley*, 6 vols., ed. William Gifford and Alexander Dyce (London: Alexander Murray, 1833), 3.201.

44 Shirley, *The Brothers*, in *Dramatic Works*, 1.239.

45 See Shirley, *Dramatic Works*, 1.v.

46 *Magnetic Lady*, in *Ben Jonson, Plays*, 2 vols., introduction by Felix E. Shelling (New York: Dutton, 1960), 2.514; Thomas Killigrew, *The Parson's Wedding*, in *Comedies and Tragedies* (New York: Benjamin Blom, 1967), 99; and Cartwright, *The Ordinary*, in Evans, ed., *Plays and Poems of William Cartwright*, 302, 314–37.

47 Among the many modern critics that have commented on Donne and theatricality since T. S. Eliot, see Gale H. Carrithers, Jr., *Donne at Sermons: A Christian Existential World* (Albany: SUNY Press, 1972), 16–21; and William R. Mueller, *John Donne, Preacher* (Princeton University Press, 1962), 111, 235, 248–49.

48 Mueller, *John Donne, Preacher*, 42–43.

49 For examples of this emphasis on personal plurality, see John Donne, *The Sermons*, 10 vols., ed. George Potter and Evelyn Simpson (Berkeley: University of California Press, 1953–62), 6.3, 7, 82; for the Trinity, 6.5–6.

50 For Solomon, see Reid Barbour, *English Epicures and Stoics: Ancient Legacies in Early Stuart Culture* (Amherst: University of Massachusetts, 1998), 105–11.

51 For Herbert on Socrates, see John Wall, ed., *George Herbert: The Country Parson, The Temple* (New York: Paulist Press, 1981), 84.

52 Barish, *Antitheatrical Prejudice*, 58–59.

53 Donne, *Sermons*, 7.6–7; 8.1–16; 9.1–3. For Milton, see *John Milton: Complete Poems and Major Prose*, ed. Merritt Y. Hughes (New York: Odyssey, 1957), 552.

54 Quoted in Barish, *Antitheatrical Prejudice*, 155.

6 NATURE (I): POST-BACONIAN MYSTERIES

1 Unless otherwise noted, Bacon's works are quoted from either John M. Robertson, ed., *The Philosophical Works of Francis Bacon* (New York: E. P. Dutton, 1905); or James Spedding, Robert Ellis, and Douglas Heath, eds., *Works of Francis Bacon* (London: Longmans, 1857–74). The Oxford edition, Graham Rees, ed. and intro., *Francis Bacon: Philosophical Studies, c. 1611–c. 1619* (Oxford: Clarendon Press, 1996), is used where possible.

2 Rees, ed. and intro., *Francis Bacon: Philosophical Studies*, xvii–xix.

3 For Rawley's biography of Bacon, see Spedding et al., *Works*, 1.33–58.

4 Graham Rees, "Bacon's Speculative Philosophy," in Markku Peltonen, ed., *Cambridge Companion to Bacon* (New York: Cambridge University Press, 1996), 121.

5 Rees, ed. and intro., *Francis Bacon: Philosophical Studies*, xlix.

6 Rees, ed. and intro., *Francis Bacon: Philosophical Studies*, l–li.
7 Rees, ed. and intro., *Francis Bacon: Philosophical Studies*, l.
8 Joseph Mede, *Works* (London, 1677), John Worthington's preface, ####2v.
9 Mede, *Works*, Worthington's preface, ###4v.
10 Bacon, *Novum Organum, with Other Parts of the Great Instauration*, translated and edited by Peter Urbach and John Gibson (La Salle: Open Court, 1994), 38.
11 Brian Vickers, ed., *Occult and Scientific Mentalities in the Renaissance* (New York: Cambridge University Press, 1984).
12 William H. Huffman, *Robert Fludd and the End of the Renaissance* (New York: Routledge, 1988).
13 Huffman, *Robert Fludd*, 1–40, 64–65.
14 Huffman, *Robert Fludd*, 54–57; cf. Reid Barbour, *English Epicures and Stoics: Ancient Legacies in Early Stuart Culture* (Amherst: University of Massachusetts, 1998), chap. 1; and Rees, ed. and intro., *Francis Bacon: Philosophical Studies*, introduction.
15 Robert Fludd, *Mosaicall Philosophy* (London, 1659), "To the Judicious and Discreet Reader."
16 James Hart, KLINIKE, *or the Diet of the Diseased* (London, 1633), 2.
17 Fludd, *Mosaicall Philosophy*, 91.
18 Robert M. Schuler, "Some Spiritual Alchemies of Seventeenth-Century England," *Journal of the History of Ideas*, 41 (1980): 293–318.
19 Sarah Hutton, "Thomas Jackson, Oxford Platonist, and William Twisse, Aristotelian," *Journal of the History of Ideas*, 39 (1978): 635–52, quotation on 646.
20 Thomas Jackson, *The Works*, 12 vols. (Oxford University Press, 1844), 4.31.
21 George Wither, *The History of the Pestilence*, ed. J. Milton French (Cambridge, Mass.: Harvard University Press, 1932), 61.
22 Henry Reynolds, *Mythomystes*, in J. E. Spingarn, ed., *Critical Essays of the Seventeenth Century*, 3 vols. (Oxford: Clarendon Press, 1908), 1.141.
23 G. H. Turnbull, *Samuel Hartlib: A Sketch of His Life and His Relations to J. A. Comenius* (New York: Oxford University Press, 1920); Hugh Trevor-Roper, "Three Foreigners: The Philosophers of the Puritan Revolution," in *Religion, the Reformation and Social Change, and Other Essays*, rev. 3rd edition (London: Secker & Warburg, 1984); and Mark Greengrass et al., eds., *Samuel Hartlib and Universal Reformation: Studies in Intellectual Communication* (New York: Cambridge University Press, 1994).
24 G. H. Turnbull, *Hartlib, Dury and Comenius: Gleanings from Hartlib's Papers* (London: Hodder & Stoughton, 1947), 36–37.
25 Trevor-Roper, "Three Foreigners," 258.
26 See Stephen Clucas, "In Search of 'The True Logick': Methodological Eclecticism among the 'Baconian reformers,'" in Greengrass, ed., *Samuel Hartlib and Universal Reformation*, 51–74.
27 Turnbull, *Hartlib, Dury and Comenius*, 343–44.
28 John Amos Comenius, *A Reformation of Schooles* (1642) (Menston, England: Scolar Press, 1969), 37, 66.

29 *Religio Medici*, in C. A. Patrides, ed., *Sir Thomas Browne: The Major Works* (New York: Penguin Books, 1977), 61.

30 Achsah Guibbory, *Ceremony and Community from Herbert to Milton: Literature, Religion and Cultural Conflict in Seventeenth-Century England* (New York: Cambridge University Press, 1998), 119.

31 *Religio Medici*, 61; cf. *Hydriotaphia*, in Patrides, ed., *Sir Thomas Browne*, 276, 278.

32 Frank Huntley, *Sir Thomas Browne: A Biographical and Critical Study* (Ann Arbor: University of Michigan Press, 1962), 78–79.

33 Barbour, *English Epicures and Stoics*, chaps. 4 and 5.

34 Geoffrey Keynes, *The Life of William Harvey* (Oxford: Clarendon Press, 1966), 358–59.

35 Walter Pagel, *William Harvey's Biological Ideas: Selected Aspects and Historical Background* (New York: Hafner, 1967).

36 William Harvey, *De Generatione Animalium*, trans. Gweneth Whitteridge (Oxford: Blackwell Scientific Publications, 1981), introduction.

37 Whitteridge, *De Generatione*, xxx.

38 They disagree, however, over the politics of this shift; for the most recent but still reductive account, see John Rogers, *The Matter of Revolution: Science, Poetry, and Politics in the Age of Milton* (Ithaca: Cornell University Press, 1996).

39 Walter Pagel, "Religious Motives in the Medical Biology of the XVIIth Century," *Bulletin of the Institute of the History of Medicine*, 3 (1935): 97–128, 213–31, 265–312.

40 Whitteridge, *De Generatione*, 85.

7 NATURE (II): CHURCH AND COSMOS

1 John Donne, *Devotions upon Emergent Occasions*, ed. Anthony Raspa (Montreal: McGill-Queen's University Press, 1975), 19–21, 25–26.

2 Cf. Edward Herbert, *De Veritate*, trans., with an introduction, by Meyrick H. Carré (Bristol University Press, 1937); and Herbert, *Pagan Religion: A Translation of De Religione Gentilium*, trans. John Anthony Butler (Binghamton, NY: Medieval & Renaissance Texts, 1996). See also D. P. Walker, *The Ancient Theology: Studies in Christian Platonism from the Fifteenth to the Eighteenth Century* (Ithaca: Cornell University Press, 1972), chap. 3.

3 Reid Barbour, *English Epicures and Stoics: Ancient Legacies in Early Stuart Culture* (Amherst: University of Massachusetts, 1998), chaps. 1 and 2.

4 Thomas Gataker, *Of the Nature and Use of Lots: A Treatise Historicall and Theologicall* (London, 1627), 172–73.

5 William Ames, *Conscience with the Power and Cases Thereof* (Leyden and London, 1639), 59–61, 244–48.

6 Henry V. S. Ogden and Margaret S. Ogden, *English Taste in Landscape in the Seventeenth Century* (Ann Arbor: University of Michigan Press, 1955), 9–13.

7 Vaughan Hart, *Art and Magic in the Court of the Stuarts* (New York: Routledge, 1994).

8 James Turner, *The Politics of Landscape: Rural Scenery and Society in English Poetry, 1630–1660* (Cambridge, Mass.: Harvard University Press, 1979), 4, 34–44.

9 Ronald Hutton, *The Rise and Fall of Merry England: The Ritual Year, 1400–1700* (New York: Oxford University Press, 1994), 185–98.

10 Hutton, *Rise and Fall*, 173.

11 Barbour, *English Epicures and Stoics*, chap. 1.

12 George Hakewill, *An Apologie or Declaration of the Power and Providence of God in the Government of the World* (Oxford, 1635), 273. For a summary of Hakewill's argument and its contexts, see Victor Harris, *All Coherence Gone: A Study of the Seventeenth Century Controversy over Disorder and Decay in the Universe* (University of Chicago Press, 1966).

13 Harris, *All Coherence Gone*, 43–84.

14 Ernest Lee Tuveson, *Millennium and Utopia: A Study in the Background of the Idea of Progress* (New York: Harper & Row, 1949), 67; Hakewill, 259.

15 John Jonston, *History of the Constancy of Nature* (London, trans., 1657), 83–84.

16 Hakewill, *An Apologie*, 302, 261–62.

17 Katharine Firth, *The Apocalyptic Tradition in Reformation Britain, 1530–1645* (New York: Oxford University Press, 1979), 245.

18 Joseph Mede, *Works* (London, 1677), 798–800.

19 For Mede's skepticism, see *Works*, A1 v, in "The Life."

20 Firth, *Apocalyptic Tradition*, 204.

21 See Firth, *Apocalyptic Tradition*, 207.

22 John Headley, *Tommaso Campanella and The Transformation of the World* (Princeton University Press, 1997).

23 Owen Hannaway, *The Chemists and the Word: The Didactic Origins of Chemistry* (Baltimore: Johns Hopkins University Press, 1975); and Brian Vickers, ed., *Occult and Scientific Mentalities in the Renaissance* (New York: Cambridge University Press, 1984), 95–155.

24 Charles Webster, *The Great Instauration: Science, Medicine, and Reform, 1626–1660* (London: Duckworth, 1975), xiii.

25 Vickers, ed., *Occult and Scientific*, 6–19.

26 See Richard G. Barlow, "Infinite Worlds: Robert Burton's Cosmic Voyage," *Journal of the History of Ideas*, 34 (1973): 291–302.

27 Robert Burton, *The Anatomy of Melancholy*, 6 vols., ed. Thomas C. Faulkner et al. (Oxford: Clarendon Press, 1989–2000) 2.54.

28 Betty Jo Dobbs, "Studies in the Natural Philosophy of Sir Kenelm Digby," *Ambix*, 18 (1971): 1–25; 20 (1973): 143–63; and 21 (1974): 1–28. Allen G. Debus, *Science and Education in the Seventeenth Century: The Webster-Ward Debate* (New York: American Elsevier, 1970), 240.

CONCLUSION: ROME, MASSACHUSETTS, AND THE CAROLINE PROTESTANT IMAGINATION

1 C. A. Patrides, ed., *Sir Thomas Browne: The Major Works* (New York: Penguin Books, 1977), 66.

2 Anthony Milton, *Catholic and Reformed: The Roman and Protestant Churches in English Protestant Thought, 1600–1640* (New York: Cambridge University Press, 1995).

3 Patrides, ed., *Sir Thomas Browne*, 69.

4 See, for example, Richard Smith, *A Conference of the Catholike and Protestante Doctrine with the Expresse Words of Holie Scripture* (Douai, 1631); Lawrence Anderton, *The Triple Cord* (1634) (Ilkley: Scolar Press, 1975); and the 1620 translation/edition of Augustine's *Confessions* (Menston, England: Scolar Press, 1972).

5 Kenelm Digby, *A Conference with a Lady about Choice of Religion* (Paris, 1638), 72–73.

6 John Fisher, *The Answere unto the Nine Points of Controversy* (1626) (Menston, England: Scolar Press, 1978), 309.

7 John Heigham, *Via Vera Tuta. Or the Truly Safe Way* (1631) (Menston, England: Scolar Press, 1975), 310; John Clare, *The Converted Jew* (1630), 13.

8 N. N., *Maria Triumphans* (1635) (Menston, England: Scolar Press, 1976), 256–57.

9 Heigham, *Via Vera Tuta*, 241.

10 Richard Smith, *A Conference*, 767.

11 James Sharpe, *The Triall of the Protestant Spirit* (St. Omer, 1630), 176.

12 Matthew Wilson, *Christianity Maintained* (1638), (Menston, England: Scolar Press, 1973), dedication to King Charles.

13 *The Judgement of an University Man Concerning M. William Chillingworth* (1639) (Menston, England: Scolar Press, 1973), 73.

14 John Floyd, *The Church Conquerent over Humane Wit* (1639?) (Menston, England: Scolar Press, 1976), 152.

15 Floyd, *The Totall Summe* (St. Omer, 1639), 100–01.

16 This controversy is catalogued in A. F. Allison and D. M. Rogers, *The Contemporary Printed Literature of the English Counter-Reformation between 1558 and 1640*, vol. 2 (Menston, England: Scolar Press, 1989).

17 Matthew Wilson, *Mercy & Truth. Or Charity Maintayned by Catholics* (1634) (Menston, England: Scolar Press, 1973), 5.

18 Christopher Potter, *Want of Charitie Iustly Charged* (Oxford, 1633), 2r.

19 William Rushworth, *The Dialogues of William Richworth* (Paris, 1640), 578–79.

20 George H. Tavard, *The Seventeenth-Century Tradition: A Study in Recusant Thought* (Leiden: E. J. Brill, 1978), 166.

21 Tavard, *Seventeenth-Century Tradition*, 169, 176.

22 George Walton Williams, ed., *The Complete Poetry of Richard Crashaw* (Garden City: Anchor, 1970), 59–60.

23 Patrides, ed., *Sir Thomas Browne*, 133.

24 See Williams, ed., *Complete Poetry*, 68–69, 212.

25 *Winthrop Papers*, 6 vols. (Boston: The Massachusetts Historical Society, 1863–92), 2.65.

26 Andrew Delbanco, *The Puritan Ordeal* (Cambridge, Mass.: Harvard University Press, 1989), 12.

27 In addition to Delbanco's notion of "ordeal," see Edmund S. Morgan, *The Puritan Dilemma: The Story of John Winthrop* (Glenville, Ill.: Scott, Foresman and Co., 1958).

28 Janice Knight, *Orthodoxies in Massachusetts: Rereading American Puritanism* (Cambridge, Mass., Harvard University Press, 1994), 3–15, 38.

29 Thomas Hooker, *The Soules Preparation for Christ* (London, 1638), 79–83.

30 Edmund S. Morgan, *Visible Saints: The History of a Puritan Idea* (New York University Press, 1963), 84.

31 Larzer Ziff, ed., *John Cotton on the Churches of New England* (Cambridge, Mass.: Harvard University Press, 1968), epistle to the reader from Thomas Goodwin and Philip Nye, 85.

32 Thomas Shepard, *Works*, 3 vols., ed. John Adams Albro (New York: Georg Olms, 1971), 2.58.

33 William Ames, *Marrow of Theology*, trans. John D. Eusden (Boston: Pilgrim Press, 1968), 233.

34 Knight, *Orthodoxies in Massachusetts*, 74; Delbanco, *Puritan Ordeal*, 31–32.

35 Shepard, *Works*, 2.377.

36 Shepard, *Works*, 2.626.

37 *Winthrop Papers*, 2.122.

38 See Morgan, *Puritan Dilemma*, 18–33.

39 *Winthrop Papers*, 2.105–06.

40 *Winthrop's Journal: History of New England, 1630–1649*, ed. James Kendall Hosmer (New York: Charles Scribner's Sons, 1908), 1. 201, 208–09.

41 William K. B. Stoever, *"A Faire and Easie Way to Heaven": Covenant Theology and Antinomianism in Early Massachusetts* (Middletown, Conn.: Wesleyan University Press, 1978).

42 *Winthrop's Journal*, vol. 1, 263.

43 David P. Hall, *The Antinomian Controversy, 1636–1638: A Documentary History*, 2nd edition (Durham, NC: Duke University Press, 1990), xi; cf. Stoever, *"Faire and Easie Way,"* 162–63.

44 *Winthrop's Journal*, 1.266, 270.

45 Stoever, *"Faire and Easie Way,"* 162–63.

46 *Antinomian Controversy*, ed. Hall, 255; cf. 298.

47 *Antinomian Controversy*, ed. Hall, 295–96.

48 Quoted in Knight, *Orthodoxies in Massachusetts*, 17–18.

49 Delbanco, *Puritan Ordeal*, 12–60, 162, 75.

50 Milton, *Catholic and Reformed*, 26–27.

Index